MW00785191

Frequency in Language

Cognitive linguists are bound by the Cognitive Commitment. They aim to provide a characterization of the general principles governing all aspects of human language in a way that is informed by, and accords with, what is known about the brain and mind from other disciplines. But what do we know about cognition that is relevant for theories of language? Which insights can help us build cognitive reality into our descriptive practice and move linguistic theorizing forward? This unique study integrates research findings from across the cognitive sciences to generate insights that challenge the way in which frequency has been interpreted in usage-based linguistics. It answers the fundamental questions of why frequency of experience has the effect it has on language development, structure and representation, and what role psychological and neurological explorations of core cognitive processes can play in developing a cognitively more accurate theoretical account of language.

DAGMAR DIVJAK is a Professorial Research Fellow at the University of Birmingham where she holds a chair in Cognitive Linguistics and Language Cognition. She is editor-in-chief of the journal *Cognitive Linguistics*, co-editor of the *Handbook of Cognitive Linguistics* (2015, with Ewa Dąbrowska) and author of *Structuring the Lexicon* (2010).

Frequency in Language

Memory, Attention and Learning

Dagmar Divjak

University of Birmingham

CAMBRIDGE
UNIVERSITY PRESS

University Printing House, Cambridge CB2 8BS, United Kingdom

One Liberty Plaza, 20th Floor, New York, NY 10006, USA

477 Williamstown Road, Port Melbourne, VIC 3207, Australia

314–321, 3rd Floor, Plot 3, Splendor Forum, Jasola District Centre, New Delhi – 110025, India

79 Anson Road, #06–04/06, Singapore 079906

Cambridge University Press is part of the University of Cambridge.

It furthers the University's mission by disseminating knowledge in the pursuit of education, learning and research at the highest international levels of excellence.

www.cambridge.org
Information on this title: www.cambridge.org/9781107085756
DOI: 10.1017/9781316084410

© Dagmar Divjak 2019

First published 2019

Printed in the United Kingdom by TJ International Ltd. Padstow Cornwall

A catalogue record for this publication is available from the British Library

Library of Congress Cataloging-in-Publication Data
Names: Divjak, Dagmar, author.
Title: Frequency in language : memory, attention and learning / Dagmar Divjak.
Description: New York, NY : Cambridge University Press, 2019. | Includes bibliographical references and index.
Identifiers: LCCN 2019010632 | ISBN 9781107085756 (hardback)
Subjects: LCSH: Frequency (Linguistics) | Language acquisition. | Psycholinguistics. | BISAC: LANGUAGE ARTS & DISCIPLINES / Linguistics / General.
Classification: LCC P128.F73 D58 2019 | DDC 410.1/835–dc23
LC record available at https://lccn.loc.gov/2019010632

ISBN 978-1-107-08575-6 Hardback

To Torkel, Knut and Oskar

Contents

Figures

Table

Acknowledgements

Cognitive linguistics is a usage-based theory of language that examines the relation between language structure, language use and general cognitive principles and mechanisms. Finding out how linguistic patterns are discovered and mentally encoded and how these representations vary with experience lies at the heart of the cognitive linguistic enterprise. Unlike many other modern theories of linguistics, cognitive linguistics also explores how language units arise from and are shaped by usage events on which general cognitive abilities act. It is precisely this combination of usage and cognition, and of cognition working on input to yield language structure, that attracted me to usage-based theories of language.

At the same time, as a cognitive linguist, I often feel torn between the cognitive and the linguistic. Cognitive linguists are bound by the Cognitive Commitment, which is the commitment to provide a characterization of the general principles governing all aspects of human language in a way that is informed by and accords with what is known about the brain and mind from other disciplines. But to what extent does this commitment influence our daily practice? I can create powerful classifications using tools that aren't cognitively realistic and I can propose classifications that are cognitively more realistic, but less powerful. Do I choose one, or do I compromise? Do I classify phenomena as economically as possible while accounting for as much of the data as possible, or do I classify phenomena in a way that is in line with what we know about human cognition? How do I really know what is in line with what we know about cognition? In fact, what do we know about aspects of cognition that are relevant for theories of language? Which insights can help us to build cognitive reality into our descriptive practice?

These were the questions that gave the impetus for this book. The bulk of the research and the writing was completed on a British Academy Mid-Career Fellowship (2015–16), followed by a semester of study leave from The University of Sheffield (2017); their financial support is gratefully acknowledged. I am also indebted to a number of colleagues for reading through manuscript drafts in various states of (in)completion. Neil Bermel, Paul O'Neill and Maciej Borowski commented on the first or final complete draft and identified many passages that needed clarification and elaboration. Nigel Gotteri, Jane Klavan and James Street focused on the technical chapters and provided guidance for making these more accessible. Nina Szymor's swift, reliable and cheerful editorial assistance took the hassle out of publishing.

Warm thanks go to Petar Milin for helping me achieve what I set out to do and, in the process, relieving me of having to criticize myself. He is, and will remain, the undisputed record holder for number of times anyone will read this book, reason why it includes a chapter on learning, unacknowledged co-author of Section 8.2.1 and creator of Figures 1.1 and 8.1.

And last but not least, there's love and kisses for the three guys to whom this book is dedicated. They ungrudgingly adopted the manuscript as family project and never inquired as to when it would (finally!) be completed. Instead, Torkel provided the cover image, and the boys set out to write their own book ... collaboratively. So much smarter!

Sheffield, 22 December 2018

Introduction

1 Frequency of Experience

What you do often, you do better and faster. This is because repetition freezes behaviour into something you can do without thinking, such as swimming, riding a bike, driving a car, and speaking your mother tongue. That is right – speaking your own language can be regarded as a behaviour that is sensitive to frequency. Children, for example, learn words sooner if they hear them often. A child's first word will typically be something they hear a lot: *mummy, daddy, teddy* are good candidates because they are frequent (and useful). Adults read and recognize high-frequency words more quickly than low-frequency words. You may have had the experience of reading a word you do not see very often, such as *blur,* and accidentally replacing it with a word like *blue* that you do encounter often. Words that are used often are also more robustly represented in memory. For example, in a noisy environment like a pub, you will have less trouble understanding a word such as *pint* that you hear often (and expect) than a word like *vine* that you encounter rarely. Or, when some letters of a written word in a newspaper are covered by coffee stains, you will find it easier to guess what it is, if it is a word like *democracy* that you read often in a newspaper than if it is a word that you see less often, such as *demagogy.* These everyday examples illustrate the powerful effects that the repetition of experience has on language cognition.

The first experimental study addressing the influence of word frequency on word recognition was Howes and Solomon (1951), run shortly after the publication of Thorndike and Lorge's (1944) list of English word frequencies. Howes and Solomon (1951) demonstrated that the visual duration thresholds for words – that is, the time it takes someone to recognize a string of letters as a word – are a function of word frequency; it takes less time to recognize a frequent word. Hall (1954) found a significant positive relationship between word frequency and recall, showing that it was also easier to recall more frequently encountered words. Scarborough, Cortese and Scarborough (1977) then showed that high-frequency words are accessed more readily than low-frequency words, while MacKay (1982) established that retrieval of high-frequency items is less subject to error than retrieval of low-frequency items.

These findings provided evidence for the assumption that repetition of experience, or frequency of exposure, is an experience that drives linguistic behaviour too. Since then, many scholarly works have investigated the extent to which different forms of linguistic behaviour could be frequency-driven. Evidence has been found for a wide range of phenomena, from processing single words to knowing which sets of verbs are used in complex argument structure constructions. Frequency does not only affect individuals during their lifetime: there is ample evidence that differences in frequencies of occurrence determine linguistic change. More frequent items tend to be the first to undergo sound changes and to be reduced or contracted, yielding *let's* and *don't*. At the same time, they are also the most resistant to analogical levelling, making it possible for irregular plurals such as *men* or past tenses such as *went* to survive (Bybee 2007).

Underlying all this is the principle that with practice – that is, repeating one and the same behaviour – you become better. Once learning has reached asymptote, the effects of frequency wear off and there is progressively less noticeable gain from further practice. By that time, a behaviour has become proceduralized or routinized; you can execute it skilfully and may do so automatically. Frequency information is collected automatically too; you do not need to remember to do it and you do not need to pay special attention to the items you are tracking. The fact that speakers' language systems are sensitive to frequencies of occurrence in language use has had a major impact on linguistic theory. Many linguists and psychologists of language have interpreted the extent of the effect that frequency of occurrence has on language users' systems and on their language processing as a refutation of Chomsky's views (Chomsky 1965). Chomsky had proposed that linguistic competence, i.e., knowledge of linguistic structures, exists separately from performance, i.e., how speakers use language and what factors influence comprehension and production. Chomsky also posited that syntax is autonomous from the rest of cognition. Frequency effects do not fit with these classic Chomskyan viewpoints: the influence of frequency on linguistic systems challenges the rigid division between knowledge of language structure and language use. Instead it suggests a dynamic model of grammar in which linguistic structure is grounded in language use.

Usage-based linguists have developed theories of how we acquire language in which frequency of occurrence, or repetition, plays a fundamental role. Information about the number of times and in which contexts you have heard something is used in a variety of ways by language learners and users. Both infants and adults use statistical properties of language input to discover structure, including sound patterns, words and the beginnings of grammar (Saffran 2003; MacWhinney 1998). This ability to extract the distributional characteristics of natural language has been argued to play a key role in linguistic development: what we learn may well be a probabilistic grammar grounded in our language experience (Ellis 2002; Bod, Hay and Jannedy 2003b). The existence of sophisticated pattern-detection abilities in human beings could circumvent the need to posit environmental triggers that set parameters, specifying a fixed set of mutually exclusive linguistic properties.

Over the last decade, the bulk of the research on frequency has focused on identifying frequency effects in an ever-growing number of areas. Frequency effects have now been documented in processing elements from about every level of linguistic analysis, i.e., phonology, morphology, morpho-syntax, syntax and lexicon, including formulaic language. It would seem that we have ample proof of the existence of frequency effects. We also know quite a bit about the facilitatory role played by frequency distributions in breaking into the language system and building up the basic structures. But the extent to which frequency effects and continua of entrenchment constrain theories of the language faculty remains controversial (see Ambridge and Lieven 2011 for discussion). This is in part due to the fact that dealing with the effects of frequencies in language use on language cognition is a discipline at the intersection of linguistics and cognitive psychology.

Disrespectfully put, psychological studies that address the theoretical status of frequency are generally carried out by research teams lacking linguistic expertise. Hence, many studies identifying frequency effects in language are based on analyses of a handful of phenomena. They typically limit themselves to counting readily identifiable forms taken out of their natural context, which significantly diminishes the richness of the input from which human beings extract distributional patterns. And they concern mostly one language, English. Driven to its extreme, this approach reduces our billion-neuron brains that enable us to adapt quickly to an immense array of stimuli to nothing more than sophisticated abacuses, used to keep tallies of all the words found in the messy 'bag of words' (see Harris 1954 for an early reference). On the other hand, many corpus linguistic studies have taken their painstakingly annotated textual data sets to be a map of speakers' minds, forgetting that what is learned or acquired by probabilistic means is not strictly proportional to the stimulus: probabilistic learning theory holds that language learning is based on complex, higher-order properties of probabilistic patterns in sensory experience, not a mere tabulation of frequency of patterns (Elman 2003).

The time has come to shift gears to theoretical questions that go beyond demonstrating frequency effects and beyond winning battles in the frequency wars. While frequency goes a long way towards explaining how language is acquired and represented, it is not well known in linguistic circles how frequency achieves these effects. The processes that lead from distribution of forms in usage to the effect of frequency on language cognition are not well understood. As we will see in this book, frequency has the effects it has because our memory is sensitive to how items are presented over time. The memory capacity of the brain is impressive, especially if we take into account what the brain likes and does not like. For example, brains cannot effectively store and recall lots of information in a short period of time. They are, however, very good at storing information that they encounter regularly. But this does not mean that they keep exact tallies: (fortunately) you do not remember how many times you checked your email account last week. Instead, repetition leaves its trace in the brain: you get better with practice. But the effect of practice wears off and as you become better at a skill, improvements become less noticeable. Eventually, repeatedly executed behaviours freeze into a skill or even a habit, something you do automatically and without thinking (and you start checking your email account without intending to).

Skills and habits are classed as memories too. Much progress has been made in the understanding of memory, and a 'memory' is now considered an emergent feature of many different parts of the brain firing in a certain way. This network of neuronal activity needs to be built up and strengthened over time with practice; it is like developing the stamina and muscle mass you need to run a marathon. Thus, practice, or frequency, can be considered the mechanism that helps commit experiences to memory. But, as we will discover in this book, the process is not as straightforward as our current theories and methods assume. There is no pure frequency effect: experience cannot be reduced to frequency as experience is filtered through attention before being committed to memory. Our experience contains too much information for us to register it all and we appear to select or pay attention to part of our experience only. Attention is another very active research area in psychology that has yielded a bewildering array of findings. Yet, empirical progress has not been matched by a consensus on major theoretical issues, which has made it challenging for linguists to incorporate attention into their theories.

No one likes complications, and scientific progress often relies on simplifications. But sustained oversimplifications such as those affecting the understanding of frequency can be harmful. Realistic considerations of the complexity involved in language cognition are vital to give frequency the place it deserves in an encompassing model of usage. They will also help us appreciate the true extent of the effects frequency has on the development, systematization and representation of language. At the theoretical linguistic level, such insights will facilitate mutual understanding between the disciplines involved and allow usage-based linguistic theory to move forward and develop further in a cognitively realistic fashion. At an individual level, exposure to 'other ways of doing things' will challenge researchers interested in language to question the foundational assumptions that their theories rest on and step beyond their customary methods of analysis. At an applied level, a better understanding of why frequency has the effect it has will be invaluable for making learning materials more strategic, both in terms of item selection and rate of presentation.

2   A Cognitive Perspective on Language

This book is written with usage-based linguists in mind, and cognitive linguists in particular, who want to gain a deeper understanding of the role repetition plays in language, and why frequency of occurrence has the effect it has, on cognition, and on linguistic theory. This is a rather unusual concern: for long, linguistic work was predominantly descriptive in nature. Linguists aimed to capture the grammar of a language as comprehensively, elegantly and economically as possible. They were not at all concerned with the mental reality of their proposals. It was not until the 'cognitive revolution', the strong reaction against behaviourism in the 1950s, that attitudes changed. For language, this refocusing on the mind's information-processing capacity was spearheaded by Chomsky. He proposed syntactic theory as an account of the cognitive processes responsible for the structural aspects of human language. Chomsky had noted that people can produce and understand an infinite number of novel sentences. This, he reasoned, means they must have internalized a grammar, or set of rules, rather than having memorized a list of responses, because – logically – an infinite number can never be listed (or memorized). Since children are not taught this grammar, they must be equipped with a 'language acquisition device' that instantiates a 'universal grammar'.

Cognitive linguistics grew out of the work of researchers, active since the 1970s, who were interested in the relation between language and mind but did not follow the prevailing tendency to explain linguistic patterns by appealing to structural properties specific to language. Rather than attempting to segregate syntax from the rest of language and from cognition by accommodating it in a syntactic component, governed by a unique set of principles and elements, they took a different approach. They examined the relation between language structure and cognitive principles and mechanisms not specific to language, yielding a new approach known as cognitive linguistics. Cognitive linguists are bound by two major commitments: the generalization commitment and the cognitive commitment (Lakoff 1990: 40). All cognitive linguists are committed (or are assumed to be committed) to providing a characterization of the general principles governing all aspects of human language in a way that is informed by and accords with what is known about the brain and mind from other disciplines. Unlike many other modern theories of linguistics, cognitive linguistics also aims to be a usage-based model of language structure. All language units arise from and are shaped by usage events through general cognitive abilities, that is, cognitive abilities that are not specific to language. These abilities include purely cognitive capacities such as perception, attention, memory, categorization and imagination, but also pragmatic and interactional principles as well as functional principles, such as iconicity and economy. It is these capacities and principles, they argue, that give language the shape it has.

Over the past decades, much attention has been devoted to categorization and imagination, as well as to pragmatic and functional principles, leaving aside attention, memory and even learning. This book aims to trigger a change that will redress the balance. And there are good reasons for wanting to achieve this. Finding out how linguistic patterns are discovered and mentally encoded and how these representations vary with experience lies at the core of the cognitive linguistic endeavour. Frequency, entrenchment and salience are therefore key concepts in cognitive approaches to language, and these relate directly to memory, attention and learning.

Linguists often overlook the fact that frequency effects are memory effects. Memory is affected by how items are presented over time, hence the way in which linguistic elements are presented over time should be a crucial consideration for usage-based linguists. The nearest linguistic equivalent of a time window is a contextual frame. Contextual frames are available at all levels of linguistic analysis: at the level of sounds that conjoin to form chunks, of chunks that form a clause and of sentences that make up the texts that capture our experiences. Context plays another role too: memory is context-dependent, and context helps retrieve memories, including linguistic memories. Therefore, context should play a crucial role in any realistic account of language cognition.

But experience cannot be reduced to frequency of exposure: information needs to be attended to – if only implicitly – before frequency can do its work; if information is not attended to, it may not be registered and encoded at all. It has been argued that attention, not frequency of repetition, determines which information is, first, attended to and, then, processed and encoded in memory. Therefore, what counts are not frequencies of events but frequencies of memories – the actual uptake by an individual speaker. The fact that repetition is not the only determinant of encoding in memory makes frequency-based measures very crude approximations of the relation between what is experienced and what is encoded.

Usage-based linguistics is predicated upon the premise that the knowledge of language emerges from exposure to usage. With our linguistic abilities believed to be rooted in general cognitive abilities, this leaves a prominent role to be played by learning. Yet, learning constitutes the language sciences' very own *elephant in the room*. A prominent learning theorist, Skinner (1957), attempted to show that the conceptual tools of behaviourism might also be useful for explaining verbal behaviour. His book aimed to provide a way to predict and control verbal behaviour by observing and manipulating the physical environment of the speaker. Chomsky's (1959) conceptually severely flawed review of Skinner's work was rhetorically highly effective and led to learning being exiled from the scene for at least three decades. Recent years have seen a resurgence in the interest in learning theory: learning models consider frequency of occurrence a fundamental force in and a powerful shaper of the language system, which remains dynamically responsive to experience throughout the lifespan.

This book proceeds from the guiding principle that any theorizing about language that aspires to cognitive reality must accord with findings from both linguistics and psychology. But researchers from these fields are separated by theoretical and methodological barriers. Jackendoff's (2007: 354) colleagues 'refused to consider linguistics a part of psychology or even of science, because linguists don't do experiments'. The divide between cognitive linguistics and the cognitive sciences can be bridged by explicitly linking work on learning, attention and memory, where the concept of frequency originated, to a usage-based analysis of linguistic complexity. How can the linguistic complexity we observe arise from the pressures jointly imposed by our need to communicate, our cultural embodiment and the constraints of our cognitive system? And how can general cognitive mechanisms provide sufficient power to explain how systems of such complexity can be learned and passed down the generations? Drawing together literature on frequency from all disciplines and using this knowledge to create a deeper understanding of the phenomenon reveals new paths along which to move the field forward. After all, in linguistics and psychology too, a failure to appreciate history dooms one to repeat the mistakes of the past.

3   What This Book Is Not About

Some will consider the decision to consider language as a mental phenomenon to the exclusion of its social dimension reductionist. As Divjak, Levshina and Klavan (2016) put it: the classical works in cognitive linguistics (e.g., Johnson 1987; Lakoff 1987; Langacker 1987; Goldberg 1995; Talmy 2000) describe the linguistic competence of the abstract idealized speaker of a language (predominantly English). Although the social basis of language was taken as a given in theory (Langacker 2016), this aspect was backgrounded in actual practice. With time, the limitations of this practice have become evident to many scholars. Croft, among others, criticizes the foundations of cognitive linguistics as being too solipsistic, that is, too much 'inside the head' (Croft 2009: 395).

The accumulation of such critical ideas has triggered a 'social turn' in cognitive linguistics (Harder 2010). This change reflects the general paradigmatic development in linguistics, also known as 'recontextualization' (Geeraerts 2010a). Recontextualization represents the return to a pre-structuralist holistic view of language, where language emerges and functions at the intersection of the cognitive, social, historical, cultural and biological domains. Indeed, there are more dimensions to language than the cognitive one that is in focus in this book. Domain-general cognitive processes shape the structure and knowledge of language alongside processes of human interaction (Beckner et al. 2009).

Language is used for human social interaction and is therefore dependent on its role in our social life: the evolution of language cannot be understood outside a social context. The nature of language follows from its role in social interaction: joint actions, so typical for socially interactive species, pose coordination problems (Lewis 1969) between the participants. These can be resolved with joint attention, for example, but communication (in itself a joint action) is by far the most effective coordination device. Humans have developed a conventional signalling system to facilitate communication. This system is to a large extent arbitrary but entrenched in a speech community. Yet, conventions are not infallible. On the one hand, and assuming that language knowledge emerges from exposure to language, there will always be a discrepancy between the prior uses that inform the speaker's choice of expression and those that inform the hearer's interpretation. On the other hand, each new situation is unique, and language typically offers multiple ways to construe the situation linguistically (Beckner et al. 2009: 3–5).

Within cognitive linguistics there are two ways in which the social dimension has been interpreted, i.e., as cognitive sociolinguistics and as social cognitive linguistics. Although these terms are often used interchangeably, there is an important difference in scope. Cognitive sociolinguistics focuses mainly on language varieties (lects), lectal variants and their cognitive representations including language attitudes (e.g., Kristiansen and Dirven 2008; Geeraerts, Kristiansen and Peirsman 2010). It argues strongly for the inclusion of a variational and sociolinguistic perspective into cognitive linguistic studies. The main aim of social cognitive linguistics, on the other hand, is to describe the social-interactional mechanisms of how usage shapes linguistic knowledge at the level of speaker and hearer. These mechanisms are rooted in general social cognitive abilities, such as joint action, coordination and convention (Croft 2009). An example of the social cognitive linguistic approach is Schmid's Entrenchment and Conventionalization Model (Schmid 2015, 2016b). The name of the model, which includes the cognitive notion of entrenchment and the social concept of conventionalization, iconically suggests that the cognitive and social aspects of language use should be treated on a par. At a more philosophical level, these aspects can be integrated with the help of phenomenology (Zlatev 2016), a discipline that focuses on human experience and helps to resolve the issues of whether language as 'experience' is individual or social, pre-linguistic or linguistic, unconscious or conscious.

4   What This Book Is About

This book is reductionist by choice. In the chapters that follow I will review research findings from across the cognitive sciences in order to gain a deeper understanding of *why* frequency has the effect it has and *what* role psychological and – to a lesser extent – neurological explorations of core cognitive processes can play in developing a cognitively more accurate theoretical account of language. The book starts with an excursion into history to reveal how information on the frequency of occurrence of words made its way into research on language and triggered a step change in how linguists think about language. However, the frequency measures that are standardly used in linguistics are rather crude: they do not acknowledge that memory encoding, storage and retrieval is a complex process, and that our experience is constrained by attention. Exploring alternative ways to track frequency that respect what we know about memory and attention will help to make theories of language cognitively more realistic. This is not the same as saying that the field of linguistics needs psychology and neurology to thrive. Linguistics has developed a range of techniques that facilitate describing the structures of a language accurately and economically. But if the aspiration is to describe language in a cognitively realistic way, then any description should accord with what we know about core cognitive abilities (Divjak 2015), and research into cognitive abilities is one of the topics psychology focuses on. Neurology provides insights that calibrate psychological theories by referring to the biological basis of behaviour.

To achieve its aims, this book consists of four parts, each of which can be read on its own, as they are devoted to introducing the main findings from work on frequency in language, memory, attention and learning. Although memory, attention and learning are all relevant for understanding language, they are ontologically different and complexly interrelated. While memory is typically thought of as a *structure* rooted in biology, learning is a *function* or a process. Memory and learning are co-dependent: more often than not we use the existence of memory traces as evidence for learning, and many indicators of memory effects are based on learning. Attention, on the other hand, is merely a construct, a useful but hypothetical 'device' which elegantly accounts for quite a divergent set of empirical phenomena that demonstrate the limits on memory and learning.

Overall, the book is aimed at readers with a background in empirical, usage-based linguistics who want to understand why frequency has played, and continues to play, such an important role in linguistic theorizing. Readers with a different background may need to read more laterally to fully appreciate the contents. The chapters provide background knowledge, as distilled from the vast (not to say overwhelming) literature on language, memory, attention and learning. They are *not* intended to be comprehensive or exhaustive in coverage. Instead, they provide a road map to relevant literature, highlighting work that best reflects the core principles and traces the progress made in these areas across a range of disciplines. The selection of literature *is* biased towards usage-based approaches of language, because those approaches have driven and have been driven by the interest in frequency in language and show most potential to integrate the findings. Since this book draws heavily on literature from the cognitive sciences, much of the evidence discussed is experimental in nature. Sometimes, this means that no clear story seems to emerge: evidence may not replicate or may be contradicted by other experiments. This is not to be seen as a weakness of experimental research, and as a reason to reject it. Rather, uncertainty constitutes the very essence of scientific investigation, and that is most certainly the case for research into an area as complex and multidimensional as language and language cognition.

In Part I, I focus on frequency. In Chapter 1, I trace the use of frequency data in the language sciences back to the introduction of word frequency lists for educational purposes. I spell out how word frequency lists were introduced into experimental work on language to control for exposure, yielding the observation of the word frequency effect. I also describe how quantitative linguists used the information contained in the frequency lists as points of departure for plotting word frequency distributions, on which the accuracy of frequency measures relies heavily. Chapter 2 looks in more detail at how the awareness of the human sensitivity to frequency of occurrence has changed the traditional view on language learning and representation and the effect it has had on the development of linguistic theories. I discuss the frequency measures that have played an important role in the development of usage-based linguistics and explain how they fit with theoretical assumptions. Chapter 3 considers the implications that the human sensitivity to frequency of occurrence could have for the nature of the language system. It discusses evidence that human cognition, including language cognition, would be captured better in probabilistic terms than by means of all-or-nothing rules.

In Part II, I zoom in on memory. In Chapter 4, I focus on the question of how frequency helps commit experiences, including linguistic experiences, to memory. After an introduction to where and how memories are stored, I review the main behavioural diagnostics of memory storage for linguistic information. In Chapter 5, I use this knowledge about how memory works to unravel entrenchment. Entrenchment is a foundational yet poorly defined concept in cognitive linguistics that captures how repeated encounters of a linguistic patterns strengthen its representation in memory.

Because frequency of occurrence does not capture actual uptake, in Part III, I move on to the brain's attention-orienting mechanisms, which influence potential uptake. In Chapter 6, I start by defining attention and discussing ways of deploying attention, before moving on to discussing how attention relates to memory and modulates the uptake of information. In Chapter 7, these insights are brought to bear on salience, a concept that usage-based linguists rely on to capture the effects of attention on language but that is characterized by a high level of terminological inconsistency. I discuss how attention is deployed during scene perception and the mechanisms language has to increase or decrease the salience of an item and guide the hearer's attention.

In Part Four, I look at approaches that could be used as stepping stones towards encompassing models that integrate frequency, memory and attention. Chapter 8 presents a number of approaches that are united by the central place they assign to prediction in explaining brain function – brains predict events – but differ in whether these predictions require stored memories. Moreover, these predictive approaches pose a new question: what type of learning mechanism is needed to yield the (particular types of) frequency effects observed? In Chapter 9, I present learning theory as an alternative to predictability-based approaches. Learning theory, regretfully conspicuously absent from the language sciences since the 1960s, accommodates frequency and its effects naturally. Learning theory describes the conditions that lead to learning, how learning proceeds and how it is translated into behaviour. Crucial for usage-based linguistics is the observation that learning increases with experience, or frequency of encounter. With our linguistic abilities believed to be rooted in general cognitive abilities, learning has a prominent role to play in linguistics.

In the final chapter, Conclusions, I map out future research avenues. For this, I rely on work from memory, attention and learning to answer the question of how and why we should be tracking and interpreting frequency to arrive at a more encompassing understanding of language structure and cognition.

Part I

1 Counting Occurrences: How Frequency Made Its Way into the Study of Language

The fundamental human capacity for learning a language has long been of interest to linguists, psychologists and neurologists alike. We take it for granted that any infant, in only a few years' time, will master at least the basics of a highly complex symbolic system. But how children accomplish this remarkable feat remains a mystery. Not only does building artificial systems with the same capability for language remain out of reach despite decades of phenomenal advances in computing, it is also far from obvious how this could be done. How is it, then, that *we* learn to communicate?

1.1 The Frequency Wars: the Role of Frequency in Nativist and Nurturist Frameworks

The lack of knowledge about the way in which language knowledge is built up has caused a rift between linguists of nativist and those of nurturist persuasions. Nativists promote a deterministic view of language: language is governed by the rules of an innate Universal Grammar, connected to a separate language faculty. Nurturists advocate a probabilistic view. Their starting point is the observation that human language systems are sensitive to frequencies of occurrence that can be dealt with by general cognitive learning mechanisms. In trying to prove one theory right and the other one wrong, advocates of both sides have turned to the way in which we become proficient language users: children achieve impressive results in a very short time while working from what appears to be very limited input.

Nativists believe that parts of the brain have evolved over time for the purpose of producing and understanding language. Most of users' knowledge of natural languages would be innate or dependent on language-specific cognitive mechanisms. Only a small part of language knowledge is 'triggered'; that is, it is acquired but not learned.[1] And what is acquired is a particular setting of

---

[1] Because the term 'acquisition' originates within generative linguistics, I will use it only in reference to work on language development and learning done within that framework. For work within the usage-based approach, I use 'language development' to refer to the process by which

15

a parameter that in itself is innate. This parameter specifies a fixed set of mutually exclusive linguistic properties, of which any given natural language can have only one. Nativists reason that grammar must be innate, considering the 'poverty of the stimulus'. The input children receive is not only ungrammatical and error-ridden (full of hesitations, self-corrections and ill-formed utterances), but also highly complex. This type of input constitutes a very poor database from which to deduce linguistic structure. The research programme of linguistic nativism or naturism therefore aims to show that very little knowledge of syntactic structure is acquired or learned from sensory stimuli. Instead, they hypothesize, infants are born with innate knowledge of how languages work and how they do not work. These innate biases allow children to figure out quickly, despite the poor quality of the limited amount of input they receive, what is and what is not possible in the grammar of their native language and allow them to master that grammar during the first few years of life.

Nurturists, on the other hand, claim that very little in language cognition depends on linguistic knowledge that is not acquired (or is acquired but not learned) or on language-specific cognitive mechanisms. Instead, they assume that infants are born possessing some basic cognitive abilities that develop through interactions with the environment but are not genetically encoded. Learning a language is thus a process in which learning mechanisms and abilities, such as pattern discovery, that are a part of a general cognitive learning apparatus play a key role; this obviates the need for an innate and specialized language-acquisition device. Over the last two decades, the nurturist approach to language has made impressive advances. Following the discovery that children's path to language is gradual and piecemeal and that adult speakers' language systems are sensitive to the frequencies of occurrence in language use, the conviction has grown that language is a dynamic and adaptive system emerging from use. At least part of the answer to the mystery of language development may thus be found in the input to which the learner is exposed.

The tension between these two points of view revolves around the simple facts that things that are innate need not be learned and things that can be learned need not be assumed to be innate. The difference between the approaches lies in their principled stance: in order to explain language cognition, do we exhaust all domain-general possibilities before making domain-specific assumptions, or do we not? Domain-general cognitive abilities are known to function in domains other than language, such as vision or motion. Some of these domain-general abilities that are crucial for language are

children learn their first language and I use 'language learning' to refer to the corresponding process for a second (or third, or . . .) language.

conventionalization   and   automation,   categorization   and   abstraction. Proponents of the usage-based approach advocate commencing the search for the cognitive abilities involved in language development, processing and representation by considering domain-general cognitive abilities rather than by assuming a priori that language requires special adaptations of cognitive functions (Elman and Bates 1996; Tomasello 2003; Bybee and Beckner 2009).

A distinctive property of human language is that the individual units and the sequences they form are highly repetitive. It is this repetition that leads to conventionalization of categories and associations, as well as to the automation of sequences (Bybee 2013: 50–1). Usage-based linguists propose that grammar is the result of the conventionalization of commonly used patterns: linguistic structure is formed through the repetition of linguistic patterns in language use. This explains why, within usage-based theory, the study of frequency effects of various sorts has contributed to the understanding of the nature of grammatical organization (Bybee 2007). Researchers working within the usage-based framework argue that sensitivity to frequency is a defining, if not the most important, feature of a successful account of language development, without positing that language development is frequency-driven or frequency-based. On a frequency-sensitive learning mechanism (which we will discuss in Chapter 9), frequency is not necessarily the main determinant of language development in all cases. Moreover, frequency may well be represented only indirectly, e.g., in the strength of neuronal connections or in the similarity structure of stored exemplars (Ambridge, Kidd et al. 2015: 240–1). Yet frequency effects are ubiquitous and attested for the development of the lexicon (single words), of morphology and of syntax (simple as well as more complex constructions). For an overview of the role frequency has played in the study of language development, see Gülzow and Gagarina (2007), Ambridge and Lieven (2011), Ambridge, Kidd et al. (2015) and Behrens and Pfänder (2016).

In an attempt to help generative linguistic theory, the main proponent of naturism, to accommodate frequency effects, Yang (2004: 451) proposed that both endowment and learning play a role in the acquisition of syntax. He argued against a domain-specific learning model of triggering and for a probabilistic learning mechanism that may well be domain-general but nevertheless operates in the domain-specific space of syntactic parameters. Phonology, lexicon and syntax – although governed by universal principles and constraints – vary from language to language and must be learned on the basis of linguistic experience. Yet no realistically efficient learning is possible without a priori restrictions on the learning space. Yang (2015: 287) casts doubt on the assertion that such frequency effects would be of any theoretical importance: in his view, a theory of language and language acquisition should not only account for what speakers say, but also for what they do not and cannot say. Ambridge and Lieven (2011: 374–5) suggest two further ways for generativists to incorporate frequency effects. Generativists could argue that (virtually) all utterances are constructed from scratch, but this process is easier, more fluent and less prone to error when items are combined that have been combined in that same way many times before. Alternatively, generativists could argue that some utterances are rote-learned and stored and function as short cuts in the production of frequent utterance types; this is especially the case when speakers are under cognitive pressure or need to reduce effort. But the dispute runs deeper than a discussion about the way in which to incorporate frequencies into linguistic theory: in fact, it goes back to the distinction between language structure (*Langue*) and language use (*Parole*) – as upheld by structuralists and adopted almost wholesale as 'competence' and 'performance' by generativists – and the assumed mutual independence between the two (Saussure 1916; but also Chomsky 1965). According to structuralists and generativists, structure trumps usage in the quest for the basic cognitive mechanisms that facilitate language.

Yet, outside linguistics, experience has long been considered a major contributor to cognitive representations. By the 1980s, a number of linguists had also begun to explore the effect that experience could have on grammar (Givón 1979; Bybee 1985). An important development here was the advent of corpus linguistics, which made it possible to investigate large(r) amounts of language than had previously been possible. Corpora not only made investigating frequencies of occurrence rather straightforward, they also showed that the strict dividing line between lexicon and grammar was untenable. After all, research on language as it is used made it clear that there are lexical constraints on grammatical structures: not all words fit all constructions, and often the choice for a lexical item limits the choice of possible constructions. For example, you *delay doing something* but you *wait to do something*. These observations fuelled the conviction that grammar was not a pre-existing, autonomous and fixed system, but an emerging one: it is fluid and continuously adapts to usage. Frequencies of occurrence are an excellent diagnostic of usage and of how usage affects the system. 'The frequency with which certain items and strings of items are used has a profound influence on the way language is broken up into chunks in memory storage, [on] the way such chunks are related to other stored material and [on] the ease with which they are accessed' (Bybee and Hopper 2001b: 3).

Newmeyer (2003) strongly objected to the claim that frequency of occurrence influences storage and retrieval. In his view, grammars may well have been shaped by real-time or online processing considerations, but their essence is not given by usage: grammar is the link between conceptualization and vocalization. It is only once language is used for communicative purposes that it begins to be shaped by the pressures of producing and comprehending language as quickly as possible. Yet the foundational conceptual structures remain part and parcel of grammatical representations (Newmeyer 2003: 684,

702). This stance appears to presume a primary function for language that is mentally oriented: language is used for thinking before it is used for communication.

The debates between nativists and nurturists are ongoing, but we will leave the comparison between the two approaches here and focus on the role that frequency of occurrence has played in the development of usage-based theories of language. Most usage-based approaches rely to some extent on frequencies of occurrence. In the following sections we will go on a short historical excursion to discover how frequency of occurrence became a topic of interest for the study of language. We will see how word frequency lists were introduced by educational psychologists with a view to improving language provision (Section 1.2). These lists proved their worth in psycholinguistics, where the observation of sensitivity to frequency gave rise to new ways of thinking about language (Section 1.3). Quantitative linguists took the art of counting words to a new level. They focused on how words are distributed across texts and laid bare some law-like regularities that help explain the learnability of language (Section 1.4).

1.2   Lexical Statistics and Word Frequency Lists

Frequency of occurrence appears to have crept into language research via word lists. *Word lists* and dictionaries were compiled as far back as the fifteenth century. The earliest lists had no frequency component but took the form of glossaries, with words grouped in categories such as body parts, animal names, names of occupations and so on. Some authors, such as Bright (1588), focused on shorthand, listing 559 words with their shorthand symbols and another 6,000 synonyms or antonyms of those 559 words. The seventeenth-century *Janua linguarum reserata* by Komenský (1631) is likely the first work to have added a frequency dimension (Těšitelová 1992: 15). *Word frequency lists* are lists that report the number of instances (*tokens*) of each word (*type*) in a collection of texts. In the early days, most of the word frequency research was applied and had an educational purpose, namely charting 'how many words were being taught and how many should be taught in spelling, reading, foreign language learning, and writing classes' (Bontrager 1991: 112). Pedagogical aims included improving spelling by 'supplying the words needed by the average person in his written expression' (Clarke 1921: 351). A representative spelling vocabulary, it was thought, could be achieved 'through the study of the words used by average persons in ordinary written discourse' (Clarke 1921: 349). Fries and Traver (1950) survey and review the efforts spent on counting words across a variety of languages during the first half of the twentieth century. They divide the word counts into four categories: (1) word counts to aid stenographers and the blind, (2) word lists for the teaching of spelling, (3) reading vocabularies and (4) measures of vocabulary size. They also include modern foreign language word counts and lists for English as a foreign language. But they did not foresee the impact word frequency lists would have on (psycho) linguistics.

1.2.1   A Brief Historical Overview of the Main Developments in Word Frequency Lists

The first frequency list in the proper sense of the word, i.e., a report that lists the number of times the form (token) of a word (type) is encountered in a particular collection of texts, was compiled by Kaeding (1898) for German. It was based on 11 million running words from legal and commercial texts; allegedly, more than 5,000 people were involved in reading, counting and tabulating letters, syllables and words (Leech, Rayson and Wilson 2014: foreword). Because the list was designed for use by stenographers, it listed the frequency of each inflected form separately: roots and root frequencies were not specific enough for the purposes of stenographers. Furthermore, frequencies of units smaller than words were also provided, e.g., syllables, prefixes, suffixes, stems, phones and letters, but word senses were not distinguished from each other.

One of the oldest and most important frequency dictionaries for English was compiled by Ayres (1915). Using a 368,000 corpus of words from commercial and private letters, he completed the first significant word count for purely pedagogical purposes, i.e., the teaching of spelling. After Eldridge (1911) had published a book listing 6,000 common English words for teachers, Thorndike, an American psychologist, educator, lexicographer and pioneer in educational research, composed three different word books to assist teachers with word and reading instruction. After *The Teacher's Word Book* (1921) that contained a list of the 10,000 most frequently used English words, two other books were published. The second book in the series, *A Teacher's Word Book of the Twenty Thousand Words Found Most Frequently and Widely in General Reading for Children and Young People*, was published in 1932, and the third and final book, *The Teacher's Word Book of 30,000 Words*, was published in 1944. The last study, also known as the Thorndike–Lorge study, was 'the culmination of half a century of effort in examining patterns of word usage' (Bontrager 1991: 92). Assisted by colleagues, Thorndike and Lorge had counted 18 million running words to provide the first large-scale frequency list of 30,000 lemmas or about 13,000 word families (Goulden, Nation and Read 1990). Note that this feat was achieved before the advent of modern computers. In 1953 the *General Service List* was published by Michael West, listing the roughly 2,000 most important words in English. The *General Service List* gives about 84 per cent coverage of general English (Browne, Culligan and Phillips 2013). The words on this list were selected to represent the most frequent words of English and were taken from a 2.5 to 5 million–word corpus of written English.[2] To maximize the utility of the list, some frequent words that overlapped broadly in meaning with words already on the list were omitted. In the original publication, the relative frequencies of various senses of the words were also included.

These word frequency lists were not intended to be given directly to students, but rather to serve as a guideline for teachers and book makers and help students move from high-frequency vocabulary and (thematic) vocabulary for special purposes to low-frequency vocabulary. Educationalists were the most important compilers and users of the word lists: they were concerned with making sure not only that native speakers learnt the meaning and spelling of the most frequent words, but also that learners acquired the core vocabulary of the language. As such, the influence of corpus-derived word lists extended to both first and second language pedagogy. Bontrager (1991: 94, 112) concludes that most of the counts were generated for pedagogical reasons, although some were designed to develop new writing systems, typically shorthand systems for stenographers. Contributions of this line of research include the discovery of a lack of systematic instruction across schools, insight into the norms and levels of knowledge facilitating educational intervention and greater objectivity in word knowledge assessment. For theoretical linguistics, one particular strand proved important. The bulk of lists drawn up before 1944 was compiled on the basis of written language, although at least one used oral data from phone conversations (French, Carter Jr and Koenig Jr 1930). These word count studies revealed that language, and spoken language in particular, was extremely repetitive (Dewey 1923): a few words occur often, while many words occur only occasionally. We will return to this observation in Section 1.4.

After 1960, word list compilation moved into a new era with the introduction of the computer, which proved exceptionally useful for compiling frequency lists. The best-known list among the early computer-assisted frequency lists is the one compiled by Kučera and Francis (1967). The corpus which Kučera and Francis derived their frequency list from, the Brown corpus, contained more than a million words sampled from 500 written texts (or 2,000 words per text) published in the United States in 1961. Since then, a plethora of corpora have been created to support diachronic and synchronic research programmes as well as research within and across languages, for native speakers and learners of a language (for an overview of influential corpora, see Xiao 2008). Alekseev (2005: 313–14) reported that more than 500 lists or dictionaries had been compiled for more than seven dozen languages, with English and Russian accounting for 30 per cent and 15 per cent of the totals respectively. Only

---

[2] The initial work was based on a 2.5 million–word corpus that was collected in 1938 under a grant from the Rockefeller Foundation: www.newgeneralservicelist.org.

about thirty of these works were based on more than a million words, and about ten of those were based on 2 million words. Lists cover different subtypes of language, e.g., written versus spoken language, the language of different genres such as fiction versus scientific writing or even specific authors.

1.2.2   Methodological Improvements that Would Influence (Psycho) linguistics

Despite the practical purpose of most of the early word frequency counts, the problems which the 'army of word counters' faced led to methodological improvements that would influence (psycho)linguistics. General issues included the choice of the unit of counting, types of sampling and corpus size. We will discuss each of these in turn.

Among the early issues that needed to be resolved was the definition of a word unit: while some compilers counted roots, others counted inflected forms and still others used in-between solutions. The rules used were often unique to a study, and this did not facilitate compiling existing lists into a larger, comprehensive one, a process piloted by Horn (1926). Fifty years on, the problem of defining the unit to be counted stood unresolved, and Allén would publish several versions of his frequency dictionary for Swedish: one for word forms (1970), one for lemmas (1971), one for collocations (1975) as well as morphemes and meanings (1980). In their paper critiquing methods and procedures commonly used when compiling word frequency lists, Faucett and Maki (1932) mentioned, among other things, the failure to distinguish between homonyms and the issue of separating words that formed established units, such as *for example.* What is typically counted is what happens to be a distinct orthographic form in the language, but these forms are often very different from what makes up a distinct form in speech (Baayen, Milin and Ramscar 2016: 1178).

Clarke (1921) compared his list of word types with Ayres's (1913) and concluded that even large samples may not be representative; it is the nature of the source material that characterizes the count, and vocabularies differ with geographical and social factors. Thorndike had in 1921 published a word list in which he championed a new measure: words were evaluated according to their mean frequencies in five samples of the material (Fries and Traver 1950: 21; Těšitelová 1992: 92). This gave a measure of the range of each word's occurrence or an indication of how widely the word is used. This insight signalled an early understanding that frequency is not the only factor determining salience and became a precursor of contemporary word dispersion measures that would soon appear, i.e., first in the work of Vander Beke (1930) and then more thoroughly in Juilland, Brodin and Davidovitch (1970). Vander Beke's

(1930) contribution was to evaluate words not only according to the frequency coefficient, but also using the distribution coefficient, that is, according to the number of texts in which the word occurs. Juilland, Brodin and Davidovitch (1970) worked with a combination of coefficients of frequency, usage and dispersion. The usage coefficient would check to which extent the usage in the corpus would differ from usage in language in general, while the dispersion coefficient would correct the absolute frequency of occurrence for distribution over subcomponents of the corpus.

Frequency list compilation yielded quantitative linguistic insights too, such as the demonstration that the reliability of the statistical approach ended at 1,000 to 1,500 words; after the first 1,000 words, variations become increasingly frequent (Fries and Traver 1950: 26). Furthermore, language was – once again – found to be highly repetitive, an observation that would lead to the study of word frequency effects, described in Section 1.3 as well as the study of word frequency distributions, introduced in Section 1.4.

1.3   Word Lists in Psycholinguistics: the Discovery of the Word Frequency Effect

Word frequency has played an important role in psychology, and the discovery of the word frequency effect is often ascribed to Cattell, who worked on the measurement of visual word-recognition thresholds. Interestingly, Cattell (1886) does not discuss the effects of frequency on recognition time, but the effects of 'connexion' or context on reaction time. He found that it takes twice as long to read 'words which have no connexion as words which make sentences, and letters which have no connexion as letters which make words'. This effect was therefore termed the word superiority effect (WSE): the existence of the word superiority effect has been taken to imply that words have an access or encoding advantage over non-words. Important insights into the origins of the word superiority effect came from Reicher (1969) and Wheeler (1970), who developed the basic experimental paradigm to study the word superiority effect, referred to as the Reicher–Wheeler paradigm. Frequency was suggested as one of the mechanisms underlying the processing distinction between isolated letters and words: real words are more frequently encountered and used. In the original study by Cattell (1886: 65), frequency is mentioned only indirectly in the description of experiments on reading a foreign language. He concluded that the 'rate at which a person reads a foreign language is proportional to his familiarity with the language'. And, of course, words that are more familiar tend to be those with higher frequency of occurrence.

1.3.1   Single Word Frequency

Although there was awareness of word familiarity as a factor to be considered in visual word-recognition threshold measurements, word frequency was never systematically varied in this research paradigm until Howes experimented with it in his 1951 dissertation (Levelt 2013: 457–8). He found correlations between the logarithm of (word) frequency (as calculated on the basis of corpora containing more than 4 million words) and recognition thresholds with correlations in the range of 75 per cent (Howes and Solomon 1951). This demonstrated that the visual duration thresholds for words are a function of word frequency with more frequent words requiring shorter presentations for recognition. Similar results were obtained in the auditory domain. Howes (1957) showed the same relation for the recognition of spoken words in noise: in noisy conditions subjects are better at identifying more frequent words. Savin (1963) added that recognition errors tended to consist of more frequent words substituting for lower-frequency words, e.g., you might misread a rarer word like *squill* as a more familiar word like *squid*.

Oldfield and Wingfield (1965) presented subjects with pictures and found that pictures with high-frequency names were named faster than pictures with low-frequency names. Wingfield (1968) showed that the effect was not replicated when subjects were asked to recognize but not label the pictures. He considered this as confirmation of the fact that the effect was caused by the frequency of the words rather than by the frequency of the pictured objects.

The lexical decision paradigm, where subjects decide whether a string of letters forms a word or not, revealed that decisions about high-frequency words are made faster than decisions about low-frequency words (Rubenstein, Garfield and Millikan 1970). Forster and Chambers (1973) used a naming paradigm, where subjects read a word out loud, to show that high-frequency words are named more quickly than low-frequency words. Grosjean (1980) showed, using a gating paradigm where the waveform of a spoken word is progressively released, that high-frequency words are recognized with less of the wave form revealed. This means that high-frequency words, such as *because*, are more likely to be recognized after less of the word has been heard than are low-frequency words, such as *beckon*.

After 1960, more sophisticated controls started to be used in psychological experiments, and frequency was one of those controls. Materials were required to be scaled, normed or rated in terms of, for example, frequency, familiarity, meaningfulness, associability and other properties, depending on the task. Bradshaw (1984) compiled a catalogue of 119 studies, most published after 1960, that provide norms, ratings and lists of verbal material for use in experiments. The materials included in his catalogue are comprehensive and were derived using rigorous objective or subjective approaches.

The objective approach relies on frequency counts of the occurrence of certain letters or words in written or spoken English. Jones and Wepman (1966) provided a count of the different words spoken by a selected sample of 54 English-speaking adults and the frequency with which each of the different words was used in the Thematic Apperception Test. Interestingly, most studies on English have relied on word frequency statistics calculated from the 1 million Brown corpus that contains texts written in 1961 and are not representative of what a contemporary, average speaker would read. This introduces, in fact, a very strong bias against finding frequency effects, yet strong and robust effects of these corpus frequencies have nevertheless been found (Jurafsky 2003: 43).

The subjective approach requires a sample group of subjects to estimate the frequency of occurrence of items or, for example, to rate them for familiarity or meaningfulness. Bradshaw (1984: 202) recommends objective measures wherever possible but points out that studies have shown that in the context of everyday language, subjects' estimated frequencies tend to match the objective occurrence of a given variable quite closely. Moreover, objective ratings may be impossible to obtain, for example, in the case of ratings for imageability or meaningfulness.

In psycholinguistics, frequencies of occurrence are now routinely considered when controlling for participants' experience with the lexicon of their language. Much of the psycholinguistic work which incorporates frequency is done in the area of single word processing (just under half of all chapters in Gaskell 2007 deals with words). Data from techniques that measure visual word recognition (see Besner and Humphreys 1991 for an overview of early work in the area) are used to answer questions regarding inflectional and derivational morphological processing.

One line of inquiry into morphological processing focused on correlations between response latencies in visual decision tasks and various frequency measures related to inflected forms, or token frequencies. Taft (1979) used the word frequency effect as a diagnostic for determining whether affixed words coming from the same stem are stored together or separately in the lexicon. Think of words that share the same stem such as *persuade* and *dissuade* that share *-suade* or *approach* and *reproach* that share *-proach*. Taft established a negative correlation between response latencies in a lexical decision task and the surface frequency of an inflected form in a corpus: more frequent forms are recognized faster, while less frequent forms take longer to process. Schreuder and Baayen (1997) found that the processing of a singular form of monomorphemic Dutch nouns is influenced by the summed frequency of the singular and plural forms. That is, words that were matched for frequency of their singular form but differed in frequency of use of the plural form were processed differently: words with low-frequency plurals such as *barks* or *breezes* were processed more slowly than words with high-frequency plurals such as *fields* or *digits*. They also found that subjective frequency ratings are strongly correlated with response latencies in visual lexical decision. Baayen, Lieber and Schreuder (1997) explored the reaction of derivational patterns with respect to stem frequency, family frequency and family size. Their experiments revealed that one specific frequency measure, morphological family size, affects processing times. The higher the number of derived words and compounds in which a noun appears as constituent, the higher the subjective frequency ratings it receives and the shorter its response latencies are. This distinguishes the recognition of words like *acid* and *pole* that belong to large morphological families from words that belong to small morphological families such as *circus* and *corpse*.

These and other studies confirmed the value of token frequencies – or other distributional factors that correlate with these frequencies – for predicting latencies in the processing of inflected forms. There is, however, much disagreement in this highly productive area of research and conflicting findings abound. Whether affixed words such as *illegible* are accessed whole or in decomposed form as a combination of *i(l)* and *legible* has been extensively discussed. Hay (2001: 1061–3) attributes the disagreement surrounding the processing of affixed words at least partially to the fact that the relation between the base form *legible* and the derived form *illegible* may affect response latencies rather than the frequency of either form separately.

It has also been argued that age of acquisition (Morrison, Ellis and Quinlan 1992; Morrison and Ellis 1995; Juhasz 2005) or cumulative frequency (Zevin and Seidenberg 2004) are more powerful determinants of recognition than overall frequency of occurrence. Age of acquisition ratings or norms are typically subjective and stem from participants indicating at which age they (think they) acquired a certain word. For example, it is expected that subjects will rate *elephant* as acquired earlier than *frequency*. How age of acquisition has an effect on word recognition remains disputed. Some argue that age of acquisition achieves its effect through cumulative frequencies: at a certain moment in time, a word learned earlier will likely have been encountered more often than a word learned later.

Evidence has now accumulated suggesting that factors which are highly correlated with repetition frequency are more strongly correlated with the observed behavioural outcomes than repetition frequency itself. Baayen, Milin and Ramscar (2016) confirmed that frequency is part of a large set of collinear predictors, including lexical properties such as word length, semantic diversity and age of acquisition, to name but a few. That is, frequency correlates strongly with these other variables, which means that those variables could equally well be responsible for effects that have traditionally been attributed to frequency. Moreover, the question of which operationalization of frequency predicts which experimental outcome best remains an area of active debate. Effects of frequency vary considerably across tasks and modalities: frequencies culled from subtitles predict response times in lexical decision and word-naming tasks better than frequencies from any other genre (New et al. 2007; Brysbaert and New 2009; but see Heister and Kliegl 2012). The problem is further exacerbated by the existence of substantial individual differences in language processing abilities that derive to a large extent from individual differences in exposure to language (Dąbrowska 2015). The experience of each language user is unique and interacts with their individual cognitive abilities.

1.3.2 Word Frequency in Context

Regardless of whether and how the dispute regarding the effect of repetition frequency on (single) word recognition is resolved, findings obtained through lexical decision tasks are only of limited interest to linguists. Psycholinguists, it seems, have a penchant for isolating words. The field has spent decades focusing on single word form (token) frequency, i.e., the frequency with which one particular stimulus is repeated in the environment. Lexical decision tasks have extremely low ecological validity since they rely on decisions language users make when they are exposed to a word in isolation, which is unlikely to happen in a realistic communicative situation.

Only in the last fifteen years have alternatives to single word repetition frequency been explored in psychology. These measures take into account the natural context in which a word occurs. One of these alternatives is the number of different contexts a word can appear in. McDonald and Shillcock (2001) proposed contextual distinctiveness as a summary measure of the frequency distribution of the contexts in which a word appears. Contextual distinctiveness was found to be a better predictor of lexical decision latencies than occurrence frequency. Adelman, Brown and Quesada (2006) simply used the number of passages or documents in which words occurred to quantify what they call contextual diversity. Even when using this very crude way to operationalize 'context', contextual diversity predicted more variance in lexical decision and naming latencies than did single word repetition frequency. This suggests that contextual diversity is the psychologically more relevant variable.

Research on explanations for frequency effects turned another corner with Johns et al.'s (2012) claim that what really facilitates lexical processing is semantic distinctiveness. Like Adelman, Brown and Quesada (2006), they counted the number of distinct documents in which a word occurred. However, they defined the similarity of any pair of documents as a function of the proportion of overlapping words in those two documents; the larger the number of words that occur in both documents, the higher the similarity between those documents. A word's semantic distinctiveness was defined as the mean dissimilarity over all the documents in which the word occurred. When used to predict lexical decision and naming times from the Balota et al. (2007) English lexicon database, semantic distinctiveness predicted more variance in response times than word frequency and contextual diversity.

Among corpus linguists, context has always been an important issue. Work on lexicography rarely uses counts of the occurrence of an individual word form in isolation: words (may) express different meanings depending on the context. Classical concordances return a list of usage examples of the item of interest and count its number of occurrences. Words are thus typically examined in their phrasal or sentential context. Indeed, collocation and colligation are core concepts in corpus linguistics. Collocations are words that are regularly used together and give rise to an association, such as *scenic route* or *winding road*. In colligations, a lexical item is linked to a grammatical one, for example the *-ing* form that is obligatory after verbs of perception *I am looking forward to seeing you* or *I heard him playing the guitar*. Raw frequencies do not provide a reliable way of distinguishing collocates or colligates objectively from frequent non-collocates or non-colligates. The combination of *the* and *review* will be rather frequent due to the frequency of *the*, but *the review* is not a collocation; *peer review*, on the other hand, is. To address this issue collocation scores are calculated that compare expected to observed frequencies and establish whether the observed frequency of co-occurrence of *peer review* is greater than what one would expect to find by chance given the frequencies with which each of the words that form the pair, here *peer* and *review*, occur. The number of association measures available within computational corpus linguistics has grown rapidly over the last decades, and I refer to Evert (2005) and Pecina (2009) for exhaustive inventories. We will look at some of these measures in more detail in Chapter 2.

Corpus linguists have also developed measures of contextual diversity, using the label 'dispersion', which we briefly touched upon in Section 1.2.2. Dispersion quantifies the homogeneity of the distribution of a word in a corpus (Lyne 1985), that is, it assesses whether a word occurs uniformly across texts or whether its occurrence is limited to a few texts instead. Is the word of high frequency because it is heavily used in a limited number of texts, or is it because it is used across a large number of texts? As we will see in Chapter 4, each scenario influences retention in memory differently. Gries (2008, 2010) provides an overview of dispersion measures, including those that penalize words for not occurring uniformly across a corpus. Behavioural data in this area is scarce, but Baayen (2010) shows that although frequency emerges as the strongest predictor in single-predictor models, it is highly correlated with many other lexical attributes. Once this correlation is accounted for, frequency does not represent a particularly important predictor in itself.

Instead, the most important predictor of lexical decision latencies is a composite, consisting, among other things, of contextual measures such as lexical diversity or dispersion and syntactic and morphological family size.

The crucial finding is that once context is taken into account, as linguists would advocate, the single word frequency effect may disappear, even in domains where it has been extensively evidenced. Raymond and Brown (2012), for example, find no evidence for the role of word frequency in reduction, once contextual co-occurrence factors have been taken into account. Baayen, Milin and Ramscar (2016: 1207) remark on the 'crudeness of our frequency counts, the absence of proper sense disambiguation and lemmatisation, and decontextualization'. Contextualized frequencies yield better predictions than isolated frequencies: the brain makes use of learned contextual regularities. This is to be expected: seminal studies from the 1970s, such as Biederman, Glass and Stacy (1973), had already demonstrated that objects are recognized faster and more accurately when accompanied by contextual information. We will return to this in Chapter 4, where it will become clear why basic requirements of memory should be taken into account when designing measures to capture exposure and experience.

But there is more to single word frequency than meets the eye. The different frequencies with which words appear in texts or are used in speech reveal interesting patterns that display law-like behaviour. Word frequency distributions have been studied for over a hundred years, but the results of this area of investigation are generally less well known in linguistics. Section 1.4 introduces the main players and summarizes key findings.

1.4   Word Frequency Distributions and the Beginning of Quantitative Linguistics

Herdan (1956, 1966) mentions a number of early yet 'noteworthy attempts' to investigate 'linguistic structure using statistical methods'. Among the early explorers that went beyond 'counting words' are Förstemann (1852, on phoneme distributions in Greek, Latin and Gothic), Drobisch (1866, on Latin hexameters), Mariotti (1880, on Dante), Lutosławski (1897, on Plato), Niceforo (1916), Dewey (1923, on English speech sounds), Yule (1944, on the distribution of nouns), Zipf (1932), Boldrini (1948, on the distribution of Italian phonemes in poetry) and Porter (1951, on the Greek hexameter). Some of these authors were engaged with literary or stylo-statistics and looked at overlaps between texts in terms of vocabulary and frequency of occurrence, while others were interested in phoneme distributions.

In France, leading stenographer Jean-Baptiste Estoup (1902) worked with seventy-five texts, totalling 30,000 words. He had taken successive thousand-word samples and counted how many *new* words appeared in each sample.

While the first sample contained 336 different words, the thirtieth and final sample contained only thirty-six new words. The histogram of these data revealed 'the characteristic hyperbolic falling curve' (Levelt 2013: 450) that would soon propel the study of the quantitative aspects of language into a new era.

In the USA, Edward Uhler Condon (1928), an employee of the Bell Telephone Laboratories, published a note in *Science* on 'an interesting functional relationship' between the frequencies of words in a text sample and the ranks of these frequencies. Using the word counts by Ayres (1915) and Dewey (1923), Condon had plotted the logarithm of the observed frequency of the nth word against the logarithm of n. The correlation that appeared was linear, and negative. He suggested that this correlation might be 'a quantitative appearance in language of the Weber–Fechner Law in Psychology'. The Weber–Fechner law describes how the change in a stimulus that will be just noticeable is a constant ratio of the original stimulus. If we notice when 1 kilogram's worth of books has been added to a suitcase originally weighing 10 kilograms but not when 500 grams of books have been added to that same suitcase, then 2 kilograms' worth of books need to be added to a suitcase originally weighing 20 kilograms for us to notice any difference. That is, the resolution of perception diminishes for stimuli of greater magnitude. Or, 'in the language of the economist, it is a quantitative law of diminishing utility on vocabulary. The frequency of use of a word measures in some way its usefulness in transmitting ideas between individuals' (Condon 1928: 300). And so the first power law for language was born.

Three of the first and most well-known researchers in the area of word frequency distributions from the Anglo-Saxon tradition were George Kingsley Zipf in the USA and G. Udny Yule and Gustav Herdan in the UK. Zipf was a philologist who turned to statistics, while Yule and Herdan were statisticians with an interest in literature. I will consider each of them in turn in the following two subsections. Focus on these three grandfathers of quantitative linguistics does not negate the contributions made by other researchers, outside of the Anglophone world. Těšitelová (1992: 82–100) summarizes more than a century of work on lexical statistics in Germanic, Romance, Slavonic, Finno-Ugric and Chinese, and the *Handbook of Quantitative Linguistics* edited by Köhler, Altmann and Piotrowski (2005) provides an excellent survey of the field, including work in syntactic and semantic statistics.

1.4.1   Zipf: a Philologist Fascinated by Word Frequencies

One of the main observations in Zipf (1935), and one that would change the field, captured the fact that there are only a few words of very high frequency and large numbers of words of low frequency, and especially many words that appear only once in a whole text. Thus, in language as it is used, there appear to be relatively few words with high frequencies of use, but large numbers of words with low frequencies of use. 'The large proportion of nouns used only once was a complete surprise' (Yule 1944: 3) and the observation gave rise to questions concerning the nature of this new, highly skewed and asymmetrical frequency distribution. Zipf was fascinated by the nearly linear relation between number of words and number of occurrences in a plot. Relying on ranks, he devised a function to capture this relation for texts of any length, and his formula has been adjusted many times over the past seventy-five years so as to generalize better (for a recent overview see Piantadosi 2014).

1.4.1.1 Zipf's First and Second Law   In any text, the most frequent word will occur approximately twice as often as the second most frequent word, three times as often as the third most frequent word, and so on. As is shown in the left-hand panel of Figure 1.1, there is a very rapid decrease in frequency amongst the most frequent words, which becomes slower as the rank grows, leaving very long tails of words with similar low frequencies (Baroni 2008: 813). Zipf formulated a first law that captures the relation between the frequency of occurrence of a word and its rank when the words are ordered with respect to frequency of occurrence. This relation can be expressed as the inverse relation between the logarithm of the word's rank and the logarithm of the word's frequency. The right-hand panel of Figure 1.1 visualizes how the frequency of any word is inversely proportional to its rank in the frequency table when both are plotted on a logarithmic scale. In other words, frequency is a non-linearly decreasing function of rank. Těšitelová (1992: 53) subsequently specified that this relation only holds for the area of the curve where rank is identical to order, i.e., where every word has its own frequency, rather than where many words share the same frequency.

Zipf made other valuable observations about the use of words. Zipf's second law describes a relation between the frequency of occurrence of a word and the number of different words occurring with that frequency: there are very few highly frequent words, but many rarely used words. This had been observed before by the creators of early word lists, who tended to remark on the repetitiveness of language: most of what we say or write is achieved with a limited number of words. The abundance of the lowest-frequency types has important consequences for the statistical analysis of word frequency data and natural language processing applications (Baayen 2001: 8; Evert 2005: 124), which struggle to make predictions on the basis of small numbers. As Herdan (1964: 19) would put it: *de minimis lex non curat* ('The law does not concern itself with trifles'). This finding is of importance for measures of collocation that have been used quite extensively in corpus-based approaches to language (see Chapter 2, Section 2.2.1).

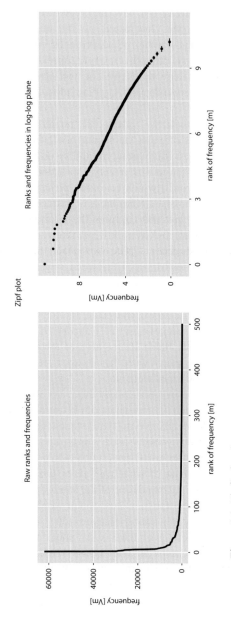

Figure 1.1 Zipf's first law

The distributional curves observed by Zipf were found to display a uniform shape for a variety of topics, authors and languages (Miller in Zipf 1935: vi/ 1968) and Zipf proposed the formula $ab^2=k$ (where a represents the number of words of a given occurrence and b the number of occurrences) to describe the word distributions of all but the most frequently used words in Latin, English and Chinese. The mathematician Mandelbrot (1953) generalized Zipf's formula by adding a second free parameter to enhance the model's accuracy for the extremes where frequency appears to be dropping more rapidly than predicted by Zipf's law (Baayen 2001: 36, 88; Baroni 2008: 815). Montemurro (2001) showed that the Zipf–Mandelbrot law zooms in on the statistical behaviour of a fraction of the total number of words contained in a corpus, i.e., in the middle-low to low range of the rank variable between 100 and 2,000. Later, it was shown that new and solid statistical regularities emerge as the sample size is increased. In large text samples with a high degree of homogeneity the power law ceases to apply between ranks 3,000 and 4,000, regardless of text length. Yet in a large corpus (of about 180 million words) that contains the collective use of language by a society of individuals, a second power law was observed for words beyond ranks 5,000–10,000. Ferrer i Cancho and Solé (2001) showed that word frequency as a function of the rank follows two different exponents. The two observed exponents divide words in two different sets: a kernel lexicon formed by a number of versatile words (5,000 to 6,000 for the British National Corpus) and an unlimited lexicon for specific communication.

1.4.1.2 Zipf's Principle of Economy and Least Effort   The reformulations and corrections to Zipf's laws do not change the fact that Zipf (1949, 1965) thought about word frequency distributions in terms of a universal property of the human mind, and searched for a principle of 'least effort' that would explain the equilibrium between uniformity and diversity in word use. He proposed that neither speakers nor hearers of a given language want to work any harder than necessary to reach understanding. Speakers minimize their production efforts by using only a few words very frequently while listeners minimize perceptual confusion by having a large vocabulary of distinct words (Baroni 2008: 816–17). Thorndike (1937) was rather sceptical of this interpretation and described Zipf's findings as a statistical effect, rather than a psychological tendency towards an equilibrium.

In an attempt to adduce more evidence for his Principle of Economy, Zipf (1949: 66) tried to formulate a third law that would capture the relation between the frequency of a word and the number of its meanings: words with higher frequencies tend to have more lexical meanings than words with lower frequencies. To be precise, the number of meanings of a word is proportional to the square root of the word's frequency, and Zipf argued that this is what we would expect if both forces, frequency and variety, are in equilibrium. Těšitelová (1992: 55) later countered that this generalization seems to hold only for formal words. Zipf (1935: 27) also proposed a law of abbreviation: the length of a word tends to bear an inverse relationship to its relative frequency.

Combining all three dimensions, Zipf (1935: 28–39) explored the relationship between high frequency, limited variety and shortness in length and discovered that more frequent words are more likely to get shortened, and this abbreviation appears intentional as it reduces effort. Joos (1936) objected that speakers may well choose shorter words to minimize effort and thereby increase the frequency of those words. However, Urrutibétheity (1972) later demonstrated on the basis of Spanish data that an increase in frequency of a word correlates with an increase in the probability of that word being functional, formal, shorter, older and belonging to the core of the lexicon. This line of research was taken further within psycholinguistics and usage-based historical linguistics. Zipf (1935), finally, provided evidence that easy phonemes should be more frequent than more complex phonemes, using data on six phonemes in twelve languages. To illustrate this claim, he used the example of the voiceless consonants *t, p, k* that are more frequent than the corresponding voiced ones *d, b, g*. Joos (1936) took issue with this finding too, claiming that a voiced stop is easier to manage as it does not require cessation of voice after a vowel.

Despite the fact that Zipf's psychological explanations were not supported, and that a satisfactory psychological explanation of why certain words are chosen at certain points remains to be proposed (Piantadosi 2014: 1127), the distribution that Zipf had discovered and popularized has been used across a number of disciplines focused on language. Skinner (1937), for example, applied Zipf's rank-frequency analysis to the thousand associations that had been given in response to each of a hundred stimulus words (as collected by Kent and Rosanoff 1910). Once hapax legomena or words that only occur once were excluded, a Zipf curve arose.

Zipf's law likewise attracted a lot of attention in quantitative linguistics. Mandelbrot (1953), relying on information-theoretic notions, did see the Zipfian distribution as a way to minimize the average cost per unit of information in a text. Yet, it was later shown that Zipfian patterns can be observed in the output of a random generation process. If we assume that word-boundary markers are scattered randomly throughout a text, then there will necessarily be a higher occurrence of short than of long words (Miller 1957: 313). But, if the underlying process is stochastic in nature, this would preclude interpreting Zipf's law in terms of general principles of language or communication such as 'least effort'. As Miller (1957: 314) put it: 'The rule is a simple consequence of those intermittent silences which we imagine to exist between successive words.'

Linguists were sceptical of Zipf's findings. Halliday (1991: 31) questioned what significance such generalizations as the Zipfian curve might have and Gross (1972: 154) concluded that Zipf's law 'has been found to be of such generality that no precise use of it can be made in linguistics'. Yet, within usage-based linguistics it has been argued that robust language learning, despite learners' idiosyncratic experience, is supported by the existence and convergence of Zipf-like distributions across linguistic form and function. Goldberg, Casenhiser and Sethuraman (2004) reported that subjects learn constructions better when the distribution of the types is more skewed. Goldberg (2006) argued that Zipfian type-token frequency distributions in natural language constructions might optimize learning by providing one very high-frequency exemplar that is also prototypical in meaning. Ellis and Ferreira-Junior (2009) tested this proposal for English as a second language. Using data from the European Science Foundation corpus, they showed that the type-token distribution of Verb Argument Constructions such as the verb locative, the verb object locative and the ditransitive in the input is Zipfian. Learners first use the most frequent, prototypical and generic exemplar, such as *put* in the verb object locative and *give* in the ditransitive. Learning is thus driven by the frequency and frequency distribution of exemplars within constructions and by the match of their meaning to the construction prototype (see also Bybee 2008; Lieven and Tomasello 2008).

Gries (2012: 503; 2015: 532–3) added that construction learning may well thrive on the Zipfian nature of the distribution because of the low-entropy environments that follow from it. A construction or a constructional category can be thought of as an exemplar cloud in multivariate or multidimensional space that is Zipfian along several formal and functional dimensions and therefore low in uncertainty along these dimensions. Uncertainty can be reduced along multiple dimensions simultaneously, such as when a child realizes that *give* is used in contexts with two human beings and an object, and the object is transferred from one human being to the other. When such a confluence of dimensions is observed, a part of the exemplar cloud is 'isolated', and this could give rise to a constructional category that linguists would label ditransitive. This process is aided further if fewer types account for more tokens, as such a ratio lowers the entropy of the distribution.

Zeldes (2012: 201–10) invoked Hebbian learning to explain why skewed distributions with few frequent types and many rare types lead to productivity. Usage physically changes the brain and makes subsequent usage along the same lines more likely. Because links between co-activated neurons are strengthened, so-called neuron assemblies emerge, which can represent perceptual categorizations and the concepts they give access to. Every instance activates that class. Such an abstract 'spurious representation' is arguably more powerful than any of the actual inputs. If a construction is acquired from a few very frequent prototypes, exemplar and abstraction only ever get activated together. If, instead, there are many rare types (each on its own too rare to build up the exemplar's representation), then the construction path expressing the communalities between the exemplars is strengthened instead and can be transferred to other instances.

1.4.2   Yule and Herdan: a Statistical Approach to Literary Style

Yule is widely known for *An Introduction to the Theory of Statistics* that appeared in fourteen editions and was translated into Czech, Polish, Spanish and Portuguese (Kendall 1952: 161). He turned to literary statistics only towards the end of his career. Yule proposed the Characteristic K, a lexical constant or measure of the repeat rate that is independent of sample size, sampling fluctuations aside. Yule initially considered using K as an index of richness of vocabulary but had to abandon that interpretation (Herdan 1964: 71).

Yule's last published book, *The Statistical Study of Literary Vocabulary*, is mainly concerned with resolving authorship disputes by reference to the richness of vocabulary. In it, Yule indicates that Zipf's work was known to him, but he does not engage with it. He merely criticizes Zipf's formula in passing as 'an unlikely sort of formula'.[3] Part of the divergence in Zipf's and Yule's results may be attributable to the long-standing and hitherto unresolved problem of deciding (or rather: agreeing) on the minimal unit of counting. Zipf (1935: 40) included all parts of speech in his research and counted every inflected form separately, whereas Yule focused on nouns and counted lexemes. Zipf's approach brings the percentage of once-words in a highly inflected language like Latin up to 64 per cent and to 49.6 per cent for English, while in Yule's calculations once-words make up just over 41 per cent of the entire word count (Yule 1944: 33).

Herdan, like Yule, was (at least initially) mainly concerned with literary style (literary statistics or stylo-statistics). He proposed an interpretation of Yule's constant, Characteristic K, as the relative fluctuation of the mean frequency of word occurrence. This enabled him to describe style in terms of a statistical concept: style is characterized by a constant ratio between uniformity and diversity of word frequencies (Herdan 1964: 71). He also specified that K was to be interpreted as a type-token statistic: a sample value of the repeat rate of vocabulary for the language in question (Herdan 1964: 151). In fact, K is

---

[3] Recall that Zipf formulated $nf^r=k$ or the number of words multiplied by an exponentiation of their occurrence equals a constant; this exponent is 2, except in very short or very long texts. Yule considered this formula problematic because it will have estimable (i.e., finite) values of mean and deviation only for a specific, narrow range of values of the exponent (r) (Yule 1944: 55).

a measure of the dispersion of vocabulary items as regards frequency of occurrence (Herdan 1964: 165).

But Herdan studied more than style. His interest was in applying statistical methods to linguistic phenomena in general. He wrote *Quantitative Linguistics* in 1964, then followed this up with *The Advanced Theory of Language as Choice and Chance* in 1966. Herdan appears to have been the first to present an overall view of quantitative linguistics and a wealth of ideas can be found in his writings. In fact, Herdan (1964: 9) made observations on the role of frequency in language that remain relevant today. He starts by mentioning that there are linguists who maintain that the frequency of linguistic forms is not a part of language but belongs to the *use* of words, and *use* is arbitrary. Herdan argues against this by referring to the fact that *language* intervenes between *langue* and *parole*, i.e., it provides the pattern for the individual utterances in *la parole*.

All laws of language except those which are basic laws of logic are statistical in nature, since they are behavioural conventions through frequency of use, but there is a difference, according to the numbers involved, between the established laws and the statistical ones in the more restricted sense of the term. Whereas the number of times which a new linguistics form has to be used to 'graduate', so to speak, as a part of *la langue* must be astronomically large, the idiosyncrasies of style which are expressed as statistical laws of *le langue* occur in much smaller numbers. This is why the statistical laws take the form of relative frequencies or, if better established, of probabilities. These are to be regarded as quantitative laws of language, in contradistinction to the conventional qualitative laws. (Herdan 1964: 18)

The discipline of linguistics is thus concerned with aspects of language which remain stable in the speech community despite inter-speaker variation. Typically, these aspects cover the three dimensions of sounds (the phonemic system), forms (the grammatical system) and meaning (the lexical system). The frequency of linguistic forms shows a comparable stability and should therefore be recognized as the fourth dimension, a fourth coordinate in Cartesian terms. Herdan (1964: 9) stresses that the similarity between adding frequency to structural linguistics and adding time to classical physics is more than an analogy since the frequency element is 'the time measured in occurrence units which a given linguistic form occupies in the whole length of the line of discourse'. In general, Herdan thought of the statistics needed to deal with language data much along the lines of the quantum statistics needed to deal with data from physics, in particular small particle physics (Herdan 1966: 431), since '[t]he masses of linguistic forms [. . .] are a part of the physical universe, and as such are subject to the laws which govern mass assemblies of any kind [. . .]' (Herdan 1960: 3). This is a rather unusual view on language. It is more standard to assume that language is about nature, but not of nature, and therefore not subject to the same laws. That is to say, language cognition is more than the physics of soundwaves or the biology of activations in neuronal tissue.

1.5   Summary and Outlook

Frequency of occurrence has a venerable history across a range of disciplines devoted to the study of language. Word frequency lists, available long before the advent of the computer, have proven foundational for the study of language across a range of disciplines. Educational psychologists introduced word frequency lists to facilitate the learning and teaching of (a foreign) language or special-purpose writing systems in classroom settings. Because the knowledge of the number of words in a language and their repeated occurrence or frequency can be used to extend pupils' vocabulary in a targeted fashion, the lists started to gain in popularity. This initiative left its mark on psycholinguistics through the methodological problems encountered during word counting: which units do we count, and how do we sample to collect information that is representative of users' language knowledge? At the same time, the availability of word frequency lists inspired mathematicians with an interest in language to approach the subject from a quantitative point of view. This led to discoveries regarding word frequency distributions that would change our view on language.

Word frequency has played an important role in cognitive psychology, where much effort went into investigating the single word frequency effect. Monsell (1991) directly considered the question of why there should be frequency effects. He argued that frequency effects follow naturally from a consideration of how words are learned. His arguments were cast in the framework of connectionist learning models, and he suggested that it was an inevitable consequence of such models that word recognition would improve the more often a word was encountered. The role of the wider context has only recently entered the picture and has contributed to aligning the interests of psychologists of language and linguists. By now, frequency effects have been found in virtually every subdomain of language that has been studied. Comprehensive reviews of frequency and its effects on first and second language learning, representation and change are available (Ellis 2002; Diessel 2007; Blumenthal-Dramé 2012; Divjak and Gries 2012; Gries and Divjak 2012). Overall, within theoretical linguistics, the finding that speakers are sensitive to frequencies of occurrence and that frequency affects language structure has had an enormous impact. It is aptly summarized in the title of Bybee's 2006 publication: 'grammar is the result of the mind's response to the repetition that is inherent in language use'.

In Chapter 2 we will focus on how grammar could be the mind's response to repetition and look at linguistic theories that rely on frequency of occurrence as a proxy for experience. We will discuss the overwhelming support for the effect of frequency on language structure and cognition that has come from usage-based theories of language. We will review the two main implementations of the usage-based idea in which frequencies of occurrence play a central role, i.e., Bybee's Exemplar View and Goldberg's Construction Grammar. We will also survey ways in which frequencies have been recorded and zoom in on those measures that have originated from within usage-based linguistics.

2   Measuring Exposure: Frequency as a Linguistic Game Changer

Frequencies of occurrence play an important role in usage-based linguistics. This is because the information contained in (co-)occurrence frequencies can be used to explain how a grammar is constructed from the ground up with nothing but general cognitive capacities that detect regularities in sensory input. Usage-based linguists hypothesize that what we learn is a probabilistic grammar grounded in our language experience; this approach diverges markedly from the generativist position that limits the use of environmental triggers to set parameters specifying a fixed set of mutually exclusive linguistic properties. In such an experience-based grammar – which is the cognitive organization of someone's experience with language – linguistic categories and linguistic structures are associated with activation or likelihood values that are determined by their relative frequencies in language use (see Elman et al. 1996 among other classics).

Research suggests that learners, even infants, also use statistical properties of linguistic input to discover structure, including sound patterns, words and the beginnings of grammar (Saffran 2003; but see Yang 2004 who criticizes this work for its 'unrealistic' laboratory setting). A major point of disagreement remains the extent to which the language environment of children provides them with enough information on the basis of which to learn a language. A bewildering array of contrasting reports has appeared regarding the relationship between the language children hear and the language they produce (for an overview see Pine 1994). Initial investigations of the facilitative role of child directed speech (CDS) focused primarily on the development of syntax, and findings remained contradictory. Studies of the role of the environment in lexical development have shown that the total amount of CDS predicts children's vocabulary size and rate of growth (Hart and Risley 1995) and the frequency of specific words within CDS predicts the age of acquisition of those words (Huttenlocher et al. 1991). Yet, Goodman, Dale and Li (2008), who conducted the first evaluation of the relation between input frequency and age of acquisition for a large sample of words, found that words used more frequently by parents are not learned first. Rather, across all words, higher parental frequency is associated with later acquisition: although nouns are least frequent in the input children receive, children tend to know nouns before they know verbs. Within lexical categories, however, higher frequency is indeed related to earlier appearance; if we look at the category of nouns, then nouns that are used more frequently by the caregivers are learned sooner by the child. Nativists were thus correct in remarking that 'it is hopeless to suppose that learning is responsive (solely) to input frequency, because the first word [that children acquire] in English vocabulary is not *the*' (Lidz, Gleitman and Gleitman 2003: 152).

In attempts to understand the nature of the mechanisms underlying language development, input-uptake correlations have the potential to provide powerful insights: if certain aspects of the input are predictive of language development and processing, such findings shed light on the nature of language-learning strategies and mechanisms, as well as on the relationship between linguistic knowledge and experience. By now, the frequency with which elements occur and the extent of our ability to extract statistical regularities from the input have played a central part in more than two decades of heated debates: how much of the ability to produce and comprehend language is programmed into our genes, and how much can be acquired through environmental stimulation? The score remains unsettled, however (see Linder and Hohenberger 2009; for a recent book-length overview see Ambridge and Lieven 2011). In what follows, we will review the two main proponents of an exposure-driven approach to language cognition (Section 2.1), and survey the main measures that have been used to capture frequency of occurrence in linguistics (Section 2.2).

2.1   Frequency and Usage-Based Theories of Language

Usage-based theories embody the surface-oriented view: 'What you see is what you get.' The term 'usage-based' was coined by Langacker (1987). The basic premise of usage-based linguistics is that experience with language creates and impacts the cognitive representations for language. Language-specific innate cognitive structures are unnecessary: cognitive representations are gradually built up by language users through encoding and decoding utterances and categorizing them on the basis of sound, meaning and context.

The roots of this usage-based view on language go back to the 1960s and the functional-typological approach to language taken by Joseph Greenberg and colleagues. It blossomed in the 1970s under the leadership of Li (1976), Givón (1979) and Hopper and Thompson (1980, 1984) who proposed that grammar is the result of the conventionalization of commonly used discourse patterns. In a position paper, Tomasello (2000) argued for a rapprochement between psychologists and cognitive functional linguists. He highlighted the fact that the theoretical freedom, offered by usage-based theories, to identify psycho-linguistic units on the basis of actual language use rather than on adult-based linguistic theory, was truly liberating. It is this marriage between linguists and psychologists of language that propagated the interest in the effects of frequency on language.

The linguistic side of the coin was elaborated in a series of nineteen now seminal papers, edited by Bybee and Hopper (2001a), that investigate the multiple ways in which frequency of use impacts cognitive representations. A recurrent theme in the volume are questions about the units of usage and the rejection of the fact that language users would come up with the same analysis as linguists do. Contributors clearly favoured the idea that the units of use, rather than the units of linguistic analysis, would be the units of mental storage and access (Bybee and Hopper 2001b: 16). Just as the speed of access to single words is affected by frequency of use, so is the speed of lexical access to larger units, such as *come on* or *you and I*.

Yet, despite the fact that speakers retain a great deal of item-specific information (Gurevich, Johnson and Goldberg 2010), they do also abstract away from particular tokens. Memory for any experience is necessarily partially abstract insofar as the richness of the experience is not recorded in all its fine detail. Moreover, memory decays over time, possibly leading to additional abstraction. Knowledge of language is typically thought to consist of a network of form-function correspondences at varying levels of specificity. One important question in linguistics is the nature of these abstractions and how the experienced instances contribute to the formation of a cognitive representation. Leading proponents of construction grammar (Goldberg 1995, 2006) and the exemplar view of grammar (Bybee 2010) have proposed different answers to this question, and have looked at different kinds of frequency information to support their claims. These frameworks will be presented in turn in the following two sections.

2.1.1   Bybee's Exemplar Theory

As far as representations of linguistic experience are concerned, exemplar theory situates itself at the concrete and detailed end of the cline. The rich memory representation that is characteristic of exemplar models is compatible with the ideas, expressed in cognitive linguistics, that linguistic or dictionary meaning is highly dependent upon and not separable from encyclopaedic knowledge, or world knowledge associated with the concept that is activated by the word (Fillmore 1982, 1985; Lakoff 1987; Langacker 1987; Croft and Cruse 2004). The representation of encyclopaedic knowledge along with linguistic knowledge emerges naturally from an exemplar model in which tokens of words or constructions are represented in memory along with the situations they are associated with in experience (Bybee 2013: 64). The level of detail assumed to be inherent in memory representations on an exemplar theoretic approach to language has also facilitated research on the role of frequency in language. The pioneering work of Joan Bybee (1985, 2001, 2007, 2010, 2015) and collaborators advanced our understanding of the different roles token and type frequency play. Bybee (2013) aptly summarizes the essence of the exemplar approach to language development, representation and change. Taylor (2012) represents the first fully exemplar-based theory of language knowledge and representation, based on a detailed analysis of corpus data.

2.1.1.1 Recording Experience   Exemplar models were not developed especially for language; rather, they apply equally to linguistic and non-linguistic categories. An exemplar model is therefore also not, in itself and on its own, a theory of language; rather, it is a model of memory representation. Such models embody the usage-based view that language is a part of general cognition and allow us to access explanations for linguistic phenomena by venturing outside language, into the domain of general cognition.

Exemplar models propose that memory for linguistic experience is like memory for other experiences (Bybee 2013: 52ff). Memory storage for linguistic experience is said to contain detailed information about the tokens that have been processed, including their form and the contexts in which they were used. Each instance of experience with language has an impact on its cognitive representation and when stored representations are accessed during encoding or decoding, the representations themselves change. Langacker (2017: 54) rightly remarks that exemplars cannot be stored – they are transient neural events. What is 'stored' is a trace of their occurrence as each occurrence adjusts synaptic connections. Chapter 4 explains in more detail how experiences, including linguistic experiences, are encoded and stored in memory.

Linguistic exemplars come in a variety of sizes, ranging from a single segment, such as a vowel, to longer stretches of text, such as poems. Tokens of experience that are judged to be the same are grouped together and form exemplar clouds. These exemplar clouds constitute the categories of a language. There is no real difference between a cloud of exemplars and a schema from cognitive grammar, a schema being a more abstract and less detailed generalization over specific patterns. The difference between clouds and schemata may well be 'more metaphorical than substantive' (Langacker 2017: 54) in that, on either account, linguistic ability resides in established patterns of activity with varying degrees of entrenchment. I refer to Chapter 5 for a more detailed discussion of entrenchment from the point of view of how memory works.

Exemplar categories are structured by similarity and frequency (Nosofsky 1988) and often exhibit prototype effects (Rosch 1975) because of differences in degrees of similarity. Note that an individual exemplar – which is a detailed perceptual memory – does not correspond to a single perceptual experience, but rather to an equivalence class of perceptual experiences (Pierrehumbert 2001). Exemplars can thus differ in strength depending on the number of tokens they contain: exemplars built up from a large number of tokens will be represented more strongly than those built up from a smaller number of tokens. The stronger exemplar or set of exemplars often forms the centre of a category and other exemplars are more or less similar to that stronger exemplar or set of exemplars.

Because exemplars are based on perceptual stimuli and contain items that are similar in some (perceptual) respect, exemplar categories can be formed on the basis of phonetic, semantic, pragmatic or contextual criteria (Pierrehumbert 2001). For any word, phrase or construction, exemplar categories from these different domains are linked, based on co-occurrence in experience. Hence, an exemplar model of language must allow for links across domains. In addition, linking or mapping also occurs among units in different contexts. In fact, the exemplar cloud of a word, for example, would include all the meanings and contexts in which the word has been experienced. This 'excessive' storage is believed to be possible thanks to our impressive neural capacity and because information is stored in a highly structured and efficient way, i.e., by forming categories (even if only as and when needed, see Nosofsky 1988) and storing similar items in proximity to one another.

In an exemplar model of language, the units and categories of grammar can emerge from the experience that is stored in memory because exemplars are categorized by similarity to one another and because contiguous experiences – such as meaning and sound – are recorded as linked to one another. Cognitive representations are built up as language users encode utterances and categorize them on the basis of sound, meaning and context. As incoming utterances are sorted and matched by similarity to existing representations, units such as syllable, word and construction are thought to emerge. Thus, grammar can be viewed as the cognitive organization of someone's experience with language (Bybee 2006). Linguists are particularly interested in how much generalization and abstraction occurs in the organization of linguistic experience. Exemplar representations contrast at all levels – phonetic, morpho-syntactic, semantic and pragmatic – with the more abstract representations of structural or generative theories, because variation and properties predictable from general principles are retained in exemplar models.

2.1.1.2 Token and Type Frequency   Exemplar models of linguistic representations, by their very nature, provide a natural record and account of the frequency of occurrence in linguistic experience. An important distinction here is that between type and token frequency, two kinds of frequencies that have been shown to play different roles in the productivity of linguistic structures (Bybee and Thompson 2000). Token frequency refers to how often a specific form appears in the input, e.g., it includes all instances of the past tense form of *read*, while excluding the present tense form (which sounds differently but is spelled identically). Type frequency refers to the number of distinct items that are used in or within the structure of interest 'whether it is a word-level construction for inflection or a syntactic construction specifying the relation among words' (Ellis 2002: 166). An example of type frequency is the number of verbs that create their past tense by changing *-ow* to *-ew*, as in *throw–threw, blow–blew, grow–grew*.

Bybee (1985) proposed that representations are strengthened by repetition, making them easier to access. This proposal applies primarily to token frequency – the number of times a particular string occurs in a text or corpus. Thus, every time a string, e.g., a construction such as *go and wash your hands*, is used, its repeated parts are strengthened. But constructions also have schematic slots, e.g., GO and VERB. These schematic slots will be represented by different exemplars such as *go and do your homework, go and get that book* which also form categories. These categories can vary in their type frequency, that is, in the number of items (*wash, do, get*, etc.) that occur in the VERB slot. All of this makes the frequency profile of a construction quite complex (Bybee 2013: 59–60).

Token frequency facilitates learning via repetition. The more often a particular token is experienced, the easier it becomes to access and use (Bybee and Hopper 2001b: 16). Because it comes with ease of access and use, token frequency can be a conservative force that protects high-frequency structures from analogical levelling. In contrast to the effects of high type frequency, high token frequency promotes the entrenchment or conservation of irregular forms and idioms; the irregular forms survive because they are high in frequency, which means that they are encountered and processed often (although an irregular form can also survive because it is highly similar to a high frequency item, e.g., *behold, forsake*).

Type frequency can guide learners to create a category out of a type (MacWhinney 1978; Bybee 1985, 1995; Bybee and Hopper 2001a). According to Bybee and Thompson (2000: 384), there are three reasons for this:

1 The more lexical items that are heard in a certain position in a construction, the less likely it is that the construction is associated with a particular lexical item and the more likely it is that a general category is formed over the items that occur in that position

2 The more items the category must cover, the more general are its properties and the more likely it is to extend to new items

3 High type frequency ensures that a construction is used frequently, thus strengthening its representational schema and making it more accessible for further use with new items.

Generally, type frequency has a positive effect on productivity: the higher the type frequency of a construction, the more likely it is to occur with a novel item (Bybee 1985; Baayen 1993). And the greater the number of types in a construction, the more bases there are for the item-based analogy that creates novel instances of the construction. Several factors modulate the tendency for constructions with high type frequency to be highly productive. First, items with very high token frequency may form an autonomous chunk and not activate the construction's exemplar cluster (Bybee 1985). As Baayen (1993) points out (see also Zeldes 2012), processing low-frequency instances of constructions requires parsing or activating the representation of the construction, which strengthens the construction. Processing high-frequency instances of constructions can occur without activating the schematic construction and therefore high-frequency items do not strengthen the schematic construction further. In other words, processing frequent items will thus not contribute to the productivity of the construction: they do not strengthen the abstract schema which is necessary for licensing novel items. Second, certain properties (formal or semantic) of the schematic slot in the construction may restrict productivity. A highly schematic slot has a broad set of properties, compatible with many items, while a less schematic slot tends to be more restrictive. Although the most productive categories have both high schematicity and high type frequency (e.g., the English regular verb formation with the suffix -ed), schematicity and productivity are to some extent independent of one another. Barðdal (2008) noted that low schematicity (i.e., strong semantic coherence) also encourages productivity, albeit in a more delimited domain.

Since type frequency relates directly to productivity, including type frequency in the mental representation of a construction is crucial (Bybee 2013: 59–63). Of course, type frequency only starts to accrue if commonalities between instances have been observed. For this reason, effects that are adequately explained by type frequency may be indicative of the existence of linguistic abstraction processes.

2.1.2   Goldberg's Construction Grammar

Strictly speaking, construction grammar is not an alternative to exemplar theory. As explained above, exemplar theory is not a theory of language; instead, it is a model of memory representation that treats linguistic experience like any other experience. Construction grammar, on the other hand, is a theory of language and one that sees grammar (morphemes, words, idioms, etc.) as pairings of form and meaning, i.e., as constructions.

Any linguistic pattern is recognized as a construction as long as some aspect of its form or function is not strictly predictable from its component parts or from other constructions recognized to exist. In addition, patterns are stored as constructions even if they are fully predictable as long as they occur with sufficient frequency. (Goldberg 2006: 5)

This insight has given rise to a family of constructionist approaches that go by the name of construction grammar. The *Oxford Handbook of Construction Grammar* by Hoffmann and Trousdale (2013) presents a complete overview of theory, method and applications of construction grammar. Goldberg's (2013) chapter contains a succinct overview of constructionist approaches.

2.1.2.1 Abstracting Constructions Constructionist approaches share the assumption that speakers' knowledge of language consists of systematic collections of form-function pairings, learned on the basis of exposure to the ambient language. Constructionists would, however, stop short of claiming that speakers do not form generalizations over these forms or that such generalizations are merely epiphenomenal.

If speakers did not necessarily form generalizations over individual words, we would expect to find languages in which the distribution of words was much less systematic than it is [. . .]. Far from being an arbitrary collection of stipulated descriptions, our knowledge of linguistic constructions, like our knowledge generally, forms an integrated and motivated network. (Goldberg 2009: 98)

A network of constructions comprises all the knowledge speakers have about their language. Constructions can in principle vary in size and complexity from a single word like *tentacle* to a full-fledged abstract construction like *the Xer the Yer* or *the more you read, the less you know*. The constructions themselves function as nodes in this network and represent speakers' detailed knowledge. Hopper (1987) remarked that viewing constructions as nodes, however, creates static representations that are divorced from active processing. Although proponents of construction grammar are firm in their claim that they did not intend to create static representations (Bybee 2013), they have not been clear on how the connections between the constructional nodes are to be envisioned (Hilpert and Diessel 2017: 71).

Constructionists view the generalizations that speakers make as a type of generalization that is naturally represented by an inheritance hierarchy (Goldberg 2009: 99). Inheritance hierarchies ensure that new elements can take on properties of old elements; for example, if there is a construction *the Xer the Yer*, then any new instance a language user encounters, e.g., *the more, the merrier*, can be classified alongside existing instances and inherit all the information shared by the other instances of that class. Generalizations can appear at different levels of abstraction and both high-level generalizations (also known as 'rules') and item-specific knowledge (often referred to as 'lists') may well be recorded and retained in memory. Langacker's (1987: 29) discussion of the exclusionary fallacy, which he terms the 'rule/list fallacy', makes this point very clearly. It may serve simplicity and economy of description to assume that particular statements or lists should be removed from grammar if a general statement or rule can be established that subsumes them. Yet, simplicity does not equal psychological reality: there is no evidence to support the assumption that the simplest description of a language phenomenon is the one favoured by language users. A similar proposal has been made in the field of categorization. The initial interest in high-level abstractions gave way to a focus on exemplars, and eventually both extremes converged on an approach that combines exemplar-based knowledge with generalizations over that knowledge (Murphy 2002; Goldberg 2006: 99; Divjak and Arppe 2013).

Speakers learn preliminary construction-level generalizations over items quickly with little input, especially when the input is skewed (Goldberg 2009: 101): a high-frequency exemplar facilitates accurate linguistic generalization both in adults and (six-year-old) children. That is, holding overall type and token frequency constant, learners generalize more easily when one type accounts for a large proportion of all tokens. It seems that the high frequency of an instance acts as an anchor point for generalization. The very frequent use of one exemplar in a pattern facilitates learning the semantics of that pattern, and this is consistent with the idea that generalizations emerge on the basis of patterns of usage.

There are other mechanisms than frequency that affect generalization. Semantic relatedness is one of them. In a study on Spanish verbs expressing *become*, Bybee and Eddington (2006: 349) asked speakers to judge the acceptability of sentences extracted from corpora.

[...] grammaticality or acceptability judgments are heavily based on familiarity, that is, the speaker's experience with language. Sequences of linguistic units that are of high frequency or resemble sequences of high frequency will be judged more acceptable than those that are of low frequency or do not resemble frequently used structures.

But how do children learn what not to say? A classic question in language development is how children construct grammatical categories and rules when adults rarely correct children's grammatical errors. This is an issue that is closely related to poverty of the stimulus arguments we touched upon earlier (Pullum and Scholz 2002), and the seeming absence of negative evidence in the input that children receive during language development has been the topic of much debate in linguistics. To explain how children avoid overgeneralization, usage-based linguists have proposed two competing mechanisms, entrenchment and pre-emption. While both mechanisms posit that children use consistent gaps in adult production to infer unattested patterns, each mechanism highlights a different aspect of the input. Entrenchment emphasizes frequency effects – exposure to more data leads to stronger constraints – while pre-emption takes the discourse context into account: failing to observe a form in a context where it would be expected leads to stronger constraints (Boyd 2014: 608). We will review statistical pre-emption and entrenchment in the next section. For further reading about the application of the principles of memory and learning in language development, see volume 42, issue 2 of the *Journal of Child Language* (2015).

2.1.2.2 Competing Mechanisms? Entrenchment versus Pre-Emption in the Selection of Constructions It has been argued that statistical pre-emption is an important factor in learning arbitrary distributional restrictions (Boyd and Goldberg 2011; Goldberg 2011b; Casenhiser and Bencini 2015). The concept of pre-emption, i.e., repeatedly witnessing a word in a competing pattern, is the most prominent attempt of usage-based linguistics to construct a theory of negative evidence that is based exclusively on the input (Stefanowitsch 2011: 114). Pre-emption is a simple but powerful mechanism based on the idea that children assume that exact synonyms do not exist. Therefore, they take the existence of a particular form in the input as evidence against the existence of synonymous forms that could potentially exist. In other words, one way that overgeneralizations can be minimized or avoided altogether takes as point of departure the idea that more specific knowledge always pre-empts more general knowledge in production, as long as either solution would satisfy the functional demands of the context equally well. This idea was first suggested by Pinker (1984).

Before we move to a discussion of pre-emption in linguistics, it should be pointed out that pre-emption is known to psychologists as 'blocking'. Kamin (1969) described how the conditioning of an association between two stimuli is impaired if, during the conditioning process, a conditioned stimulus (e.g., a tone) is presented together with another conditioned stimulus (e.g., a light) that has already been associated with the unconditioned stimulus (e.g., a shock). This effect was explained by the Rescorla–Wagner model (more about this model in Chapter 9) that predicts that if one conditioned stimulus (a light) already fully predicts that the unconditioned stimulus (a shock) will come, nothing will be learned about a second conditioned stimulus (a tone) that accompanies the first conditioned stimulus (the light). The term 'blocking' was introduced into linguistics by Aronoff (1976: 43) who defined it as 'the non-occurrence of one form due to the simple existence of another'. He used the concept to approach the variation in noun triplets, e.g., curious–curiosity–curiousness (for which there is no related form *cury) versus glorious–glory–gloriousness (for which there is no *gloriosity). Blocking has a proven track record in inflectional morphology, too (Clark 1993: 81): from forms like *walked*, *crawled* and *danced* a child might deduce that the past tense is formed by adding *–ed* to a verb. Hearing the past tense *went* but not *goed* in the input will serve as evidence that the *–ed* addition rule does not apply to *go*.

Although the term blocking persevered within morphology (Rainer 2016), usage-based linguists rebranded the same phenomenon as pre-emption and have used this mechanism in their theorizing to explain how children would retreat from overgeneralizing argument structures (Goldberg 1995, 2006). Stefanowitsch (2011) provided the first corpus-based evidence of what he calls 'preemption by contextual mismatch'. For this he relies on the analysis of corpus data concerning the dative alternation, i.e., the ditransitive *She gave the girl a toy* versus the prepositional dative *She gave a toy to the girl*. He argues that it is not the occurrence of alternative forms as such that has a pre-emptive effect, but that the context within which those forms occur plays a crucial role. Functional similarity here is not the same as functional identity. Even near-synonymous or synonymous constructions are rarely fully interchangeable; they typically differ in terms of the information-structural contexts they prefer. Many grammatical constructions have information-structural restrictions that determine the discourse contexts in which they may occur. When the discourse context does not fit, speakers have to use alternative constructions. If speakers fail to use the alternative that the discourse context calls for, the language learner will take this as evidence that that option is not available. For example, if the prepositional alternative is produced with a specific verb, i.e., *They donated toys to the charity shop*, even though the context requires the ditransitive, language users will conclude that *They donated the charity shop toys* is not a suitable option for the verb *donate*. Thus, the occurrence of a construction in a context typical for another construction should pre-empt that other construction. Yet, the results of the corpus analyses reported in Stefanowitsch (2011) showed that there are no significant differences in the information-structural profile of alternating and non-alternating verbs in the prepositional dative. This makes it unlikely that such differences could serve as a source of information for determining which verbs alternate and which ones do not. Moreover, individual verbs appeared to differ with respect to the degree with which they adhere to the information-structural constraints of the constructions they occur in. Finally, this degree of adherence was found to be independent of whether alternative constructions are available or not.

Goldberg (2011a: 138–40) countered that these findings did not invalidate pre-emption as a protective mechanism because the wrong conditional probabilities had been considered. Stefanowitsch (2011) looked at the probability of certain information structure properties, given the dative construction, rather than at the probability of encountering a dative construction, given certain information-structure properties. Goldberg argued that the strength of pre-emptive evidence can be determined by how high the probability of encountering one alternative is, together with the frequency of any pre-emptive expressions. Frequency plays a role in the process of statistical pre-emption because pre-emption is probabilistic: a speaker can learn only upon repeated exposures to one construction instead of another related construction that the latter construction is not conventional. If a given pattern does not occur with sufficient frequency, no stable conclusions can be drawn. Yet, the confidence with which language users can conclude that one construction pre-empts another is not a simple linear function of frequency. The relation between the two is better captured by the natural logarithm function, which makes the effect of additional examples level off the more examples are encountered.

The probabilistic nature of pre-emption does imply that this proposal may not be sufficient to account fully for children's retreat from overgeneralizations: pre-emption does not provide a solution for cases where the target construction is of such low frequency that it could not be expected to appear, or cases in which there is no construction that is related closely enough to the target construction (Goldberg 1995: 126–7). In other words, low-frequency or novel non-alternating verbs are not covered by statistical pre-emption since pre-emption presupposes hearing the verb multiple times. Constructions may be either too low-frequency or too semantically or pragmatically specialized for another construction to effectively pre-empt their appearance.

Hearing a pattern with sufficient frequency has, indeed, been argued to play a key role in constraining overgeneralizations (Braine and Brooks 1995; Brooks and Tomasello 1999; Theakston 2004). Learning from positive evidence will create verb-argument structures which have a strength proportional to how often a verb has been heard with that argument structure. Like other researchers working within this tradition, Braine and Brooks (1995: 368) did not take a stance on the precise quantitative relation between representational strength and frequency of usage. They merely noted that with age there appears to be an increase in flexibility in switching between sentence constructions to meet conversational demands (e.g., to have particular arguments as subject or as object).

On Braine and Brooks's (1995) 'entrenchment hypothesis', attending to frequently occurring constructions can mitigate against the lack of negative evidence. Repeated presentations of a verb in particular constructions (e.g., *The rabbit disappeared*) cause a child to infer probabilistically that the verb cannot be used in non-attested constructions (e.g., **The magician disappeared the rabbit*). Stefanowitsch (2008) approached the issue of overgeneralization from the point of view of negative evidence. He proposed the concept of negative entrenchment and argued that, given a sufficiently sophisticated understanding of frequency, negative evidence can be inferred from the positive evidence in the linguistic input. It is possible to discriminate mathematically between combinations of linguistic items that are accidentally absent from a given corpus and combinations whose absence is statistically significant. And if a corpus linguist can calculate expectations of co-occurrence based on information about the individual occurrence of properties and elements to predict their frequency of co-occurrence and then compare the prediction to the actual observations, a language learner may well be able to do the same thing subconsciously:

Assuming such a statistically-driven model of entrenchment, the availability of negative evidence is a natural consequence: the stronger an expectation of co-occurrence is, the more noticeable its absence will be. The continued non-occurrence of a given expected configuration of linguistic categories would thus lead to a negative entrenchment of the combination of features in question. This negative entrenchment could serve as direct negative evidence for constraints on rules or schemas. (Stefanowitsch 2008: 522)

There appeared to be a large and statistically significant correlation between negative evidence and acceptability ratings, and it was found that degrees of significant absence correlate with degrees of unacceptability. No statistically significant correlation between pre-emption scores and acceptability ratings seemed to exist. From this it follows that pre-emption is an unlikely source of negative evidence in learning grammatical constructions even if pre-emption is (re)conceptualized in probabilistic rather than all-or-nothing, categorical terms. Entrenchment fares considerably better.

One implication of the entrenchment view is that, when an argument structure has been learned to a stable level of entrenchment, it will pre-empt alternatives, unless they have been independently witnessed. This creates a challenge for explaining how speakers deal with newly witnessed or rarely attested alternatives: since they have been independently witnessed they should no longer be pre-empted on a strict entrenchment account, but given their low frequency, they will not be well-entrenched either. Divjak (2017) reports results from acceptability ratings for low-frequency *that*-constructions with adult native speakers of Polish. A wide frequency spectrum was covered, with verb frequency ranging from 0.393 to 1,516.32 instances per million, and the *that*-complement being of very low frequency for the majority of those verbs (<0.66 instances per million). She found that the degree to which a verb depends or relies on a grammatical pattern, relative to occurrence of the same verb in other grammatical patterns, predicts the acceptability of that verb in that pattern. The learning theories we will discuss in Chapter 9 would explain this finding in terms of background rate (Rescorla 1968): the extent to which a relationship between a verb and a pattern is learned depends on how often the verb is coupled with the construction and how often it occurs on its own. If the construction frequency is kept constant, the more frequently the verb occurs on its own, the less well it predicts that construction. Furthermore, a lower- and upper-word frequency threshold were identified where an increase in conditional probabilities starts or stops causing an increase in acceptability of a verb in a *that*-clause (see Erker and Guy 2012). It is the middle 50 per cent of the data (i.e., the middle quartiles of verb unigram frequency) that shows the effects of frequency on acceptability most strongly; in her sample, the middle quartiles for unigram frequency spanned occurrences between 10 and 140 instances per million words. Speakers seem to entertain another strategy for the lowest-frequency verbs (i.e., verbs in the bottom quartile of verb unigram frequency, occurring fewer than six times per million words), and they rely on information gleaned from pattern transparency for guidance. The highest-frequency verbs, occurring more than 188 times per million words in the sample, are likewise more resistant: they are possibly so well-engrained that properties in addition to co-occurrence need to be respected (see Bybee 2006: 715). Overall, her findings support an entrenchment rather than a pre-emptive account; no effect of pre-emption was found unless there was a very strong preference for, or entrenchment of, one of the two constructions.

A second implication of the entrenchment view is that overgeneralizations will be less common, and will subjectively be less acceptable, for high-frequency verbs than for semantically matched lower-frequency verbs. For example, *The magician vanished the rabbit* feels slightly more acceptable than *The magician disappeared the rabbit*, since the inference from absence is stronger for the higher-frequency verb *disappeared*. Theakston (2004) discusses experimental data showing that children were more likely to overgeneralize verbs that were used infrequently (e.g., to use *giggle* transitively) than verbs that are highly frequent (e.g., to use *laugh* transitively). High-frequency verbs are thus less likely to be overgeneralized than low-frequency verbs. Ambridge (2013) confirmed that children were more accepting of low-frequency verbs being used in novel high-frequency constructions, than of high-frequency verbs being used in alternative constructions. For constructions that are considered to form alternations, such as the dative and locative constructions, the effects are less pervasive (see Ambridge and Lieven 2011: 252–4).

As discussed in Section 2.1.1.2, Bybee (1985) had already proposed that type frequency correlates with productivity, and it generally does. At the same time, the degree of relatedness or similarity of new instances to instances that have been witnessed is likely to play at least as important a role as type frequency. Constructions that have been heard with a wide variety of verbs are more likely to be extended than constructions that have been heard with a semantically or phonologically specific set of verbs (Tomasello 2000). Type frequency and degree of variability are often confounded in real language samples, since the degree of variability is likely to increase as the number of attested types for a given construction increases (see also Barðdal 2008). The greater the degree to which previously attested instances fill the semantic or phonological space that includes the potential target instance, the more confident speakers will be in using the target instance (Brooks and Tomasello 1999). Suttle and Goldberg (2011) experimentally manipulated the morpho-phonological and semantic variability of the test set, its similarity to an attested instance, as well as type frequency and variability. All other things being equal, the higher the type frequency of a pattern, the higher the productivity (Bybee 1985; Goldberg 1995; Clausner and Croft 1997; Tomasello 2003; Barðdal 2008). That is, argument structure constructions that have been witnessed with many different verbs are more likely to be extended and used with additional verbs. Experiments by Robenalt and Goldberg (2015) replicated the stronger dispreference for a novel use with a high-frequency verb relative to its lower-frequency counterpart, but only for those sentences for which there exists a competing alternative phrasing. When there is no consensus about a preferred way to phrase a sentence, verb frequency is not a predictive factor in sentence ratings. In other words, while speakers prefer familiar formulations to novel ones, they are willing to extend verbs creatively if there is no readily available alternative way to express the intended meaning. Goldberg (2009: 103) argues that this finding is consistent with the idea that it is pre-emption that prevents overgeneralization, not entrenchment, if pre-emption is operationalized as the frequency of the verb in itself. That is, the pre-emptive context in which *laugh* might have been expected to occur transitively but instead is witnessed intransitively occurs more frequently than the same pre-emptive context for *giggle*. Upon repeated exposures to one construction instead of another construction with a closely related meaning, the learner can infer that the second construction is not conventional. An older additional explanation to account for low-frequency cases invoked categorization as a mechanism that supplements pre-emption (Goldberg 1995: 126–40; 2006: Chapter 5). Boyd and Goldberg (2011) experimentally tested the hypothesis that speakers pick up on a distributional restriction and tentatively generalize beyond their experience to apply it to other instances of the same category. For example, English *a*-adjectives cannot be used prenominally, making *the asleep boy* infelicitous. Speakers pick up on this restriction and learn to avoid this formulation if an alternative that fulfils the same function, such *the boy is asleep*, is consistently witnessed.

In subsequent research, the pre-emption and the entrenchment account have been pitched directly against each other. Boyd, Ackerman and Kutas (2012) report that adult learners use both entrenchment and pre-emption to infer grammatical constraints. They arrived at this conclusion on the basis of a novel verb learning task conducted on thirty-six undergraduate students in which the effects of entrenchment and pre-emption were orthogonalized. In the intransitive-only group the experimenter described each video clip seven times using a novel verb in simple intransitive constructions (e.g., *Look! The apple is yadding!*). In the mixed group the verb was modelled using a mixture of four simple intransitives and three periphrastic causatives per video clip (e.g., *The apple is yadding* and *The squirrel really made the apple yad!*). The mixed group exhibited stronger constraint learning than the intransitive-only group in both the production and ratings tasks. This suggests an independent pre-emption effect, since entrenchment (operationalized as overall frequency) was held constant across groups. The ratings task did not provide evidence of constraint learning by the intransitive-only group, but the production data of this group, as contrasted with the control group, yielded significant evidence for learning that is consistent with an independent entrenchment effect.

In an experiment with 214 participants (six-year-olds, ten-year-olds and young adults), Ambridge, Kidd et al. (2015) again disconfirmed the advantage for pre-emption: while entrenchment appeared to be a robust solution to the problem of the retreat from error that generalizes across different error types, no such evidence was found for pre-emption. That is, no support was found for the prediction of the pre-emption hypothesis that the greater the frequency of the verb in the single most nearly synonymous construction, the lower the acceptability of the error. Support was found, however, for the prediction of the entrenchment hypothesis that the greater the overall frequency of the verb, regardless of construction, the lower the acceptability of the error, at least for the two older groups of participants. This finding generalized beyond the particular verbs and constructions used in the materials. Divjak (2017) also found that, in adult speakers, lexico-syntactic variation trumps pre-emption; the less surprised raters are to encounter a *that*-clause after a verb that is also (and in the majority of cases more frequently) followed by an infinitive, the higher the rating for the *that*-paraphrase. This is in line with Braine and Brooks (1995: 368) who described that, with age, there appears to be an increase in flexibility in switching between sentence constructions to meet conversational demands.

The debate about which account captures best how learners avoid over-generalization errors is ongoing. Ambridge et al. (2018) present evidence from a large study, including reanalyses of Ambridge, Pine and Rowland (2012), Ambridge (2013), Ambridge et al. (2014), Ambridge, Bidgood et al. (2015) and Blything, Ambridge and Lieven (2014) and an extended replication of *un*-prefixation with adults. The reanalyses were run using more appropriate measures of pre-emption and entrenchment that relied on the chi-squared statistic instead of on the frequency of the occurrence only of the favoured construction. Errors in the statistical modelling of the data were also corrected, and in one case a large corpus was consulted to obtain more reliable frequency estimates. They found that pre-emption and entrenchment effects are rarely dissociable for errors of verb argument structure overgeneralization, due to collinearity. The effects of pre-emption and entrenchment could only be disentangled for errors of reversative *un*-prefixation. A meta-analysis of all studies suggests that both effects exist and that pre-emption increases with age.

By way of summary, it should be noted that both 'entrenchment' and 'pre-emption' are merely labels for particular effects that are outcomes of the construction competition process, rather than cognitive mechanisms in their own right. The implication is that the solution to the retreat from error lies not with specialized cognitive mechanisms, but rather in a probabilistic process of construction competition. Of course, taking frequency of occurrence as a direct indicator of strength of memory and potential for pre-emption dangerously oversimplifies the effect that frequency has on memory. We will return to this issue in Chapter 5, after we have reviewed the basic mechanisms of memory storage and retrieval in Chapter 4. In Chapters 8 and 9 we will look in more detail at frameworks that naturally incorporate the human sensitivity to frequency into more encompassing frameworks of cognition.

2.2 Frequency Measures that Have Played an Important Role in the Development of Usage-Based Theories of Language

What is striking in the discussions about the role frequency plays in the emergence of structure from usage is the relative simplicity – bordering on naivety – of the association measures used to capture frequency of occurrence and co-occurrence. Although it was clear early on that language learning is based on complex, higher-order properties of probabilistic patterns in sensory experience, and not a mere tabulation of frequency of patterns (Elman 2003), usage-based linguists tend to gravitate towards raw counts of occurrence and co-occurrence. However, a variety of measures of association between words, as well as between words and constructions, are available for import from computational linguistics, and some have been developed with specific linguistic questions in mind, as we will see in Section 2.2.1 and Section 2.2.2. For an extensive discussion of the basic principles of statistical language processing and an overview of the possible applications I refer the reader to classics in the natural language processing area, i.e., Manning and Schütze (1999) and Jurafsky and Martin (2014).

It will also become clear that, despite the interest usage-based linguists have displayed in measuring association strength, considerations regarding the adequacy of any measures used to capture the strength of association between linguistic items in an objective and verifiable way have played a subordinate role. Similarly, there is a dearth of work investigating the cognitive mechanisms – if any – these measures would capture, even though this could reveal the reasons why some of them perform better than others.

2.2.1   Collocational Statistics

One strand to the quantitative approach to language has focused on measuring the degree to which two words are associated with one another. Collocations are very important for usage-based linguists because collocations are a type of multiword expressions, prefabricated strings that have become conventiona-lized through repetition frequency. Although typically adjective–noun combi-nations (such as *strong tea* and *scenic route*) will come to mind first, the same mechanism operates on other parts of speech, and verb–object compounds such as *have fun* and *make (no) sense* also exist. Word–word combinations could well form the basic units of a probabilistic theory of word combinations that reflect the users' experience with language (Thompson and Hopper 2001). As Divjak (2017) showed, some constructions, such as the *that*-construction, can be identified on the basis of their subordinating conjunction (i.e., the word *that*). This makes it possible to apply the techniques typically used for measur-ing the association between words and to capture the attraction between words and constructions. Such multiword units, which may include word-construction combinations, could also scaffold the learning of a grammar from the ground up, by facilitating the detection of patterns at ever higher levels of abstraction (Dąbrowska 2000, 2004, 2008).

2.2.1.1 Lexical and Semantic Associations between Words   There are a range of associations possible between words. Theoretical linguists have mainly been interested in semantic associations between words while corpus linguists favour lexical associations.

Semantic associations capture relations between the concepts lexical items give access to. Typically, five types are distinguished: synonyms, antonyms, meronyms (part–whole relationships), hyponyms (subordinate concepts) and hypernyms (superordinate concepts). Semantic associations have been studied extensively in linguistics because speakers' awareness of their existence makes it possible to deduce information about the organiza-tion of the so-called mental lexicon. Within usage-based linguistics, hypo-nyms and hyperonyms have received much attention in the context of prototype theory (Rosch 1975), where the approach to the data has been largely introspective or experimental (for a first book-length application of insights from prototype theory to linguistics, see Taylor 1989/1995). Synonyms and, to a lesser extent, antonyms, on the other hand, have attracted a great deal of attention from usage-based linguists working in a corpus-based fashion. Two book-length treatments can be named here: Divjak (2010) presents an extensive investigation of synonymy within a cognitive linguistics framework. Based on corpus data, the traditional model of synonym pairs is rejected and replaced by a more gradual view on synonymy that revolves around clusters of verbs sharing the same network of constructions. Experimental evidence provides support for the cluster-based approach and for the Behavioral Profiling method used (Divjak and Gries 2006) to pinpoint differences between clusters and between verbs in one cluster. In a similar vein, Jones et al. (2012) investigate antonymy using corpus and experimental data to build a theoretical picture of the antonymy relation, its status in the mind and its construal in context.

Lexical associations have been in focus within corpus linguistic approaches, in particular to English, and are generally referred to as collocations (which we already encountered in Chapter 1, Section 1.3.2). Fixed word expressions such as *strong tea* rather than *powerful tea* are not restricted to adjective–noun combinations; there are phrasal verbs (*pick up; lay off*), noun–noun compounds (*car oil; ice cream*) and idioms (*kick the bucket; spill the beans*). The simplest way to discover recurrent word associations or collocations in a corpus of texts would be to count their co-occurrence. The assumption that collocations are combinations of words that occur together more frequently than arbitrary word combinations is part of most definitions of what a collocation is. Raw co-occurrence data (i.e., the observed frequency signatures or contingency tables) provide some evidence for recurrent word combinations, mainly in the form of co-occurrence frequencies (Evert 2005: 42–4). However, the plain numbers are difficult to interpret, especially since the high frequency of some word combinations is merely accidental: highly frequent words, such as the article *the*, are expected to co-occur very often with a number of other words, even if they do not form collocations (Pecina 2009: 24). Moreover, any conclusions drawn from raw data are only valid for the the corpus from which the data were extracted. When extraction involves automatic linguistic pre-processing or analysis, the observed frequencies will also be affected by the errors that these programmes make (typical error rates range from 2 per cent for a well-trained part-of-speech tagger to almost 50 per cent for broad-coverage syntactic analysis) (Evert 2005: 42).

Statistical analysis helps overcome these problems and distinguishes between random combinations that occur together just by chance and those that might form more stable collocations. More generally put, statistical analysis has three main goals (Evert 2005: 42): (1) to interpret the observed frequency data as an indicator of statistical association between words and to quantify the strength of this association, (2) to generalize results beyond the particular source corpus from which the co-occurrence data were obtained and (3) to filter out noise introduced by automatic pre-processing and extraction. All three tasks are related in their underlying logic, which assumes that the object of interest – the statistical association between the components of a pair type – is a hidden quantity that is reflected in the frequency table.

Table 2.1 *2-by-2 contingency table for* peer review

	Word *review* or construction present	Word *review* or construction absent	Row totals
Word *peer* present	Cell 1	Cell 2	Total frequency of *peer*
Word *peer* absent	Cell 3	Cell 4	
Column totals	Total frequency of *review*		Total corpus size

2.2.1.2 Some Measures of Association   Language researchers are particularly interested in the statistical association between the words that make a pair, that is, they are interested in pairs where the sample provides clear evidence that the words co-occur more frequently than expected by chance. This association should be a property of the language as a whole, and our goal is to make inferences about the language using information from the sample we can observe (Evert 2005: 50; Pecina 2009: 42). In order to measure the statistical association between two words, also called 'bigrams', the data extracted from the corpus are interpreted as a random sample from an infinite population. This assumption comes with desirable properties that make analysis straightforward: if the population is infinite, we can sample with replacement and the words that we sample remain independent. Such an infinite population contains all possible bigram types whose probabilities are considered unknown parameters of the population. Any inferences concerning these parameters can be made only on the basis of the observed frequencies obtained from the sample (Evert 2005: 44; Pecina 2009: 39–40).

There are many approaches to measuring the association between two units. A first significant step towards compiling an exhaustive list of available association measures was made by Evert (2005). His efforts focused on measures applied to 2-by-2 contingency tables of the type shown as Table 2.1, representing co-occurrence frequencies of word pairs or word–construction combinations. Say, for example, that we are interested in the words *peer* and *review*. Cell 1 contains the number of times both *peer* and *review* are observed together in a sample; cell 2 lists how many times *peer* was observed with other words than *review*; cell 3 contains the number of instances where *review* was used together with other words than *peer*; and cell 4, finally, lists the number of words in the sample that are neither *peer* nor *review*.

2-by-2 contingency tables are standard fodder for many statistical tests that assess the significance of the difference between the values in the cells. If there is a significant difference in the values for *peer* depending on whether *review* is present or absent, there is contingency or dependence between *peer* and *review*. Computing the *significance of the association* and the *degree of association* are the two most popular ways of approaching the relation between words or between a word and the construction it occurs in. Both approaches rely on the information that is available in bigrams, but they differ in the question they ask, and in the bias they show while answering that question.[1] Let us explore this in a bit more detail.

Significance measures ask the question: 'How much evidence is there for a positive association between the words, no matter how small the effect size is?' Measures of the significance of word association are derived from statistical hypothesis tests; these tests calculate the probability (expressed as a p-value) that the observed values (the occurrence frequencies observed in the sample) would be due to chance. Association measures that rely on significance testing thus aim to quantify the amount of evidence that the observed sample provides against the null hypothesis of independence, i.e., against the non-association of a given pair type. This question is operationalized as: 'How unlikely is the null hypothesis that the words are independent?' (Evert 2008: 1228). If the p-value is low (below a significance level α, typically set to 0.05), the null hypothesis is rejected in favour of the alternative hypothesis (at the significance level α), which states that the two words do not co-occur by chance alone and are hence likely to be found together in other samples as well. If the p-value exceeds 0.05, the null hypothesis that the association between the words is merely an artefact of sampling is retained as a plausible explanation of the words' co-occurrence. Because the probability estimate is or can be expressed in the form of a p-value the association scores can be compared directly. Measures of the significance of word association come in different types and can be further subdivided into exact statistical hypothesis tests, likelihood measures and asymptotical statistical hypothesis tests (see Evert 2005 for details). Test statistics calculate the probability that the observed frequencies would occur if the null hypothesis were true. Likelihood values, on the other hand, test the null hypothesis by comparing its likelihood to the likelihood of the alternative hypothesis. In principle, all these tests should compute (more or less) the same p-values. Most experts seem to agree that Fisher's test produces the most meaningful p-values (see Yates 1984), hence the Fisher association measure is often taken as a reference point for the significance of association group (Evert 2005: 110). Measures of the significance of association have one important drawback: a high association score, corresponding to a large amount of evidence against independence, can result

---

[1] Pecina (2009: 44–5, 48) provides a comprehensive list of eighty-two association measures. It needs to be mentioned that many of these measures produce very similar results. Levshina (2015: Chapter 10) reports on a study involving the Russian ditransitive construction, e.g., *buy someone a book*. Twenty different association measures were used to calculate the relation between the verb and the construction and high correlations were detected between many of the measures, yielding several distinct groups of very similar association measures.

either from a high degree of association between the components of a pair type or from a large amount of evidence being available (Evert 2005: 84; 2008: 1228). In other words, significance measures show a bias for high frequencies: if the number of observed frequencies is sufficiently large, even a small effect size, i.e., a small relative difference between observed and expected frequencies, can turn out highly significant.

Effect-size measures ask: 'How strongly are the words attracted to each other?' This is operationalized as: 'How much does observed co-occurrence frequency exceed expected frequency?' (Evert 2008: 1228). This family of measures estimates one of the coefficients of association strength from the observed data. They are concerned more with the degree of association (quantified by any one of the coefficients of association strength) than with the amount of evidence supporting it (Evert 2005: 110ff). Degree of association measures do not rely on null-hypothesis significance testing; instead, they assess how much more likely one hypothesis is compared against the other. The level of significance is typically ignored, and the test statistics are used as methods for determining the strength of association instead, i.e., as an estimate for the *effect size*, with their scores directly used as the association scores for ranking. Measures of association strength are divided into point estimates and conservative estimates. This group is much more diverse than the significance of association group. Since the various coefficients have quite different properties, there is no obvious group prototype (Evert 2005: 116). Yet, they are all biased towards low frequencies and cannot account for sampling bias, yielding high effect sizes for low observed frequencies.

In addition to association measures based on significance and effect size, there are also *context-based association measures* that look at information available around the bigrams (Pecina 2009: 42). Generally, a context is defined as a bag of word types occurring within a context window, i.e., a predefined distance, from any occurrence of a given bigram or word token in the corpus. The main idea of using this concept is to model the average context of an occurrence of the bigram/word type in the corpus, i.e., to find word types that *typically* occur in its neighbourhood. Collocations occur in different contexts than their component parts – association measures that implement this principle are adopted from the fields of mathematics (vector distance) and information retrieval (vector similarity). Several techniques have been proposed to quantify the similarity between two contexts by comparing their vector representations (Frakes and Baeza-Yates 1992). Established implementations of vector semantics are latent semantic analysis (LSA) (Landauer and Dumais 1997) which considers the document as context and yields topical information. The hyperspace analogue to language (HAL) (Lund and Burgess 1996) uses a ten-word window and yields information that is more similar to what linguists would consider as semantic. For an accessible comparison of LSA and HAL, see

Sahlgren (2006). A recent addition to the word vector family with improved computational efficiency and accuracy is Word2Vec, created by Mikolov et al. (2013) at Google. Information-theoretic concepts such as entropy and mutual information have also been used. After all, collocations occur as units in environments that are considered noisy from the perspective of information theory. Entropy is expected to be lower within collocations (uncertainty as to which word comes next is low) and higher outside them (uncertainty as to which word comes next is high). We will return to entropy in Chapter 3, Section 3.3.

2.2.1.3 Challenges for Association Measures: the Random Sample Model and Its Assumptions   All association measures that compute the significance or degree of association between two units are based on a number of assumptions that do not necessarily hold in language. Inference is most reliable when the assumptions of independence and homogeneity made by the random sample model about the data are met: (1) the pairs of random variables are statistically independent, i.e., their occurrences have no influence on each other and they occur independently of each other and (2) their distributions are identical to (or only negligibly different from) the prototype, the idealised theoretical model, as mathematically defined. These assumptions can be violated by real-world data in various ways and for various reasons (Evert 2005: 57ff).

Kilgarriff's (2005: 72, 270) paper highlights the major sticking point in the linguistic literature: statistical hypothesis testing uses a null hypothesis, which posits randomness, but 'language is never ever random'. Words in a text are not randomly selected, and our corpora are not randomly generated, hence when we look at linguistic phenomena in corpora, the null hypothesis will never be true. Because of this lack of randomness in sampling, and because of the size of the corpora we have access to, the fact that the relation between two phenomena is non-random does not support the inference that it is not arbitrary. For this reason, 'hypothesis testing is rarely useful for distinguishing associated from non-associated pairs of phenomena in large corpora. Where used, it has often led to unhelpful or misleading results' (Kilgarriff 2005: 273).

Evert (2005: 59) submits that the null hypothesis is highly unrealistic for natural language data. Although this does not affect the validity of the random sample model, it will affect the interpretation of association scores. By the same token, only those violations of the random sample assumption which have a substantial influence on the multinomial sampling distribution are problematic for a statistical model. Gries (2005a: 82, 84, 281), too, is less pessimistic and points out that the situation is much improved by post-hoc correction for multiple testing: once correction is applied to the p-values derived from the chi-square tests, the random baseline of 5 per cent false hits is not exceeded. Furthermore, the introduction of effect sizes helps weed out the accidentally significant by singling our significant differences that are practically of limited importance.

Schmid and Küchenhoff (2013: 538) bring up the issue of independence of observations, a point that is, in essence, closely related to Kilgarriff's observation about the non-randomness of language. Independence of observations refers to the notion that the value of one part of the data is unrelated to any other part. In other words, knowing the value of one observation gives you no information about the value of any other. But it also means that the sampling of one observation does not affect the choice of the second observation. When more than one measurement is taken from an author, the two measurements are not independent since the score on the first measurement is likely to be related to the score on the second measurement. All the observations belonging to a given author usually have similar values, at least when compared with values from other authors. In corpora, typically multiple observations stem from one and the same author or speaker who each have their favourite ways of putting things. Unless a repeated-measures analysis or mixed model is used, this lack of independence of observations results in incorrectly narrow confidence limits and incorrectly small p-values: effects appear more significant and reliable than they are because the effective sample size is smaller than the one that is assumed.

Currently, no association measure seems to be able to deal directly with the interdependence of observations. A simple and straightforward way to avoid this problem is ensuring that the observations are truly independent.[2] Truly random sampling also excludes bias as an alternate explanation for an association. Bias is any trend in the collection, analysis or interpretation of data that can lead to conclusions that are systematically different from the true conclusions that should have been drawn. Unlike random error, which results from sampling variability and which decreases as sample size increases, bias is independent of both sample size and statistical significance. Bias can cause estimates of association to be either larger or smaller than the true association. In extreme cases, bias can give rise to an association which is the direct opposite of the true association. In corpora, bias is inherent at the data-collection stage: unless each author is entitled to make one and only one contribution, the danger exists that expressions favoured by better-represented authors will dominate the findings.

---

[2] Baayen (2011: 311–12) points out that one way of quantifying a verb's preference for a dative construction – in the particular case described in the paper – is to use the random intercepts of a generalized linear mixed model fit to the data in order to predict the chosen dative construction. A positive random intercept (the adjustment of the baseline log-odds for the construction) for a verb would signal that verb's bias towards that construction. Random intercepts for subjects could be employed in a similar fashion to signal subject-specific biases in preferring one dative construction over another.

The final issue with existing association measures concerns the tendency to use the results of significance testing to draw conclusions about association, as discussed above in Section 2.2.1.2: a range of contingency-based measures rely on null-hypothesis significance testing to establish the strength of the association. It has been argued in the linguistic literature (Schmid 2010: 111–15; Gries 2012) that measures with the capacity to relate observed to expected frequencies would be superior to those that do not include this information, if only from a mathematical point of view. Yet significance tests were designed for small numbers of observations, which makes them ill-suited for most linguistic purposes: given the large number of observations available, even very small deviations from independence would yield statistically significant results. This would, however, merely be significant evidence of an insignificant association as p-values measure strength of evidence, and not evidence of strength of association, which is ultimately the evidence that linguists seek.

2.2.1.4 Measure Validation   While certain measures have been established as de facto standards in certain sub-disciplines (e.g., log-likelihood in computational linguistics, t-score and mutual information in computational lexicography), a theoretically justified choice would consider that different measures highlight different aspects of collocativity and will therefore be suited for different tasks. Yet, very little research has been done on determining which measures works best under what circumstances.

In 1964 at the Symposium on Statistical Association Methods For Mechanized Documentation (Stevens, Giuliano and Heilprin 1965), Giuliano advocated a better understanding of the measures and their empirical evaluation (as cited by Evert 2005: 19):

[First,] it soon becomes evident [to the reader] that at least a dozen somewhat different procedures and formulae for association are suggested [in the book]. One suspects that each has its own possible merits and disadvantages, but the line between the profound and the trivial often appears blurred. One thing which is badly needed is a better understanding of the boundary conditions under which the various techniques are applicable and the expected gains to be achieved through using one or the other of them. This advance would primarily be one in theory, not in abstract statistical theory but in a problem-oriented branch of statistical theory.

[Secondly,] it is clear that carefully controlled experiments to evaluate the efficacy and usefulness of the statistical association techniques have not yet been undertaken except in a few isolated instances ... Nonetheless, it is my feeling that the time is now ripe to conduct carefully controlled experiments of an evaluative nature, ... (Giuliano 1965: 259).

Evert (2005: 30) notes that 'it is amazing to see how little progress has been made in the understanding of word co-occurrences, association measures and their relation to collocations in the forty years that have passed since the Washington Symposium'.

Addressing this issue from a theoretical and from a practical point of view yields contradictory findings. Theoretical discussions about the suitability of particular association measures are concerned with their mathematical properties, and, while the so-called significance measures are not satisfactory as measures of significance, practitioners find that these measures appear to have linguistic merits that justify their use as heuristic measures for collocation identification (Evert 2008: 1238). Practically, measures can be evaluated in a number of ways, e.g., by running comparative evaluation experiments under different conditions, by replicating analyses using different measures or different parts or types of corpora and so on, but also by comparing the corpus-based results with native-speaker intuitions and behaviour, either as laid down in dictionaries and grammars or behaviour as measured in online or offline experiments.

Lisac and Milin (2006) were among the first to test two measures of association – the T-test and mutual information, proposed by Church and Hanks (1990) – against behavioural data probing language perception. While the T-test represents the difference (expressed in standard units) between the observed probability of co-occurrence and the probabilities of observing both words independently (chance), mutual information expresses a ratio, i.e., the number of times the observed mutual probability is larger than would be expected if words occur independently and would co-occur randomly, and this is expressed in logarithmic units. If there is a genuine association, the joint probability is much larger than chance co-occurrence. Association values were calculated on the basis of a newspaper corpus, and behavioural data were obtained through two primed lexical decision tasks, one in which the prime preceded the stimulus and one in which they were both visible on screen. It was found that, with increasing mutual information, lexical decision latencies shortened, and more so in noun–noun combinations than in adjective–noun pairs; no effect was observed for T-test values, thereby reducing its relevance for linguistic approaches that value cognitive reality.

Evert (2008: 1238–42) presents a case study on the identification of multi-word expressions using different association measures, where all members of an n-best list (a list of likely possibilities) were evaluated by a professional lexicographer or terminologist. Their annotations were used to calculate the *precision* of the n-best list, i.e., the proportion of true positives among the candidates. An alternative way of assessing the measures' performance relies on a geometric visualization technique that obviates the need for manual verification and goes straight to the mathematical cores of the measures. It interprets observed and expected frequencies as two-dimensional coordinates that can be used to represent each word pair in a data set by a point in Euclidean space. For statistical association measures, three-dimensional plots are needed (Evert 2005: Section 3.4).

While earlier experimental work focusing on a selection of association measures reported behavioural support for these measures (Gries, Hampe and Schönefeld 2005; Ellis and Ferreira-Junior 2009; Ellis and Simpson-Vlach 2009; Colleman and Bernolet 2012), research contrasting a range of association measures with conditional probabilities (Divjak 2008, 2017; Wiechmann 2008; Blumenthal-Dramé 2012; Shaoul 2012; Levshina 2015) shows that conditional probabilities are the favoured predictors for a range of online and offline linguistic behaviours. The conditional probability of encountering an event is the probability that the event will occur given the knowledge that another event has already occurred. In this case, the events are not (assumed to be) independent, and this may well be why conditional probabilities yield better predictions than association measures that require independence of events, an assumption that is rarely, if ever, met in natural language.

Wiechmann (2008) surveyed forty-seven competing variants of association measures and tested their predictivity against experimental data from online sentence comprehension as measured in an eye-tracking experiment. He found that Minimum Sensitivity outperforms any of the other measures in predicting reading behaviour across local syntactic ambiguities. Minimum Sensitivity is a two-way or bi-directional conditional probability that selects the best of the two available conditional probabilities, i.e., in the case of a verb and a construction it would consider both the probability of encountering a construction given the verb, that is P(verb|construction), and the probability of encountering a verb given the construction or P(construction|verb).

For cognitive linguists, the question is whether uni- or bi-directional measures capture the cognitive reality of a user's linguistic knowledge more adequately. While the former measures calculate, for example, how likely the construction is given a verb or P(verb|construction), the latter would supplement this information with a calculation of how likely a verb is given the construction and compute both P(verb|construction) and P(construction|verb). To date, there is little research probing this issue. Divjak (2008, 2017) obtained sentence acceptability ratings on dispreferred and often low-frequency Polish combinations of verbs and constructions. Levshina (2015) used offline gap filling and sentence production tasks on the Russian ditransitive. Both studies surveyed a number of association measures as well as conditional probabilities and found that uni-directional probability measures explained behavioural performance at least as well as bi-directional measures. In a similar vein, Blumenthal-Dramé (2012) studied the online processing of complex word forms in English, using a variety of tasks and both reaction time as well as fMRI measurements. Her conclusions confirmed those obtained for offline tasks: (the logarithm of) relative frequencies (the ratio between surface – that is, root plus affix – and base – or root – frequencies) predict entrenchment best.

Ellis (2016) and Ellis, Römer and Brook O'Donnell (2016: 176–84) summarize experimental work requiring lexical decisions and meaningfulness judgements on verb argument constructions (VACs) that partially supports this finding: while all of the experiments show effects of verb frequency and verb–VAC frequency, lexical decision is additionally driven by semantic prototypicality (but not by the probability of the construction given the verb), whereas meaning judgement is affected by the probability of the construction given the verb (but not by semantic prototypicality). Ellis (2016: 415) explains the effect of contingency on judgements of meaningfulness as follows:

Comprehension (etymologically, 'together catching') requires the assemblage of fragments of meaning, and this is done faster when the pieces go together well. High verb-VAC contingency, as reflected by ∆Pcw [the probability of the construction given the word – DD], speeds the dynamic competition among the massively parallel constituency of the unconscious mind to elect a current oneness to the fleeting stream of conscious experience.

Interestingly, none of the probability-based measures that outperformed the other measures on the tasks described related observed frequencies to expected frequencies in order to perform null-hypothesis statistical significance testing. Gries and Ellis (2015: 525) argue that by omitting null-hypothesis statistical significance testing the ability is lost to determine whether a word occurs more in a construction than would be expected given the word's frequency in the corpus. But is information on a word's overall frequency, and on the relation between observed and expected occurrence, crucial for speakers? Küchenhoff and Schmid (2015: 543) point out that:

[i]t is unreasonable and futile to ponder which of the two rankings is more or less appropriate or convincing, because they give two different pieces of information. The FYE [Fisher–Yates exact test – DD] ranking is headed by verbs which are both frequent enough and sufficiently attracted by the [. . .] construction to find their way to the top of this list; in contrast, the log OR [logarithm of the odds ratio – DD] ranking reflects the verbs' propensity to occur in the construction, more or less irrespective of their absolute frequency.

Yet, as mentioned, conditional probabilities that ignore absolute frequency predict behaviour at least as well as odds ratios that incorporate absolute frequencies, and better than methods relying on significance testing. The information gained from relating observed to expected frequencies the way this is done in statistical null-hypothesis testing may well be of low psychological relevance for speakers. Nevertheless, comparing observed and expected frequencies is core to collostructional analysis, which we will look at in the next section.

2.2.2   Collostructional Statistics

In addition to measures that originated within corpus-based computational lexicography, there are measures of association that arose from within usage-based linguistics and were designed with specific linguistic questions in mind. Collostructional analysis, one of the most popular association measures in usage-based linguistics, is one such measure (for an overview see Stefanowitsch 2013). In fact, it is a family of methods that make it possible to measure the attraction between words and constructions where constructions are defined as form–function pairings in the Goldbergian tradition (Stefanowitsch and Gries 2003; Gries and Stefanowitsch 2004; Stefanowitsch and Gries 2005). There are three different methods (Gries 2015: 506), each answering a different research question:

1 Collexeme analysis measures the degree of attraction/repulsion of a lemma to a slot in one particular construction, such as the attraction or repulsion of the verb *give* to the ditransitive (as in *He gave her a book*);
2 Distinctive collexeme analysis measures the preference of a lemma to one particular construction over another, functionally similar construction, such as the preference of the verb *send* for the ditransitive (*She sent him a book*) or for the *to*-dative (*She sent a book to him*). Multiple distinctive collexeme analysis extends this approach to more than two alternative constructions;
3 Covarying collexeme analysis measures the degree of attraction of lemmas in one slot of a construction to lemmas in another slot of the same construction, as is the case in the *into*-causative construction (such as *mislead into believing* or *tricked into revealing*); this can be item-based or system-based.

Collostructional analysis requires frequencies as input and is similar in spirit to a number of the collocation statistics that were surveyed in Section 2.2.1.2, in that observed and expected frequencies are compared. In addition to observed co-occurrence frequencies of words and constructions, it also provides a comparison of the observed frequency to the one expected by chance and, based on this, outputs a measure of the strength of the attraction or repulsion that relies on the log-transformed p–value of a Fisher–Yates exact test.

Overall, collostruction strength has been criticized on the same points as other association measures, i.e., the directionality of the measure, the inclusion of contingency information and the (ir)relevance of statistical null-hypothesis testing (Divjak and Caldwell-Harris 2015: 67–8). Bybee (2010: 97–101) objects to the fact that the overall token frequency of an item, used for normalization, detracts from its attraction to a construction. She also objects to the fact that the computation of collostruction strength relies on the frequency of all constructions in the corpus, which is notoriously difficult to estimate (what counts as a construction?). This information is typically presented in the fourth cell of a contingency table (see Table 2.1). Schmid and Küchenhoff (2013) criticize collostructional analysis, among other things, for its reliance on this 'fourth cell' and for its use of a p-value as evidence of strength, since in reality a p-value provides an estimate of the strength of the evidence. As mentioned above, a p-value captures how strong the evidence against the null hypothesis is; it does not evaluate the strength of the relation between two variables.

Collostructional analysis techniques have also been critiqued on a more theoretical basis: Bybee (2013: 62) points out that collostructional analysis 'rolls token and type frequency into one measure along with controls for overall frequency of the lexical item and a count of constructions in the language'. Gries (2012: 498–502) uses this remark as a point of departure to sketch a two-dimensional cross-tabulation of all occurrences of a word and a construction, i.e., the word in the construction, the word in all other constructions and the construction with all other words. This approach would take into account type frequencies, token frequencies and type–token distributions and thereby represent the reality of the learning environment more accurately. Ideally, it would be supplemented with information on the dispersion of these items (Ambridge et al. 2006: 175), i.e., how widespread the co-occurrences are in language, because learning is better when it is spread out instead of massed.

As would be expected from a usage-based linguist, Bybee (2010: 100–1) finds it problematic that no cognitive mechanism has been identified that would correspond to what is measured by collostructional analysis. 'By what cognitive mechanism does a language user devalue a lexeme in a construction if it is of high frequency generally?' she asks. This is, indeed, a question that collostructional analysis must answer. Papers have appeared refuting a number of reported problems (Gries 2012, 2014), and Gries (2012: 496) has countered that constructional strengths are based on conditional probabilities – p(verb|construction) and p(construction|verb) – and the frequencies giving rise to these probabilities. Unfortunately, most of the counter-arguments Gries lists merely adduce examples of cases in which collostructional analysis has successfully predicted behavioural data, and this in comparison with a generally very small number of alternative association measures.

One might wonder, for example, why collostructional strength seems to work, despite its mathematical and conceptual issues (that it may well share with other association measures, see Section 2.2.1.3). It has been argued that, what 'seems to make collostructional analysis work most of the time' is the fact that the 'elsewhere-uses' of the word of interest follow a Zipfian distribution and are, especially in the case of a high-frequency word of interest, much rarer than the word of interest. Therefore, the elsewhere-uses do 'not distort the data much' (Gries 2012: 503). But this assumes a traditional approach to language development that is not based on learning. Baayen et al. (2016: 115–16) have argued that a Zipfian power law is not necessary for discriminative learning to be effective. Discrimination learning does not mind diversity in the signal as long as the (co-)occurrence exhibits a systematicity that allows for reliable predictions to emerge. In fact, 'uneveness' of word frequency distributions may be optimal for learning as the objects, states and events that words encode tend to follow the same power law of occurrence. In other words, we talk about experiences with a frequency proportional to their relevance.

2.3   Summary and Outlook

Frequencies of occurrence have played an important role in usage-based linguistics. On a usage-based approach to language, grammar is the cognitive organization of someone's experience with language. It consists of linguistic categories and structures that are more or less likely depending on their relative frequencies in language use. Information contained in (co-) occurrence frequencies can explain how a grammar could be constructed from the ground up, given our ability to extract statistical regularities from the input. Speakers abstract away from the tokens they have encountered in use. One important question in linguistics is the nature of these abstractions and how the experienced instances contribute to the formation of a cognitive representation. Exemplar grammarians have produced an extensive description of the effects of token and type frequency on the productivity and longevity of language structures. Construction grammarians have made considerable progress in understanding how overgeneralization is avoided by focusing on the raw frequencies with which competing forms occur in context.

What is striking in the discussions about the role frequency plays in the emergence of structure from usage is the relative simplicity – bordering on naivety – of the measures used to capture frequency of occurrence and co-occurrence: raw counts of occurrence and co-occurrence were long considered sufficient. The past two decades have seen a surge in measures of association strength; the vast majority of these measures were imported from computer science where the focus was on the association between words, but a few were designed with linguistic interest in mind and measure the association between words and constructions.

Up till now, there has unfortunately been little reflection on the adequacy of any of the measures used to capture the strength of association between linguistic items in an objective and verifiable way. Yet, to ensure that the results of our text-based analyses are reliable, we need to understand the properties of the measure we use and how it captures or interacts with the properties of the data. Furthermore, there is a dearth of work investigating the cognitive mechanisms these measures would capture – if any. To advance our understanding of language cognition and the role frequency plays in this, we need to put the linguistics back into the frequencies and relate frequency distributions properly to the workings of the mind. In Chapter 3 we will review a number of theories of language cognition that rely heavily on repetition frequency and explore the effect that frequency of use has had on how cognitive scientists approach language.

3 More than Frequencies: Towards a Probabilistic View on Language

In the previous two chapters we have seen how information about occurrence frequency made its way into research on language and led to the observation that language users are sensitive to the frequency with which forms occur in their linguistic environment. Linguistic theories have built this sensitivity into their foundations, yielding usage-based approaches that dispense with innate structures and instead allow language knowledge to emerge from exposure to usage and to change with usage. We have also surveyed a number of measures that have been used to capture the association between words or between words and constructions.

In this chapter we will explore how frequency of occurrence could support the emergence of structure. Frequencies of occurrence and co-occurrence fluctuate: they are sample-dependent and should hence not be expected to be the same on every occasion. But over time, patterns emerge in these fluctuating (co-)occurrence frequencies. Given enough data, (theoretical) probabilities can be calculated on the basis of sample-dependent co-occurrence frequencies, and these probabilities are (more or less) stable. This finding has led to the hypothesis that language cognition might be probabilistic. Taking a probabilistic approach to language is a very sensible thing to do for other reasons too: the language we hear and produce is unsegmented, ambiguous and noisy. Probability theory is the best normative model we have for decision making under such conditions of uncertainty. Of course, our best normative model may still be a poor descriptive model for language (see Jurafsky 2003: 39), and this needs to be taken into account when considering the adequacy of a probabilistic approach to language cognition.

We will review some of the evidence that has amassed to support viewing human cognition, including knowledge and use of language, as relying on probabilistic processing. Probabilities play a role in comprehending and producing language. We can rely on probabilistic and information-theoretic models to explain how, in comprehension, probabilities affect access (more probable structures are accessed more quickly, with less effort or with less evidence), disambiguation (the more probable interpretation is more likely to be chosen) and processing difficulty (difficult sentences or passages may have low probability or require a sudden switch of probabilistic preference between alternative interpretations). Similar observations have been made for production where highly likely structures are produced faster, more easily or with more confidence and are chosen more frequently.

3.1 Constructing a Grammar from the Ground Up

'"[R]ules" of language, at all levels of analysis – from phonology, through syntax, to discourse – are structural regularities which emerge from learners' lifetime analysis of the distributional characteristics of language input' (Ellis, Römer and Brook O'Donnell 2016: 35). Frequency of occurrence and co-occurrence play a fundamental role in this process: patterns each have their own activation or probability values that are determined by their relative frequencies in language use. Research suggests that human beings are quite adept at determining underlying frequency distributions and central tendencies and extract this information automatically; this also applies to linguistic events.

A research finding on which much of usage-based linguistics builds is the human ability to extract statistical regularities from the world around us to learn about the environment (for a review, see Gómez 2007; Rebuschat 2013). Section 3.1.1 explains how learners, even infants, can use statistical properties of linguistic input to discover structure, including sound patterns, words and the beginnings of grammar. Section 3.1.2 then sketches how these regularities or patterns could initially be stored as exemplars and form the basis for later generalization, resulting in the linguistic structures and categories of an experience-based grammar.

3.1.1 Detecting Patterns Statistically

One topic that has attracted much attention is the ability to segment a continuous speech stream into words. This is no small feat, as unlike written language, spoken language does not have any clear boundaries between words: spoken language is a continuous stream of sound rather than individual words with silences between them. One proposal for how learners segment the continuous input stream into segments starts from the assumption that human beings are attentive to the distributional properties of language. In an artificial grammar learning study with adult participants, Saffran, Newport and Aslin (1996) found that participants were able to locate word boundaries and, e.g., identify the word *infant* based only on *transitional probabilities*, that is, on the likelihood of encountering *-fant* after having heard *in-*. This builds on the observation that, in language, some sounds are less typically used at the beginning of a word than at its end, making it possible to identify words in continuous speech. This experimental outcome suggested that adults are capable of using statistical regularities in a language-learning task.

Saffran, Aslin and Newport (1996) also showed that very young learners, eight-month-old infants, can likewise exploit transitional probabilities between syllables in order to segment continuous speech into words in an artificial language. The grammar of this language consisted of four words, each composed of three nonce syllables such as *bidaku*, *padoti*, *tupiro* or *golabu*. During the experiment, infants were exposed to a continuous speech stream consisting of these words, presented in a monotone synthesized voice. There were no other cues (e.g., pauses, stress, and intonation) to word boundaries than the statistical probabilities. Within a word, the transitional probability of two syllable pairs was set to one: in the word *padoti*, for example, the syllable *do* always immediately followed the syllable *pa*, and *ti* always followed *do*. Between words, however, the transitional probability of hearing a syllable pair was only 33 per cent as any one of the three remaining words (in this case, *bidaku*, *golabu* or *tupiro*) could follow *ti*, the last syllable of the word *padoti*. Although many factors play a role in segmenting speech into words, this specific statistical learning mechanism is powerful and can operate over a short timescale; typically, infants were exposed to the artificial language for only two minutes.

To exclude the interpretation that infants were learning serial-order information, i.e., that one syllable never follows another, and were not actually picking up on transitional probabilities between words, infants were tested on legal words (e.g., *bidaku*) or words that exist in the artificial language versus illegal words that did not exist in the artificial language (such as *dalapi*). They were also tested on legal versus illegal syllable combinations (syllable sequences composed of the last syllable from one word and the first two syllables from another, e.g., *dakugo*). In both cases infants showed a novelty preference or dishabituation effect and listened longer to novel words or syllable combinations. These results were replicated when the frequencies of the syllables within versus across words were equal while maintaining the differences in transitional probabilities (Aslin, Saffran and Newport 1998). This confirmed that transitional probabilities among three-syllable sequences were tracked, not serial order information or frequencies of co-occurrence of the syllables in these sequences.

This study was followed up by many others that described statistical learning abilities in the auditory and visual domains more generally. Saffran (2003) reviews evidence suggesting that infants rapidly capitalize on the statistical properties of their language environments, such as the distributions of sounds in words and the orders of word types in sentences, to discover important components of language structure. Infants track such statistics, for example, to discover speech categories (e.g., native-language consonants, see, e.g., Maye,

Werker and Gerken 2002), word boundaries (e.g., Saffran, Aslin and Newport 1996), and basic syntax (e.g., Gomez and Gerken 1999; Saffran and Wilson 2003). More recently, Pelucchi, Hay and Saffran (2009) showed that the conclusions reached on the basis of data from studies with eight-month-old infants using artificial languages (where the stimuli are continuous streams of synthesized syllables that are highly simplified relative to real speech) do scale up to natural language learning of Italian in real-life situations. Rabagliati, Ferguson and Lew-Williams (2019) conducted a meta-analysis of sixty-three experiments on infants' pattern learning. They found that infants were most likely to detect and generalize patterns from stimuli that are relevant to their experience of language, people and objects. For an extensive review of the theory and validity of a statistical learning account of language development, see Erickson and Thiessen (2015).

The accumulation of evidence for the existence of computational abilities that extract structure so rapidly was a real game changer in the discussions between nativists and nurturists. Human beings appear to extract probabilistic information automatically from their environment, and this includes linguistic information. Guided by the statistical properties of linguistic input, structure is discovered and a probabilistic grammar based on our language experience emerges from the ground up. This ability to extract and entrench the distributional characteristics of natural language underpins usage-based theories of grammar. Yet Yang (2004: 451–2) argued that statistical learning does not reliably segment words in a realistic setting of child-directed English without knowledge of phonological structure, because in principle an infinite range of statistical correlations exist and could be tracked (e.g., the probability of two adjacent syllables rhyming and of two adjacent vowels being nasal). The performance of Yang's computational model improved dramatically with knowledge about phonological structure such as the fact that each word only has one primary stress. From this Yang (2004: 455) concluded that language acquisition can be viewed as a form of innately guided learning, whereby universal grammar instructs the learner what cues they should attend to.

But why would children be listening out for nasal vowels, for example? Statistical learning abilities appear to be very powerful and constrained by human learning mechanisms (along with constraints on human perception, processing and speech production), such that some statistical patterns are more readily detected and used than others. Saffran (2001a) established that infants were not learning statistics but were using statistics to learn language: twelve-month-olds can first segment novel words and then discover syntactic regularities relating the new words – all within the same set of input (Saffran and Wilson 2003). This would not be possible if the infants formed mental representations only of the sequential probabilities relating individual syllables, and no word-level representations. In fact, humans appear to learn sequential structures better when they are organized into subunits such as phrases than when they are not (Saffran 2001b, 2002). These findings point to another benefit of statistical language learning: the mental representations produced by this process are not just sets of syllables linked by statistics, but new units that are available to serve as the input to subsequent learning processes.

An interesting question to ask is whether children are seeking to discover word boundaries at all? Baayen et al. (2016: 16, 24, 113) argue that adopting a discriminative stance, rather than a decompositional one, may better characterize the challenges children face. They reason as follows: let us replace the assumption that children would be aiming to segment words out of the sound stream with the hypothesis that children are trying to identify the lexical equivalent of their experience, whatever the size of that lexical equivalent might be. Maybe children are not hunting for words like *I, want* and *some* that they can then put together to express an experience. Maybe they are happy to go with units of any size, such as *I want some*, as long as these units capture a relevant experience. This obviates the problem that linguists and psychologists have been debating for decades, i.e., that 'bootstrapping' word boundaries from transition probability troughs is computationally infeasible due to the existence of many word boundaries with high-transition probabilities. It is also in line with findings from first language development that highlight how children benefit from starting big, i.e., from multi-word units (Arnon and Clark 2011). Baayen et al. (2016) use a Rescorla–Wagner network to model a discriminative stance. Their network is designed to predict the lexical expression of an experience, as it is encoded in the signal, instead of the boundaries between word forms. From such a discriminative perspective, low-transitional probabilities are not 'separators', but 'binders': they are excellent cues for discriminating between the lexical expressions of experiences. Ultimately, human learning mechanisms may themselves have played a prominent role in shaping the structure of human languages. We will return to models of human learning, and the Rescorla–Wagner model in particular, in Chapter 9.

3.1.2   Conventionalizing Common Patterns

Sounds that occur together frequently can be considered components of words, or words and word boundaries can be posited at points where low-frequency transitions between sounds are observed (Saffran, Aslin and Newport 1996). Yet, the mechanism by which children are said to discover words does not only detect legal words of the type you would find in a dictionary. A child performing segmentation in this fashion is likely to arrive at an inventory of segments containing words as well as multi-word sequences (Bannard and Matthews 2008). And this may well be a blessing: the ability to detect multi-word sequences opens up the possibility of discovering the beginnings of grammar by the very same statistical learning mechanism that would help children detect words. In an experience-based grammar, linguistic categories and linguistic structures are the result of the conventionalization of commonly used patterns. According to this account, children initially remember the utterances they hear as holophrases: they begin with a restricted set of utterances taken directly from experience and learned via domain-general skills, including imitation and intention reading. Child learners advance to productive syntax by generalizing over the exemplars they have stored.

This account relies on certain controversial assumptions. The most fundamental is that children are able to store whole sequences of words taken directly from the input. Bannard and Matthews (2008) were the first to test this assumption experimentally. Following the logic of Taft's (1979) approach to the acquisition of plural morphology, they used a repetition task to probe children's knowledge, expecting them to repeat high-frequency combinations such as *Sit in your chair* more easily and accurately than closely related low-frequency combinations like *Sit in your truck*. Their expectation was confirmed and appeared to be independent of any effect of syntax, of the frequency of the component words or of transitional probabilities between pairs of words.

Tomasello (2003) has argued that children form productive constructions through a process of schematization. This is achieved when children hear repeated uses of one form, e.g., *throw*, along with varied use of another form (e.g., noun phrases referring to whatever is thrown: *throw the ball*, *throw teddy* and *throw your bottle*) in similar contexts. The outcome is a linguistic construction that contains a minimum of one lexical item and one "slot" (*throw* X). Important here is the fact that children are exposed to a range of patterns that are partly fixed, partly flexible, such as *Would you like some water/milk/juice?*, which allows them to use both recurrence and novelty to break into the system via low-level generalizations of the type *Would you like some X?* Matthews and Bannard (2010) confirmed that children are indeed likely to detect an opportunity to substitute alternative words into the final position of a four-word sequence if it is difficult to predict the fourth word, given the first three words and the words observed in the final position are distributionally similar. After all, the statistical history of events is built from information on frequency of co-occurrence.

A probabilistic approach may help to understand how, and to what extent, learners infer language structure from linguistic input. Because the process is driven by input and input differs for each individual, children's knowledge of the structure of the language they are acquiring will differ according to the input they have received. Overall, children will perform better on tasks when they are asked to make use of a frequently encountered and therefore stored string such as *I want it* or a lexical schema *I'm X-ing it*, than on equivalent transitive structures such as

Harry met Sally. Cognitive abilities such as categorization and analogy formation then come into play and operate on these extracted patterns or holophrases to yield, first lexical schemas, and later higher-level generalizations. This process of abstraction is protracted but can in principle begin as soon as children have two stored exemplars across which to abstract. Even when children have formed adult-like abstract constructions, they will be better at utterances that constitute prototypical instances of those constructions. There is ample empirical evidence supporting this account, and as yet the predictions it makes remain to be falsified (Ambridge and Lieven 2015).

At the same time, the constructivist approach to language learning faces many challenges. First and foremost, it will need to address how exactly children progress from holophrases to abstract constructions; appealing vaguely to categorization and analogy formation is insufficient for creating a testable model. Proponents of a constructivist approach also disagree as to whether these abstractions would be stored or created as and when needed. On a radical exemplar account (Ambridge 2018), new forms are produced or processed by on-the-fly analogy across multiple stored exemplars. These exemplars are weighted by their degree of similarity to the target, taking into account the communicative goal or the task at hand. There are no stored abstractions such as noun or verb, subject or transitive clause, hence these do not need to be learned; learning a language therefore boils down to storing exemplars, and frequency of encounter plays a straightforward but crucial role in this process, as we will see in Chapters 4 and 5.

Putting aside the discussion as to whether abstractions are or are not stored (the majority of researchers working on language rightly or wrongly assume that they are stored; more about this in Chapter 9), there is agreement that taking a probabilistic standpoint makes learning language overall look more tractable: learning no longer requires (re)constructing one grammar with certainty, merely approximating it with sufficiently high probability. Unfortunately, Chomsky had formulated (misinformed) arguments against probabilistic approaches to languages that had led the field to believe that there was nothing interesting about statistical approaches to language, and it took the language sciences decades to recover.

3.2   Probabilistic Grammar

The interest in probabilistic grammars for natural languages was reawoken by Patrick Suppes (1970) who used the notion of a probabilistic grammar to account for the child's developing knowledge of grammar. He started out from the observation that 'a fully adequate grammar for a substantial portion of any natural languages does not exist', but discussions about how to choose between several competing partial grammars abound (Suppes 1970: 1). He proposed to use the 'objective probabilistic criteria of a standard scientific sort' to select a grammar because '[i]n any application of concepts to a complex empirical domain, there is always a degree of uncertainty as to the level of abstraction we should reach for' (Suppes 1970: 3). After all, the 'criterion for acceptance of the grammar' can be 'just a standard statistical one', that is, 'the selection of a grammar can follow a standard scientific methodology of great power and wide applicability, and methodological arguments meant to be special to linguistics – like the discussion of simplicity – can be dispensed with' (Suppes 1970: 11–12).

The problem that plagued and still plagues linguistics is this: 'At the present time, the main tendency in linguistics is to look at the deviant cases and not to concentrate on a quantitative account of that part of a corpus that can be analysed in relatively simple terms' (Suppes 1970: 5). Although Suppes disarmed a number of common objections to considering probabilistic grammars, the resistance against a probabilistic approach to language would be around for a long time. As Halliday (1991: 31) put it:

It had always seemed to me that the linguistic *system* was inherently probabilistic, and that frequency in text was the instantiation of probability in the grammar." [...] "It turned out that some people felt threatened by this suggestion, regarding it as an attack on their freedom as individuals to choose what they wanted to say. It was rather as if by stating people's probable sleeping behaviour one would be denying them the freedom to lead a nocturnal existence if they chose. But there was an interesting contrast here. Occurrence in vocabulary had been being counted for some time, and the results had been used, by Zipf (1935), to establish general principles such as the relationship between the relative frequency of a lexical item and its place in the rank order [...] Why, then, the resistance to quantitative patterns in grammar?

Abney (1996: 21–2) discussed how probabilistic models are sometimes seen as nothing but 'stop gap' approximations: they serve until better descriptions of missing factors or information that is difficult or impractical to collect reveal the deterministic nature of the phenomenon.

But this argument is flawed. If we have a complex deterministic system, and if we have access to the initial conditions in complete detail, so that we can compute the state of the system unerringly at every point in time, a simpler stochastic description may still be more insightful. To use a dirty word, some properties of the system are genuinely emergent, and a stochastic account is not just an approximation, it provides more insight than identifying every deterministic factor. Or to use a different dirty word, it is a reductionist error to reject a successful stochastic account and insist that only a more complex, lower-level, deterministic model advances scientific understanding.

Linguistics would come around, but only after cognitive scientists had proven the value of probabilistic models for language learning and processing. For this, they relied on the work of computational linguists who aimed to advance our scientific understanding of language cognition by better understanding the computational properties of language. This was not without its problems.

> In caricature, computational linguists believe that by throwing more cycles and more raw text into their statistical black box, they can dispense with linguists altogether, along with their fanciful Rube Goldberg theories about exotic linguistic phenomena. The linguist objects that, even if those black boxes make you oodles of money on speech recognizers and machine-translation programs (which they do not), they fail to advance our understanding. This paper, then, is essentially an apology, in the old sense of apology. I wish to explain why we would do such a thing as to use statistical methods, and why they are not really such a bad thing, maybe not even for linguistics proper. (Abney 1996: 3)

In the next two sections we look at the role probabilistic approaches to language have played in language science, first in cognitive science (Section 3.2.1), and then in linguistics (Section 3.2.2). Although probabilistic methods are often associated with empiricist views of language development, the framework is equally compatible with nativism – after all, there could be prior constraints on the class of language models. Probabilistic methods should be viewed as a framework for building and evaluating theories of language development and use, and for concretely formulating questions concerning the poverty of the stimulus, rather than as embodying any particular theoretical viewpoint. This point arises throughout cognition; although probability provides natural models of learning, it is an open question whether initial structure is crucial in facilitating such learning (Chater and Manning 2006: 342–3).

3.2.1   Probabilistic Approaches to Language Cognition in the Cognitive Sciences

Probabilistic approaches have a venerable history in the cognitive sciences. Over the past decade, several journals have devoted special issues to precisely this topic. Two such issues that are of particular interest are *Trends in Cognitive Sciences* (Volume 10, Issue 7, July 2006) on probabilistic models of cognition, alongside *Trends in Cognitive Sciences* (Volume 14, Issue 8, August 2010) on approaches to cognitive modelling.

3.2.1.1 *Theoretical Discussions*   Chomsky (1965) had argued that the learning problem is unsolvable without strong prior constraints on the language, given that the linguistic stimulus is poor, i.e., partial and full of errors. Gold (1967) provided mathematical evidence that, assuming a context-free grammar (a type of formal grammar, consisting of production or rewriting rules that describe all possible strings in the language and apply regardless of the context), learners cannot converge on a language from positive evidence alone 'in the limit', even as the corpus becomes indefinitely large. Manning (2003: 311)

clarifies that Gold's results depend on the assumption that, for any language in the hypothesis space, and for any order of sentence presentation, a correct language must be returned after a finite period of time. Because learners may observe an unrepresentative sample of the language for any period of time, they may not be able to settle on the 'correct' version of the language in time unless they are provided with negative evidence. Of course, we can also assume that each incorrect grammar is rejected after a finite period of time rather than that the correct grammar is accepted after a finite period of time. Under this weaker criterion of approachability in the limit, both context-free and context-sensitive grammars are learnable from positive evidence alone (Feldman et al. 1969). Horning (1969) showed that the class of stochastic context-free grammars is learnable from positive evidence alone, provided we assume a denumerable class of possible grammars with a prior distribution over their likelihood. A probabilistic grammar puts probability distributions over sentences. Any high-probability phenomenon is likely to occur, hence lack of occurrence provides negative evidence: a grammar that frequently generates structures that are not actually encountered becomes increasingly unlikely as the amount of observed data grows (Manning 2003: 311; Stefanowitsch 2008).

Taking a probabilistic standpoint makes learning look more tractable: learning no longer requires (re)constructing one particular grammar with certainty; it merely requires approximating it (speakers might, for example, learn slightly different idiolects) with sufficiently high probability (Abney 1996: 24; Chater and Manning 2006: 340). But Chomsky (1957, 1965) had formulated arguments against probabilistic approaches to languages that had led the field to believe that there was nothing interesting about statistical approaches to language. Abney (1996: 22–4) refutes these arguments by pointing out that Chomsky misrepresented Shannon's discussion of nth order Markov models, which define the conditional probability of encountering a word, given n (preceding) words. It may be true that neither the grammatical sentence, 'Colourless green ideas sleep furiously,' nor the ungrammatical sentence, 'Furiously sleep ideas green colourless,' have occurred in English. But the point of Shannon's approximations is that, as sample size increases, the total mass of ungrammatical sentences that are erroneously assigned a probability other than zero decreases. In other words, the number of ungrammatical sentences that are predicted to occur with some likelihood by the model will decrease as more data accumulates. Of course, many linguistic structures are too rare for their probability to be computed by counting the number of times they have occurred in a training sample, and in these unique cases we would not expect to see direct evidence of frequency. Yet, frequency of occurrence comes into play indirectly: it is possible to estimate the probability of one larger, complex structure from the counts of many smaller objects (see Jurafsky 2003: 42). Moreover, as Abney points out, Chomsky was arguing against the finite-state aspect of Markov models, not against their statistical nature. None of Chomsky's arguments applies to stochastic models more generally. The *n*th order Markov models do suffer from one major structural drawback, and that is that they can only capture dependencies up to *n*. Words depend on other words that may be quite far back in the stream, and if they are beyond *n*, they are inaccessible to the model (Hale 2016: 399).

3.2.1.2 Computational Implementations   Explicit mechanisms of probabilistic processing have been pursued most vigorously by connectionists, an area of study that was shaped by the seminal work of McClelland and Rumelhart (McClelland and Rumelhart 1981; Rumelhart and McClelland 1982). Connectionist models instantiate a particular kind of computational model of cognition that moves away from the computer metaphor which had yielded the information processing approach that dominated cognitive psychology in the 1970s, and to which we will return in Chapter 5. Connectionist models mimic properties of the brain, without necessarily aiming at (high levels of) biological realism. These models represent processing as patterns of activation across simple processing units that act together and act simultaneously to process information and connect together into complex networks; that is, cognition can be understood as a network of connections between units or nodes that look and act like neurons. If one node is activated, the activation travels to the other nodes depending on the strength of the connections between the nodes. Knowledge, and thus memory, is stored in the strength of the connections between the units, hence the name 'connectionism'. Connectionist models are also known as artificial neural network models or as parallel distributed processing models. For an excellent summary of connectionist models of cognition and an overview of the work that has been done in this tradition, see Thomas and McClelland (2008).

    Connectionist work is known within linguistics because the models have been trained on language phenomena, i.e., letter perception (McClelland and Rumelhart 1981; Rumelhart and McClelland 1982), the English past tense (Rumelhart and McClelland 1986), spoken word recognition (McClelland and Elman 1986) and sentence processing (Elman 1990, 1991). These models showed that multiple influences work simultaneously and in parallel to shape the system's response. They also demonstrated that rule conformity can arise without the explicit representation of the linguistic rule: as long as there are regularities in the statistical structure of a problem domain, these regularities can be learned and extended to new situations. Because the behaviour of the system is flexible and context-sensitive, it can accommodate regularities and exceptions within a single processing structure. Furthermore, the network could induce structured representations containing grammatical and semantic information from word sequences only, which prompted the view that associative learning mechanisms might play a more central role in learning than previously acknowledged (Thomas and McClelland 2008: 33, 37–8, 42). Although the network architecture in itself is biologically implausible (Dror and Gallogly 1999), the fact that 'a very simple network of processing units can perform a linguistic mapping' gave the field 'a powerful scientific metaphor for how neurons in the brain might accomplish linguistic mappings' (Baayen 2003: 231). Monsell (1991: 150) credited connectionist models with giving 'frequency of occurrence [...] its rightful place as a fundamental shaper of a lexical system always dynamically responsive to experience ...'.

The use of probability theory in computational modelling became more prevalent over the next two decades, and tempted psycholinguists to move from looking at frequency effects for single words to collecting evidence that frequency plays a role in more complex relationships such as those between words and between words and syntactic structure (for an overview of probability in psycholinguistics, see Jurafsky 2003: 41–63; for an overview of early computational models in psycholinguistics, see Jurafsky 2003: 63–89). In this area researchers had used both the joint probability of two words occurring together (or its simpler version of raw joint frequency) and the conditional probability of encountering a word given the previous word (a.k.a. transitional probability). Jurafsky (1996) approached the problem of retrieving a linguistic structure from a mental grammar and choosing among these structures to parse linguistic input from a probabilistic perspective. He showed that a single probabilistic algorithm could handle both tasks, thereby allowing a more uniform representation of linguistic knowledge. Important for linguists is his finding that a probabilistic model differs in its predictions from the frequency-based models traditional in psycholinguistics, with true probabilities essential for a cognitive model of sentence processing. Narayanan and Jurafsky (1998, 2002) expanded these insights into a Bayesian net model of human processing that combines probabilistic knowledge sources from lexical, idiomatic and syntactic/semantic domains.

This line of research has given rise to probabilistic grammar-based models (we will encounter these again in Section 3.3 of this chapter on information theory). Probabilistic grammar-based models typically use a probabilistic context-free grammar to encode information about lexical and structural preferences. The model incrementally assigns a probability to each possible analysis using grammar rules, for which the probabilities are estimated on the basis of a training corpus. Crocker and Brants (2000), for example, present an incremental probabilistic parsing model that ranks preferred analyses during parsing, using estimates from a parsed corpus. The assumption is that, when processing language, human beings consider all possible analyses that have received a probability exceeding a certain threshold. Processing difficulty arises when a sentence analysis that was dispreferred when one part of the sentence was available turns out to be correct when more of the sentence becomes available. Probabilistic grammar-based models thus account both for the generation of alternative analyses in case of an ambiguity and for processing difficulty that can arise from resolving such ambiguities. Their robustness and wide coverage stems from the fact that they use large, probabilistic grammars induced from a treebank, a syntactically annotated training corpus (Padó, Crocker and Keller 2009: 795–6).

Many computational linguists see the possibility of putting probability distributions over the 'hidden' syntactic structure that results from any linguistic model as a distinct advantage (Manning 2003: 296, 308). The psychological evidence for non-lexical syntactic structure, i.e., constituency, remains very weak (Jurafsky 2003: 94), however. It is, moreover, problematic that probabilistic approaches that do not rely on parsing do not scale up well and perform poorly on large data. Distributional approaches, on the other hand, fare a lot better in this respect (Chater and Manning 2006: 341–2).

Another common shortcoming of probabilistic grammar-based models is that they do not naturally integrate factors beyond the lexico-syntactic information encoded in a probabilistic context-free grammar. In real life we rely on pragmatics, understanding of social relationships and other elements of world knowledge to determine what people might say or mean. It needs to be borne in mind, though, that much of the development in probabilistic models was not driven by an interest in modelling human language processing but by the need to create practical computational systems for language processing (see Abney 1996: 2) – for recognizing speech, analysing or retrieving information in texts, question answering and machine translation. This focus on solving practical problems, and on problems that are solvable given the current state of technological progress, explains why certain aspects of language were prioritized over others. Moreover, pointing out that computational models do not concern themselves equally with all dimensions of language would be unfair: theoretical linguistic models, which are not at all hampered by practical implementational concerns, do not (yet) try to integrate information from phonology, morphology, syntax, semantics and pragmatics either.

3.2.2   Probabilistic Approaches to Language Cognition in Linguistics

Frequencies of linguistic structure, especially structure that is related to lexical items, undeniably play an important role in language processing. Grammatical rules may be associated with probabilities of use, capturing what is linguistically likely, not just what is linguistically possible (Chater and Manning 2006: 335). From this viewpoint, probabilistic ideas can augment symbolic models of language. Yet this complementarity does not imply that probabilistic methods merely add to symbolic work, without modification. The 'probabilistic turn', broadly characterized, has led to some radical rethinking in the science of language.

Statistical methods bear mostly on all the issues that are outside the scope of interest of current mainstream linguistics. In a broader sense, though, I think that says more about the narrowness of the current scope of interest than about the linguistic importance of statistical methods. Statistical methods are of great linguistic interest because the issues they bear on are linguistic issues, and essential to an understanding of what human language is and what makes it tick. We must not forget that the idealizations that Chomsky made were an expedient, a way of managing the vastness of our ignorance. [...] To a significant degree, I think linguistics has lost sight of its original goal, and turned Chomsky's expedient into an end in itself. [...] Linguistic data other than structure judgments are classified as "performance" data [...] Performance is considered the domain of psychologists, or at least, not of concern to linguists. (Abney 1996: 5–6)

Bod, Hay and Jannedy (2003b) were the first to focus on the value of probabilistic models for linguistics. They questioned the idea that had dominated linguistics since the 1950s, i.e., that language is categorical and linguistic competence discrete. Each case study in their volume illustrates that discrete linguistic categories do not account for observed variation, or at least do not account for anything but the extremes of the continuum. Probabilistic models, on the other hand, account for both categorical and continuous data, and thereby capture the observed behaviour of real speakers and real languages better. Interestingly, Bod, Hay and Jannedy (2003a) explicitly state that they do not reject categorical approaches to linguistics but aim to integrate the progress made by linguists working within these frameworks with insights from probabilistic approaches that make it possible to capture the gradient middle ground adequately. In fact, linguistic constraints can be thought of as statistically robust generalizations, learned from limited language exposure. Depending on the individual and the language sample the individual has been exposed to, these generalizations will be arrived at in different ways and to different extents.

This insight sparked an interest in probabilistic statistical classification models in linguistics, the use of which had been pioneered by Sankoff and Labov (1979). Fitting models to predict constructional and lexical choice is a growing trend in usage-based linguistics. It is a method widely applied in semantics (e.g., Arppe and Järvikivi 2007; Arppe 2008; Divjak 2010; Divjak and Arppe 2013), syntax (e.g., Gries 2003; Bresnan 2007; Bresnan et al. 2007; Bresnan and Ford 2010; Kendall, Bresnan and Van Herk 2011; Klavan 2012), morphology (e.g., Antić 2012; Baayen et al. 2013), phonetics and phonology (e.g., Erker and Guy 2012; Raymond and Brown 2012), and in areas as diverse as sociolinguistics (e.g., Grondelaers and Speelman 2007), historical linguistics (e.g., Gries and Hilpert 2010; Szmrecsanyi 2013; Wolk et al. 2013) and language development (e.g., Ambridge et al. 2012). Klavan and Divjak (2016b) critically survey this line of research and report that the majority of research in this area relies exclusively on the statistical modelling of corpus or experimental data while only a minority combines textual and behavioural data. This limits the conclusions that can be drawn for language: the mere fact that a pattern is attested in a corpus or is picked up by participants from a limited set of simplified experimental items does not mean that it is detected and exploited by language users, who are exposed to a vastly more complex system in real life.

Joan Bresnan has done much work to develop and test probabilistic models of how grammar varies in the individual and in speaker groups across space and time. In a series of papers on the dative alternation, Bresnan elaborated a probabilistic and gradient view on syntax. Starting from a multivariate corpus-based model (Bresnan et al. 2007), designed to predict the binary dative alternation using data from the 3 million–word Switchboard collection of recorded telephone conversations, she showed that language and linguistic choices are more probabilistic than had been recognized in theoretical linguistics. Her model included fourteen linguistic predictors, covering the semantic class of the main verb, accessibility of the recipient, accessibility of the theme, pronominality of the recipient, pronominality of the theme, definiteness of the recipient, definiteness of the theme, animacy of the recipient, person of the recipient, number of the recipient, number of the theme, concreteness of the theme, structural parallelism in dialogue (the existence of the same kind of structure in the same dialogue) and length difference (i.e., the difference in number of graphemic words between the theme and recipient as a measure of their relative weight). In a mixed effects logistic regression model, all of the model predictors (except for number of recipient) were found to be significant. Bresnan was also the first to evaluate such a model experimentally (Bresnan 2007, but also Bresnan and Ford 2010 and Ford and Bresnan 2013). In Bresnan (2007) a scalar rating task was used to evaluate the correlation between the naturalness of the alternative syntactic paraphrases and the corpus probabilities. Bresnan found that subjects' scores of the naturalness of the alternative syntactic paraphrases correlate well ($R^2 = 0.61$) with the corpus probabilities and can be explained as a function of the same predictors. Language users' implicit knowledge of the dative alternation in context thus reflects the usage probabilities of the construction. Ford and Bresnan (2010, 2013a, 2013b) investigated the same question across American and Australian varieties of English. They ran a continuous lexical decision task (Ford 1983) and found, fitting a mixed effects model to the data, that lexical-decision latencies during a reading task reflect the corpus probabilities: more probable sentence types require fewer resources during reading, so that reaction times measured in the task decrease in high-probability examples.

While a probabilistic approach was being elaborated for syntactic choices, lexical semantics was undergoing a similar change in approach. For book-length treatments I refer readers to Arppe (2008 and references therein) and Divjak (2010 and references therein). Building on earlier work by Divjak (2003, 2004, 2010), Divjak and Arppe (2013) used a dataset of 1,351 tokens to train a polytomous logistic regression model, applying the one-versus-all heuristic, to predict the choice between six Russian verbs that, when combined with an infinitive, can all be translated with the English verb *try*. Eighteen predictors (eleven semantic and seven structural) were used in the model, derived from seven different variables encoding the TAM (tense–aspect–mood) marking on the verb, the semantics of the subject and infinitive, and properties of clause and sentence. The model predicts the probability for each verb in each sentence and reveals how strongly each feature individually is associated with each verb. The overall accuracy of 51.7 per cent (50.3 per cent when tested on unseen data) is three times better than chance. The model's performance was tested against speakers' behaviour in a series of three studies, including offline and online tasks.

Divjak, Dabrowska and Arppe (2016) report on the offline forced choice task with sixty sentences, spanning the entire probability space; as a consequence of this, the testing set contains a larger proportion of verbs in highly variable contexts than would be the case in a random sample. The corpus-based model was retrained on the annotated sample minus the sixty training sentences and the probability of the six *try*-verbs in the sentences used for the forced choice task was computed. The verb with the highest predicted probability for a given context was taken to be the model's response on the forced choice task. The 'correct' response was taken to be the verb which actually occurred in the original corpus sentence. Overall, although both model and speaker perform 2.5 to 3 times better than chance, they still made the 'wrong' choice in more than half of all cases. But, in contrast to speakers, the model had no access to information about the token frequencies of individual verbs other than their frequencies in the corpus sample, which were roughly equal by design. After frequency information was included into the model by multiplying the predictions of the original model by the square root of each verb's relative frequency, the model performed exactly at the same level as the average human participant. Divjak, Arppe and Baayen (2016) describe the online self-paced reading task on attested corpus sentences to ascertain whether TAM marking, which came out of the corpus model as the strongest predictor, plays a role in the online processing of the three most frequently used *try*-verbs. Using a generalized additive mixed model, they showed that the preferential TAM marking of a verb is picked up by native speakers and plays a role in the online processes captured by a self-paced reading task: words are read more quickly if they are presented with their preferred TAM marking. The story is, however, more complicated than this, and individual learning styles turned out to play an important role in explaining readers' behaviour (Milin, Divjak and Baayen 2017).

Taken together, the studies by Bresnan and Ford on constructional alternations, and by Divjak and Arppe on lexical synonyms confirm that there is no difference between lexicon and grammar: in both cases distributional patterns, enriched with frequency of contextual co-occurrence information, are extracted from usage and appear predictive of a range of language behaviours. Such probabilistic approaches to language learning, processing and representation have done much to dispel the idea that language is rule-based and that language knowledge is discrete. These insights, together with the common language provided by quantification, have made it possible for linguists to engage more closely with researchers from other disciplines interested in language. In the next section, we will look in more detail at one such cross-disciplinary engagement, i.e., the interaction with information theory, which has yielded valuable insights for the understanding of language processing.

3.3   Probabilities Link Linguistics to Information Theory

Although many cognitive scientists believe information processing to be central to cognition, it is not always clear what is meant by 'information'. It seems generally accepted that stimuli that are more 'informative' increase 'cognitive load' and should therefore require more 'mental effort' to process. Some researchers have 'gone beyond the metaphor' (Frank 2013: 475) and have brought concepts and insights from information theory to bear on explanations of cognitive phenomena. The usefulness of probabilities had long been known within information theory, where measures such as surprisal and entropy originate. An excellent tutorial introduction to information theory is provided by Stone (2015); the standard reference is Cover and Thomas (2006).

In 1948, Claude Shannon published *A Mathematical Theory of Communication*, in which he describes information as a well-defined and measurable entity.

Shannon's theory of information provides a mathematical definition of information, and describes precisely how much information can be communicated between different elements of a system. This may not sound like much, but Shannon's theory underpins our understanding of how signal and noise are related, and why there are limits to the rate at which information can be communicated within *any* system, whether man-made or biological. (Stone 2015: 2)

This insight transformed our understanding of information and marked the dawn of modern telecommunication: it helped reveal fundamental limits on signal-processing operations such as compressing data and on reliably storing and communicating data. Information theory is fundamentally about the problem of 'reproducing at one point, either exactly or approximately, a message selected at another point' (Shannon 1948: 379). If information contained in data is thought of as a useful signal and the rest of the data as distracting noise, then mathematically, information can be defined as the logarithm of the inverse of the probability that the event will occur:

$$I_e = log\left(\frac{1}{Pr(e)}\right)$$

This formula can be rewritten as the negative logarithm of the same quantity (given that the logarithm of a product or a division of two quantities is the sum or the difference of the logarithms of those two quantities, respectively):

$$I_e = log(1) - log\Big(Pr(e)\Big) = 0 - log\Big(Pr(e)\Big) = -log\Big(Pr(e)\Big)$$

The probability of an event allows us to determine how accurately a message will be reproduced: reproduction is easy if the message is expected, but hard if the message is unexpected. The Shannon information of an outcome, also called surprisal (Tribus 1961; Barlow 1990) or surprise ratio, measures how unexpected a specific outcome is, given the probabilities of each outcome in the set. The average Shannon information is called entropy (it is the average surprise of a probability distribution of a random variable). Entropy quantifies the uncertainty involved in predicting the value of a random variable and is thus a measure of uncertainty, or of the unpredictability of information content: something that is predictable has low entropy, whereas something that is unpredictable has high entropy. When our uncertainty is reduced, we gain information so entropy and information are two sides of the same coin.[1]

Information theory is a mathematical model of information transmission and a valuable tool for understanding the difficulties associated with such transmission. As such, it does not concern itself with 'meaning', a fact which is off-putting for many linguists. Yet, entropy and surprisal have been used to some extent in psycholinguistic models of morphological processing (Kostić 1991; Moscoso del Prado Martín, Kostić and Baayen 2004; Milin, Đurđević and del Prado Martín 2009 for morphological processing; Milin et al. 2009 for an overview) and of syntactic processing (Hale 2001; Levy 2008; Jaeger 2010; Frank 2013). While most studies have focused on language comprehension using experimental designs, some have considered language production using data from spoken natural language corpora. Insights from information theory have also been implemented in computational emergentist models (e.g.,

---

[1] The maximum amount of information associated with a discrete variable is the logarithm of the number of equally probable values it can adopt. Because a binary variable can adopt two states, it conveys up to 1 *bit* of information (Stone 2015: 43–4). For this reason, many publications on information theory have a title that refers to *bit(s)*.

Automatic Distillation of Structure by Solan et al. 2005). We will review these studies in the following sections.

3.3.1   Morphology

The introduction of insights from information theory to morphology was spearheaded by Kostić who quantified the amount of morphological information conveyed by a word form by using and adapting measures from information theory designed to capture uncertainty and measure uncertainty reduction. Kostić (1991) studied the processing of inflected nouns in Serbian, a morphologically rich language that boasts a system of seven cases. In a series of experiments conducted on Serbo-Croatian nouns it had been observed that when subjects were presented with inflected nouns in isolation, the nominative-singular form had the shortest lexical-decision response latency; no difference was found among the other (i.e., oblique) forms of a noun, which were all approximately equal in decision latencies (Lukatela et al. 1978; Lukatela et al. 1980). The processing hypotheses that held sway at the time could not account for this observed variation. Kostić (1991), who replicated the finding, therefore adopted the assumption that variation in word-recognition latency among the inflected forms of a noun would be accounted for by the amount of information each form contains. A series of experiments confirmed that the processing cost of an inflected variant is predicted by its frequency and functional load (Kostić 1995; Kostić, Markovíc and Baucal 2003). Subsequent refinements consider other dimensions of variation in order to isolate the factors that contribute to processing cost.

The insight that the amount of information conveyed by a unit is negatively correlated with the probability of occurrence of that unit and positively correlated with its processing costs, or in other words, that the cost of retrieving information from long-term memory is proportional to the amount of information retrieved, further inspired research on lexical processing from an information-theoretical point of view. Building on Kostić's work, Moscoso del Prado Martín, Kostić and Baayen (2004) proposed a mathematical formulation of the morphological complexity of a word, its *information residual*. This measure contains the combined influences of the amount of information conveyed by the target word and the amount of information carried by its morphological paradigms. The information residual is the difference between the cost of recognizing a word and the support for a word provided by its morphological paradigms (both measured on the logarithmic scale, i.e., in bits). A reanalysis of existing visual lexical decision response latencies on monomorphemic, polymorphemic and compound words in Dutch showed that the effects on response latencies, which had previously been attributed to frequency counts (such as surface frequency and base frequency, inflectional ratio, cumulative root frequency and morphological family size), were accounted for in a more parsimonious manner using the information residual of a word. The apparent processing differences between the three types of words arise naturally as consequences of the probabilistic distributions found in different types of morphological paradigms. This work 'extended Kostić's findings from inflectional to derivational morphology and compounds while at the same time using a more standard measure of the amount of information carried by a paradigm' (Moscoso del Prado Martín, Kostić and Baayen 2004: 16). From a theoretical linguistic point of view, the generalizations make it possible to subsume the family size information that correlates with type-frequency effects and the inflectional information that correlates with token-frequency effects under a single measure (Blevins 2013: 367).

Milin, Ðurđević and del Prado Martín (2009) investigated the relevance of inflectional paradigms and inflectional classes for lexical processing using data from Serbian. They hypothesized that the probability distribution of the inflected variants of a given lexeme can differ substantially from the probability distribution of the case endings at the level of the inflectional class. If that is the case, the corresponding entropies would differ substantially from each other as well. In order to capture this difference, they extended the inventory of entropy-based measures used in the study of morphological processing with *relative entropy* (or Kullback–Leibler divergence). Relative entropy is a measure of the dissimilarity between the frequency distributions of two of the paradigms to which a word belongs: the paradigm it belongs to according to its stem (i.e., the inventory of case-endings a word can take), and the more general paradigm of the stem's nominal class (i.e., the words that share one set of case-endings). After controlling for other variables, the divergence between these two paradigms was positively correlated with response latencies and error counts in a visual lexical decision task: the larger the divergence, the slower the respondents were in recognizing a word and the more errors they made. This shows that context, including word-level context such as the endings a word typically takes, plays a crucial role in how we process language. The results were interpreted as traces of the simultaneous influence that both the word stem and its inflectional paradigm have on lexical processing. Of course, entropy measures defined over full paradigms are cognitively implausible because of the Zipfian nature of the input. They do, however, reveal that the degree of contextual variability in which an item is encountered affects the representation of the item.

The information-theoretic approach to modelling morphological structure has also given rise to the formal rehabilitation of the complex system perspective of traditional word and paradigm (or WP) models. As Blevins (2013: 372) explains, a classical WP model acknowledges words because the uncertainty associated with a word is less than the sum of the uncertainty of its parts. The same holds for paradigms: paradigms are allowed to play a role in the model because the uncertainty associated with a paradigm is less than the sum of the uncertainty of the members of the paradigm. In both cases, conditional entropy is ideal for modelling the reduction in uncertainty that results from the inter-dependencies between the parts and the wholes. A general morphological model that develops these claims is outlined in Blevins (2016).

3.3.2   Syntax

Similar to what was found for morphology, the general insight that information theory contributed to the study of syntactic processing is that words that convey more information take longer to read. Work in this area shares the core assumption that each word is interpreted immediately and sentence processing is incremental. At the same time, different researchers have provided different answers to the crucial question of what to define the information measures over: as a result, there is work defining these measures over words, parts of speech and syntactic tree structures. Yet, syntactic categories are theory dependent and it is not at all clear whether such a (or, for that matter, any) categor-ization is cognitively relevant. Despite significant progress in the area, the question remains which underlying cognitive mechanism is responsible for longer reading times on words that convey more information (see Frank 2013: 487).

Hale (2001)'s starting point is a probabilistic phrase-structure grammar, a probabilistic grammar defined in terms of a stochastic process that rewrites strings of grammar symbols according to the probabilities on the rules of the grammar. Each sentence in the language of the grammar has a probability equal to the product of the probabilities of all the rules used to generate it. He proposed the hypothesis that cognitive load can be defined in terms of the total probability of structural options that have been disconfirmed at some point in a sentence. Put simply: if we assume that at each word a number of structural hypotheses are disconfirmed, then the more hypotheses need to be discon-firmed, the more time it takes to move on to the next word, resulting in longer reading latencies. Instead of calculating this probability at the sentence level, i.e., for complete sentences, Hale calculated so-called prefix probabilities at the word level using Stolcke's (1995) algorithm. This algorithm determines, at each word, the sum of the probabilities of all possible sentence continuations that are compatible with the part of the sentence seen up until that word.[2]

---

[2] If the grammar is consistent (and the probabilities of all possible continuations add up to 1), then subtracting the prefix probability from 1 gives the total probability of all the analyses that the parser has disconfirmed.

In a self-paced reading task, a person's difficulty perceiving syntactic structure (e.g., garden path and subject/object relative asymmetry) can be modelled by word-to-word *surprisal* in the context within which it appears. Surprisal at a specific word equals the logarithm of the ratio of the prefix probability before seeing the word to the prefix probability after seeing it. Surprisal offers a way of understanding language processing in terms of a mathematical theory. It allows us to quantify how difficult it is to process a linguistic expression, word by word, as that expression is produced over time (Hale 2016: 397–8).

Hale (2003) puts his model explicitly on an informational theoretical footing. Information theory would view sentences as random events and words as symbols that appear with a certain probability. Each time a word is revealed, that word's information value can be quantified. The greater the information value of the word, the greater its processing difficulty is hypothesized to be (Hale 2016: 398). This approach suggests that cognitive load is related to the reduction in the perceiver's uncertainty about what the producer meant. Sentence processing is seen as entropy reduction: the reduction in uncertainty from one word to the next is the information conveyed by that word. The number of bits conveyed per word is a determinant of reading times and other measures of cognitive load. The more bits of information are transacted at a specific word, the longer it will take to process that word, signalling the effort that the system has to do to specify the representation.

The surprisal theory of Hale (2001) and the entropy reduction hypothesis of Hale (2003) differ in a crucial respect. In the former, the difficulty of a word is determined by the number of sentence continuations that are compatible with the part of the sentence seen up until that word. In the latter, the difficulty of a word is linked to a change in the (un)certainty of how the sentence should be analysed syntactically. These two quantities need not be related (see Levy 2008: 1128).

Levy (2008) proposes a probabilistic, expectation-based theory of syntactic comprehension, unifying the idea of the work done in incremental probabilistic disambiguation with expectations about upcoming events in a sentence. He explores the role of resource allocation and reallocation during parallel, incremental, probabilistic disambiguation in sentence comprehension as a source of processing difficulty. To measure processing difficulty, he used response times from reading time experiments on syntactic ambiguity resolution. In Levy's (2008) model, all possible interpretations of a sentence are allocated a probability of occurrence that together form the probability distribution for the interpretations of the sentence. The difficulty experienced while processing a particular word stems from the need to update the probability distribution; the degree of difficulty is determined by the degree to which the preference distribution over interpretations of the sentence that the word requires has to be updated. To quantify the degree of difficulty associated with the update,

Levy (2008) uses the Kullback–Leibler divergence or the relative entropy of the updated distribution with respect to the initial distribution (compare here the use of relative entropy in morphology by Milin, Đurđević and del Prado Martín (2009)): the greater the difference between the two distributions, the greater the relative entropy. On this approach, the predicted difficulty of a word is equal (Levy 2008: 1130–1) to the surprisal associated with encountering that word given the context, as defined by Hale (2001); note, however, that in Levy (2008) surprise is derived via relative entropy. 'Expectations about upcoming words in a sentence need not be explicitly calculated; rather, they are implicit in the partial parse of an incomplete input' (Levy 2008: 1132).

An important point concerns the question of how strongly surprisal theory is committed to full parallelism, i.e., that all possible structural analyses of a sentence are maintained during online comprehension (Levy 2008: 1136–7). As Levy (2008: 1135) points out:

[F]ull parallelism becomes less tractable as a wider variety of information sources is brought to bear in probabilistic disambiguation. This leads to the possibility that parallelism in the human parser is limited: more than one, but not all, of possible analyses are maintained in the course of online comprehension. Without full parallelism, the strict equivalence between relative entropy and conditional word probability (and together with it the causal bottleneck property, if one takes the relative entropy measure as primitive) is lost. However, evidence from the probabilistic parsing literature (Henderson 2004; Roark 2001) suggests that in typical sentences, most of the probability mass is focused on a small number of highly ranked analyses. To the extent that this is true, the relative entropy/surprisal equivalence will be approximate [...].

Jaeger (2010) proposes a principle of efficient language *production* based on information-theoretic considerations. His uniform information density (UID) predicts that language production is characterized by a preference to distribute information uniformly across the linguistic signal, i.e., to keep the amount of information per amount of linguistic signal constant and avoid peaks and troughs. Assuming that speakers aim to transmit information uniformly, and stay close to, but not exceed, the channel capacity '[w]ithin the bounds defined by grammar, speakers prefer utterances that distribute information uniformly across the signal (information density). Where speakers have a choice between several variants to encode their message, they prefer the variant with more uniform information density (ceteris paribus)' (Jaeger 2010: 25).

The predictions this hypothesis generates were tested against data on *that*-omission in English from a corpus of spontaneous speech. If the complementizer *that* is expressed at the onset of a complement clause, the same amount of information is distributed over one more word, which lowers the clause's information density. Therefore, everything else being the same, speakers should be more likely to produce full complement clauses (clauses with *that*) than reduced complement clauses (clauses without *that*), if the information of the complement clause onset in its context is higher (Jaeger 2010: 28). Information density emerged indeed as a strong predictor of *that*-mentioning in a representative sample of English speech, even after controlling for a large number of effects that had been identified as predictive in previous accounts of syntactic production. In other words, syntactic reduction appears to be affected by information density, which is consistent with the hypothesis that syntactic production is organized to be efficient. Given that information is an inherently probabilistic notion, the observed sensitivity to information density also suggests that syntactic production is probability-sensitive (Jaeger 2010: 46).

Frank (2013) examined the relative entropy hypothesis, which claims that the cognitive processing difficulty of a word in sentence context is determined by the word's effect on the uncertainty about the sentence, for actual words rather than their part of speech or syntactic categories. He used a recurrent neural network for estimating entropy and a self-paced reading task for obtaining measures of cognitive processing load. Entropy was computed over four-word sequences (for a 7,754-word vocabulary), which has the advantage that it does not rely on any particular grammar or other assumption about how sentences are interpreted or parsed. Entropy reduction is a significant predictor of reading time, over and above many other factors. Results show a positive relation between reading time on a word and the reduction in entropy due to processing that word, supporting the entropy reduction hypothesis. Moreover, increasing suffix length improves model fit, suggesting that what really matters is uncertainty about the complete sentence. This effect of relative entropy was found to be independent from the effect of word surprisal, yet no evidence was found of a dissociation between surprisal and relative entropy. The difference between the two effects does not correspond to a difference between subjects, sentences, parts of speech or content versus function words. As a consequence, there is no evidence (yet) to conclude that these two measures correspond to cognitively distinct processes.

3.4 Summary and Outlook

The success of probabilistic methods in computational linguistics suggested that human language development and processing might exploit probabilistic information. 'Language displays all the hallmarks of a probabilistic system. Categories and well-formedness are gradient, and frequency effects are everywhere' (Bod, Hay and Jannedy 2003a: 10). Probabilities, therefore, need to be integrated everywhere: in language development, processing and representation. Much evidence has accumulated that favours a probabilistic view on language. Knowledge of language does not need to be understood as a minimal set of categorical rules or constraints, but as a (possibly redundant) set of gradient rules, which may be characterized by a statistical distribution (Bod, Hay and Jannedy 2003a: 7, 10).

The effectiveness of probabilistic techniques in accounting for language processing indicates that probabilities might, indeed, account for an important component of human language learning. Probability might thus prove important as a unifying theoretical concept for understanding how the cognitive system makes the uncertain inference from speech signal to message, and vice versa. It may also help understand how, and to what extent, learners infer language structure from linguistic input (Chater and Manning 2006: 339–40).

How exactly a probabilistic level is implemented is a different question. In linguistics, the need to address this issue has not been felt strongly due to a tendency to favour theory over implementation. Researchers working within an information-theoretic approach share the same attitude. Hale (2003: 119) points out that he sees information theory as a way of 'breaking the endless circle of appealing to frequency as an explanation for performance', but 'the issue of what cognitively or neurally plausible processing architectures actually reduce entropy (as specified here) is very much open'. This feeling is echoed by Milin et al. (2009: 216) who state that 'we do believe that the concepts of information science provide us with excellent tools to probe the *functional organization of the mental lexicon*, but we shall remain agnostic about how paradigmatic structures are implemented in the brain'. In computational circles, the most common assumption is that probabilities are realized either as an activation level of a mental structure or as a distributed pattern of activation, whereby stored frequencies or probabilities are encoded as resting activation levels or as weights on connections. Stone (2018), however, goes much further. He argues that the way in which neurons communicate in their respective biological neural networks is designed to achieve maximum efficiency at minimal metabolic cost. And this trade-off can be formalised in terms of Shannon's information theory. Such efficiency, Stone argues, cannot be a mere accident but must be an evolutionary necessity.

This discussion leads us to the next question: which brain mechanisms could support the registration of frequency information, and how might brain structures respond to repetition? In Chapter 4, we will consider how the brain responds to frequency of occurrence and relies on repetition to commit experiences to memory.

Part II

4   Committing Experiences to Memory

We have seen in the previous chapters that frequency of occurrence plays an important role in many contemporary approaches to language. Frequency of occurrence is, in essence, the repetition of an experience; and hearing or reading language is an experience too. Human beings are sensitive to the frequency with which they experience something and repeated experiences are laid down in memory with a strength that relates to the extent of the exposure. Surprisingly, knowledge about memory formation and consolidation has barely influenced linguistic theories. But if we consider exposure to language as a linguistic experience, our knowledge of language could, and should, be described as a complex system of memories.

How does frequency help commit experiences to memory? In this chapter we will take a closer look at memory and explore the brain mechanisms that respond to the repetition of experiences. It is important to investigate where frequency effects occur in the sequence of events going from environment to neural representations. This is knowledge we need in order to constrain our linguistic theories to those that can account for the types of structures that might emerge from this sensitivity to repetition. It is precisely these structures that are worth pursuing on a usage-based, cognitive linguistic approach to language development, processing and representation.

After a brief introduction to memory in general, different classifications of memory systems will be introduced. Section 4.2 delves into the physiology of memory and asks where and how memories are stored. In Section 4.3, memory processes, i.e., encoding, storing and retrieving, are discussed while Section 4.4 focuses on diagnostics of memory traces for language.

4.1   What Is Memory?

Memory is a cover term for the ability to make what is learned persist through time. Although fundamental to our existence and experience, memory – like time – cannot be directly observed. We do know that our experiences modify our brain; aspects of that modification are retained in our brains and make up knowledge. Because the exact nature of memory processes eludes us, researchers have turned to metaphors to guide their investigations. But the metaphors have been so powerful that they have taken on lives of their own; this is why we standardly define memory as the ability to encode, store and retrieve information.

4.1.1   Changing Metaphors and Methods in the Study of Memory

Metaphors help us think: they make it possible to conceptualize an unknown, intangible concept in terms of a known and often tangible entity (Lakoff and Johnson 1980). Think of the many languages and cultures that use space to conceptualize time and talk about time using spatial metaphors (Lakoff and Johnson 1980; Núñez and Cooperrider 2013; Moore 2014). We talk about the duration of time using words for size ('a short weekend') while the passage of time is described using verbs of motion ('the week flew by').

Different metaphors have supported different ways of thinking about memory too and have led to new types of explanations of memory phenomena. The dominant functional metaphor for memory has long been one of storage and retrieval. Completed by the search metaphor, these three concepts have spilled into theories and models of memory to the extent that memory is typically conceptualized as a container that can be searched to retrieve one of the many memories it stores. Furthermore, analogies have been called upon to account for the observed memory processes. The most prominent analogies refer to the ways we have invented to record, preserve and reproduce information. Following technological developments closely, analogies have been drawn with anything from Plato's wax tablet to present-day computers. Everyday terms for remembering and forgetting reflect this analogy too: we have 'impressions' (as if memory were a block of wax) and events can be 'etched' onto our memory (as if memory were a surface). Some of us are said to have a 'photographic' memory, and what we have forgotten has been 'erased' from memory. The influence of technological development has been so strong that nineteenth-century theories of visual memory, for example, reflected the succession of new optical processes (Draaisma 2000: 3). The metaphors and analogies that have supported thinking about memory have given rise to many hypothetical mental representations or processes that are only loosely tied to behaviour (Roediger 1980). Take the computer analogy, for example: computers are infallible, and this infallibility is their greatest shortcoming in serving as analogy for research into human memory. Equally limiting may be the inventory of terms that is automatically activated through the computer and information-processing metaphors. Computers operate on symbolic representations of the world. They have physical memories where they store and retrieve information for processing. Do we, therefore, too (Epstein 2016)? Do we store words and rules for combining words into sentences? Do we create representations of auditory or visual stimuli? Do we move information from short-term memory to long-term memory for later retrieval? In fact, many metaphor-induced defects in the formulation of theories of memory have been corrected multiple times over the course of the centuries, but psychology 'seems to suffer from a memory loss that borders on the pathological' (Draaisma 2000: 5).

   Like the metaphors that have shaped thinking about memory, available investigative techniques have shaped findings. For example, the older, 'specific location' interpretation of memory, which assumed that memories were held in one place in the brain, dates back to an era when most of the knowledge of memory came from studying memory disorders, arising from relatively restricted brain damage. By studying the different forms these disorders could take, it became possible to observe defects in individual subsystems of the brain's memory systems and hypothesize their function in the normally working brain. Recent advances in neuroimaging techniques have revolutionized the field by making it possible to study not only structure, but also function, i.e., the workings of the healthy and intact living brain in real time. Neuroimaging techniques are correlational, however, which means that they show correlations between cognitive performance and areas of brain activity, and correlation is not causation. Despite this limitation, it is now generally accepted that memory representation relies on a network, a connection between disparate areas in the brain: stored memories are distributed throughout the brain and rely on connections across spatially separate areas of the brain rather than on any specific area (Conway et al. 2003). Within the current network view of memory (Fuster 2009), memories are thought of as activation patterns of neuronal tissue, formed by experience. Different stimuli may activate different networks that could partly overlap. Research suggests that there may be specific neural circuits for particular memories, including for morphological knowledge (Marslen-Wilson and Tyler 2007; Nevat et al. 2017) and syntactic constructions (Allen et al. 2012). The evidence remains circumstantial, at best, and much more work is needed before the inventory of linguistic functions can reliably be mapped onto the inventory of neurological structures (Poeppel 2012). This challenge is compounded by the standard approach in digital brain mapping of merging brain maps of individuals into an 'average' or 'normal' brain that is then used to make claims that are applied to individuals. Yet, as always, averages do not necessarily correspond to any one single individual, and care needs to be taken when interpreting claims made on the basis of aggregated data.

4.1.2 Changing Foci in the Study of Memory

In addition to the many metaphors and analogies that have guided research on memory, the topic has also been of interest to researchers from different disciplines. Over the centuries, memory has moved from philosophy to psychology and more recently to biology, and with each of these moves, the locus of interest shifted. Philosophers describe how the mind creates associations between ideas. Psychologists study how memory 'works', whether there are different kinds of memory and how these interact; and they have done so within several frameworks, most notably behaviourism and cognitivism. Biologists examine where and how we store what we learn as memory.

Hermann Ebbinghaus (1885b), a historian and philosopher by training, is often said to have been the first to apply the scientific method to the study of memory (although experiments on memory were conducted at least 150 years before that, see Draaisma 2000: 93). Inspired by Fechner's work on psychophysics that captured the relation between the strength of a physical stimulus and the intensity of a sensation in mathematical laws, Ebbinghaus set out to achieve the same for memory (Draaisma 2000: 94). He contributed important insights to memory research, including the learning and forgetting curve (Ebbinghaus 1885b). Using himself as subject, Ebbinghaus memorized lists of meaningless syllables (trigraphs). He varied the length of the lists between six and twenty items and experimented with the length of the retention interval between time of study and time of test. He found that shorter lists were easier to remember and that testing soon after completing memorization results in more accurate retrieval. His 'forgetting curve' captures the power function that relates probability of recall and recency, showing that half of what is memorized is forgotten twenty-four hours later. In a sense, Ebbinghaus studied memory by measuring forgetting. For this he also looked at what he called the 'savings score', i.e., he measured the reduction in the time required to relearn a previously learned list. Although savings diminished as the retention interval grew larger, there were always savings. Ebbinghaus also found that overlearning would make the forgetting curve less steep: if you continue to learn something past the point of mastery, long-term retention improves. Bahrick (1984) later showed that forgetting 'stops' after five years. He tested 773 subjects on their high school Spanish and found that the forgetting curve levels off after five to six years; it then remains stable for a quarter of a century after that. In other words, forgetting is rapid initially, but levels off with time and corresponding reduction in knowledge.

Interestingly, although Ebbinghaus (1885b) may have introduced a marked change in the methods used to study memory, the theories guiding the research remained unaffected. During the first half of the twentieth century, while behaviourism held sway, the study of memory remained the study of learning and forgetting. Since behaviourists were interested in observable behaviour only, to the exclusion of unobservable mental events, they mainly looked for empirical relations governing the acquisition, transfer and extinction of habits, or implicit memories. Although their ban on non-observable processes also partially removed the necessity for metaphors, metaphors were still used (Draaisma 2000: 138). A frequent behaviourist metaphor for memory is the metaphor of the telephone exchange where incoming signals are linked via one-to-one switches to outgoing responses; this was sufficient to capture the connection between stimulus and response. Other popular, neo-behaviourist, metaphors were the maze and the map (see the work of American psychologist Edward Tolman) that derived from instruments popular in research into learning but later also structured thinking about learning. There was also the lure of the psychic machine (see Tolman's contemporary, Clark Hull), which served as an early articulation of the logic of simulation research (Draaisma 2000: 140).

The middle of the twentieth century witnessed the invention of the computer. As Draaisma (2000: 57, 138) puts it: '[n]o new technology since the invention of photography and the phonograph captured human imagination as much as the computer did.' It encouraged philosophers, psychologists and mathematicians to reflect on the relationship between human and machine intelligence, and before long the computer had become the dominant metaphor in the psychology of memory. Terminology developed for describing computers, such as input and output, encoding and address, working memory and temporary or back-up storage, was borrowed and started being used for describing human memory. But Alan Turing (1969: 13) argued that the analogy between the brain and the computer should be directed at the level of information rather than at the level of physiology. The focus on information processing put the idea of the flow of information and the transformations that this entails at the core of theorizing about cognition and memory. Because of this metaphor, the study of encoding became the study of how information was transferred from short- to long-term memory. The transition from associationism to information processing also led to the separation between storage and retrieval processes. While mid-twentieth-century 'memory was still a matter of acquisition, retention, transfer and interference between stimuli and responses,' a mere ten years later, retrieval processes such as recognition and recall were studied separately from storage processes and this shaped theories and experiments (Tulving and Thomson 1973: 352).

The idea of the computer as a suitable metaphor for memory remains controversial today. On the one hand, thinking of memory as a computer does solve the problem of infinite regress. In many theories of cognition, representations are posited that need manipulating. An example here are Chomskyan rules that act on representations. Who applies these rules? Rule application, a form of representation manipulation, is done by other and typically higher-level representations. But these higher-level representations, typically, need manipulating too (and the representations above them as well, ad infinitum). If we see memory as a computer, we can replace representations with data structures that rely on simpler data structures, requiring less intelligence each time the task is broken down further, rather than more. Yet, unlike a personal computer that excels at doing one thing at the time and does it very fast, the brain is a parallel device that does many things at once. Paraphrasing Dennet (1979: 122–4), Edelman (2008: 170) explains how, in (some) computational models of memory, this idea is implemented as a collection of expert modules, all fed by a gating device that acts as a router. The gating device and the expert modules are trained in parallel. The router learns three things: first, it learns to subdivide the solution space into relatively homogeneous regions, that is, it performs a rough classification. Next, it learns to associate each class of inputs with one of the regions. And finally, it learns to direct the data accordingly so that it ends up in the appropriate region. The expert modules, trained on subsets of the data, are specialized, i.e., 'tuned' to a region of the possibility space, and hence perform better than if each of them had to cover the entire possibility space. They are also less likely to suffer from interference among memory traces. Imamizu et al. (2004) present data from a computational simulation, supported by fMRI-based evidence, that such a model may indeed be implemented in the human brain. Dividing the labour imposes structure and efficiency on the network of neurons, which is in this model of expert modules conceptualized as a distributed computational system. These tuned units play a central role in the machinery that interfaces between an attractor network's dynamic memory and the rest of the cognitive system. A causal connection to the rest of the system (and eventually to the world) is crucial: a memory is a memory of something by virtue of being evoked by a signal from a tuned unit and, in turn, being interpreted by one.

The most recent revolution, also known as the biological revolution, combines a molecular and a systems component (Squire and Kandel 2009: 7). For long, psychologists had believed that they could not borrow anything useful from neurologists: the gap between the behaviour of neurons and that of people was deemed too wide to bridge. Yet it is the synthesis of biological and psychological approaches that promises a new level of understanding. This insight followed from the publication of John Hopfield's (1982) paper on the emergent collective computational abilities of networks. Heralding the connectionist revolution, Hopfield (a theoretical physicist) proved that 'in a network of simple homogenous elements relatively permanent patterns of equilibrium are created, which can function as a physical substratum for the storage of information' (Draaisma 2000: 191). Most theorists now focus on associative models of memory: we represent information in memory in terms of connections among units of information. A node is a unit of information that is connected to other nodes. Activation that transfers from one node to another is called *spreading activation*; the further it spreads, the more it weakens until it eventually dissipates. Although this brain metaphor is inspired by the structure of brain tissue, its popularity was fuelled by the increase in computational power made available through parallel computing. The similarity between neuronal tissue and neural networks remains as tentative as that between computer memory processes and functions, however.

4.1.3 Classifications of Memory: the Multi-Store Model

Classifications of memory tend to take one of three approaches: they either classify memory by duration of encoding, by encoding of information type or by temporal direction. The first two are depicted in Figure 4.1.

When we look at memory systems from the point of view of the *duration* for which each system can hold a memory, as the American philosopher William James proposed, we can roughly distinguish between sensory memory, short-term memory and long-term memory. Sensory memory is the shortest element of memory. It enables the retention of sensory impressions after the stimulus has passed, to allow cognitive processing prior to conscious access. It is thought that there is a separate sensory memory system for each perceptual system, e.g., iconic memory for visual information, echoic memory for auditory information and so on. Generally, traces of sensory stimuli are expected to vanish in under one second, except traces of echoic information, which are said to last up to four seconds. We will discuss the other two types of memory, working memory and long-term memory, in detail below. Memory systems can

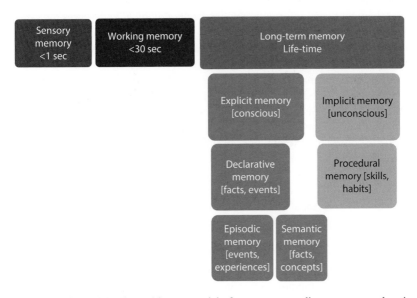

Figure 4.1 The multi-store model of memory according to memory duration

also be classified by encoding of *information type*. There is declarative memory, which is explicit and consists of semantic memory for general facts and of episodic memory that contains memory for personal facts; the information can be accessed intentionally and consciously. There is also procedural or implicit memory, which enables us to perform tasks and can be attested through change in behaviour; it is acquired and used unconsciously. Memory classifications that take into account *temporal direction* recognize retrospective and prospective memory (not depicted in Figure 4.1). Retrospective memory involves remembering what we know about something and is high in information content. Prospective memory focuses on when to do things and is low in information content. These three different classifications of memory are often combined.

A core type of memory that appears to be missing from Figure 4.1 is short-term memory. What is now known as *working memory* comprises what was first known as primary memory (James 1890) and then as short-term memory. First, the idea of a passive primary memory was replaced by more dynamic accounts of temporary information storage and information processing, such as the working-memory model. Next, the work of Baddeley and Hitch (1974) and of Baddeley (1986) not only changed the terminology used to describe working memory, but also the way in which working memory was construed. Instead of thinking of working memory as one system, Baddeley and Hitch proposed multiple memory systems that subserve working memory. They reserved one memory system for every major perceptual modality: the *visuospatial sketchpad* is there for visual information while the *phonological loop* serves the same function for auditory information. These systems maintain information for temporary use. The *episodic buffer* coordinates overlap between these two systems and links working memory to long-term memory (Baddeley 2000). An attentional mechanism, the *central executive*, coordinates the working memory components. Recent neuroscientific work has established that areas in the prefrontal and medial temporal lobes appear to be the neural regions mediating working memory and that the multiple components of Baddeley's model are housed in different lobes of the cerebral cortex (Schwartz 2011: 82).

Working memory can be defined as the neural structures and cognitive processes that maintain the accessibility of information for short periods of time in an active conscious state (Schwartz 2011: 59–60). In spite of controversy, there is agreement that working memory displays three properties. First, working memory is a short time memory system: information is held for somewhere between fifteen and thirty seconds unless it is continually refreshed (rehearsed). Information is lost due to interference, i.e., new information that enters working memory displaces the information that was present. Second, the capacity of working memory is limited. It was initially set to 'the magic number seven' (plus or minus two units) by Miller (1956). Yet, it is possible to chunk bits of information in several ways to aid memory, thereby extending one's working memory capacity. Moreover, word length and pronunciation time also affect the amount of information that can be maintained in working memory. The estimate has been revised several times since, and Cowan's (2001) lower estimate of four items (plus or minus one) seems to be promising for linguistics (see Chapter 6, Section 6.3.1). Third, the (current) contents of working memory are thought to be equivalent to consciousness (see Section 4.2.1 below), but at the same time it has also been suggested that working memory is nothing but attention working on and activating structures held in long-term memory (Cowan 1988; Oberauer 2002). The limit of four items would thus be a limit on the capacity of the focus of attention (Cowan 2001: 110).

In contrast to short-term memory, *long-term memory* stores limitless amounts of information for long periods even when not rehearsed, and it may even be difficult to retrieve it into an active form. There are different types of long-term memory, each associated with different cognitive behaviour and supported by different neural regions: the two main distinctions are between declarative or explicit memory and between procedural or implicit memory. Endel Tulving (1972) has been credited with proposing the idea that long-term memory involves multiple systems. Although this proposal was initially heavily criticized, it is now accepted in one form or another by memory researchers, and is neurocognitively supported (Cohen and Squire 1980; Ullman 2004: 234; Schwartz 2011: 91–3).

Declarative memories can be consciously retrieved while procedural memories comprise motor and perceptual skills, conditioned behaviours and automatic processes. In fact, it has been proposed (Ullman 2004) that both memory systems are active when processing language, with the declarative system handling sounds and words, and the procedural system supporting the combination of these elements into more complex structures. This fits a generative account where pre-existing abstract syntactic rules operate on acquired words. On a usage-based account, the dividing line would fall in a different place: words only exist and express meaning in context, and abstractions or generalized templates are derived from exemplars encountered during learning. This would imply that more of language could or would be handled by the procedural system: while the selection of the message to convey will most likely be a conscious decision and resort under the declarative system, the production of sounds and forms for the lexical items that convey the message and their combination into chains could be procedural. We will discuss this in more detail in Section 4.3.4.

Within declarative memory, there is a further distinction between semantic memory and episodic memory. Semantic memory is the neurocognitive memory system that encodes, stores and retrieves information relating to knowledge of the world; this information need not be personal. It consists of facts, associations between facts and stories that we create as we learn about the world and abstract commonalities from similar episodes. Episodic memory, on the other hand, handles personal, individual experiences linked to a specific temporal and spatial context. Both types of memories interact: for example, deep encoding strategies enhance memory for lists of words (Craik and Lockhart 1972), most likely because semantic information becomes associated with episodic memories.

4.2   The Physiology or Neurobiology of Memory

How exactly memory for language works at the physiological level remains largely unknown. Research on memory for language cannot benefit from invasive but highly informative techniques that are used in the domain of animal learning. Much of what we 'know' about memory and language thus remains a 'best guess', and I will highlight those findings that are reasonably well established and are important for language cognition and linguistic theory.[1] As mentioned above, we should be mindful of the conceptual 'trap' laid out by the metaphors used to guide inquiry about memory.

4.2.1   Remembering Experiences

It is generally accepted that memories of experiences are stored in the brain. The human brain is light but oxygen-greedy: it weighs about 1.36 kilograms, i.e., about 2 per cent of the average adult's body weight, but consumes 25 per cent of the oxygen used by the body at any given moment. The brain is made up of an estimated 100 billion nerve cells and the interconnections between these nerve cells are even more numerous. The brain is composed of a number of separate anatomical and functional areas. Memory functions appear to reside mostly in the subcortical structures, the areas of the brain that rest below the cortex or brain surface and that are shared with non-human animals. The most important brain areas are depicted in Figure 4.2; note that the medial view does not allow identifying all areas accurately.

The brain's functions can be studied in many ways, and for long the effects of brain damage to a region were the main indicators for the function of that region. Think for example of the Broca and Wernicke areas that have been associated with speech production and comprehension respectively ever since Pierre Paul Broca and Carl Wernicke reported impairments in their patients. Yet, technological progress has made imaging techniques available that allow us to study healthy brains in real time. Of course, each technique has its own

---

[1] The neurobiological information presented in this section is based on the accounts given by Schwartz (2011, chapter 2) and Squire and Kandel (2009, chapters 2 and 5).

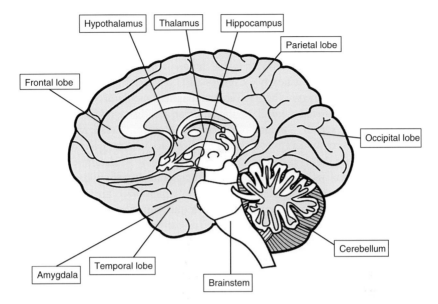

Figure 4.2 Structures situated by approximation on the medial aspect of the cortical and subcortical areas of the human brain. Courtesy of Filipović-Đurđević and Zdravković (2013).

limitations which affect the conclusions that can be drawn. The four major imaging techniques currently used are EEG, PET, (f)MRI and MEG; some provide good spatial resolution, showing where activity takes place, while others are temporally more accurate and reveal the flow of information in real time.

Electroencephalography (EEG) measures the electrical output of the brain using electrodes put on the scalp; active areas generate more energy than inactive areas. Measurements can be made very quickly, which makes it possible to track changes that occur in the brain as the task unfolds. EEG thus provides accurate temporal characterization. *Positron emission tomography* (PET) traces radioactive chemicals injected into the blood stream; active areas require more blood. Measurements are at least thirty seconds apart due to the time it takes to get a good picture of the brain, so it is not helpful in determining the flow of information, but PET provides accurate spatial localization. *(Functional) magnetic resonance imaging* (fMRI and MRI) use large magnetic fields to align the molecules in the brain, the organization of which is again disrupted as blood flows into areas of the brain that are used in a task. In structural MRI, changes in structures in water molecules are looked for to produce a map of the brain. In fMRI it is the oxygen molecules in the blood that are traced. In other words, fMRI signals reflect brain activity indirectly, by measuring the oxygenation of blood flowing near active neurons. Measurements are relative to reference neuronal activity hence fMRI provides accurate spatial localization. With this technique, a picture can be taken every half a second, making it nearly as fast as EEG and certainly safer than PET. *Magnetoencephalography* (MEG) records magnetic fields produced by electrical currents occurring naturally in the brain, on a millisecond-by-millisecond basis using very sensitive magnetometers. Different from fMRI, MEG signals are obtained directly from neuronal electrical activity and show absolute neuronal activity that is not dependent on the choice of a referent. Only MEG provides temporal and spatial information of equal quality about brain activity.

For now, much disagreement remains as to which brain area fulfils which function. Given this, let us focus on the larger question at hand: can any mental process be localized to a specific region (or combination of regions) in the brain, or should we subscribe to a network view on which brain functions are distributed across all brain regions? Are both approaches mutually exclusive? Karl Lashley (1930), a behaviourist, defended the view that the brain is composed of identifiable, localized parts and all functions can be related to particular brain regions. The brain area involved in processing a memory may determine where memories are stored. For example, memories of visual information are likely stored in the visual cortex. Donald Hebb (1949) countered that mental functions are not localized to specific brain regions but instead are global properties that arise from the integrated activity of the entire brain. Hebb's idea of a distributed memory store was farsighted and underlies today's understanding that memory is widely distributed: different areas store different aspects of the whole with little redundancy or reduplication of functions across areas. Evidence from vision, for which the neural sequence from perception to memory is best understood, casts doubt on the wisdom of insisting on any extreme positions in this debate (Squire and Kandel 2009: 77–80, 143). Whenever an object is perceived, neural activity occurs simultaneously in different brain areas, i.e., perception is dependent on distributed but coordinated activity in different areas of the cortex. The result of these brain changes is called an *engram*. The engram is also how and where memories are stored: the same areas that are involved in perception and processing are involved in remembering. Yet, each region contributes differently to the representation, depending on what type of perception and information processing they are specialized for.

Recent research on anaesthesia and consciousness provides further evidence for the opinion that a network-view is indispensable because memory resides in the brain's ability to *integrate* information. General anaesthesia has been used to induce unresponsiveness and amnesia during surgery for nearly two centuries. It is also thought to extinguish consciousness, yet the extent to which it does this is harder to establish. Despite different mechanisms and sites of action, most anaesthetics are assumed to induce unconsciousness by targeting, directly or indirectly, a posterior parietal area in the brain, and possibly also a medial cortical core (Alkire, Hudetz and Tononi 2008: 876). This has two possible causes: evidence from anaesthesia and sleep states converges to suggest that loss of consciousness is associated with a breakdown of cortical connectivity and thus of integration, or with a collapse of the repertoire of cortical activity patterns and thus of information. Why should this be the case?

It has been suggested that information and integration may be the very essence of consciousness, and unconsciousness seems to occur due to the brain's (temporary) inability to integrate information (Alkire, Hudetz and Tononi 2008: 880). On an information-theoretic account, information is the reduction of uncertainty among alternatives: a coin falling on one of its two sides provides 1 bit of information, whereas a die falling on one of six faces provides ~2.6 bits. Given the countless experiences we could have, having any conscious experience is extraordinarily informative. At the same time, every experience is an integrated whole that cannot be subdivided into independent components. A healthy brain cannot experience visual shapes independently of their colour. In other words, 'the die of experience is a single one – throwing multiple dice and combining the numbers will not do' (Alkire, Hudetz and Tononi 2008: 879). Zhou et al. (2015) present a theoretical model – without considering biological details – of loss of consciousness under general anaesthesia to understand the dynamic nature of sensory activity and information integration in a hierarchical network. The model successfully reproduces key spectral features, clinically observed in EEG scalp recordings, of transitions from conscious to unconscious brain activities during general anaesthesia.

4.2.2 How Do Experiences Change the Brain?

A closely related question that has long puzzled scientists is the question of how memories are stored. Just over a century ago, Santiago Ramón y Cajal performed groundbreaking work that revealed the neuron or nerve cell, shown in Figure 4.3, as the primary functional unit of the nervous system. He was awarded the Nobel Prize in Physiology or Medicine in 1906 for his 'neuron doctrine'.

Neurons are biological cells that specialize in the transmission and retention of information in the brain. They form networks of communicating cells in the brain and connect to neurons in the nerves and the muscles of the body. What distinguishes neurons from other biological cells are the electricity-conducting fibres that extend from their cell body or soma: one into the neuron (the dendrite), and one out of the neuron (the axon). These fibres make it possible to transmit information across the brain or nervous system. Neurons are

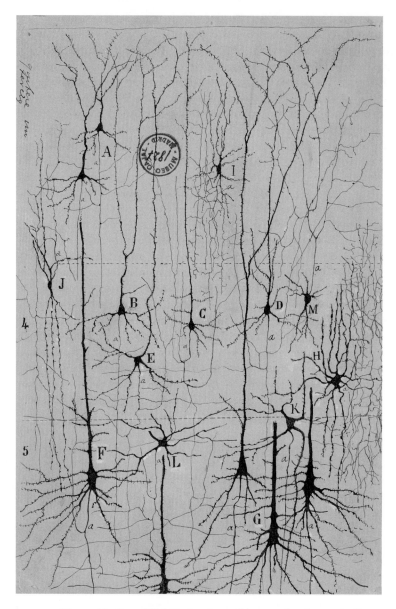

Figure 4.3 One of Cajal's drawings of the neural pathways in the cortex. Courtesy of the Cajal Institute, 'Cajal Legacy', Spanish National Research Center (CSIC), Madrid, Spain.

dynamically polarized, so that information flows in a predictable and consistent direction within each nerve cell.

Dendrites, of which a neuron can have hundreds, are those parts of neurons that receive information from other neurons in the form of electrical pulses that either increase or decrease the voltage or electrical potential within the cell. Electrical information transmission along dendrites is instantaneous, but works only over short stretches. The various inputs sum at the cell body or soma and can cause a cell to start a signal to another cell via the neuron's sole axon, which can be up to 1 metre long (e.g., the axon in the spinal cord) and can branch out and connect to hundreds of neurons. Transmission in an axon happens via an electrochemical process known as *action potential*. This process keeps the electrical potential constant, regardless of the length of the axon.

The axon of one neuron does not touch the dendrite of the other neuron. There is a gap, called a synapse, between the two. This gap is bridged in a chemical way: when the electrical signal reaches the terminal buttons of the axon, neurotransmitters are released that cross the synapse and induce an electric flow in the next dendrite. Neurotransmitters are proteins, produced by the nervous system. Our brains use amino acids or their derivatives such as dopamine and serotonin, the most famous from a list of hundreds of different chemicals, to convey information from one part of the brain to another. They can increase activity (i.e., excite), or decrease activity (i.e., inhibit), in the dendrite, and may have a different effect depending on the neural circuit they participate in: one and the same target cell will typically have excitatory receptors for some transmitters and inhibitory receptors for others.

The different learning capabilities of different animals are related to the number of nerve cells they have and the way in which they are interconnected. Each of the estimated 100 billion neurons in the human brain makes about 1,000 connections to other neurons via synaptic connections. The resulting 10^{14} connections provide a rough indicator of our maximal memory storage capacity (Squire and Kandel 2009: 22, 30–1). The remarkable thing about neuronal signals is that they are the same, regardless of which information (visual, auditory, olfactory, etc.) they carry, and whether they are incoming or outgoing. One of the key principles of brain function is that the nature of the information conveyed by a nerve signal is determined not by the nature of the signal but by the particular pathways that the signal travels in the brain: the brain analyses and interprets patterns of incoming electrical signals along specific and dedicated pathways.

How exactly neurons encode and represent information is still being unravelled. But we may assume that each step on its own must be simple to allow execution by 'mindless entities' such as neurons (Edelman 2008: 30).

A first insight was gained after discovering that in most regions of the brain mature nerve cells have lost their capacity to divide, so we do not add many new nerve cells to our brain during our adult life. Ramón y Cajal concluded that learning cannot *cause* the growth of new nerve cells. Therefore, he proposed that learning might cause existing nerve cells to strengthen their connections with other nerve cells, thereby making communication more efficient (Squire and Kandel 2009: 17). Depending on the type of learning, the nerve cells involved can make either more and stronger connections or fewer and weaker ones.

The chemical signal at the synapse is graded and modifiable, while the electric impulse in the axon (the action potential) is all-or-nothing (see Bear, Connors and Paradiso 2016). Ramón y Cajal (1894) developed this idea further and proposed the synaptic plasticity hypothesis: neural activity can modify synaptic strength, and learning makes use of this malleability. In other words, the learning process might alter the patterns and intensities of electrical signals that constitute the brain's activity. Learning would produce prolonged changes in the strength of synaptic connections through growth of new synaptic processes, and the persistence of these could serve as the mechanism for memory. This has led to research at the intersection of biology and psychology that unravels how nerve connections change during learning and how those changes are maintained over time as memory.

One possible cellular mechanism of learning that exists in both a short-term and a long-term form is long-term potentiation (LTP), which changes the connection strength between neurons; note that LTP has currently only been attested in laboratory settings. A functional modification in the ability of neurons to signal to each other forms the cellular basis of short-term memory storage. Short-term memory storage is transient, does not require anatomical change to be retained and does not require the synthesis of new proteins. Long-term memory, on the other hand, can only be stabilized by anatomical changes, and these changes require new protein synthesis. LTP is a lasting change at synapses that occurs when long-term memories form. LTP can be non-associative (i.e., when it occurs either pre- or post-synaptically) or associative (when it requires concomitant activity both pre- and post-synaptically) (Squire and Kandel 2009: 124–7). In associative LTP, due to the constant signalling between two neurons, the synapses become more responsive and the threshold at which a postsynaptic dendrite will begin sending electrical signals is lowered, as Hebb predicted (Squire and Kandel 2009: 127; Schwartz 2011: 39).

Hypotheses on how learning would happen at the cellular level are also available from computational neuroscience. Edelman's (2008: 44, 55, 57) account, briefly introduced in Section 4.1.2, is particularly suitable for modelling language. It will be discussed in more detail in Chapter 8, Section 8.1.3.

4.3 Memory Systems, Memory Processes and Neural Mechanisms of Memory Storage

Major lessons have been learned about our memory systems, and the very bio-neurological basis of the storage mechanisms seems to have been unravelled. Despite significant progress, we still know very little about how complex information is processed and represented in the brain. Much of what is known about memory in human beings stems from artificial lab-based experiments involving trivial information; it is plausible that more important things are less susceptible to remembering and forgetting (Bouton 1994: 226). Memory processes are typically subdivided into three types. Encoding captures the learning process. Storage or representation refers to the phase when information is not in use. Retrieval, finally, refers to our ability to activate and access information when we need it. In this section, we will look at how information held in the different memory systems, in particular the declarative and procedural systems, is encoded, stored and retrieved. Both systems are part of long-term memory, which is thought to reside in the changes in neurons across the sensory and motor systems that are involved in learning about the world.

4.3.1 How Experiences Become Neurally Encoded and Long-Term Available as Declarative Memories

Declarative memory is flexible, relational memory that can be accessed consciously and intentionally to guide behaviour in new situations. In declarative memory, the metaphorical move from short-term to long-term memory requires the involvement of the medial temporal lobe system. This system, comprised of the amygdala, the hippocampus and surrounding cortex, is needed at the time of learning, but also during the lengthy period of reorganization and stabilization that accompanies the establishment of the memory in the cortex. This slow fixation process allows other cortical areas to change gradually by incorporating information about the world into their representations. Slow modification protects against instability and vulnerability to interference.

In order to turn short-term memories into long-term memories, new proteins must be synthesized (and this within a specific time-window) and genes must be switched on to facilitate synaptic connectivity. This – and this is important for language – happens only after repeated learning trials: only repeated pulses of neurotransmitter (serotonin) allow the active component of protein kinases to travel to the cell nucleus, where they bind to DNA and activate the genes needed for forming long-term memories. The consolidation phase during the formation of long-term memory is thought to be the moment when the proteins encoded by the activated genes are synthesized. Before this step is completed, memory can be blocked by inhibitors of protein synthesis (for a review of the role of protein synthesis in memory consolidation, see Hernandez and Abel 2008).

Except in habituation where there is pruning of synaptic terminals, there tends to be an increase in the number of synaptic terminals per neuron which generally improves effectivity in exciting other neurons. That is, for memories to be available long-term, there needs to be a coordinated structural change in both the pre- and post-synaptic cells (Squire and Kandel 2009: 55, 57–8, 144–52). Due to these anatomical changes a newly minted, long-term memory can be maintained for a significant period of time.

4.3.2 How Experiences Become Neurally Encoded and Long-Term Available as Procedural Memories

Non-declarative, procedural or implicit memory is memory for habit, for rather inflexible, consistent relationships between stimulus and response; it is not accessed consciously and intentionally. It is less well understood than declarative memory but knowledge about the neural basis of procedural memory can be gleaned from research on non-associative and associative learning.

Two key concepts in the area of non-associative learning (which we will return to in Chapter 9) are habituation, or learning about a benign or unimportant stimulus, and sensitization, that is learning about a harmful or threatening stimulus. Short-term habituation is the result of a functional reduction in the transmitter released by each action potential. Habituation is thus embedded in the neural circuit that produces the behaviour and involves a transient decrease in synaptic efficacy. Short-term sensitization leads to a functional increase in synaptic strength, however. This means that, at different times, the same set of synaptic connections can be modulated in opposite directions by different forms of learning. As a result, the same set of connections can participate in storing different memories but decreases and increases are achieved in different ways: while decreases are homosynaptic and affect only targeted synaptic pathways, increases are heterosynaptic, meaning that both pathways that were targeted and those that were not targeted undergo changes (Squire and Kandel 2009: 53).

Important concepts in the field of associative learning are temporal contiguity, where one event *precedes* the other, and contingency, where one event *predicts* the other. Predictive rules resemble cause-and-effect rules that govern the external physical world. It is therefore plausible to assume that animal brains have developed neuronal mechanisms designed to recognize events that predictively occur together from those that do not. An animal that acquires knowledge through learning can respond better to a far greater variety of stimuli than one that is limited to an innate programme of knowledge. The nervous mechanisms underlying learning that requires temporal pairing of stimuli remain incompletely understood. What is known is that for behavioural conditioning to occur the trigger and the response must excite the same sensory neurons, not only in sequence (as is the case with sensitization), but also within a critical interval. This precise timing of the stimuli results in a larger injection of the transmitter, and several theories exist as to how exactly that would be the case (Squire and Kandel 2009: 62–3, 65–6). We will return to this in Chapter 5, Section 5.4.2.

4.3.3   How Experiences Are Retrieved

Errors can be introduced into memory at the stage of encoding, storage and retrieval. This is because, when retrieving a memory, we do not simply reactivate the distributed fragments that make up the engram: what is reactivated depends on the cue that is available.

The British psychologist Frederic C. Bartlett (1932) started the study of memory in naturalistic settings and showed that remembering is not the same as retrieving traces from storage; it is an active reconstructive process, and it is possible that a reconstructed activity is accepted as accurate even though it is not an exact reproduction. This insight gave rise to a change in the study of memory: the study of memory moved from a more behavioural approach of studying stimuli and the responses they elicit to a cognitive approach of paying attention to the processes that intervene between a stimulus and a behaviour. Tulving and Schacter (1990) confirmed, using priming experiments, that having a strong memory does not guarantee successful retrieval: you need cues for retrieval, and the best cues are those that awaken the best-encoded aspects of the memory you are trying to retrieve. If the cue is weak or ambiguous it is possible that only parts of the engram, or even the wrong engram, are activated. Interestingly, the act of remembering tends to improve subsequent memory because remembering provides an opportunity to rehearse information. But sometimes the opposite happens and remembering impairs later memory: bringing to mind some information associated with a cue will inhibit the recall of other information associated with that same cue (this is known as retrieval-induced forgetting, which is typically temporary – Anderson, Bjork and Bjork 2000). Retrieval is also context dependent, and influenced by mood, state of mind and environment – see Section 4.4 below.

Memory is most accurate when the gist is being tested rather than details and when no leading questions are asked, or false suggestions are made. With time, memory strength decreases and details disappear, but this forgetting of details aids memory because it allows us to generalize over particular individual instances, abstract over peculiarities and assemble general knowledge. From studies on animals with relatively simple nervous systems we know that forgetting does imply the actual loss of information because some of the synaptic modifications that were made during learning regress, probably because new information storage resculpts existing representations. Some associated procedural memories may, however, persist (e.g., preferences that formed as the result of a forgotten event) because they are supported by synaptic changes in other parts of the brain.

4.3.4   Computational Models of Memory for Language

As mentioned before, research on memory for language cannot make use of the invasive techniques that have revealed much of what we know about memory. Instead, several computational models for memory of language have been proposed, among which the declarative/procedural model of language by Ullman and colleagues (Ullman 2001, 2004) and the complementary learning systems account of Davis and Gaskell (2009).

Ullman (2001, 2004) presented the declarative/procedural (DP) model of language that assigns the lexicon to the declarative system and grammar to the procedural system. This strict distinction between lexicon and grammar is pervasive in much work on the brain and cognition and does not mesh with usage-based and emergentist approaches to language that start from the assumption that grammar and lexicon are part of the same continuum. The DP model assumes that the brain system subserving declarative memory also underlies the mental lexicon. It rapidly stores all arbitrary, idiosyncratic, word-specific information. The likelihood for this type of information to be memorized increases with the item's frequency and the subject's declarative memory abilities. Generalizations across representations (e.g., of phonologically similar irregular stem pairs) is achieved by a super-positional associative memory (Ullman 2004: 245). The brain system underlying procedural memory handles already-learned rule-based procedures, in particular those that involve sequential and hierarchical structures; this property makes the procedural system ideal for dealing with grammar. Note that both systems may be involved in encoding the same or similar information: sequences of lexical forms that are stored in declarative memory could provide the database from which grammatical rules are gradually abstracted (Ullman 2004: 247). Early on in learning the declarative system appears more important than the procedural system, but over time the balance may shift.

A second proposed model, specialized for word learning in adults, is the complementary learning systems (CLS) account of Davis and Gaskell (2009). It revolves around rapid initial familiarization supported by temporal and hippocampal learning, followed by slow lexical consolidation in neocortical areas. The complementary learning systems model posits that a new memory is first encoded by the hippocampal memory system, before it moves to the neocortical memory system. This process stabilizes and integrates novel information into long-term memory without causing interference with existing knowledge. On this account, hippocampal involvement would decrease over time while neocortical integration gradually increases. While there is strong support for gradual neocortical integration (Takashima and Bakker 2016: 191), the available evidence from lexical learning does, however, not support the decrease of hippocampal involvement after consolidation. This has led researchers to suggest that the neocortex may need to be thought of as a system that is dependent on prior knowledge, rather than one that learns slowly (McClelland 2013): new information that is consistent with knowledge previously acquired by a cortex-like artificial neural network can be learned rapidly and without interfering with existing knowledge while inconsistent new knowledge causes so-called 'catastrophic interference'.

4.4   Behavioural Diagnostics of Memory for Language

While the account in Sections 4.2 and 4.3 was based on evidence from neurobiology that we can – at least for now – only tentatively link to language, work in behavioural and computational psychology has revealed a number of valuable principles that affect memory. If language depends on brain systems that subserve other cognitive functions, as usage-based linguists propound, these principles should apply to language learning too. Curiously, the importance of memory formation and consolidation has barely influenced linguistic theories (for a preliminary overview see Takashima and Bakker 2016: 192) and the relation between memory processes and grammar systems remains virtually uncharted territory (an exception is Dahl 2013). In this section, we will review a few well-known memory effects that have been shown to play a crucial role in language learning, i.e., the frequency effect, the spacing effect and the serial position effect.

4.4.1   Frequency

A central diagnostic for the presence of long-term memory traces has been the word frequency effect. The brain mechanisms that underlie entrenchment in memory specify a major role for repeated experience, whether it is overt experience in the environment or mental rehearsal during silent rumination. More frequent words are recognized more easily and processed faster and more accurately (for reviews see Monsell 1991; Divjak and Caldwell-Harris 2015; Baayen, Milin and Ramscar 2016). How does frequency achieve these effects? The contemporary account holds that diverse aspects of the neural networks which encode words have become shaped, via repeated exposure and learning, so that processing is more efficient based on this repeated exposure. More mental processing is believed to create efficient representations which are more easily processed, compared to stimuli that are rarely processed. How could this work?

4.4.1.1 Quantity of Processing

Psychologists have traditionally assumed that frequency of occurrence affects entrenchment because repeated frequency provides speakers with greater exposure, which means more opportunities for experiencing the stimuli and hence more mental processing. Due to the lack of neurobiological studies in this area, I will briefly review some of the most well-known computational models that have been used to shed light on this question.

Morton's (1969) logogen or word-detector model, which influenced researchers for decades, contains the earliest mechanistic account of how frequency could influence mental structures. The logogen model assumed that word frequency becomes encoded as part of a word's mental representation. Logogens were defined as simple processing units that behaved like neurons and accumulated input from multiple sources and fired outputs. In other words, they were a simplification of the neural processes that were thought to mediate word recognition. In the logogen model, each word in the lexicon has a dedicated feature counter, or logogen. As perceptual information comes in, the counts in matching logogens increase. A word represented by a logogen is said to be recognized when incoming activation is sufficiently strong to pass the logogen's activation threshold. Frequency effects are explained by assuming that high-frequency words have higher resting levels (or equivalently, a lower threshold) than low-frequency words. High-frequency words can therefore be identified on the basis of fewer perceptual features than low-frequency words (but see the critique in Forster 1976). Morton assumed that each logogen's own recognition threshold could be affected by context; this explained the facilitatory effect context has on recognition. The threshold could also be permanently lowered by successful recognitions, which accounted for both frequency and repetition effects.

Logogens anticipated the neurally inspired processing units of connectionist models developed in the 1980s. One of the early connectionist models is McClelland and Rumelhart's (1981) interactive-activation model of letter and word recognition. This model incorporated frequency-dependent baseline activation levels: high-frequency words were assumed to have higher baseline activation levels than low-frequency words. Later connectionist models (e.g., Seidenberg and McClelland 1989) implement entrenchment as the result of frequency-sensitive learning. Strength of representations can correspond to several things in a connectionist network, such as heavily weighted connections from some input features to processing units inside the networks' architecture, large numbers of connections or other types of redundant representations. Weighted connections between processing units function akin to the dendrites and axons of neurons:

specific links between processing units that frequently match inputs to their expected outputs are strengthened, inspired by the Hebbian learning principle in neuroscience that 'neurons that fire together wire together' (Hebb 1949). Crucially, later models diverged from earlier ones because of their auto-associative learning ability (McClelland and Rumelhart 1985), that is the ability to form connections among input units and identify patterns, rather than transcode input patterns into output patterns.

Connectionist models have been used to describe how human languages might draw on both the procedural and declarative memory systems for learning (Rogers and McClelland 2004; Gupta 2012). Short-term retention of specific episodes is believed to be part of the declarative memory system, mediated by the hippocampus and medial temporal structures (Cohen and Squire 1980). This declarative memory system performs speedy and one-trial learning, but material in it decays. However, if these events recur, they can be learned via the procedural system, mediated by neocortical structures (Gupta 2012). Here, slow learning allows information to be incrementally integrated into long-term memory structures, where they have rich associations with many patterns. This is said to facilitate the generalization and abstraction that language knowledge is thought to rely on.

The procedural system is most efficient at encoding systematic mappings using distributed representations. In distributed representations, multiple patterns are stored across the same set of processing units. This makes it possible for regularities to be extracted and for generalizations to be made. If systematicities are lacking, as is the case when we learn arbitrary mappings, such as the link between word forms and meanings, non-distributed (also called sparse or localist) representations fare better. It has been proposed that hippocampal structures use sparse representational structures to implement arbitrary associations, including episodic and short-term memories (Rogers and McClelland 2004). Arbitrary associations can be permanently learned only with considerable exposure. It is thought that, with continual rehearsal and learning, these associations are gradually displaced from the fast-learning hippocampal system and integrated into the neocortical procedural system.

Learning lexical items, morphological patterns and syntactic constructions is a complex endeavour that relies on the integration of the procedural and declarative brain systems (see review in Gupta 2012). Learning a new morphological variant can usually be handled by the procedural system because it involves minor adjustments to established sound-to-motor patterns. Novel mappings, such as learning a new word, require creating new pathways between inputs and outputs and may initially be stored as part of declarative memory. If the novel word is never encountered again, the weighted connections that represent it will be overwritten when new patterns are encountered.

But if the word is repeatedly encountered, each exposure provides another training trial in which it can be integrated into procedural memory structures.

4.4.1.2 Quality of Processing   So far we have discussed the fact that, usually, some frequency or repetition is needed to ensure encoding in long-term memory, but quality of encoding plays a role too. What affects the quality of the encoding? A different approach to memory, that does not assume the existence of multiple memory stores, is the *levels of processing* approach. On this approach, memory is what happens as a result of processing information. More meaningful handling of information leads to better encoding of that information.

While studying incidental learning, i.e., learning as by-product of perceiving and understanding the world, Craik and Lockhart (1972) found that the manner in which information is first encountered and rehearsed leads to a difference in depth of processing; this affects how well the information is encoded. Deep or meaningful processing of information in working memory leads to better and longer information retention than shallow sensory-based processing. Sensory-based processing only involves maintenance rehearsal, i.e., repeating information over and over, while meaningful processing requires elaboration rehearsal or associating words with images, other words or existing knowledge. This hypothesis was first experimentally confirmed by Craik and Tulving (1975) and replicated in a long series of studies. Participants were presented with sixty words about which they had to answer one of three questions. Some questions required the participants to process the word in a deep way (e.g., semantically) and others in a shallow way (e.g., structurally and phonemically). Questions were, for example, 'Is the word written in capital letters or small letters?' (to test visual processing), 'Does the word rhyme with ...?' (to test auditory processing) or 'Can you use the word in this sentence ...?' (to test for meaningful processing). Participants were then given a list of 180 words into which the original words had been mixed and were asked to pick out the original words. They recalled more words that had been semantically processed, compared to words that had been processed visually or auditorily. Of course, deeper processing goes hand in hand with more time and effort spent processing, so it is difficult to pinpoint the exact cause of the memory advantage.

Yet, robust memories can be formed with single-trial learning. A language example is fast mapping, whereby children and adults infer the meaning of a word from context (Carey and Bartlett 1978). But a strong mental representation will be formed from a single instance only in special cases, such as those associated with intense emotions. Emotions may also affect memory for items and events in general (Erk et al. 2003). Emotions or emotional states themselves are memories: they are states associated with certain experiences. Heightened emotions can lead to experiences crystalizing into long-lasting and vivid memories. Think of flash-backs (resulting from the inability to suppress information) or flash-bulb memories that are highly detailed but not always entirely accurate memories of important events. These happen because stimuli of emotional significance instinctively attract our attention (Schupp et al. 2007), and we tend to remember by focusing on an event, as we will see in Chapter 6.

4.4.2   Spacing

Contemporary views of the brain's multiple memory systems also help explain why exposures that are widely spaced in time and occur in different contexts are more important than raw frequency. Spacing is known to (corpus) linguists as dispersion, a concept that was discussed in Chapter 1, Section 1.3.2.

Spaced repetition is a learning technique that incorporates increasing intervals of time between reviews of previously learned material. The spacing effect refers to the observation that items on a list are learned better if they are not presented consecutively or massed but spread out in time or spaced. Ebbinghaus (1885a) already experimented with the distribution of study time. He contrasted massed practice (when all study occurs in one block of time) with distributed practice (when study is spaced out over time). The two approaches yielded different saving scores: if the amount of study time was kept constant, distributed practice yielded higher saving scores than massed practice. This effect has become known as *the spacing effect*: more learning (as evidenced by better retention) occurs when practice is distributed even though equal amounts of time may have gone into study.

Bahrick et al. (1993) calculated that retention of foreign language vocabulary was greatly enhanced if practice sessions were spaced far apart. For example, '13 retraining sessions spaced at 56 days yielded retention comparable to 26 sessions spaced at 14 days.' Banaji and Crowder (1989: 49) concluded that 'a repetition will help most if the material had been in storage long enough to be just on the verge of being forgotten'. This 'lag effect' makes optimal use of the spacing effect: recall after long lags between learning is better than recall after short lags, and by gradually increasing the spacing between practices you learn even better. The best time to practice is when you are on the verge of forgetting. Pimsleur (1967) was the first to devise a rigid memory schedule of half-lives (the time it takes for a quantity to fall to half of its initial value) that he used in his language-learning programs: practice again five seconds after the first practice, then twenty-five seconds, then two minutes, ten minutes and so on. Leitner's system for learning with flash cards, described in his 1974 popular science book 'So lernt man lernen', doubles the half-life each time you remember correctly and cuts it in half each time you are incorrect. In other words, each time a word is successfully retrieved the period of time increases before the word is revisited while each unsuccessful retrieval decreases the time until the next presentation. Duolingo, the popular language learning app, has developed half-life regression (Settles and Meeder 2016) that relies on data collected via their app to individualize the forgetting curve and tailor the frequency of word presentation to individual learners' performance.

Spaced practice thus leads to more robust and enduring learning than massed practice (Anderson and Schooler 1991; Carpenter et al. 2012). Several theories exist as to how this effect would arise. On the *deficient processing* view, massed repetition leads to only one representation of the material in memory, whereas spaced repetition creates a new representation for the second presentation, thus bolstering the memory. Repeated stimuli that occur close together in time will be treated by the brain as a single episode. Repeated experiences thus have less chance to participate in the slow procedural learning, which facilitates integration into long-term memory structures. '[R]emembering experiences involves updating or strengthening neural circuits. Extremely similar experiences would impact the same circuits, and the cumulative effect of exposure need not be linear' (Pierrehumbert 2006: 525). In other words, redundant experiences are not registered as strongly as unique experiences. It has been suggested that this may be the case because of the small contextual differences that accompany learning when trials are spread out in time. According to the *encoding variability* view, spaced repetition is likely to entail some variability in each individual presentation; this then leads to a more robust memory which is more connected to other ideas. Johns, Dye and Jones (2016: 1215) found that repeated presentations of a word at learning stage only benefit subsequent processing speed if the presentation is accompanied by a change in context. Tulving and Thomson (1973) contributed the finding of *encoding specificity*, after encountering the so-called extra-list cuing effect, that is facilitation of recall of a list item by a retrieval cue that was not explicitly a part of the input list. What is stored is determined by what is perceived and how it is encoded, and what is stored determines what retrieval cues are effective in providing access to what is stored. They found that retrieval is better when it occurs in situations that match the conditions under which the memory was encoded. These conditions can refer to the context in which the information was encoded, including the physical location or surroundings, as well as the mental or physical state of the individual at the time of encoding.

Another interpretation of context looks at context on the level of language. The number of contexts a word occurs in is typically captured by a word's contextual diversity (see Chapter 1, Section 1.3.2). Contextual diversity significantly influences how a word is learned and remembered. Words that are present in a greater diversity of contexts are acquired more rapidly in early learning (Hills et al. 2010) and are processed more quickly and accurately in naming and lexical decision (Schwanenflugel and Shoben 1983; Adelman,

Brown and Quesada 2006). Likewise, in standard episodic memory tasks, high diversity benefits recall (Lohnas, Polyn and Kahana 2011) but impairs recognition (Steyvers and Malmberg 2003). These findings supplement the influence of contextual diversity on the benefit of spaced practice over mass practice (Verkoeijen, Rikers and Schmidt 2004).

4.4.3   Primacy and Recency: Serial Position Effects

Likewise important for the study of memory and language are the serial position effects; these were popular in research on memory conducted in the 1960s but have since been sidelined. Serial position effects capture the findings that, when people are given a list of words to memorize and are asked to recall them immediately, they tend to remember the first items and the last items well, but they make mistakes on items that appeared in the middle of the list. This effect is well documented in humans and has been observed in animals as well, yet theories struggle to account for serial position effects (Pearce 1997: 163). Let us look at both effects in turn.

The recency effect is the observation that memory is usually superior for items that are recent, i.e., at the end of a serial position curve. The recency effect was first described by Mary Calkins (1894). Calkins extended Ebbinghaus's research by studying the retention of pairs, where subjects were asked to memorize word–word, word–picture, syllable–word or syllable–pictures pairs. She then tested how well subjects remembered the second item (the target), if they were given the first (the cue). She found that, the greater the overlap in meaning between cues and targets, the easier it was for the subjects to learn and retain the information. Prior familiarity with the pairs also helped. Overall, in immediate recall (i.e., testing immediately after learning), items that had been learned most recently were retained better. The recency effect has been demonstrated in a number of animals too (e.g., in dolphins by Thompson and Herman 1977, but also in monkeys, pigeons and rats).

The primacy effect is the observation that memory is usually superior for items at the beginning of a serial position curve. That is, words at the beginning of a list are remembered more frequently than words lower down the list. Different from the recency effect, the primacy effect has been much harder to establish in animals. Harper, McLean and Dalrymple-Alford (1993) used a maze-learning task to evidence both primacy and recency effects in rats, thereby showing that similar cognitive processes support list learning in both animals and humans.

Generally, the primacy effect appears to be more robust than the recency effect: for example, if time is allowed to elapse between memorizing a list and being tested on it, then the primacy effect remains but the recency effect is reduced (Glanzer and Cunitz 1966). The same reduction was observed if subjects were asked to count backwards between memorization and recall (Roediger and Crowder 1975). The differential effect of these interventions on primacy and recency also suggests that the factors triggering the primacy effect are not necessarily those triggering the recency effect. The primacy effect is thought to arise because early items receive more processing (the first item can be rehearsed by itself while the second item needs to be rehearsed alongside the first and so on), which facilitates encoding of early items into long-term memory. The recency effect was long thought to be caused by the maintenance of items in short-term or working memory, yet recency effects have been observed in long-term memory too. Baddeley and Hitch (1993: 148) therefore proposed an alternative account of recency that assumes that memory representations of recent inputs have increased levels of activation, which facilitates reactivation.

In this way, the recency effect is similar to the priming effect, which has a long and rich history in morphological and syntactic processing (Forster 1981), and refers to the greater availability of an item due to prior presentation – for a recent overview and discussion see Branigan and Pickering (2017) and the comments on this article. Sociolinguists have long known the phenomenon under the name of accommodation: speakers tend to adapt to each other, for example, by aligning their pronunciation (Giles 1973). Priming or persistence has also been observed at the syntactic level, both in spoken and written language production. Levelt and Kelter (1982) observed in an experimental situation that the form of the question influences the form of the answer in Dutch: the question *To whom did Paul show his violin?* tended to be answered with a prepositional phrase *to John* whereas the (in Dutch also grammatical) question *Who did Paul show his violin?* tended to elicit the answer *John.* Within a usage-based framework, Szmrecsanyi (2006) presents an extensive study on morpho-syntactic persistence in spoken English; he analyses comparisons (*more ready* versus *readier)*, genitives (*the university's budget* versus *the budget of the university*), future markers (*is going to* versus *will*), particle placement (*She looked the word up* versus *She looked up the word*) and complementation (*began wondering* versus *began to wonder*) in spontaneous discourse. Calude and Miller (2009) showed that, in spontaneous, unplanned conversation, speakers (of New Zealand English) emulate each other's grammar: if one speaker uses a cleft construction such as *It was my mother who rang the other day,* others are likely to do the same. In written production, Gries (2005b) provided evidence for the existence of priming effects for the dative alternation and particle placement with transitive verbs. He found that priming effects are verb-specific in that some verbs support or resist priming more than others. Like Szmrecsanyi, Gries (2005b) found persistence to decay logarithmically, and this differs from experimental findings. Hartsuiker's (2008) experiments in written and spoken dialogue show that this divergence may be due to the fact that the syntactic priming effect is long-lived while the lexical boost that comes with the prime is short-lived.

Much has been written about the effect that priming has on the language system or on the user's knowledge of the language. Pickering and Branigan (1998) consider it a transient, local phenomenon that is relevant only to language production in progress and has no effect on memory. Bock and Griffin (2000), on the other hand, think of the priming effect as a learning mechanism that contributes to being able to use and produce language; this skill is fine-tuned in every episode of adult language production. We will return to the mechanisms underlying memory for experiences in Chapter 5, Section 5.3.

The primacy effect has also been linked to attention: subjects are likely to focus at the beginning of a task but their attention may then drift. The drift of attention may be linked to the fact that they are processing the information they have been given earlier or rehearsing it if they anticipate being tested on the material later on.

4.4.4   An Adaptive Perspective

It has been argued that the way in which memory functions is extremely well adapted to the structure of the environment. It is possible to see a causal link here and conclude that memory has the structure it has precisely because the environment is structured the way it is (Anderson and Schooler 1991: 405).

The effects of frequency, spacing and serial position can be predicted from the statistical properties of information use. Anderson and Schooler (1991) looked deeper into the behaviour of forgetting. They analysed newspaper headlines, emails and parental speech to children and found that the probability that a word appeared on a particular day was a lawful function of the number of days since it had last appeared. That is, a word is most likely to occur if it has occurred the day before. After that, its probability of occurrence declines as a function of days since its last occurrence, with a curve trajectory resembling a traditional forgetting curve. Items are forgotten as their probable usefulness declines. Forgetting information reduces the risk of information overload: an organism can only cope with so many items at a time and forgetting keeps the risk of interference from related but irrelevant information at bay.

In other words, human memory may well have the form it has because it is adapted to the environment: the contents of memory would be organized in such a way that information that is needed can be accessed quickly and reliably. At any point in time, memories vary in how likely they are to be needed and the memory system tries to make available those memories that are most likely to be useful. According to the Principle of Likely Need (Anderson and Milson 1989), the accessibility of an item in memory is not simply a function of its current match to a retrieval cue but is also strongly influenced by its history of use. Items that have previously been retrieved in a variety of different contexts are more likely to be needed in the processing of a yet unknown future context; hence, they should be easier to access. The memory system can use the history of use of a memory to estimate whether the memory is likely to be needed next. The probability that a memory will be needed shows reliable relationships to frequency, recency and pattern of prior exposures. Memory thus infers a so-called need probability, which is the probability that we will need a particular memory trace.

The fact that the memory system is adapted to the structure of the environment also explains the practice, retention and spacing effects that have long defied mechanistic explanation. Memory mirrors the structure of the environment and both display retention and practice functions that are at least approximately power laws, i.e., one varies as a power of the other. Retention and practice effects are approximately additive, i.e., their combined effect is equal to the sum of their individual effects. We will come back to this insight in Chapter 9, Section 9.2.2.

4.5   Summary and Outlook

The study of memory has a long history and has over the centuries been guided by a variety of metaphors that have helped as well as hindered progress. From studying memory through learning and forgetting, to viewing memory as information flowing between different stores, the field has now moved to considering memory as reliant on networks of interconnected neurons. Yet, past metaphors continue to hold sway, and evidence remains circumstantial, leaving practitioners to navigate between competing and conflicting accounts.

For linguists, the time has come to delve deeper into research on memory. Because memory for linguistic information is like memory for other information, frequency effects in language are memory effects and we need to understand how frequency achieves these effects. Knowing how memory works is indispensable: memory limitations are reflected in language use and in structures derived from language use. Constraining the types of structures linguists posit to those that might emerge from usage is important because it is this kind of structure that is worth pursuing on a usage-based, cognitive linguistic approach to language development, processing and representation. Also, knowing how reliably frequency of occurrence diagnoses encoding and ensures recognition and retrieval is crucial for assessing the value of frequency information for linguistic theory.

So, how is memory thought to work? As we have seen, there is declarative and procedural memory. We commonly use both memory systems together. Each of these two systems has its own function: conscious recall versus unconscious performance. Each of these two systems has its own neural systems, but there are clear similarities. Both the declarative and procedural systems have a short-term form of memory lasting seconds and a long-term form of memory lasting days or longer. Information is briefly held in short-term memory, where it gets overwritten by new incoming information unless it is (continually) rehearsed. Both short- and long-term forms of memory rely on a change in synaptic strength. Short-term storage needs a transient change in synaptic strength while the activation of genes and proteins is necessary for converting short-term memories into long-term memories. Long-term memory is stabilized through the growth of presynaptic terminals and dendritic spines. Despite the assumed existence of several types of memory, synapses use only a limited number of mechanisms in various combinations to accomplish change: it is not what kinds of molecules are made at synapses that determine what is remembered but rather what and along what pathways the synaptic change occurs. The location of the synaptic changes determines the specifics of the stored information while the permanence of the information depends on the structural changes that affect the geometry of contact between cells.

Slow learning that is spread out in time and over different contexts is key for information to become or remain available long term. Information that is used in many contexts is retained better, and it has been argued that this would be evolutionarily advantageous: information that occurs in many contexts is more likely to be needed in yet unknown future contexts. If similar experiences occur close together, they are treated as one and are less likely to become part of long-term memory. Repeated experiences are integrated into long-term memory as memories of what generally happens. Less useful memories are forgotten to prevent interference from related but irrelevant information. Forgetting is not necessarily bad: while it means loss of information, it also allows us to abstract over peculiarities and assemble general knowledge.

Long-term memory stores limitless information but (some of) it can be difficult to access. Accessing a memory is easier when it occurs in situations that match the condition under which the memory was encoded. Meaningful cues help retrieve memories – if a cue is weak or ambiguous, the memory may be reconstructed inaccurately. Interestingly, retrieving a memory can strengthen the memory trace because retrieval provides an opportunity to rehearse the information. The memory system is functionally organized in such a way that it tries to make available those memories that are most likely to be useful. Frequency plays an important role in this, but not an exclusive one. The probability that a memory will be needed is also related to recency and the pattern of prior exposures.

An important insight to take with us into the next chapter is that frequency alone does not ensure a memory trace is left. First encounters may leave a trace for some words and not for others; multiple encounters may have differential effects depending on spacing between presentations position in the series and overall quality of processing. Unfortunately, this has been overlooked or neglected in much theorizing about the role of frequency in language and in applications of frequency-based findings in linguistics. The fact that simple repetition is not the only determinant of registration in memory makes frequency-based measures very crude approximations of the relation between what is experienced and what is encoded.

5   Entrenching Linguistic Structures

Usage-based linguistics is predicated on the assumption that language knowledge emerges from exposure to language use. It seems generally accepted that, through repeated exposure, units of varying size are identified and gradually become encoded and differentially entrenched in memory. Key to this is the assumption that frequency-sensitive learning results in mental representations, if not optimized then at least suited for a particular environment. It may seem odd to equate these mental representations, i.e., mental traces of linguistic forms with something as prosaic as memories, but they must be memories: memories capture information that has been encoded and can influence future processing. There is no requirement for memories to be conscious or to be recallable, and they are not restricted to any one dimension of our experience, nor do they exclude any dimensions.

The process by which linguistic experiences are mentally encoded and committed to memory is called 'entrenchment'. Because cognitive linguists aim to endorse a sophisticated view of learning and memory-based processing, the notion of entrenchment is frequently invoked in linguistic research. Yet, the concept is not well defined, and neither has its relationship to frequency been clearly spelled out. While a single exposure may leave memory traces strong enough to persist, memory formation and consolidation typically require repetition. Frequency as indicator of the number of times an event is repeated in the environment is the most straightforward interpretation of the effect that repetition might have on the encoding and storage of a given event in memory. Decades of research on learning and memory have singled out frequency as one of the most robust predictors of human cognitive performance in general.

Ever since the surge of corpora in the 1990s, the extent of a speaker's experience with language has typically been operationalized as frequency of occurrence in a representative sample of the language. For some time, it was thought that frequency in text would instantiate entrenchment in the cognitive system (Schmid 2000). Some experimental studies appeared to yield findings that converged with the results of corpus analysis, while many others reported findings that diverged, and claims to a strong correlation between text and mind were revoked (Schmid 2010). As recently as 2010, Schmid (2010: 125) concluded his chapter on the relation between frequency in the text and entrenchment in the mind by saying that 'so far we have understood neither the nature of frequency itself nor its relation to entrenchment, let alone come up with a convincing way of capturing either one of them or the relation between them in quantitative terms.' Instead, it was recognized that the relationship between frequency of occurrence (especially as measured in a sample) and strength of representation in the mind is far from straightforward (for a recent overview see Baayen, Milin and Ramscar 2016).

While Chapter 4 outlined in general how experiences are committed to memory, this chapter starts from a description of the term entrenchment and how it relates to frequency. Since Langacker (1987) it has become generally accepted in usage-based circles that with repeated use or higher frequency, a novel structure becomes progressively entrenched, to the point of becoming a unit. Despite the apparent simplicity of this commonly accepted assumption, Section 5.1 shows that opinions diverge on the exact interpretation of the term entrenchment. In Section 5.2, three possible interpretations of entrenchment are distilled from the definitions that have been most influential. Section 5.3 delves into the question of how repeated linguistic experiences should be captured, while Section 5.4 relies on knowledge about memory to answer some of the most frequently asked questions regarding the role of frequency for memory and language.

5.1   Entrenchment in the Mind, or in Society?

It has been claimed that language is a social fact, an observable regularity in the language use realized by a specific community. But it is also a cognitive fact, because the members of the community have an internal representation of the existing regularities that allows them to realize the same system in their own use of the language. A key objective of cognitive linguistics is to determine whether and how the structure of language can result from patterns of usage. It was thus an important step in the foundational writings by cognitive linguists to discuss how linguistic patterns are mentally encoded, and how these representations vary with experience. Entrenchment was introduced to cognitive linguistics as a theoretical construct by Langacker (1987), who used the term to explain how linguistic structures are created and shaped through use. This section, expanding on Divjak and Caldwell-Harris (2015), reviews what linguists mean by entrenchment and connects their theoretical ideas with contemporary views of memory.

5.1.1   Linguistic Views on Entrenchment

In his seminal book, *Foundations of Cognitive Grammar*, Langacker (1987: 59) made the case for a 'continuous scale of entrenchment in cognitive organization'. In Langacker's view, a structure becomes more entrenched each time it is used, but extended periods of disuse can reverse that effect. With repeated use and corresponding progressive entrenchment, a structure can turn into a unit. These units themselves are variably entrenched, and their degree of entrenchment depends on the frequency of their occurrence. Langacker's definition of entrenchment thus focuses on the role of entrenchment for representation, looking at the storage and organization of structures in our mental inventory. This characterization of entrenchment is noteworthy on two accounts: it states explicitly that increasing frequency of occurrence deepens entrenchment and that increasing entrenchment can lead to *qualitative* differences in representation, as when a frequently co-occurring sequence becomes a unit in memory. From a cognitive point of view, the first point can be interpreted in terms of memory formation and consolidation, while the second is reminiscent of Gestalt formation (see Section 5.2.2). More recently, Langacker (2008: 16) elaborated on unitization in terms of automatization, a process when 'through repetition or rehearsal, a complex structure is thoroughly mastered to the point that using it is virtually automatic and requires little conscious monitoring'. One could say that, at this point, use of the structure has become a habit.

Bybee's characterization also emphasizes how repeated use leads to a strengthened representation that facilitates ease of access. She, too, refers to the automatization that comes with repeated use. In addition, she highlights the increased fluency or fluidity of processing, which leads to fusion of the units (2007: 324 on parts of noun phrases; see also 2007: 10, 279). Important in Bybee's definition is the addition of the idea of fusion: separate entities can fuse into one larger unit, a phenomenon that exceeds chunking. Chunk status implies that the unit can be retrieved from mental storage as a whole rather than by accessing the individual component parts and parsing them on the basis of rules or schemas (see De Smet and Cuyckens 2007: 188). Fusion takes this one step further as the elements of a word or chunk start merging into one, i.e., the 'extent to which the phonological shape of two morphemes are co-mingled or co-determined' (Bybee 1994: 248). This can happen across constituent boundaries (Bybee 2007: 316), such as when *going to* fuses into *gonna* and *want to* becomes *wanna*. Like Langacker's, Bybee's definitions of entrenchment implies that gradedness is an inherent property of chunking and fusion. Paraphrasing the essence of Hebbian learning, Bybee concluded that 'items that are used together, fuse together'.

Frequency has traditionally been considered the main driver of entrenchment (Bybee 1985: 117; Langacker 1987: 59; Bybee 2003; Krug 2003; Lieven 2010), and Croft and Cruse (2004: 292) stress the idea that the impact of frequency continues to be felt beyond the initial phase, i.e., that with increasing use, structures continue to accrue representational strength and increase in automaticity 'even beyond the minimum threshold required for independent storage'. In usage-based approaches to computational modelling, similar views have been expressed that explicitly tie the entrenchment of pattern or construction-like units to the corpus frequency of the corresponding subunit sequences. Edelman (2006: 434) operationalized unitization in terms of joint probabilities, which is reminiscent of how word–word collocates were distinguished from non-collocates in Chapter 2, Section 2.2.1. That is, if the probability of the joint appearance of two elements is higher than the product of the probabilities of their individual appearances, they may be considered a unit. Coding such elements as a unit also results in a more concise mental representation. Blumenthal-Dramé (2012: 68f) argued that, crucially, the continuous properties associated with entrenchment seem to be related to processing, that is, to changes in the *use* of stored entities, rather than the *inventory* of stored entities, as they imply that the process of fusing separate entities becomes easier and more fluid.

Some linguists have even postulated a direct link between raw frequencies extracted from corpora and mental representation and have elevated it to the status of principle. Schmid (2000: 39) proposed the from-corpus-to-cognition principle, according to which 'frequency in text instantiates entrenchment in the cognitive system'. That is, inspired by Halliday's (1993: 3) claim that frequency in text instantiates probability in the linguistic system, Schmid suggested that entrenchment would link directly to frequencies as obtained from a corpus and hence that corpus frequencies would provide a shortcut to mental structures. Edelman (2006: 434) has drawn similar conclusions for the patterns detected by ADIOS, a computational algorithm for the automatic distillation of structure that learns from raw text (and that we will encounter again in Chapter 8). Edelman reasons that, because the entrenchment of pattern- or construction-like units depends on the corpus frequency of the corresponding subunit sequences, the patterns postulated by the algorithm must be psychologically real. The from-corpus-to-cognition principle has been criticized in the literature as being too simplistic (Gilquin 2006; Arppe et al. 2010), a fact later acknowledged by Schmid (2010).

Once a unit is established and entrenched in the system and constitutes a conventional unit in the grammar, it can sanction other usage events. The extent to which it does so is a matter of degree and speaker judgment. Sanction measures the well-formedness of a structure, i.e., 'how closely it conforms to linguistic convention, in all its aspects and dimensions' (Langacker 1987: 66). The mention of linguistic conventions brings in the social perspective of entrenchment. Entrenchment as a cognitive process is to be distinguished from the societal process of conventionalization. On a usage-based view, what is entrenched in the mind of the speaker must have been acquired through engaging with a community of speakers who prefer certain patterns over others. How do cognitive and social entrenchment relate?

5.1.2   Entrenchment in the Mind, or Conventionalization in Society?

Geeraerts, Grondelaers and Bakema (1994) have argued that frequency of use does not determine cognitive entrenchment at all. Instead, frequency of use only matters with regard to a specific meaning or function, in comparison with alternative expressions of that meaning or function. Entrenchment should be considered a 'socially structured feature of observed language use' (Geeraerts 2017: 154). On this definition, the frequencies needed to capture entrenchment are the relative frequencies of competing expressions, not absolute or normalized frequencies of use. Text frequencies merely capture the combination of the number of times a concept or idea is discussed in a text or collection of texts, the number of times a construal is chosen to express that concept or idea and the number of times an expression is chosen to put the concept or idea into words (Geeraerts 2017: 169).

Mukherjee (2005: 225) explicitly stated that frequency counts in a corpus reflect, more or less directly, degrees of conventionalization of linguistic units or structures, rather than their entrenchment. Entrenchment is a mental phenomenon that differs from speaker to speaker. This conclusion was echoed by Schmid (2015, 2016b: 551) who proposed the entrenchment and conventionalization (EC) model that unites both sides of the cognitive linguistic entrenchment coin. He defines entrenchment as encompassing three types of cognitive processes: association, routinization and schematization. Conventionalization contains four types of processes, i.e., innovation, co-adaptation, diffusion and normation. Entrenchment and conventionalization are contingent upon each other, and Schmid refutes the idea that conventionalization would be nothing but a form of distributed entrenchment, i.e., that the more people have an entrenched representation of a given linguistic structure, the higher its degree of conventionalization would be. He argues that entrenchment is a psychological process that takes place in speakers' minds and operates on patterns of associations and activities involved in usage. Conventionalization, on the other hand, is a social process that takes place in societies and speech communities and operates on utterance types (or utterances that have some elements in common).

[T]he separation of entrenchment and conventionalization allows for a more precise description of the cause-and-effect feedback-loop fashion in which frequency of usage acts upon linguistic structure: the usage frequency of a conventional utterance type supports the routinization of patterns of associations, which increases the likelihood of their activation and in turn the likelihood of repetition, which contributes to increasing conventionality. Since patterns of associations entail competition between the different types of associations, frequency in this feedback loop is never frequency of use as such, especially when it comes to using it as a proxy for measuring entrenchment, but frequency of use in social situations serving communicative and social functions. (Schmid 2016a: 20–1)

The list of forces that are said to act upon the cognitive and social processes that shape language is long and the EC model is designed as a cognitively and neurologically plausible, functional, interactional, socio-cognitive, variational, dynamic, emergentist and usage-based model of linguistic usage, structure and knowledge. The question of how this framework will be implemented in practical analyses of language remains unaddressed. The range of dimensions to consider reads 'like a rough compendium of everything that is known or at least suspected to affect language use (and structure) in the fields of cognitive linguistics, pragmatics as well as interpersonal and variationist sociolinguistics' (Schmid 2016a: 9). Schmid (2016b) represents a first step in this direction, but operationalization of the EC model is in its infancy, and the framework is far from being of direct use to cognitive linguists in their daily descriptive and analytical practice.

Does the social angle invalidate the vast amounts of research that have been done into entrenchment using corpus frequencies? Conventionalization does not operate in a vacuum: instead, agreement on how to solve a communicative task can only be achieved using structures that have been entrenched by individuals. The focus in the remainder of this chapter is on 'individual' or 'cognitive' entrenchment, i.e., the regularities that individual speakers extract and entrench in memory. This process does presuppose contact with other speakers, but the alignment remains partial – individual differences in language knowledge and use do exist (for a recent overview see Dąbrowska 2015). The abstraction over these alignments is what we call the 'system'. A radical usage-based approach would seem to do away with the notion of system altogether, yet 'accounts of language usage, language acquisition and language change are impossible without an assumption about what it is that is being used, acquired, or subjected to change' (Boye and Engberg-Pedersen 2010). Furthermore, 'individual usage events are realizations of an existing systemic structure, but at the same time, it is only through the individual usage events that changes might be introduced into the structure' (Geeraerts 2010b: 237).

By linking behaviour as encoded in texts to behaviour as registered using experiments, it becomes possible to measure entrenchment. In a study tracing the locus of a system for constructional alternations using acceptability ratings, Divjak (2018) found that it was rather the result of conventionalization in society than of entrenchment in the mind. Language is very likely a complex adaptive system (Beckner et al. 2009), in which knowledge of the system's individual parts does not imply knowledge or understanding of the system. Although cognitive linguistics has recently undergone a 'quantitative turn' (Janda 2013), it still awaits its 'experimental turn', and work that combines textual and behavioural evidence remains the exception rather than the norm.

5.2 Three Types of Entrenchment

The brief survey of definitions used to capture the essence of the elusive concept of entrenchment presented in Section 5.1 reveals the family resemblance structure among the various characterizations of entrenchment. What these characterizations have in common is the belief that *entrenchment refers to a process of strengthening memory representations*. This may result in a general reduction in processing effort or automatization (Section 5.2.1), Gestalt formation or 'unitization' à la Langacker (Section 5.2.2) and chunking accompanied by formal reduction or 'fusion' à la Bybee (Section 5.2.3). It should be borne in mind that highlighting three types of entrenchment for ease of presentation imposes artificial boundaries on a phenomenon that is inherently graded. Moreover, automatization can apply to patterns of different size, which affects what is susceptible to unitization and chunk formation or even fusion. One approach, rather traditionally linguistic in nature, is to start from the smallest units such as individual sounds of phonemes and proceed to forming morphemes and words. Another approach, more compatible with usage-based and discriminative approaches to language learning, would be to start big and progressively identify smaller units on an as needed basis.

5.2.1 *'What You Do Often, You Do Faster and with Fewer Errors': Entrenchment as Reduction in Cognitive Effort and Increase in Automatization*

Since the development of the information-processing paradigm in psychology in the 1960s to 1980s, it has become accepted that frequency is among the most robust predictors of human performance in general (Howes and Solomon 1951; Broadbent 1967; Hasher and Zacks 1984): what you do often, you do faster and with fewer errors. Human beings are also surprisingly good at providing frequency estimates for a range of language stimuli (these estimates do seem to relate to raw frequencies but are contaminated by many of the lexical dimensions that correlate with frequency such as emotionality, see Baayen, Milin and Ramscar 2016). This suggests that frequency information accumulates automatically (Hasher and Zacks 1984; Jurafsky 1996; Saffran 2003).

Frequency has also proven to be a robust predictor of performance across a wide variety of linguistic tasks, and frequency effects have been found in virtually every subdomain of language that has been studied. For instance, high-frequency words show a uniform advantage in perceptual and production tasks, with shorter response latencies and higher accuracy in tests of perceptual identification (Morton 1969), word naming (Forster and Chambers 1973) and lexical decision (Scarborough, Cortese and Scarborough 1977). Comprehensive reviews of frequency and its effects on language structure exist (Diessel 2007; Divjak and Caldwell-Harris 2015). Overviews of frequency effects in L1 are presented in Ellis (2002, 2012), for L1 development they are summarized in Lieven (2010) and Behrens and Pfänder (2016) and for L2 in Ellis and Larsen-Freeman (2006).

Seeing entrenchment in terms of representations of varying strengths calls for a memory-based origin. While a single exposure may leave memory traces strong enough to persist, memory formation and consolidation typically require repetition. The standard interpretation of frequency, and the one assumed here, indeed equates the frequency with the number of times a stimulus is repeated in the environment, henceforth 'repetition frequency'. Frequency as indicator of repetition is the most straightforward interpretation of the effect that frequency of occurrence has on the encoding and storage of events in memory, and one that has a long history in the study of learning. Rehearsal resulting from repeated exposure and use yields memory formation and consolidation, while (extended) periods of disuse cause decay and attrition. Many models of lexical access are built on the assumption that repetition is key to entrenchment in memory, such that the more times an item is encountered, the more easily it will be processed or accessed. This principle of repetition is often formalized as a mental counter, which may bias detection of an item (by lowering its resting state threshold – Morton 1969; or by raising its baseline activation level – Coltheart et al. 2001), or which may increase its accessibility in a serial access system (Murray and Forster 2004). Yet, for repetition to work, the retention of memory traces from one communicative event to the next is required (see Schmid 2017b: 18–19). In fact, repetition happens ideally in different (communicative) situations, as we saw in Chapter 4, Section 4.4.2. Given the importance of context, the extent to which pure repetition matters independently of other factors has been questioned, as we will see in Section 5.4.4 further on in this chapter.

Behaviour that is executed repeatedly becomes less demanding (requiring less effort), less prone to error, and at the same time also faster. This is so because a high frequency of behaviour repetition increases the likelihood that the behaviour will be frozen into habit and will be *automatically* chosen in subsequent decisions (Sedlmeier and Betsch 2002: 10). The key aspects that define automatic task processing are a decrease in effort, an increase in speed, independence of voluntary control and no interference with concurrent processes (De Pisapia, Repovš and Braver 2008: 443). Prevailing models of automaticity explain automatic processing as faster processing than controlled processing. Yet, functional imaging studies support an alternative account of automaticity as efficient, elegant and economical, but not fast: global activation is reduced and activation is shifted from cortical to subcortical areas once automaticity has been achieved. If automaticity would equal faster processing, functional imaging would indicate greater activation when an automatic task is performed (Saling and Phillips 2007).

Automaticity may not explain the decrease in processing time. Fluency of composition, on the other hand, could explain why higher frequencies yield shorter response times, i.e., faster processing: for this we need to assume that frequency affects the connection weights between the constituent parts of a sequence. Some neuroimaging work in this respect has been done on morphology (Blumenthal-Dramé 2012). Here, fluency affects the weights between the constituent morphemes of multi-morphemic units but not the morphemes themselves, i.e., morphemes are stored units that are more or less quickly accessed and assembled, dependent on their frequency of usage. But assuming morphemes as basic building blocks goes against the basic tenets of usage-based approaches to language where unanalysed exemplars constitute the input in which morphemes may be discovered and over which constructions could be abstracted; yet different patterns altogether may be called for.

5.2.2 'Units that Occur Together, Refer Together': Entrenchment as Unit Formation for Access and Retrieval

It has been common to study frequency effects using single isolated words, and indeed the (single) word frequency effect is one of the most robust findings in experimental psychology (Monsell 1991). Gestalt formation has been invoked to explain why the mind would prefer units, and why sometimes the whole is more than the sum of its parts (Von Ehrenfels 1890). Over almost a century of development, Gestalt theory has inevitably attracted criticism (Gobet 2017: 250), which could be summarised as targeting the very 'first principle of Gestalt': despite the fact that the overarching Good Gestalt principle appears as unifying and parsimonious, it also remains abstract, lacking in clarity and operationalizability. Furthermore, Gestalt theory, for some authors, remains descriptive rather than explanatory in nature. Yet, it seems that the abstractness and descriptive nature of the theory itself has boosted its attractiveness and apparent applicability to other domains. The law of figure–ground segregation, whereby the figure is in focal attention and stands out from or against the ground, has been fruitfully applied to syntax within cognitive linguistics. Usage-based linguists have been less successful in explaining the size of letter or word sequences that would be ideally suited for obtaining Gestalt status, and they tend to remain agnostic as to how the co-occurrence frequencies that purportedly support this process should be recorded.

Furthermore, the most commonly used diagnostic, frequency, runs into problems when moving beyond the single word. Wray (2002: 25–31) discusses how problematic frequency counts are in establishing formulaic sequences: when searching for multi-word strings, a decision has to be made about the size of the search window and how frequent the association has to be for it to count as one. Such frequency thresholds are inevitably arbitrary and often chosen in function of the size of the corpus that is searched, the quantity of the data that is needed and the size of the chunks under scrutiny. Several ratio measures have been proposed to capture frequently co-occurring items, that balance the frequency with which an item occurs in a pattern with the overall frequency it has in the corpus. Yet, these do not (and cannot, unless the corpus is annotated for utterance function) capture the ratio of message-to-message expression or the frequency with which a particular message is verbalized using a certain expression. Moreover, often the results of these searches have to be subjected to post hoc manual analysis and additional decisions need to be made about which associations to discard. Sometimes these decisions are straightforward, e.g., when sentence boundaries have been ignored, but at other times the decision is more subjective, which undermines the added value of an objective computerized search. Moreover, corpora are unable to capture the true distribution of rare or short-lived formulaic sequences and are in general unlikely to be representative of the linguistic experience of any one individual.

At the same time, going beyond the single word is important. We have seen in the previous chapter that context plays an important role in memory encoding. A linguistic example of this would be the finding that children are more likely to correctly produce irregular plurals such as *feet* or *teeth* if they are asked to produce them in typical contexts such as *on your [feet]* and *brush your [teeth]* (Arnon and Clark 2011). Contextualized frequency yields better predictions than isolated frequencies and this can be expected: the brain makes use of learned contextual regularities. Seminal studies from the 1970s, such as Biederman, Glass and Stacy (1973), demonstrated that objects are recognized faster and more accurately when accompanied by contextual information. Yet, this leads to what Mitchell et al. (1995) have called the 'grain size issue': frequencies can be estimated at multiple levels of linguistic analysis (e.g., syntactic construction, syntactic construction given a verb, syntactic construction given a verb and object). What is the relevant grain size for a given calculation and how should different frequency measures be integrated? Mitchell et al. (1995: 472) point out that finer grain sizes will increase precision but may be costly in terms of storage and computation because more information needs to be stored and manipulated. They might also lead to a situation in which no predictions can be made because the reader or listener has never before encountered that precise structure. Coarse records would be easier to maintain, but the pooling of information would lead to loss of precision. This leaves the interpretation of entrenchment as unit formation with quite a number of practical problems to solve.

5.2.3 'Units that Occur Together, Blur Together': Entrenchment as Chunking, Possibly Resulting in Fusion

Usage-based linguists may have popularized chunking, but the idea is much older. Wray (2002: 7–8) traces the history of 'unexpected levels of fixedness in language' back to the middle of the nineteenth century with John Hughlings Jackson, who was fascinated by the ability of aphasic patients to produce greetings, prayers and rhymes although they were unable to construct new utterances. References to the chunkiness of language can be found in the writings of many influential linguists, i.e., de Saussure (1916/1966: 177), Jespersen (1924/1976: 85), Bloomfield (1933: 181), Firth (1937/1964: 83) who speaks of the 'holophrase' as the unit of actual speech, Bolinger (1976: 1) and Fillmore (1979: 92).

If entrenched expressions are mental representations of language forms which are either implicit or explicit memories, then any form can be entrenched including single words, complex phrases, lexical items and even abstract schemas. Frequency effects have indeed been found for phonemes, morphemes and multi-word expressions, and have been attested for items across the low- to high-frequency range as well as for random four-word sequences (see Bannard and Matthews 2008; Arnon and Snider 2010; Tremblay and Baayen 2010; Tremblay et al. 2011; Caldwell-Harris, Berant and Edelman 2012; Snider and Arnon 2012; Divjak 2017 for recent work on these effects in low-frequency structures). Once items form a unit, they are on the path towards chunking and possibly even fusion. Linguists usually invoke three mechanisms to explain chunking and fusion:

1 High token frequency leads to a *tightening of syntagmatic bonds*, which conditions phonological reduction and the loss of identity of the formerly separate components (Bybee 1985: 41, 95). The phonological reduction of English auxiliaries, such as *I've, I'm* and *I'll*, is a well-known illustration of this mechanism.
2 High token frequency results in a *loosening of paradigmatic bonds* (Bybee 2007: 301) which means that individual component parts become dissociated from previously related forms, which can be paradigmatic alternatives or semantically related forms. An example here would be the phrase *a lot of*, which does not tolerate any other nouns instead of *lot*.
3 High token frequency detaches a string from more abstract constructions, thereby *resisting analogical alignments* with higher-level schemata, which

eventually yields a conservation effect. Typical examples here are irregular past tense forms, such as *went* instead of *goed.*

Chunking illustrates the power of grouping information for human cognition. Both deliberate and automatic chunking exists; while deliberate chunking is considered as a way to bypass the limits on short-term memory, automatic chunking has been observed in relation to long-term memory processes and indicates the effect of frequency on the way information is learned. Green (2017) presents evidence from text corpora, showing that the number of units in n-grams, phrasal verbs, idioms, intonation units, phrasal categories and clause structures consistently remains below four, across languages as diverse as English, Chinese and Inuktitut. This would be expected given that working memory is a fundamental cognitive capacity for information storage and processing; its limitations should be reflected in language use and any structures derived from use.

In fact, large short-term memories could be a disadvantage early on in language learning. Newport (1990) has argued that 'less is more': developmentally immature language learners can grasp only fragments of the ambient speech at any one time, which breaks up a complex language structure into smaller, more manageable parts. Mature learners with larger short-term memories no longer need to do so, which would put them at a disadvantage for learning. Elman (1993) found that his implementation of a parallel distributed processing model learned complex language structures more easily if the short-term memory capacity model was initially set to small and increased later in learning. In other words, chunking can be considered as more than a way of grouping elements together: it is a form of information compression (Miller 1956). Learning, as formalized by computational models, may not be optimal, but is highly adaptive: early on, small chunks are learned that impose few constraints and can be reused often. With experience, chunks or the building blocks of further knowledge, become larger and so learning becomes faster. There is a trade-off between the amount of information captured by a chunk and how often it can be used, and frequency can be used to establish a workable compromise (Gobet 2017: 260–1).

A more difficult question is whether entrenchment *necessarily* implies chunk *storage*. It has become standard practice to view frequency effects associated with a unit as proof of the existence of corresponding mental representations. If frequency effects are found for a specific morpheme sequence, then researchers feel justified in viewing that morpheme sequence to be mentally represented as a discrete unit. For example, Blumenthal-Dramé (see also Bannard and Matthews 2008) concluded from her study of the processing of multi-morphemic words that the effects of token frequency at different levels of language description attest to the necessity of positing full storage of tokens, irrespective of whether they are complex or simple (Blumenthal-Dramé 2012: 193). An interesting take on the chunking question comes from the discussion about the relationship between storage and computation. It continues to be debated whether frequency effects are observed because a frequent multi-morphemic word or multi-word expression is stored as a unit or whether its pieces are more rapidly assembled. Tremblay et al. (2011: 595) provided evidence for holistic storage but noted at the same time that behavioural research may not be able to distinguish between holistic retrieval and speeded online computation. Blumenthal-Dramé (2012: 187) argued that '[...] highly independent representations will be holistically retrieved rather than analytically processed'.

Recent computational modelling casts doubts on the wisdom of interpreting frequency effects as indications of storage. Baayen's (2010, 2011) naive discriminative learner model contained no representations corresponding to whole words or phrases, only letter unigrams and bigrams. The model nevertheless showed frequency effects for multi-word units. Based on this demonstration, Baayen (2011) argued that specific morpheme sequences (including multi-word expressions) show frequency effects because the model develops its own representations that are frequency sensitive, as a by-product of learning form-to-meaning mappings that vary in frequency (see also Baayen and Ramscar 2015). Other researchers have suggested that the tension between storage and computation is unnecessary. Shaoul (2012: 171) proposed that the graded effect of probability is a side effect of the emergent nature of n-gram processing. In other words, the neural patterns which mediate language processing contain probabilistic expectations of how patterns will be completed. Any given sound or syllable encountered in a speech stream activates expectations for a subset of all possible following sounds or syllables based on prior processing (Elman 1993; Baayen and Hendrix 2011; Geertzen, Blevins and Milin 2016). Expectations are activated quickly and effortlessly, as if the predicted sequence was stored separately as a ready-made unit. This view of expectation generation and expectation-based processing rather than chunk storage is consistent with the workings of a probabilistic grammar (see also Chapter 9). Given this, and the fact that frequency effects have been observed where they were not expected, frequency effects are unlikely reliable evidence or diagnostics of unit storage.

5.3 How Are Repeated Experiences Recorded?

We now turn to some empirical work in cognitive and evolutionary psychology that may shed light on the question of how repeated experiences are recorded, and hence how formal markers of entrenchment could be determined. This section will draw on insights from decision making under uncertainty and from memory to underpin cognitive linguistics.

Hasher and Zacks (1979) proposed the automatic coding hypothesis. Frequencies appear to be encoded fairly automatically – at least by 'rats, pigeons and sophomores at elite institutions', in a process that requires little or no attentional capacity and works without awareness or intention. At the same time, frequencies are mere approximations, in the sense that they reflect tendencies rather than precise quantities; this is illustrated by the observation that people, when asked to provide subjective estimates of frequencies, are unable to do so accurately (Gernsbacher 1984) (but compare here Bradshaw 1984: 202, who found that subjective frequency ratings are rather reliable). Research has shown that people are sensitive to frequencies across a wide range of conditions, but not to all kinds of frequencies, and that the effects of manipulations are mostly small. Frequency information is registered in memory, regardless of age, ability or motivation; training and feedback do not improve the ability to encode frequency. Neither does the ability to encode frequency decrease with old age, depression or multiple task requirements. Yet, the memory of frequencies is less invariant than was originally suggested since some factors, such as deeper processing, spaced repetitions and repetition in the same context, have a reliable impact on frequency estimates. Looking back on years of work, Zacks and Hasher (2002: 27, 32) defined frequency, space and time as fundamental organizing dimensions of behaviour. The innate ability to automatically encode frequency, spatial location and temporal order serves an adaptive function because frequency, space and time are fundamental attributes of experience that define the flow of events in our environment and that enable us to solve critical problems.

Evolutionary psychology postulates the existence of cognitive algorithms that are specifically tuned to frequency information and exploit the frequency information that is present in the environment. We can only achieve our goals in an uncertain world by learning and applying information about frequency distributions. The conceptual distinction between the probability of a single event ('There is a 33 per cent chance that a funded grant application has a female PI') and a frequency (e.g., 'Three out of the ten funded grant applications had a female PI') is fundamental to mathematical theories of probability. Gigerenzer proposed the frequency format hypothesis, or the idea that the brain understands and processes information better when presented in frequency format than in a probability format. He demonstrated that most reasoning fallacies resulted from working with probabilities rather than frequencies: natural frequencies, not probabilities of single events, facilitate Bayesian reasoning, i.e., the estimation of a posterior probability from observation (Gigerenzer 2002: 59, 62). In other words, the use of frequency information as input for decision tasks yields much better results than the use of probability information. This finding has sparked bio-evolutionary arguments claiming that nature could not develop a sense for detecting single-event probabilities because they are unobservable; instead, frequencies are observable and therefore these would be more likely candidates for input (Cosmides and Tooby 1996: 15).

That people's intuitions would therefore not follow a calculus of probability (Cosmides and Tooby 1996: 2) is, however, not generally accepted in psychology today. Evidence has been presented for the existence of a cognitive statistical inference system that requires data in frequency format in order to operate according to probabilistic principles. Evolutionary approaches to judgment under uncertainty have shown that subjects, untutored in probability theory, reliably produce judgments that conform to many principles of probability theory when (1) they are asked to compute a frequency instead of the probability of a single event, and (2) the relevant information is expressed as frequencies (Brase, Cosmides and Tooby 1998: 3).

If humans have cognitive adaptations for inductive reasoning, one might expect them to be good at picking up frequency information incidentally (Hintzman and Stern 1978; Hasher and Zacks 1979) and at using it to make probability judgments. An individual can easily observe the frequency with which events occur ('It rained on six out of the last ten days when there were cold winds and dark clouds,' or 'We were successful one out of the last ten times we applied for research grants'). Under conditions of natural sampling, only the absolute number of hits and false alarms is needed. Base rates, or the underlying probability of an event not conditioned on prior probabilities, are sometimes needed for calculating the conditional probability. This is the case in designed experiments in which two samples are taken, and the size of each is set in advance: in such designed experiments, likelihoods contain no information about base rates (Brase, Cosmides and Tooby 1998: 6). Once frequency representations have been acquired, there are advantages to maintaining them. Important information is lost when a frequency (e.g., 'Three out of the ten funded grant applications had a female PI') is converted to and stored as a proportion or single-event probability ('There is a 33 per cent chance that a funded grant application has a female PI'). When this happens, the absolute frequencies of the two component events cannot be recovered. As a result, (1) it is difficult to update the database as one encounters new instances; (2) the sample size is lost, and with it a basis for indexing how reliable one's estimate is (300 observations provide a more reliable database than 3); (3) more data needs to be stored (including likelihoods and base rates); and (4) the original data cannot be recategorized to construct novel reference classes after the fact, as they become useful. Sample size is important for learning: on Gallistel's (1990) model of classical conditioning, animals use sample size to compute the

statistical uncertainty associated with an estimate of the rate of the unconditioned stimulus in the presence of a conditioned stimulus. Their learning curve
increases monotonically and reflects the decrease in the statistical uncertainty
as the sample size increases. We will return to learning in Chapter 9.

Yet, there is disagreement about how these experimental results should be
interpreted. Evans and Over (1996) have argued, against Cosmides and Tooby
(1996) and Gigerenzer and Hoffrage (1995), that there is a need to distinguish
between implicit and explicit cognitive systems and that probabilistic information may be represented by both the implicit and the explicit cognitive systems
with different psychological consequences. Since reasoning about quantitative
word problems is an explicit process, there is no evolutionary reason to assume
that quantitative word problems will be easier when phrased in terms of
frequencies rather than in terms of probabilities. In fact, the reported findings
disappear when stimuli are properly matched on interest and interpretability
and the expectations of the task are made explicit (O'Brien et al. 2007: 76–9).
A more conceptual explanation refers to how the explicit reasoning system
operates, i.e., via the construction and manipulation of mental models representing possible states of affairs. Frequency formats and probability formats
yield equal performance in statistical word problems if they are presented so as
to cue a simple mental model of set inclusion (Evans et al. 2000: 198). In fact, it
is interesting that each question format produces a different kind of bias. The
most often cited bias in the literature is base rate neglect (see also Kahneman
and Tversky 1972). Base rate neglect is a formal fallacy. If respondents are
presented with both base rate or generic information and with specific information, they neglect the generic information. Yet, the opposite is also observed,
and Evans et al. (2000) have reported a bias to give the base rate as the answer
to the posterior probability question, neglecting the diagnostic evidence.

Brase, Cosmides and Tooby (1998: 5) have argued that the ability to make
well-calibrated probability judgments depends on the ability to count, which in
turn depends on the ability to see the world as composed of discrete entities. It
has been argued that our frequency computation systems are designed to
produce well-calibrated statistical inferences when they operate over representations of whole objects, events and locations. It could be that the frequency-
computation system is simply incapable of taking anything other than whole
objects as input. If this were the case, then there would be a strong interaction
between format and parsing: the frequency format would have a much smaller
effect for conditioning events parsed arbitrarily than for conditioning events
parsed as whole objects. This does not appear to be the case, however, and the
results suggest an alternative view: the input to a frequency-computation
system must be representations of tokens rather than types (Brase, Cosmides
and Tooby 1998: 3, 12). The system is, in principle, capable of counting tokens
of arbitrarily parsed entities, but such arbitrary parsings are rarely fed into the

system as input. This is because representations of the physical world are built by other systems, and these systems were designed to individuate and imagine transformations of whole objects; this is reminiscent of the Gestalt theory in Section 5.2.2.

In language, things are different, however, and entities of any size can be detected in the speech stream. Although linguists have traditionally cut down language into its smallest meaning bearing units, i.e., morphemes, evidence of frequency effects for words and even multi-word sequences does exist. The multi-word frequency effect shows up regardless of whether the sequences are compositional (non-idiomatic) four-word phrases such as *don't have to worry* (Arnon and Snider 2010; Snider and Arnon 2012) or four- or five-word non-phrasal (i.e., more or less arbitrary) sequences (Tremblay and Baayen 2010) such as *in the middle of*. Given that frequency effects are typically considered as evidence for storage (but see Section 5.2.3), this finding has sparked interest in the role multi-word sequences could play in L1 and L2 development, processing and representation and the implications this would have for linguistic theorizing. For an overview and discussion of the main findings regarding the role of multi-word units, I refer readers to the special issue of *TopiCS* (2017, volume 9, issue 3, edited by Christiansen and Arnon).

Moreover, there is a paucity of work exploring the optimal entity size of linguistic entities. Geertzen, Blevins and Milin (2016: 28) pursued the hypothesis that units such as words are 'abstracted on the basis of recurrent statistical patterns, specifically patterns of syntagmatic and paradigmatic interpredictability'. They used an approach based on Kolmogorov complexity to explore the relation between boundaries of various unit types (morphemes, words and sentences) and the amount of information that each type conveys, across four languages (isolating English, fusional Estonian and agglutinating Finnish and Hungarian). The informativity of boundaries appeared to differ across types and, to varying degrees, across languages. Across the languages sampled, sentence boundaries added relatively little information; word boundaries were the most informative, especially in English; morph boundaries lie between these extremes. Words can be considered 'optimal-sized units for describing the regularities', and it is their maximal productivity that makes them suited to serve 'as primary focus of grammatical abstraction for the speaker'. Curiously, written word boundaries do not straightforwardly map onto pauses in the speech stream. As mentioned before, identifying words in speech is a challenging task for both human learners and computer algorithms. What is less well known is that identifying word boundaries in writing is also difficult for beginning readers for reasons that link in with the work of Brase and colleagues: children who count halved objects as wholes tend to violate space boundaries in forming words (Meltzer and Herse 1969). These difficulties shed doubt on the choice of words as optimal-sized units for those striving towards cognitive reality in description.

5.4   Frequently Asked Questions

Frequency has long been identified as the main determinant of entrenchment. This is because the input to the processing of frequencies is repeatedly encountered events or objects (that have been categorized to avoid each perception being idiosyncratic). That is, frequency is basically repetition, and the importance of repetition for the formation of memory traces is well known (see Chapter 4). The question of how repeatedly occurring events are processed and how the resulting frequencies of events influence cognition dates back to the beginning of psychology. Ebbinghaus (1885b) and James (1890) already studied how the frequency with which an event occurs determines how well we remember it, and the frequency with which two events co-occur determines how strongly they are associated. Also, as we all know from experience, memories for all types of sensory input can be lost (through forgetting) when that information is not reinforced by repetition or recency.

The frequency with which events co-occur thus became a cornerstone of memory models (Hebb 1949) and played a central role in the probability learning paradigm (Estes 1950). Yet, a few questions remain. This section takes up some of the most frequently asked questions concerning the role of frequency in usage-based theories of language, and answers them with the help of the knowledge we have gathered in the previous chapters. The questions address the types of units that are entrenched (Section 5.4.1), whether there is a threshold for entrenchment (Section 5.4.2), whether some frequency measures are better for predicting entrenchment (Section 5.4.3) and whether frequency itself triggers entrenchment (Section 5.4.4).

5.4.1   What Is Entrenched?

What exactly can be entrenched has remained underspecified in the literature. Given that entrenchment results from repeated exposure to input, in principle anything can be entrenched, from a single sound over a multi-morphemic word to a formulaic expression.

In linguistics, morphemes, the alleged smallest meaning bearing units, are typically considered the atoms or basic building blocks of language. The past three decades have seen an influx of first psycholinguistic and then neurolinguistic work on the processing of multi-morphemic sequences (see Blumenthal-Dramé 2017 for an introductory overview). Although this research did not set out to measure the usage-based theoretical concept of entrenchment, the findings it has produced could be used to draw inferences about entrenchment.

On a usage-based view of language, there are no primordial building blocks, however. There is only language use. Units are used and learned in context and therefore never achieve absolute autonomy, just different degrees of decontextualization. They are abstracted from usage events through reinforcement of commonalities (Langacker 2017: 52). As mentioned in Section 5.3, there is some evidence from computational modelling to show that words may be useful units to abstract for an isolating language like English (Geertzen, Blevins and Milin 2016). At the same time, Baayen et al. (2016) have argued that children may well be trying to identify the lexical equivalent of their experience rather than be aiming to segment words out of the sound stream (see Chapter 3, Section 3.1).

How would language users delineate relevant units? A probability-based approach to unit identification underlies psycholinguistic and computational approaches to word recognition. Baayen et al. (2016) have argued that adopting a discriminative stance, rather than a decompositional one, may better characterize the challenges children face. Using Rescorla–Wagner networks, they tried to predict the lexical expression of experience – regardless of its length – encoded in the signal instead of the boundaries between word forms. This approach fits well with the usage-based tenet that structure is emergent and linguistic units are not independent components from which larger expressions are constructed. Instead, they are themselves abstracted from larger structures (see Bloomfield 1914). Yet, it is very different from traditional linguistic approaches to classification such as word classes (Matthews 1972: 160ff). In dynamic, usage-based models, structures reside in overlapping patterns of activity and units are established patterns (processing routines). Rule application is nothing but co-activation of overlapping patterns of different levels of abstractness (Langacker 2017: 53–4). Surprisingly, cognitive linguists typically take traditional classifications as the starting point for their analyses without questioning their cognitive reality (Divjak 2015).

Schmid (2017a) proposed that entrenchment operates, not on units, but directly on the traditional four dimensions of the association between form and meaning, that is, the symbolic, syntagmatic, paradigmatic and pragmatic ones. But these four types of associations do not all function at the same level. The syntagmatic level, where words that co-occur get associated with each other, sets things in motion. The paradigmatic level, where alternatives are considered, comes into play at later stages only since paradigmatic knowledge is gradually abstracted through commonalities in syntagmatic input. The symbolic level is always present, but may well depend on the syntagmatic one for clarification, since words render meaning in syntagmatic context. And to some extent this syntagmatic context is modulated by the pragmatic level, once a speaker has become sensitive to pragmatics.

5.4.2   Is a Threshold Number of Occurrences Required for Entrenchment?

Since people do not remember all events, but tend to remember highly frequent information well, it has been customary to assume that stimuli need to occur some number of times before they are unitized, after which they can grow in strength as a function of our experience with them. However, this view lacks empirical linguistic support (Gurevich, Johnson and Goldberg 2010) and little remains known about lower or upper bounds of frequency needed to ensure entrenchment. Yet, as we saw in Chapter 4, Section 4.3.2, to turn short-term memories into long-term memories, new proteins must be synthesized (and this within a specific time window) and genes must be switched on to facilitate synaptic connectivity. This relies on a chemical process that requires repeated pulses of neurotransmitter (serotonin) and therefore happens only after repeated learning trials.

There is, as yet, no research that links findings from biology directly to language. And even within linguistics, researchers have not been able to agree on what might be a frequency threshold for multi-morphemic or multi-word utterances (Arnon and Snider 2010; Caldwell-Harris, Berant and Edelman 2012). Alegre and Gordon (1999) have proposed a threshold of six occurrences per million words for inflected forms, but frequency effects have been observed well below that threshold (Baayen, Lieber and Schreuder 1997; Baayen, Wurm and Aycock 2007; Arnon and Snider 2010; Blumenthal-Dramé 2012; Caldwell-Harris, Berant and Edelman 2012; Divjak 2017) and are found for all frequency ranges for morphologically simple controls (Alegre and Gordon 1999). Divjak (2017) found frequency effects for rare lexico-syntactic combinations in Polish (< 0.66 instances per million) but showed that these effects are driven by words that themselves occur at least six times per million words. In other words, a lower word-frequency threshold was identified where an increase in conditional probabilities starts causing an increase in acceptability of a verb in a *that*-clause.

This does not imply that items below this threshold would not leave traces in memory. If a single exposure is below the threshold where a counter begins accruing evidence, then the counter of exposures remains set to zero, and logically no experience can accumulate. Without such initial traces, the threshold at which frequency becomes a force to be reckoned with would never be reached. In other words, it may be more fruitful to assume that evidence accrues from the first exposure, but that speakers cannot formulate reliable hypotheses about the acceptability of configurations until sufficient evidence has accumulated, which seems to be around six instances per million words. Erker and Guy (2012), too, proposed thinking of frequency as a gatekeeper or potentiator:

some constraints on subject personal pronoun use in Spanish are activated or amplified by high frequency.

5.4.3   Which Frequency Measure Is Ideal for Predicting Entrenchment?

A key question that has received attention only recently is which frequency measure or family of measures is best suited to predict entrenchment? Do different frequency measures correlate with different incarnations of entrenchment?

Schmid (2017b: 11–12) focuses on the way in which different types of frequency counts and measures may affect different types of entrenchment. He undertakes an explicit attempt to present the many ways in which frequencies can be counted and calculated and distinguishes types and tokens; words, morphemes, phonemes and syntactic constructions; isolated words, words in contexts and words in patterns or schemas; relative and absolute frequencies, observed and expected frequencies and frequencies as interpreted by further statistical tests; in experiments and in corpora, etc. He also lists the many ways in which the notion of entrenchment can be understood, i.e., as reduction in cognitive effort and increase in automatization; as unit-forming type of access and retrieval; as chunking, possibly resulting in fusion; as pre-emption/blocking. Taken together, this list shows how different ways of measuring frequencies relate to different ways of understanding entrenchment. On his account, for frequency counts of individual linguistic items to be meaningful in terms of conventionality and entrenchment, they have to be measured and interpreted relative to frequencies of syntagmatic companions (cotextual entrenchment), to frequencies of paradigmatic competitors, and to frequencies of pragmatic competitors (contextual entrenchment). Filipović-Đurđević and Milin (2019) quantified the trade-off between information carried by the syntagmatic and paradigmatic axes. They found that words (in this case adjectives) need to be predictable from context, or the number of lexical options that could fit in a constructional slot needs to be limited: in a large corpus, they did not find any adjectives that were simultaneously highly unpredictable along both the syntagmatic and paradigmatic axes.

Leaving aside the issue of the nature of the units that would deserve consideration and the properties of the measures or algorithms used to track them, including the wider context of use in any frequency-based analysis seems a sine qua non. Seminal studies from the 1970s, such as Biederman, Glass and Stacy (1973), had already demonstrated that objects are recognized faster and more accurately when accompanied by contextual information. This translates straightforwardly to language, and linguists have indeed focused on frequency effects in language varying in size from phonological to morphological and syntactic contexts. Even disciplines that have been preoccupied with frequency counts, such as corpus linguistics, have borne this principle in mind. Indeed, core concepts in corpus linguistics are collocations, i.e., words that are regularly used together giving rise to an association, and colligations, where a lexical item is linked to a grammatical one. Issues that are currently debated in assessments of the usefulness of existing frequency measures include the uni- or bi-directionality of the measure along with the inclusion of contingency information and the relevance of statistical null-hypothesis testing (see Chapter 2, Section 2.2.1 for details).

In Chapter 2, Section 2.2.1.4, we discussed in detail how earlier experimental work supported association measures as reliable predictors of entrenchment (Gries, Hampe and Schönefeld 2005; Ellis and Ferreira-Junior 2009; Ellis and Simpson-Vlach 2009; Colleman and Bernolet 2012). However, research contrasting association measures and conditional probabilities (Divjak 2008, 2017; Wiechmann 2008; Blumenthal-Dramé 2012; Shaoul 2012; Levshina 2015) shows that conditional probabilities are the favoured predictors for a range of more natural linguistic behaviours than recognizing (isolated) words. Wiechmann (2008), for example, surveyed a wide range of association measures and tested their predictivity using data from eye-tracking during sentence comprehension. The best measure at predicting reading behaviour was minimum sensitivity. This measure selects the best of the two available conditional probabilities, i.e., P(verb|construction) and P(construction|verb). Recent studies have compared uni-directional probability measures to bi-directional measures; while the former calculate, for example, P(verb|construction) or how likely the construction is given a verb, the latter would supplement this information with a calculation of how likely a verb is given the construction and compute both P(verb|construction) and P(construction|verb). Divjak (2008, 2017) obtained sentence acceptability ratings on dispreferred and often low-frequency Polish combinations of verbs and constructions. Levshina (2015) used gap filling and sentence production tasks on the Russian ditransitive. Both studies surveyed a number of association measures, including conditional probabilities, and found that unidirectional probability measures explained behavioural performance at least as well as bi-directional measures. In a similar vein, Blumenthal-Dramé (2012) studied the processing of complex word forms in English, using a variety of tasks and both reaction time as well as fMRI measurements. Her conclusion was that (log) relative frequencies (the ratio between surface [root + affix] and base [root] frequencies) predict entrenchment best.

Likewise, computational psycholinguists have demonstrated that conditional probabilities (defined as the likelihood to encounter a word given its context, for example) are more appropriate than frequencies for explaining language processing in general, and Elman (2009) contains an excellent overview of work in this tradition. Recall that Jurafsky (1996) showed that a probabilistic model differs in its predictions from the frequency-based models traditional in psycholinguistics, with true probabilities essential for a cognitive model of sentence processing. The usefulness of probabilities has been well known within information theory, which we discussed in Chapter 3, Section 3.3, where measures such as entropy and surprisal have been developed. Entropy is a measure of the unpredictability of information content: something that is predictable has low entropy, whereas something that is unpredictable has high entropy. In a similar vein, the surprise ratio, also called 'surprisal' (Barlow 1990), measures how unexpected a sequence is, given the probabilities of its components. Surprisal has been used in psycholinguistic models (Hale 2001; Levy 2008; Frank 2013) and in computational emergentist models (e.g., ADIOS, see Solan et al. 2005).

Moreover, none of the probability-based measures that outperformed the others on the tasks described above related observed to expected frequencies in order to perform null-hypothesis statistical significance testing. The information gained from relating observed to expected frequencies, in the way this is done in statistics, may have low psychological relevance to speakers and should therefore not be pursued at all costs in cognitive linguistics.

There has also been quite a bit of discussion in the literature about the types of texts that would yield the most accurate frequency estimates. In psycholinguistic work, frequency estimates from a representative corpus are used as proxies for a subject's prior experience with language. Much has been written about the 'ideal' source from which to draw frequency estimates, and corpora of movie subtitles seem to fare better than any traditional corpora (New et al. 2007). Heister and Kliegl (2012) reported that frequency estimates from a tabloid yield similarly predictive values and suggested that it is the emotional charge of language used in movies, rather than its similarity to spoken language, which makes subtitle frequencies better predictors.

5.4.4   Is Repetition Frequency Itself Causal?

Is it really frequency that is causing the observed processing advantages that have led to certain conclusions about mental representation? The frequency with which words occur is strongly correlated with other characteristics (Cutler 1981). Highly frequent words tend to be short in length, concrete rather than abstract, easily imaginable and they are acquired at an early age (Whaley 1978). Word frequency also correlates positively with many lexical attributes that have been quantified from corpora, such as orthographic neighbourhood density, syntactic family size, noun–verb ratio and number of meanings (Baayen 2010; Balota et al. 2012). A key confound of frequency is environmental: high-frequency words are not only experienced more often, they are also likely to have been experienced more recently (Scarborough, Cortese and Scarborough 1977) and in a greater variety of contexts (Dennis and Humphreys 2001). Words that are spread more evenly across contexts behave differently from those that cluster more densely (Church and Gale 1995), and these differences appear to have important consequences for processing. Using graphical modelling, Baayen, Milin and Ramscar (2016) dissect the role of frequency in lexical processing, aiming to disentangle the set of highly collinear predictors it is part of. They concluded that frequency of occurrence is not a primal causal factor for reading latencies in lexical decision tasks. Frequency appears to be shaped by meaning, constraints of production effort (as captured by word length) and word co-occurrence.

Researchers have long suspected that these correlated factors, rather than the extent to which people have been exposed to words, may contribute to the processing advantage found. Over the past fifteen years, evidence has accumulated that factors which are highly correlated with repetition frequency are more strongly correlated with behavioural outcomes than repetition frequency itself. One of these factors is the typical context of occurrence of words. Recall from Chapter 1 that the discovery of the powerful effect of context (McDonald and Shillcock 2001; Adelman, Brown and Quesada 2006; Brysbaert and New 2009) emerged from data-mining large corpora to extract frequency counts and other values associated with words. Because many words are part of multiword utterances, researchers sought to understand how much of lexical learning is contextual in nature. McDonald and Shillcock (2001) used relative entropy to measure the amount of information a word conveys about its context (its contextual distinctiveness), while Adelman, Brown and Quesada (2006) used the number of passages or documents in which a word occurred (its contextual diversity). Even when operationalizing context in this very crude way, contextual diversity predicted more variance in lexical decision and naming latencies than did repetition frequency, suggesting that contextual diversity is the psychologically more relevant variable. Yet, these results are not always replicated: Heister and Kliegl (2012) found that contextual diversity does not explain more variance than type frequency for a range of German corpora.

More recently Jones, Johns and Recchia (2012) have claimed that what really facilitates lexical processing is semantic diversity. Improving on Adelman, Brown and Quesada (2006), they counted the number of distinct documents in which a word occurred but defined the similarity of any pair of documents as a function of the proportion of overlapping words in those two documents. This continuous measure scores a word that has appeared in multiple semantically distinct contexts more highly than one that has occurred in more redundant contexts, even when the two are balanced on both document and frequency counts. A word's occurrence is weighted relative to the information overlap between the current context and the previous contexts in which it has occurred. A word's semantic distinctiveness was defined as the mean dissimilarity over all of the documents in which it occurred. This makes the measure dynamic: the value for a specific document depends on how much new information it contributes about the word beyond what has previously been encountered (Johns, Dye and Jones 2016: 1215). When used to predict lexical decision and naming times from the Balota et al. (2007) English lexicon database, the *semantic distinctiveness count* predicted more variance in response times than word frequency and contextual diversity. Jones, Johns and Recchia (2012) found that occurrence in more semantically variable contexts has limited effect for the processing of low frequency words. This is because frequency is a necessary condition for variability to exist: compared to their high-frequency counterparts, lower-frequency words have a more limited event history, and hence are less likely to have been sampled as broadly. The semantic distinctiveness count was empirically validated with an artificial language experiment. Johns, Dye and Jones (2016) followed their experiment up with a natural language-learning paradigm to examine the semantic representations that are acquired as semantic diversity is varied. Subjects were incidentally exposed to novel words as they rated short selections from articles, books and newspapers. When novel words were encountered across highly distinctive discourse contexts, subjects were both faster and more accurate at recognizing them than when they were seen in similar, i.e., redundant, contexts. However, learning across redundant contexts promoted the development of more stable semantic representations.

To determine how increased usage itself may be responsible for frequency effects, studies have been carried out with people who could reasonably be expected to have different usage histories. One method has been to compare the lexical processing by persons from different occupations or social groups. In a lexical decision study using nurses, law students and engineers, each group responded more quickly to words relevant to their area of expertise (Gardner et al. 1987). This finding at the word level was replicated for phrases: religious Jews have faster processing of religious phrases than secular Jews (Caldwell-Harris, Berant and Edelman 2012). These findings establish that at least part of the frequency effect is in fact due to language users' actual experience with those words and phrases, but it is not the whole story.

5.5   Summary and Outlook

The notion of entrenchment is frequently invoked in linguistic research, but the concept remains vague. What it means for something to be represented in the mind remains undecided and the process of entrenchment has been defined in various ways. Although the characterizations share the belief that entrenchment refers to a process of strengthening memory representations, there is disagreement as to how this would happen and what the end result would be.

Langacker (1987) used the term entrenchment to explain how linguistic structures are created and shaped through usage. This idea has taken firm root in usage-based linguistic theory where it is loosely understood as capturing the fact that repeatedly encountered linguistic patterns become progressively encoded in memory. It is based on the observation that repeated exposure to or use of a pattern strengthens its representation in memory, making it easier to access and process. Within cognitive linguistics, entrenchment may result in a general reduction in processing effort or automatization, in Gestalt formation or 'unitization' (Langacker 1987) or in chunking accompanied by formal reduction or 'fusion' (Bybee 1985).

The frequency of a unit's occurrence, as estimated on the basis of corpus data, has been linked to that unit's entrenchment in memory. Various types of frequencies, from raw frequency to conditional probabilities and dispersion, have been used to capture entrenchment. Recently, linguists have started to explore which frequency measure or family of measures would be best suited to predict entrenchment. Some suggest that different frequency measures relate to different ways of understanding entrenchment, while others question the validity of interpreting frequency effects as an indication of entrenchment and storage in memory altogether. It remains, indeed, unclear how frequencies would be counted by the cognitive system and how many exposures are required for items to become entrenched. Some linguists set arbitrary frequency thresholds but evidence that such thresholds exist is limited. It has been suggested that each instance of an item is recorded in memory and frequency effects kick in when sufficient information has accumulated.

The assumption that entrenchment of linguistic units results from stimulus repetition alone has been challenged too. Entrenchment of mental representations can also result from single exposure, e.g., when associated with strong emotions. Repetition alone does not ensure entrenchment; spaced exposure in separated contexts leads to more enduring learning than massed exposure even if the number of repetitions is held constant. Furthermore, the processing advantage found for frequent words may result from factors correlated with frequency, not frequency itself. Among the most powerful factors correlated with frequency are contextual and semantic diversity. A word's context of occurrence predicts more variance in data than frequency alone. And the salience and relevance of a stimulus for learners' goals may be more important than frequency per se. We will explore in the next two chapters to what extent language uptake and use are affected by attention (or the lack of it) and whether all dimensions of language (traditionally termed phonology, morphology, syntax and semantics) are equally affected.

In other words, although important, frequency is not the be all and end all in memory, and it should therefore not be the be all and end all in linguistics either. Moreover, repetition frequency quantifies only part of the input, i.e., positive evidence, but it is important to quantify negative evidence as well to account more fully for learning. Linguists have tentatively dealt with this using negative entrenchment, which we encountered in Chapter 2. We will see in Chapter 9 that theories of learning propose principled solutions for incorporating negative evidence.

Part III

6   The Brain's Attention-Orienting Mechanisms

In the previous chapters we have discussed how frequency of occurrence is one of the most reliable predictors of human behaviour, including producing and comprehending language. It comes as no surprise then that frequency of occurrence and co-occurrence has played a crucial role in the development of usage-based linguistics, which grounds language knowledge in exposure to usage. But the chapter on memory concluded by stating that frequency is not the be-all and end-all for language:

> Exemplar models are not sensitive to frequencies of ambient events per se, but rather to frequencies of memories. In between physical experience and memory lies a process of attention, recognition, and coding which is not crudely reflective of frequency. (Pierrehumbert 2006: 525)

In other words, counting frequency of occurrence (however sophisticated the measure) may only very crudely reflect a generalized (average) environment, at best; it may not capture the actual uptake, let alone the actual uptake by any individual speaker. One important factor that influences potential uptake is attention:

> Clusters of exemplars do not reflect undifferentiated raw experience, but rather experience as it has been encoded and stored. The role of differential attention in coding and memory is well-documented in psychology, and attention is not a simple function of frequency. In the widely used preferential looking paradigm for infants, the infants appear to pay the most attention (as indexed by eye fixations) to events which are right at the edge of the learning envelope; neither so familiar that they are boring, nor so novel that they cannot be coded and assimilated (Jusczyk 2000). More generally, it appears that people are adapted to events that are most informative. Events that are attended to are in turn more likely to be remembered. (Pierrehumbert 2006: 525)

Psychologists have argued that attention, not repetition frequency, determines which information is encoded in memory. The reasoning behind this is that information needs to be attended to before frequency can do its work; if information is not attended to, it may not be registered and encoded at all. And attention tends to be paid to items that are 'just right' in terms of information richness, not the most frequent ones, and not the rarest ones. But what is 'just right'? What captures our attention? In fact, what is attention?

This deceptively simple question taps into a massive body of research. The recently published *Oxford Handbook of Attention* (Nobre and Kastner 2014b) provides a thorough overview of the major research questions pursued within the domain of attention studies. Surprisingly, not a single chapter in the 1264-page handbook is devoted to the interaction between attention and language. Although much experimental work on attention relies on language, there is a dearth of research on attention that focuses on language, with the notable exception of Mishra (2015) and Mishra, Srinivasan and Huettig (2015). This compartmentalisation is in no small part due to the modular approach to cognition proposed by Fodor (1983), which justified a strict separation of cognitive capacities.

6.1   Grasping the Phenomenon: What Is Attention and What Does It Do?

Attention is an important modulator of cognition, and the relationship between attention and language is intricate. To understand how attention is deployed in language and how it affects the selection of linguistic elements, knowledge about event perception and representation is a sine qua non. The selective nature of visual attention is crucial for language use: speakers need to select the entities they want to communicate and choose between competing words and syntactic constructions (Bock and Ferreira 2014; Langacker 2015). Yet, the necessity of attention for the development of language runs deeper: there is developmental and neurological evidence showing that attention and language are intimately linked.

Many critical insights into the relation between language and attention stem from studies of language development and use in those affected by cognitive disorders (Mishra 2015: 75): if attention is key to language development, then its impairment can cause delays in linguistic development. The importance of attentional control for language development suggests a strong link between the distribution of attention over the environment and the organization of language used to talk about the environment. Establishing the attention–language interface is a prerequisite for developing more complex mappings from event semantics to syntactic structure. A crucial link in this process is the development of joint attention. Joint attention refers to a state where child and caregiver both attend to the same thing and are aware that they are doing so. Scaife and Bruner (1975) were the first to map this ability in infants under the age of one. It has since been suspected that joint attention between child and caregiver plays a crucial role in language development because it promotes linking words and sentences with objects and events (Bruner 1978; for a first review see Baldwin 1995). The joint attentional state makes it easier for the child to infer what the caregiver is talking about, and hence to pick up new words. Initially, this ability is fragile and word learning is most successful when the caregiver scaffolds learning by talking about things the child is already attending to. At around eighteen months children become more able to monitor the caregiver's eye gaze and use this new ability to infer what their caregivers are talking about (Matthews and Krajewski 2015: 392). This might well explain why word learning receives a boost at around that same age. In the domain of segmentation, prosody imposes an intonational phrase structure on the sound stream, and the edges of these units are a critical factor in learning sequential structure (Shukla, Nespor and Mehler 2007; Shukla et al. 2012). At an analytical, grammatical (rather than lexical) linguistic level, Perruchet and Poulin-Charronnat (2012) argue that associations between elements will only be learned if they are held within the same attentional chunk; associations between elements that straddle an intonational phrase boundary, for example, are not learned.

But what is attention? Research into attention started with the definition of attention provided by William James (1890: 404):

Everyone knows what attention is. It is the taking possession by the mind, in clear and vivid form, of one out of what seem several simultaneous possible objects or trains of thought. Focalization, concentration, of consciousness are of its essence. It implies withdrawal from some things in order to deal effectively with others . . .

Contemporary definitions of attention echo James' original definition and, at their core, consider attention as 'the prioritization of processing information that is relevant to current task goals' (Nobre and Kastner 2014a: 1204). Yet, Nobre and Kastner (2014a: 1206) admit that the field has not provided an explicit and consistent definition of its object of study: the term 'attention' is often used in a vague manner and many definitions exist alongside each other and are used inconsistently. Many other core concepts, including those that are relevant for linguistics, such as automaticity, salience, top-down and bottom-up processes suffer from the same definitional indeterminacy, making it extremely challenging to understand and compare findings.

To this day, attention researchers typically define attention as the selection of information (Wu 2014: 14–16). The most influential definition of attention presents attention as selective focusing on some aspects of the environment. Because attentional capacity is limited and the input to the perceptual system is too rich for processing, information selection is essential. Broadbent (1958), inspired by communication theory from the 1950s, proposed to use the technical language and mathematical precision of information theory to characterize information processes that are capacity-constrained and can only handle a limited amount of information at a time. Although the methodological side of this proposal did not become embedded in psychology, capacity limits are typically appealed to in order to explain why the introduction of a theoretical construct like attention would be necessary: selective attention is key to acquiring robust information from the environment.

Attention comprises several processes such as remaining focused, ignoring irrelevant distractors and monitoring the ongoing activities for better performance (Mishra 2015: 25). This selection of a subset of information can occur in the interest of further processing (attention for perception) or in the interest of action (attention for action).

[...] the amount of information coming down the optic nerve – estimated to be on the order of 10^8 bits per second – far exceeds what the brain is capable of fully processing and assimilating into conscious experience. The strategy nature has devised for dealing with this bottleneck is to select certain portions of the input to be processed preferentially, shifting the processing focus from one location to another in a serial fashion. Despite the widely shared belief in the general public that 'we see everything around us', only a small fraction of the information registered by the visual system at any given time reaches levels of processing that directly influence behaviour. This is vividly demonstrated by change blindness (Simons and Levin 1997; O'Regan, Rensink and Clark 1999) in which significant image changes remain nearly invisible under natural viewing conditions, although observers demonstrate no difficulty in perceiving these changes once directed to them. Overt and covert attention controls access to these privileged levels and ensures that the selected information is relevant to behavioural priorities and objectives. Operationally, information can be said to be 'attended' if it enters short-term memory and remains there long enough to be voluntarily reported. Thus, visual attention is closely linked to visual awareness (Crick and Koch 1998). (Itti and Koch 2000: 1489)

Bottlenecks in the information processing stream have always been assumed to exist and the search for their nature and locus has fuelled much research in the field of attention. After a brief historical excursion into early work on the role of attention in auditory (Section 6.1.1) and visual (Section 6.1.2) perception, Section 6.2 discusses two main ways of deploying attention that have been relevant for research on language production and comprehension. How stimuli become goals and how our attentional mechanisms select them for attention remains debated; one of the most widely spread hypotheses (which has also made it into linguistics) proposes that selection happens through competition as a result of the interaction between top-down and bottom-up factors. In Section 6.3, finally, we integrate findings from research on attention with what we know about memory and language.

6.1.1   Attention and Auditory Perception

Attention can be seen as a type of selection, i.e., filtering, that occurs at a specific moment in perceptual processing to handle capacity limitations

(Wu 2014: 19). The selective attention account provided the background for the first major debate in the study of attention, i.e., at what point in perceptual information processing (early or late?) does attentional selection occur? Serences and Kastner (2014) provide an extensive overview of research into selective attention.

Early research on auditory language processing had demonstrated the existence of a processing capacity limit. Using a dichotic listening paradigm during which different information is presented to each ear, Cherry (1953) – and later others – showed that subjects attend to only one stream at a time although they could perceive abrupt changes in lower-level physical properties in the other information stream. Higher-level properties such as semantics were typically not registered, although some material would be noticed, such as the subject's name (Moray 1959). This led Treisman (1960) to hypothesize that information from the non-attended channel is not blocked but attenuated, and possibly only filtered out at later processing stages. This would mean that all information is available to perception, but not necessarily processed. The question therefore became whether selection in perceptual processing occurs early (Broadbent 1958) or late (Deutsch and Deutsch 1963).

However, there appears to be quite a bit of flexibility in prioritizing relevant information. Another important finding, and one that led away from the early versus late selection debate, was that the nature of the experimental task seems to affect when attention is deployed. Kahneman and Treisman (1984) discovered a strong parallel between empirical evidence for early versus late selection and experimental tasks in which perceptual information streams competed strongly with each other (Cherry 1953). If perceptual information does not compete strongly, this effect is not present. An example of a task where competition is weak is the Stroop task (Stroop 1935). Words for colours are printed in a non-matching colour, e.g., the word green is printed in blue, and participants are asked to name the colour (i.e., blue), and ignore the printed word (i.e., green). They concluded that bottlenecks might reflect points of competition and therefore move with task demands.

Lavie and Tsal (1994) later proposed that all processing resources are standardly put to use but may not be needed: if the information channel attended to does not exhaust all resources, some resources can be redirected to the unattended channel. This has become known as the load theory of attention (Lavie 2005; Lavie and Dalton 2014), and it explains differences that were initially ascribed to early versus late processing: early selection effects are observed in situations where perceptual load is high and consumes all available processing, while late selection effects are seen when perceptual load is lower, leaving resources available for processing unattended channels. Under low perceptual load conditions, it is necessary to draw on executive control functions to maintain processing priorities. Recent evidence from neuroimaging and electrophysiological studies confirms that attention deployment is neither late nor early; instead, deployment depends on the demands the subject's behavioural goals place on the processing machinery (Serences and Kastner 2014: 97).

6.1.2   Attention and Visual Perception

While early experimental paradigms in the 1950s relied on auditory tasks and verbal shadowing tasks in particular, in the 1960s interest shifted towards visual paradigms. Two different types of visual attention can be distinguished; these are known as pop-out search and serial search. An item can pop out because it stands out along one dimension (e.g., a red apple in a box of green apples) of the many that are accessed during initial parallel processing. Or, it can be discovered because attention is deployed serially, and focused on one object at the time. A comparable finding results from work using the spatial cueing paradigm developed by Michael Posner (1980) with which the existence of overt versus covert attention was investigated. While overt attention requires conscious eye movements that direct and focus the eye on a target, covert attention does not. Posner's spatial cueing paradigm has inspired research on language and attention, which we will discuss in Chapter 7.

In the area of visual attention, Treisman and Gelade (1980) proposed a feature integration theory (FIT), which has been modified many times since. The basic assumptions of FIT are as follows: each scene is initially coded along a number of basic visual dimensions such as colour, brightness, shape and motion, that are then bound together to ensure the correct synthesis of features for each object. On this approach, attention is viewed as the *outcome* of processing: serial processing with focal attention can be seen as 'binding' visual features together into objects. The binding problem is the problem of combining information from many different sources – the constructivist view of perception is that we form hypotheses about the most likely interpretation of the available information, and these hypotheses act top-down to construct what we 'see' (Styles 2005: 5–6, 71, 87–93). In this tradition, attention is seen as selection for object representation, and from there for conscious awareness of objects (Wu 2014: 23).

Feature integration theory thus treats visual attention as the glue that binds the separable properties of objects together. The underlying assumption is that sensory properties such as colour, orientation and size are encoded automatically and put onto the corresponding feature maps, in parallel and without the need for focal attention. These features are then combined, and this can happen in three different ways: either the features fit into object frames that have been predicted using stored knowledge; or, focal attention selects a location on the map that represents where all features are located (but does not know *which* features are where) and the active features can be compared to objects stored in long-term visual memory for recognition; or, features can conjoin on their own (often resulting in illusions). So, features are coded pre-attentively in parallel over the visual display, and it is the conjunction of features that requires serial search with focal attention.

There are many theories that compete with FIT. Attentional engagement theory (Duncan and Humphreys 1989, 1992) proposes that selection by visual attention is not spatially based but perception- or object-based. Search efficiency relies on similarity as the grouping factor: how easily do targets and distractors fall into separate perceptual groups (compare here the Gestalt principle we discussed briefly in Chapter 5), making it easier or harder to reject them as irrelevant. Guided search theory (Wolfe, Cave and Franzel 1989) relies on both space and perceptual grouping to explain visual attention search. Without going further into detail, it is clear that much disagreement remains about what attention is and does, making it hard for researchers from neighbouring disciplines to build on the findings.

6.2   Ways of Deploying Attention

Since James (1890) shifts of attention are known to have different possible origins. Wu (2014: 29–38) discusses five different divisions or functions of attention, i.e., (1) top-down versus bottom-up attention, (2) endogenous (to the perceiver) versus exogenous attention, (3) goal-directed versus stimulus-driven attention, (4) controlled versus automatic attention and (5) voluntary versus involuntary (or automatic) attention. There are two central dichotomies, i.e., bottom-up versus top-down attention, which is tied to how attention comes about (stimulus-driven or not), and controlled versus automatic attention, which is linked to the features of attention (involving intention or not) (Wu 2014: 34). Understanding the contribution that each of these types of attention makes to behaviour and finding out how they overlap and interact remains of interest to researchers in the field (Nobre and Kastner 2014a: 1208). Within linguistics, the bottom-up versus top-down distinction is the one that has found application, in particular in relation to the discussion on salience, and we will focus on that opposition in the next section. Psycholinguists, on the other hand, have focused on the workings of automatic versus voluntary attention. This opposition is discussed in Section 6.2.2.

6.2.1   Attention: Bottom-Up or Top-Down?

How is the selection of one particular item accomplished? Research in visual cognition has focused on pinning down factors that drive attention (Mackworth and Morandi 1967; Loftus and Mackworth 1978). The assumption is that there are two different ways of deploying attention (see Itti and Koch 2000 for a review) and behavioural evidence has accumulated in favour of a two-component framework. There would be a bottom-up, fast, primitive mechanism that biases the observer towards selecting stimuli based on stimulus salience. This bottom-up mechanism is complemented with a second slower, top-down mechanism with variable selection criteria, which directs the 'spotlight of attention' based on goals and tasks under cognitive, volitional control. Note that there is some evidence to suggest that this bottom-up versus top-down distinction, which was defined at the behavioural level, does not seem to be supported at the neurological level (Wu 2014: 27).

When we speak of bottom-up attentional control we mean attentional control that is driven by factors external to the observer, such as stimulus salience (e.g., pop-out stimuli that contrast strongly with surrounding items based on a simple feature value). These are typically 'early' features of the visual stimulus, such as colour, intensity and orientation, which are claimed to drive pre-attentive selection. The basic mechanism can be strongly influenced top-down. Behaviourally, this is manifested by the ability to *guide search* more efficiently towards visual targets if their appearance is known in advance, and to ignore irrelevant distractors more efficiently. Top-down attentional control is driven by factors that are 'internal' to the observer, such as current goals, task relevance and rewards.

Both modes of attention can operate at the same time and visual stimuli have two ways of penetrating to higher levels of awareness: they can wilfully be brought into the focus of attention, or they can win the competition for saliency. Awh, Belopolsky and Theeuwes (2012) remarked that in the opposition between bottom-up and top-down salience, the former is determined by physical salience and the latter by current selection goals, but this leaves out the effect of selection history:

The key problem we highlight with this construct is that grouping together control signals that are 'internal' (i.e., unrelated to stimulus salience) conflates the effects of current selection goals and selection history (i.e., priming). Because current goals and selection history may generate conflicting selection biases, we argue that they should be viewed as distinct categories of control.

Although these (three) effects could in principle operate in a coordinated fashion, various studies have demonstrated that they can also work in direct opposition to one another. This suggests that they are distinct sources of selection bias (Awh, Belopolsky and Theeuwes 2012: 441).

How does attention operate when we view real-life scenes? What guides visual search in the real world? Core questions here relate to attention deployment in real-life scene perception, and opinions diverge. Itti, Koch and Niebur (1998) showed support for the bottom-up view, i.e., that scene saliency attracts eye movements. Henderson (2003) defends the top-down view that the cognitive goals of the perceiver guide scene perception: depending on what information you are looking for, you will look around the scene in a particular manner. Top-down processes can also refer to predictive processes that, for example, allow readers to anticipate what is coming, depending on their background knowledge and reading fluency (Mishra 2015: 244). Mishra et al. (2012) found that, in high literates, visual objects and linguistic forms are activated simultaneously, which explains how language input can drive attentional mechanisms towards matching visual objects automatically.

What neural activity is observed when we pay attention? As we have seen in Chapter 4, when neurons are stimulated (neurons in the visual areas will be stimulated by light or colour), they will generate spikes at a specific firing rate to carry information about the signal (Chelazzi et al. 1993). As in much brain research, in investigating the source of attention control, the focus has shifted from individual brain areas to large-scale networks. Studies of the contributions made by individual brain areas are supplemented by investigations of how information across different network regions is coordinated and integrated. As mentioned above, there is recent evidence to suggest that the simple binary bottom-up versus top-down distinction may not be supported at the neurological level (Wu 2014: 27). Corbetta and Shulman (2002: 201–2) used imaging work to propose the following:

Visual attention is controlled by two partially segregated neural systems. One system, which is centered on the dorsal posterior parietal and frontal cortex, is involved in the cognitive selection of sensory information and responses. The second system, which is largely lateralized to the right hemisphere and is centered on the temporoparietal and ventral frontal cortex, is recruited during the detection of behaviourally relevant sensory events, particularly when they are salient and unattended.

Although things may turn out to be more complex, linguists have nevertheless used the tension between bottom-up and top-down attention productively to determine the salience of an item. We will discuss salience in linguistics in more detail in Chapter 7, Section 7.2.2.

6.2.2 *Attention: Automatic or Voluntary?*

Can linguistic processes take place without deliberate effort? If so, which processes require voluntary control, and which ones are automatic? The majority of psycholinguistic studies examining whether sentence processing is automatic or voluntary look at attention as a limited resource. We appear to activate knowledge automatically upon hearing words (Salverda and Altmann 2011); but what about syntax and semantics? There is evidence that these two aspects of comprehension are affected differently: selective attention to different aspects of a sentence modulates brain networks differently (Rogalsky and Hickok 2009).

Using an ERP paradigm, Gunter and Friederici (1999) manipulated attention selectively and found by analysing N400 (a negative deflection in the EEG signal that peaks around 400 milliseconds after the onset of the stimulus) and P600 (a positive deflection in the EEG signal that peaks around 600 milliseconds after the onset of the stimulus) that attention capture by external stimuli, i.e., exogenous attention, affects syntax and semantics differently. Hahne and Friederici (1999), using the same ERP paradigm, specified on the basis of the ELAN effect (early left anterior negativity, a negative deflection in the EEG signal that peaks around 200 milliseconds after the onset of the stimulus) that attentional manipulation had little to no effect on early syntactic processing, which could therefore be considered automatic. Hahne and Friederici's (2002) study added that sentences with structural violations were never analysed semantically. In other words, we process syntax automatically, but proper semantic processing would require voluntary attention (Friederici 2011). Interestingly, Hahne and Friederici (1999) also found that participants selectively attended to infrequently presented information, yet the manipulation of trial proportions in their set-up was later criticized (Steinhauer and Drury 2012) for not guaranteeing that attentional processes themselves were manipulated; this leaves the findings susceptible to doubt.

Researchers have also studied language processing while engaging attention in some other modality. They did so by analysing the mismatch negativity (MMN) effect from an ERP signature: the MMN is automatically generated when a deviant stimulus is detected. Pulvermüller et al. (2008) let subjects listen to (un)grammatical sentences in the right ear, while playing tones varying in intensity in the left ear; at the same time, the participants watched a silent video film of their choice. Critically, the tones heard in the left ear overlapped with elements that made the sentence played in the right ear (un)grammatical; for example, the tone overlapped with the –s of both grammatical *he comes* and ungrammatical *we comes*. No evidence was found of syntactic processing being affected by exogenous cues demanding attention; this, too, was taken as an indication of early and automatic processing of syntax.

Dual task conditions have also been used to investigate whether sentence processing might rely on central executive resources instead, such as working memory (Caplan and Waters 1999). Attention is sometimes considered the executive control component of working memory (Barrouillet et al. 2007) or controlled attention (Engle et al. 1999), and keeping something in working memory is assumed to be equivalent to attending to it. Waters, Caplan and Yampolsky (2003) asked university students to listen to syntactically simple and complex sentences under increasing working memory load, i.e., they had to judge sentences while performing a digit span task. Although the digit span task affected sentence processing, it did so regardless of complexity. Gordon, Hendrick and Levine (2002) conducted a similar experiment, but asked subjects to remember a list of nouns instead of a string of digits. The linguistic items in working memory caused interference with complex sentence processing, especially if the words that had to be held in memory were similar to those used in the sentence. Yet, evidence from neuropsychological work with Parkinson's patients suggests that it is executive control mechanisms, rather than attention specifically, that are responsible for and play a critical role in language processing (Lee et al. 2003).

In the area of production (for a detailed overview see Mishra 2015, chapter 5), it was long believed that attention was automatic, but more recent research shows that selective attention may be at work here too. Data from naming tasks documents the existence of what has been termed 'spreading activation': a picture or word seems to activate several related concepts as a norm (and more if there are many phonological and/or semantic competitors, see Kan and Thompson-Schill 2004). This would mean that executive control is needed to select the correct response. Picture naming latencies show some delay, indeed, which has been considered the result of this competition (Bock and Levelt 2002). This interpretation fits with a serial view of name generation: name generation involves a series of incremental steps, i.e., visual perception, lemma retrieval (including semantic and syntactic properties) and phonological form retrieval (Indefrey and Levelt 2004). On such a serial account of language production, semantic and phonological interference would be observed at two different stages in processing (Mishra 2015: 106). This is precisely what Schriefers, Meyer and Levelt (1990) found: semantic facilitation was observed within 150 milliseconds, and phonological facilitation after 150 milliseconds. WEAVER++ ('*w*ord *e*ncoding by *a*ctivation and *ver*ification') is a computational model designed to explain how humans plan the production of spoken words, and it assigns a role to attention in this process (Roelofs 1997). The model aims to make explicit how language users 'weave' together the many dimensions of declarative knowledge ('knowing that') and procedural knowledge ('knowing how') while producing spoken words. It also makes it possible to examine how word production tasks differ in the dimensions they weave together and how they achieve this.

Yet, there are alternative proposals, and these run on an interactive architecture and parallel processing, such as the interactive two-stage model proposed by Dell et al. (1997). In these models, different properties (such as phonological and lexical properties) can influence each other: phonological information is activated in a cascaded fashion and during phonological processing, feedback connections are active and lead back to the lexical level.

Dell (1986) already contained evidence supporting this position: conceptualization processes influence articulation, and articulatory features affect conceptualization.

Although both parallel and incremental theories would predict a different role for attention, on either account central attention is required for naming pictures, i.e., for generating words. Data from dual tasks suggests that the ability to name visually presented pictures is affected by concurrent linguistic tasks (Mishra, Srinivasan and Huettig 2015: 115). Even if syntactic processing would be automatic (semantic processing is not), this does not mean that attention would not be required for syntactic computation in production (Mishra, Srinivasan and Huettig 2015: 238–9): at the very least, some form of top-down control from cognitive goals is necessary to ensure that sentences adequately capture an event or situation and communication is successful.

6.2.3   Attention in Language: from Object Recognition to Scene Perception

By extension from object recognition, attention is crucial in scene perception, and work on language has looked at scene perception. Hintz and Huettig (2015: 42) summarize that when we simultaneously process spoken language and visual input, representations from either modality can match phonologically, semantically and visually. The listener's fixation behaviour during a language-mediated visual search, as recorded in eye-tracking experiments, seems to be determined by a tug of war between all these types of word knowledge. The exact level of representation at which word–object mapping takes place appears to be determined by the timing of processing in both the language and the visual processing system, the temporal unfolding of the speech signal and the nature of the visual environment. We will discuss each of these areas in turn below.

The visual world paradigm is often used for the investigation of language–vision interaction (Cooper 1974; Tanenhaus et al. 1995; see Huettig, Rommers and Meyer 2011, for a review). In the visual world paradigm participants hear spoken language while they look at a visual scene related to the spoken utterance. Participants' eye movements are recorded for analysis. A special issue of *Acta Psychologica* (volume 137, issue 2, June 2011) provides an extensive overview of the literature on 'Visual search and visual world: Interactions among visual attention, language, and working memory' while Knoeferle, Pyykkönen-Klauck and Crocker (2016) contains a comprehensive collection of reviews of visually situated language comprehension research using the visual world paradigm. For an account of individual differences with respect to visual perception and language comprehension, see Knoeferle (2015).

Allopenna, Magnuson and Tanenhaus (1998) showed that word–object mapping may occur at the phonological level of representation. The participants in their study looked at computer displays showing, for example, the pictures of a beaker (the target object), a beetle (the phonological onset competitor), a speaker (the phonological rhyme competitor) and a carriage (the unrelated distractor), while hearing the spoken instruction, 'Pick up the beaker.' The participants were more likely to fixate both the image of the beaker and the image of the beetle while the initial phonemes of the word 'beaker' were pronounced. After the first syllable, when the acoustic information of 'beaker' stopped matching 'beetle', the likelihood of looks to the 'beetle' decreased. Towards the end of the word 'beaker', when it resembles 'speaker', looks to the picture of a 'speaker' started to increase in frequency instead.

In the absence of phonological relationships between the spoken words and the visual objects, word–object mapping can also take place at a semantic-conceptual level of representation. Huettig and Altmann (2005), among others, found that the semantic properties of words can direct eye gaze towards objects in the visual field in the absence of any associative relationships between targets and competitors. That is, participants direct their visual attention towards a depicted object (e.g., a 'trumpet') when they hear a semantically related but not associatively related target word (e.g., 'piano'), and that the likelihood of fixation was proportional to the degree of conceptual overlap. This means that the more the concepts that are shown and played have in common, the more likely participants were to fixate on the visual object. Huettig et al. (2006) observed that corpus-based measures of word semantics (e.g., latent semantic analysis, Landauer and Dumais 1997) correlated well with such fixation behaviour. Based on those studies, language-mediated eye movements appear as a sensitive indicator of the degree to which the semantic information available in speech and the conceptual knowledge retrieved from the visual objects overlap.

Finally, there is experimental evidence suggesting that word–object mapping occurs at a perceptual level of representation in the absence of phonological and/or semantic mapping. Visual mapping, that is, increased looks to entities that are, for instance, related in visual shape, has been observed when participants were presented with the picture of a cable while listening to the spoken word 'snake'. The likelihood of looks to the picture of the cable increased while the word 'snake' acoustically unfolded (Huettig and Altmann 2004, 2007; Dahan and Tanenhaus 2005).

Huettig and McQueen (2007) concluded that the listener's fixation behaviour during language-mediated visual search reflects the tension between matches at phonological, semantic and visual levels of representation. In four eye-tracking experiments, they presented participants with displays including either four visual objects or the printed word names of the same objects and concurrent spoken sentences including a critical target word (e.g., 'beaker'). The target word was preceded by on average seven words but the sentence preceding the critical word was contextually neutral (i.e., participants could not predict the target word from the sentential context). Three of the four entities in the display were related to the target word: one was related in meaning (e.g., a fork, and unrelated in phonology and visual shape), one was similar in visual shape (e.g., a bobbin, and unrelated in phonology and semantics) and the name of the third object overlapped phonologically in the first syllable with the target (e.g., beaver, and was unrelated in semantics and visual shape).

Unfortunately, the visual world paradigm typically uses impoverished stimuli, that is, a simple image is displayed in each corner of the computer screen. Andersson, Ferreira and Henderson (2011) addressed this issue by presenting participants with real-life photographs of cluttered scenes while playing three-sentence passages that were varied in speech rate. This way, the ecological validity of the experiment was improved. They found that the participants directed their gaze towards objects mentioned in speech even when the speech rate was high. Hintz and Huettig (2015) tested explicitly how the increased complexity of semi-realistic scenes impacts phonological and semantic processing and shapes word–object matching. They showed objects in visually simple and complex environments, and participants were asked to indicate whether the object that was being named was displayed. More complex visual scenes reduced the likelihood of word–object mapping at the phonological level of representation. This may be because enhanced visual complexity boosts visual processing, thereby shifting word–object mapping preferences to the disadvantage of phonological mapping. The expectation is that semantically coherent visual scenes (e.g., a kitchen scene) would boost word–object mapping at a semantic level of representation. The selection of items in crowded images and the inhibition of phonological processing under these circumstances predicts an important role for control mechanisms, and hence attention, in visual search.

6.3   Attention and Memory: Encoding and Retrieving Information

As has become clear in the previous sections, what we know about attention stems mainly from the study of perception, and of visual perception in particular. The relationship between attention and perception is close: attention improves perception. Yet, this relationship is triadic: attention also leads to better memory, another insight that dates back to James (1890). Unfortunately, the behaviourists' focus on the relationship between stimulus and response caused psychologists to abandon research into the relation between attention, perception and memory. Interest in the relation between memory and attention was reinvigorated by connectionist and parallel distributed models.

6.3.1   The Relation between Attention and Working Memory

Despite the fact that attention plays an important role in controlling the activation, maintenance and manipulation of representations in working memory, and that working memory has been thought of as a means of maintaining representations to voluntarily guide perceptual selective attention, working memory and attention have been studied largely in isolation from each other. It was mentioned in Section 6.2.2 that attention can be considered the executive control component of working memory (Barrouillet et al. 2007) or controlled attention (Engle et al. 1999), and keeping something in working memory is assumed to be equivalent to attending to it. Kiyonaga and Egner (2013) propose that, in reality, attention and working memory should not be considered as separate constructs; instead, we should think of them as part of a shared cognitive resource for prioritized processing (this resource has traditionally been called attention) focused on either internal information (traditionally labelled working memory) or external information (traditionally considered selective attention). In other words, working memory and attention may well be competing and impacting on each other because they rely on the same limited resource. The extent to which this resource is dedicated to one domain more than to the other can be influenced by task goals and other internal representations, which determine which external stimuli are selected for processing. Conversely, because working memory and attention domains influence each other, externally selected stimuli can also alter internally maintained representations, including task goals.

The hypothesis that there would be a relation between attention and short-term memory is not new. Both the supervisory attention system in the memory model proposed by Norman and Shallice (1986) and the central executive from the model by Baddeley and Hitch (1974) assign an important role to attention. Baddeley (1993: 168) speculated that the working memory system could or should be considered working attention, as it would be concerned with attention and coordination rather than with storage. Cowan (1988), Fuster (2009) and Oberauer (2009) have also challenged the idea that working memory would be a separate system dedicated to short-term storage and instead contend that attention controls the activation of long-term memory representations for use in the short term. Working memory is thus seen as attention acting on long-term representations. In this conceptualization, a number of long-term representations can be activated in working memory, but only one receives the focus of attention and becomes the subject of current processing. In a similar vein,

Postle (2006) and later also Theeuwes, Belopolsky and Olivers (2009) stated that working memory arises as a result of the recruitment of multiple brain systems by attention.

A number of complementary theoretical frameworks have been proposed to conceptualize the relation between memory and attention. Chun, Golomb and Turk-Browne (2011) argue for a distinction between externally oriented attention (directed to perceptual stimuli in the environment) and internally oriented attention (focused on thoughts and memories). They complement this bifurcation with the insight that memory encoding focuses on the results of externally oriented perceptual attention while memory retrieval represents internally oriented reflective attention. In Knudsen's model (2007), attention reflects the combined contributions of four distinct processes. First, there is working memory, a highly dynamic type of memory that temporarily (i.e., for a few seconds) stores selected information for detailed analysis (Baddeley 2003). Second, there is competitive selection or the process that determines which information gains access to working memory: working memory holds only a limited amount of information and multiple types of information compete for control over the neural circuits subserving working memory at any one time (Desimone and Duncan 1995). Working memory does more than only accept, store and manipulate information; it also improves the quality of the information by modulating the sensitivity of the neural circuits that represent the information. Sensitivity control is a top-down process that regulates the relative signal strengths of the different information channels that compete for access to working memory (Egeth and Yantis 1997). But top-down bias signals are not the only way for information to gain access to working memory: salience filters work bottom-up and automatically enhance responses to stimuli that are infrequent in space or time or are of instinctive or learned biological importance (Koch and Ullman 1985). According to Knudsen (2007), the engagement of these processes leads directly to increased behavioural sensitivity and shortened response latencies (the traditional metrics of attention) as well as to the cognitive benefits that we associate with attention.

6.3.2   The Role of Attention in Encoding and Retrieving Information

Memory is subject to processing constraints and hence requires selection: we cannot attend to every aspect of our experience, we cannot commit all aspects of our experience to memory, and neither can we retrieve all encoded information at the same time. Because of this, we selectively orient our attention. This affects what we later remember. It has been argued that the ways in which we form, retrieve and work with our memories are acts of attention (Chun and Johnson 2011). Framing memory in this way highlights the processing limits inherent to memory and the related need for selection.

Miller (1956) presented evidence that there is a limit on information that can be remembered in the short term. This information needs to be kept active (e.g., by rehearsing) for the memory to be preserved. Broadbent (1971: 325) argued that the need for rehearsal shows the close relation between attention and memory in a limited capacity system: while attention is directed at the material and the material is rehearsed, it remains in conscious awareness. As soon as attention is diverted, the information is lost unless there has been sufficient rehearsal for the information to have been encoded into long-term memory. Once in long-term memory, attention is no longer required to maintain information in conscious awareness. Here we encounter the top-down and bottom-up influences again from the previous section. Bottom-up attention is captured by aspects of our experience that are very salient, and these salient elements bias how attention is allocated and what we remember. Top-down attentional control is essential for encoding relevant information and for preventing the encoding of irrelevant information; our goals determine what properties of an experience we attend to and consequently remember. Top-down attentional control is also important for retrieval. Because the main obstacle to successful retrieval is interference between memories, we need selective attention to retrieve those memories that are goal-relevant (Anderson and Spellman 1995; Chun and Turk-Browne 2007; Chun and Johnson 2011).

While attention to an event is required for later intentional use of memory (explicit memory), attention does not seem necessary for automatic use of memory (implicit memory). Information that remains unattended to tends to be poorly remembered, yet some learning does seem to occur, depending on concurrent task type and task difficulty (Kuhl and Chun 2014: 813–15). Unattended information may or may not influence future perception: there is evidence to suggest that repeated unattended information is learned latently but only influences behaviour when it becomes relevant to the task at hand (Jiang and Leung 2005). This would be a fascinating area of research for linguists to pursue: how much of language do we learn incidentally?

Viewing the encoding and retrieval of memories as acts of attention also allows us to relate the neural mechanisms that support memory and attention (Kuhl and Chun 2014: 806). Encoding factors that promote successful remembering have been elucidated using the subsequent memory paradigm. Research done using EEG or fMRI suggests that relationships between neural encoding response and remembering reflect contributions of attention (Kuhl and Chun 2014: 808–9). The brain regions that show memory effects are partially dependent on how subjects attend to encoded information, i.e., what aspect of the experience they focus on (such as sound versus meaning, Paller and Wagner 2002): variation in neural activity just before an experience predicts memory for that event (Turk-Browne, Yi and Chun 2006; Guderian et al. 2009).

This finding has received support from intracranial recordings of oscillatory power in theta and gamma bands in humans. Brainwaves result from synchronized electrical pulses that emerge when neurons communicate with each other. They are divided into bandwidths to describe their functions, but it needs to be borne in mind that brainwaves reflect different aspects when they occur in different locations in the brain. (Cortical) theta brainwaves are high-amplitude, low-frequency (four to seven cycles per second) that appear during meditative, drowsy, hypnotic or sleeping states (but not during the deepest stages of sleep). Gamma brainwaves are high-frequency waves (typically around 38 to 42 hertz) that have been hypothetically related to neural consciousness via the mechanism for conscious attention. Oscillatory power on theta and gamma wavelengths has been associated with the creation of memories and consciousness respectively (Singer and Gray 1995). It also appears to be positively correlated with probability of subsequent remembering, including remembering linguistic information. Prat et al. (2016) showed that higher beta and gamma power predicted faster second language learning. Beta waves have a frequency between 12.5 and 30 cycles per second and are split into three levels – low beta waves, beta waves and high beta waves; they occur during normal conscious states. Individual quantitative EEG measures extracted from eyes-closed resting-state EEG data, in particular right-hemisphere low beta power, explained 60 per cent of the variability in second language learning. Traditional behavioural indices of fluid intelligence, executive functioning and working memory capacity were not correlated with learning rate. These findings stem from a study involving sixteen monolingual English subjects (twelve of which were female) participating in an eight-week online intensive course of French.

6.3.3   *Memory, Attention and Language*

There are more observations on the relation between memory and attention that are directly relevant to the study of language. Some pertinent findings stem from the study of contextual cueing while other results stem from research on divided attention.

Often, regularities in perceptual experience are learned and this learning biases subsequent attention allocation. A prime example of this is contextual cueing: it is easier to locate an object if it is predictable from its surroundings (Chun and Jiang 1998; Chun 2000). There appear to be two types of context effects: intrinsic and extrinsic ones (Hewitt 1973). While the former refers to properties that are intrinsic to the stimulus at the time of encoding, the latter refers to properties of the environment that were present at the same time as the stimulus but are not part of the stimulus. This insight has been implemented in language models. Johns et al.'s (2014) semantic distinctiveness model (SDM) is a distributional model which incorporates a mechanism to weight the attention that is given to a new entry. This mechanism is activated whenever a new context entry is encoded into a word's semantic vector. More specifically, the model compares a new context to those already contained in the word's semantic vector (i.e., all the previous contexts the word has been encountered in). If the new context is congruent with the expected meaning, the new context is encoded at a weaker intensity than if the new context is surprising. The predictions of the SDM fit with predictive accounts of language processing (see Chapter 8), in which speakers construct expectations about future linguistic input based on current context. Words that are low in contextual variability are supported by consistent contextual cues and can be weighted less strongly in memory, since they will be more predictable in context. Conversely, words that are high in contextual variability should be represented more strongly in the lexicon, since they are less associated with any given context, and thus lack contextual scaffolding. On this view, lexical access is a dynamic process, where both past experience with words and their current context combine to support retrieval. The model was validated with an artificial language experiment (Jones, Johns and Recchia 2012) and with a natural language learning paradigm (Johns, Dye and Jones 2016). Interestingly, this effect is dependent on frequency. High-frequency words were shown to be processed more efficiently when a word occurred in more semantically variable contexts. The reason for this is unlikely to be mere repetition. Rather, frequency is a necessary condition for variability to exist. Compared to their high-frequency counterparts, lower-frequency words have a more limited event history, and hence are less likely to have been sampled as broadly (Johns, Dye and Jones 2016).

Research on divided attention (e.g., caused by distractions or multi-tasking) has shown that episodic encoding is impaired when attention is divided. All tasks involving divided attention appear to have some detrimental effect on word-list retrieval but monitoring words or word-like material (Fernandes and Moscovitch 2002) has a larger distracting effect than card sorting (Baddeley et al. 1984), digit monitoring (Fernandes and Moscovitch 2002) or visuo-spatial tasks (Craik et al. 1996). Divided attention mainly affects the binding of elements: memory for items is less affected than memory for associations between items (Castel and Craik 2003). Furthermore, divided attention affects explicit memory, leaving implicit memory virtually unaffected (Mulligan 1997, 1998; Wolters and Prinsen 1997). These findings highlight the differences in attentional demands associated with various types of memory encoding and the differential effect they will have on memory for language.

If divided attention leaves implicit memory unaffected, divided attention tasks can be used as diagnostic for determining the more habitual aspects of language. Given that attention to language is often divided – we rarely produce or comprehend language without doing something else concurrently – those aspects of language that can be freely produced or comprehended while another task is being performed are likely handled by the implicit memory system. This predicts differences in performance depending on whether the linguistic knowledge involved requires more or less or no attention.

6.4   Summary and Outlook

The term 'attention' is typically used in a vague manner, including within psychology, where it originated. There are many definitions of what attention would be or could capture, and they are used inconsistently. There appear to be four major theoretical positions from which to view attention (see De Pisapia, Repovš and Braver 2008: 423): (1) attention filters the information stream to make it possible for our limited processing capacities to meet the computational demands (Broadbent 1958); (2) attention solves the binding problem, i.e., focusing on a limited set of features facilitates binding features correctly into higher level object representations (Treisman and Gelade 1980); (3) attention selects those aspects of the environment that will enable efficient and optimized processing and behaviour (van Der Heijden and Bem 1997); and (4) (which we did not discuss) attention is an emergent phenomenon of neural mechanisms, i.e., attention is seen as activation dynamics that arise in systems where inhibitory competition and constraint satisfaction are ubiquitous network components (Desimone and Duncan 1995; Duncan 1996). In research on language, attention tends to be seen as a filter on sensory experiences that selects relevant information for preferential processing.

Attention is important for linguists because some have argued that attention, not repetition frequency, determines which information is encoded in memory. Attention plays a role for language in at least three respects. First, there is developmental and neurological evidence that attention and language are intimately linked. Attention may well be crucial for language development as it promotes linking words and sentences with objects and events. Through joint attention, a child infers what the caregiver is referring to and picks up new words and structures. Secondly, although all encountered information is available to perception, not all information can be processed due to capacity limits. Thanks to attention, relevant information is selected from the environment and processed or used for further action. To capture a visually complex situation in words, speakers need to attend to one or more components of that situation. Regularities in perceptual experience bias subsequent attention allocation: predictable contexts make objects easier to locate. Attention thus influences perception and conceptualisation, affecting the encoding of conceptual structure into language. Thirdly, attention does not appear to be necessary for the encoding of all types of memories: whereas explicit memories do require conscious attention during encoding, implicit memories do not. Due to this difference, frequencies of occurrence might be more reliable predictors of encoding and encoding strength for some types of linguistic knowledge than for others.

It has been argued that items that are 'right' in terms of information richness, not the most or least frequent ones, tend to attract attention. Linguists use the term 'salience' to describe the way in which attention captures items in the environment. Like attention, the term 'salience' is characterized by a high level of terminological inconsistency. Some argue that an item's salience is affected by frequency of occurrence while others link salience to context of occurrence. Moreover, attention to a particular aspect of a situation can be the result of the speaker's own goals and expectations or of the referent's physical properties. We will see in the next chapter how attention is deployed during scene perception and we will learn that languages have mechanisms to increase or decrease the salience of an expression's parts, reference or context. This enables speakers to use linguistic devices to guide the hearer's attention in a desirable way.

7 Salience: Capturing Attention in and through Language

Attention tends to be paid to items that are 'just right' in terms of information richness, not the most frequent ones, and not the rarest ones. But what is 'just right'? What captures our attention? As explained in the previous chapter, attention can be attracted by stimulus properties (such as loudness or brightness) or by the organism's goals (e.g., stimuli that signal events of biological significance, which aids survival). For example, Mackintosh (1975) claims that organisms will pay attention to, and hence readily learn about, stimuli that are good predictors of important events (such as food or pain). Thus, stimuli with high associative strength, in particular stimuli that have a higher predictive value than all other stimuli present, receive most attention. Pearce and Hall (1980) proposed that controlled attention will be directed to those stimuli that need to be learned about; how much learning needs to be done is determined by the surprisingness of the event that follows. In other words, organisms will pay least attention to and learn most slowly about those stimuli that are followed by a correctly predicted event, while incorrectly predicted and hence surprising events are learned about more readily.

Because language is auditorily or visually perceived, findings from research on attention in the visual and auditory domain are, in principle, transferable to language. As an aside it is interesting to note that much psycholinguistic research on the interplay between language comprehension and visual perception was undertaken in order to examine the claims about the procedural modularity of the language and vision systems. Mishra (2015: 70) attributes an important role to embodied theories in carving out a place for attention in research on language. Embodied theories of cognition hold that cognition resides in our sensory and motoric experiences. In that sense, these theories predict a direct link between language and perceptual and motor processes via sensorimotor activations. This includes roles for the motor system, the attentional system and vision.

In usage-based linguistics attention capture is described through the notion of salience. Like entrenchment, the concept of salience has been used by linguists to refer to different phenomena. In this chapter, we will first tease apart the different ways in which linguists and psychologists have approached attention in language (Section 7.1). Section 7.2 will then look at salience in language, how it has been treated in linguistics and how it relates to frequency.

7.1   Capturing Attention in Language: Linguistics versus Psychology

'[I]f language helps express thoughts, attention selects the most relevant ones to work on' (Mishra 2015: 1). To capture a visually complex situation in words, speakers need to attend – selectively – to the different components of that situation. Does attentional focus on one referent influence linguistic choice in visually mediated language production? Tomlin and Myachykov (2015: 32) break down the overarching question of how attention biases language structure, production and comprehension into three sub-questions that help us understand how grammar is employed during visually situated language production.

1 How is attention deployed during event conceptualization?
2 Are speakers/hearers guided by attention in their expression/interpretation of a scene?
3 How do different languages formalize possible correspondences between attention and expression?

While there is agreement that attention biases event perception and conceptualization and thereby affects the translation of a conceptual structure into language, psychologists and linguists tend to focus on different aspects of how linguistic and attentional processes interact (Tomlin and Myachykov 2015: 32). Linguists are interested in those aspects of a situation that capture attention and guide the choice between competing grammatical encodings, while psychologists prioritize the role of attention in changing the information flow during language processing.

7.1.1   Attention in Linguistics

Linguists working within cognitive and functional frameworks regard attention as a crucial ingredient in the structure, development and use of language. Despite this conviction, there is a dearth of work exploring how attention and language relate. Generally, linguists are not so much interested in the nature of attention-orienting mechanisms as in the existence of attention and some of its characteristics (Langacker 1987: 115). They typically work back from the linguistic expression to determine how attention was deployed within the scene.

Langacker (1987: chapter 3) focuses on the cognitive abilities implicated in language; attention is one of them. To Langacker, attention equals focused processing, which is necessitated by the richness of our experience. Much of our mental life is related only indirectly to perception and to perceived reality;

it is our conception and experience of reality, more than reality itself (in as far as reality can be perceived), that is relevant to language. Our experience of reality unfolds across a number of domains simultaneously; there is perception across the visual, auditory and tactile domains; there are motor events, mental processes such as emotions and so on. We do not and cannot attend in equal measure to each of these input channels to our experience; instead we focus or concentrate on a small number of areas. Due to this focus or attention, i.e., a heightened level of cognitive processing, inputs from those areas are perceived as being more prominent or salient (Langacker 1987: 115). Langacker (1987: 116) thus sees attention as 'superimposed on the intricately woven fabric of our mental experience and selectively augments its salience; it is not prerequisite for such experience'. The cognitive ability of focusing attention is active in a number of operations that are highly relevant from a linguistic point of view.

Langacker's notion of 'construal', the relationship between the speaker/ writer and the situation they represent, embodies the role attention plays in language. Experience is so rich that there is no single way to represent a situation. The grammar of a language provides users with a range of constructions, which differ subtly in meaning and satisfy varying semiotic and interactive goals. Construal reflects the user's ability to adjust the focus of attention by altering the mental imagery representing a situation. These differences can be obvious (when contrasting *Scotland lies to the north of England* with *England lies to the south of Scotland*) or very subtle (when comparing *The author sent a message to his readers* and *The author sent his readers a message*). Cognitive grammar also depends on the notion of 'profiling', which refers to the effect that construal has. Profiling captures the fact that, for any linguistic act, some entity stands out in profile against a background; that entity is called the figure. The contrast between figure and ground plays a prominent role in cognitive grammar where the figure within a scene is that substructure that stands out against the ground and receives prominence as pivotal entity around which the scene is organized and for which the scene provides the background. The figure/ground organization is not predetermined for a given scene, and it tends to be possible to structure the scene around different figures. Yet, the figure is not by definition in the focus of attention: figure/ground arrangements are likewise registered in domains we are not attending to (Langacker 1987: 120–2). In usage-based linguistics some of the most extensively investigated attention-directing devices are those that highlight the conceptual distinctions of containment versus support, path versus manner and source versus goal (Jackendoff 1983; Talmy 1985, 2000, 2007; Lakoff 1987; Choi and Bowerman 1991).

The fact that speakers of a language are predisposed to process certain structures over others has important implications for theorizing about language change as well. Fennell (2001: 6) argues that one language-internal factor in English shedding its case system and becoming an analytic language is that speakers developed a fixed stress on the nuclear syllable. This drew attention away from the final syllable and ultimately brought about the loss of inflectional endings. In contrast, languages within the Indo-European family that allowed major stress on any syllable, such as Russian, preserved their inflectional characteristics. Over generations, learners of English automatically began to focus attention on syntactic placement, because word order became for them the primary means of determining grammatical relations. In other words, orienting attention to the nuclear syllable of a word meant being alerted to changes in syntax rather than changes in morphology.

Talmy (2007: 264) explains how we can attend to the linguistic expression, to the conceptual content of that expression or to the context at hand. Different aspects of the expression, content and context have different degrees of salience: languages have mechanisms to increase or decrease the salience of the parts of an expression, its reference or context. The speaker employs this system in formulating an expression; the hearer, largely on the basis of such formulations, allocates their attention in a particular way over the entities. These entities are typically the semantic referents of constituents, but the phonological shape of a constituent or the vocal delivery of the utterance can also be fore- or backgrounded. Oakley (2009) describes how selective attention explains Talmy's (1995, 2000) notions of 'windowing' and 'gapping'. Given a kind of referent scene, for example, a motion event with a conceivable initial, medial and final image schematic organization, the options available to discourse participants are threefold: windowing all features, windowing two and gapping one or windowing one and gapping two.

Crucially, languages differ in how they implement attention-focusing mechanisms. Linguists have studied the relation between attention and grammatical encoding cross-linguistically to arrive at generalizations about attention and language (Halliday 1976; Chafe 1979, 1994, 1998; Givón 1983, 1988, 1992; see Tomlin et al. 2010 for a review). Linguistic attention is gradient and organized hierarchically: attention is more focused on the overall literal meaning of a sentence than on the meanings of its individual words and still more on the contextual import of that sentence's meaning than on the literal meaning of the sentence (Talmy 2007: 266). Crucially, the attentional properties found in language do not map perfectly onto attentional properties in other cognitive systems (Talmy 2007: 266). While greater magnitude along a cognitive parameter tends to attract greater attention to the entity manifesting it – compare here stronger stress on a linguistic constituent and the large size or bright colour of an object in visual perception – morphological topic and focus markers have no counterpart in perceptual systems. In the same fashion, abrupt change along any sensory parameter is one of the main mechanisms in the perceptual modalities for attracting attention to the stimulus, but this plays a minimal role in the attentional system of language.

As it does in cognitive grammar, attention places a crucial role in mental space grammar (Fauconnier 1985; Oakley 2009): while cognitive grammar provides a rich model for studying the link between semantic (meaning) structure and phonological (sound) structures, mental spaces provide a rich model for understanding the real-time use of these structures in specific situations. Different from the majority of work on attention in linguistics, Oakley (2009) does not begin with structure but with models of interpersonal use. To him, as to Chafe (1994), languages are semiotic systems for directing and harmonizing the attention in others. To this end languages develop and maintain their own systems for selecting, sustaining and controlling attention. Oakley relies on mental space models to elaborate his account. Mental spaces are partial assemblies constructed as we think and talk for purposes of local understanding and action. They correspond to possible worlds in truth-conditional semantics, but a mental space does not contain a faithful representation of reality; instead, it is an idealized cognitive model. It has been hypothesized that at the neural level, mental spaces are sets of activated neuronal assemblies and that the connections between elements correspond to coactivation bindings. On this view, mental spaces operate in working memory but are built up partly by activating structures available from long-term memory. With respect to mental space grammar, selection of attention applies to all three space types: base space, viewpoint space and focus space. Base space, also known as reality space, presents the interlocutors' shared knowledge of the real world. Viewpoints and foci shift as the discourse develops and shifts attention.

7.1.2   Attention in Psychology of Language and Psycholinguistics

Work by psychologists of language on the relation between attention and grammar explores a number of related issues. The question of whether the order in which situational components are encountered affects the order in which they are mentioned in language is of most direct relevance to usage-based linguistics. Assuming that there is a significant relation between form and function, is this relation exploited by speakers and hearers when they interact? Does the distribution of a speaker's attention over the elements of the situation translate directly into structural choices? In this research, pragmatic information such as topic, focus and given versus new information plays an important role.

Myachykov et al. (2011: 97) start from the assumption that the first step in transitioning from viewing a scene to talking about it involves the creation of a conceptual message, i.e., determining who did what to whom. During this phase, the attentional system may act as filter, highlighting more salient referents for preferential processing. Although attention can be endogenous (resulting from the speaker's own goals and expectations) or exogenous (resulting from the referent's physical properties), psycholinguistic research on attention and language has focused on the latter type, i.e., exogenous attention. Two paradigms have dominated the field (Myachykov et al. 2011; Tomlin and Myachykov 2015: 37–44): referential priming and perceptual priming, and we will survey both in turn.

7.1.2.1 Referential Priming Studies   In studies using the referential priming paradigm, subjects preview a visual referent before the target event involving this referent appears on the screen. The visual, semantic and structural information associated with the previewed or primed referent makes the referent easier to process. In production, for example, the primed referent is more likely to be the starting point of the sentence used to describe the event. In a verification study, a participant in an experiment is more likely to identify a sentence as describing an event if the sentence begins with the primed referent.

Prentice (1967) investigated how attentional focus on the referent as a consequence of referent preview affects the use of the active versus passive voice in English. He found that if participants previewed the referent that would become the agent, they were more likely to produce active sentences; if they previewed the referent that would become the patient, they were more likely to produce passive sentences. In other words, the participants were primed to use the previewed referent in sentence-initial position. The effect was stronger for the active voice than for the passive voice, which indicated how canonical choices such as the preference for the active voice can constrain the extent to which perception can influence linguistic choices.

Turner and Rommetveit (1968) conducted a memory experiment with forty-eight children from nursery school to third grade. They hypothesized that focusing the children's attention on the agent or patient of an event during storage and retrieval of sentences describing that event would influence the choice for the active or passive construction during recall. The hypothesis was confirmed, but the effect was smaller for focused attention during storage than during retrieval. Overall, when the agent or the complete event was presented as a retrieval cue, active sentences tended to be recalled as presented (i.e., as active) while passive sentences tended to be transformed into the active voice. When a picture of the patient was presented, active voice sentences tended to be transformed into the passive voice and passive sentences tended to be recalled correctly.

Tannenbaum and Williams (1968) started from the assumption that the choice between an active and a passive construction follows from the attentional characteristics of the encoding situation: when the agent is in focus, active sentences that put the agent in sentence-initial position are preferred, while passive sentences are preferred when the focus is on the patient. The experimenters manipulated conceptual focus by means of a six-sentence preceding paragraph which highlighted the subject or the object. They asked participants to describe the situation with both active and passive sentences. The differences in response latencies (here, the time elapsed between the end of the stimulus presentation and the completion of the response) between the production of active and passive served as an index of the participants' readiness to use either form, with shorter latencies signalling increased ease of production. They found that, when the participants' attention was directed to the receiver of the action (i.e., the logical object), the time required to generate a passive description was equal to that required to generate the active; when the participants' attention was directed to the actor, the logical subject, the passive sentence took longer to generate than the active one. These findings confirmed the existence of a functional distinction between two forms of encoding (active and passive) that stem from the demands of the encoding situation.

Olson and Filby (1972) conducted a comprehension study of active and passive sentences and found that the ease of processing one or the other structure is a function of prior coding of the event. On the basis of a series of five experiments, including sentence verification and question/answer tasks, they established that reaction times were faster when there was a match between the form of the picture coding and the surface structure of the sentence; that is, the active sentence was verified more quickly when the picture was coded in terms of the agent (active coding) and the passive sentence was verified more quickly when the picture was coded in terms of the patient (passive coding). Yet, overall, the passive sentence in the passive picture-coding condition took longer to verify than the active sentences in the active picture-coding condition. They concluded, quite contrary to the transformational linguistic convictions of the time, that comprehending a passive sentence in the logical object–verb–subject word order does not require recovering its equivalent active sentence base structure.

7.1.2.2 Perceptual Priming Studies   These early referential priming paradigms made more than just perceptual information available (Myachykov et al. 2011: 99). Researchers soon switched to perceptual priming paradigms to investigate the relation between attentional processing and sentence organization, or the assignment of syntactic roles in a clause.

Osgood and Bock (1977) proposed that a referent's salience, which they took to mean vividness, might predict its position in a sentence, with the most salient referents occupying the most prominent sentential positions. MacWhinney (1977) suggested that the most salient referent is put in sentence-initial position, which determines the structural organization of the sentence. Tomlin (1995, 1997) hypothesized instead that salient referents tend to occupy the most prominent syntactic role. Of course, in English, a language with rather strict subject–verb–object word order, the most prominent sentential positions are reserved for the most prominent syntactic roles. Tomlin's proposal was tested using a very strong variant of the perceptual priming paradigm known as the FishFilm. The FishFilm is a psycholinguistic adaptation of the cueing paradigm (Posner 1980), in which subjects' attention is directed to an uninformative cue while they view events (for a description and visualization of the task, see also Myachykov, Tomlin and Posner 2005; for a critique of the methodology, see Bock, Irwin and Davidson 2004). Agent-cued trials yielded virtually 100 per cent active sentences while patient-cued trials resulted nearly always in passive sentences. Gleitman et al. (2007), who used a much subtler implicit cueing procedure and tested a range of syntactic constructions, confirmed Tomlin's findings, although the effects were much weaker. Overall, the participants tended to assign the cued referent a position early on in the sentence, revealing a potentially hybrid system playing on grammatical-role assignment and linear positioning. Similar results had been obtained by Forrest (1996), who investigated the visually cued production of locative sentences in English.

Myachykov, Garrod and Scheepers (2012) followed this experiment up with a production study that investigated how perceptual, structural and lexical cues interact to affect structural choices during English transitive sentence production. They relied both on the cueing (Posner 1980) and priming (Bock 1986) paradigms. Visual cueing facilitates choice between two alternatives by marking the target with a visual cue (e.g., a pointer). Priming increases sensitivity to a stimulus through prior exposure and is considered a form of implicit memory. It can be used as a way of cueing participants to choose one alternative over the other (Myachykov, Garrod and Scheepers 2012: 305). In the three experiments, twenty-four participants described transitive events in different combinations of (1) visual cueing of attention towards agent or patient, (2) structural priming for active or passive and (3) with and without semantic match between the verb in the prime and the target event. Speakers had a stronger preference for passive-voice sentences (1) when their attention was directed to the patient, (2) after reading a passive-voice prime and (3) when the verb in the prime and target matched. The verb-match effect was the by-product of an interaction between visual cueing and verb match, however: the increase in the proportion of passive-voice responses with matching verbs was limited to the agent-cued condition. Matching verbs appear to suppress the effectiveness of agent cueing in its ability to promote active-voice descriptions. Myachykov, Garrod and Scheepers (2012) also tested whether informative versus uninformative cueing with respect to subject properties affect choice in the production of English transitive sentences. While informative cues allowed subjects to preview the referent and determine its crucial properties (e.g., animacy), uninformative cues revealed the referent's location. They found that, even in the presence of structural or semantic manipulations, cueing locations boosted the use of passive constructions. This shows that attentionally driven syntactic choices are the result of a direct and automatic mapping from attention to sentence. Perceptual information plays an integral and self-sufficient role during the assignment of structural roles alongside available lexical and structural information.

The problem with using English as the target language is that English has a fixed subject–verb–object word order, making the grammatical subject occupy sentence-initial position. Studies on languages with flexible word order such as Russian (Myachykov and Tomlin 2008), Finnish (Myachykov, Garrod and Scheepers 2010) and Korean (Hwang and Kaiser 2009) make it possible to disentangle the grammatical-role assignment versus linear positioning explanations. Myachykov and Tomlin (2008) ran the Tomlin (1995) study for Russian. Although they found that Russian speakers produced 20 per cent more object-initial active voice sentences when the patient was cued, the effect of the manipulation was much smaller than for English. Myachykov, Garrod and Scheepers (2010) used the Gleitman et al. (2007) design on Finnish. They replicated the effect for the English portion of their data, but no effect was found for Finnish even though, judging by the results for English, the cueing manipulation was clearly effective. Hwang and Kaiser (2009) obtained similar null results for Korean, where an effective cueing manipulation did not influence syntactic choice. Perceptual priming effects appear to be weaker in flexible word order languages. Tomlin and Myachykov (2015: 42) hypothesize that this shows that the grammatical-role assignment mechanism is the primary syntactic device for representing attentional focus, and that linear ordering comes into play when grammatical-role assignment is tricky, due to the range of linguistic structures that are available in any one particular language. In English, both routes lead to the same solution, amplifying the cueing effect. In Russian and Finnish, only the linear ordering route is available, and this is likely due to the general disuse into which the passive has fallen. This topicalization route has detrimental effects on processing speed and reduces the priming effect.

Of course, many other forces play a role, such as syntactic and lexical priming, thereby complicating the picture further. This was investigated in Myachykov, Garrod and Scheepers (2012) who focused on English transitive sentence production and combined all three priming manipulations, i.e., perceptual, lexical and syntactic. They found robust perceptual priming effects across all three manipulations. Crucially, there was no interaction between perceptual and syntactic priming, only between perceptual and lexical priming; perceptual and syntactic priming effects were of equal magnitude. Perceptual information about the referents can affect subject assignment independently and in parallel. Norcliffe and Konopka (2015) review the (relatively small) body of research on languages other than English to draw conclusions about whether and how the planning processes involved in producing whole utterances are fine-tuned to language-specific properties.

7.1.2.3 Tracking Eye Movements   Ibbotson, Lieven and Tomasello (2013) investigated in a non-technical way, whether the social cue of the attention-directing eye gaze could be used to learn to infer the function of grammatical subject, which can be grounded in terms of attention and information structure. Using the active/passive alternation, they examined whether children can choose the subject or focus in a way that is consistent with the eye gaze of the speaker (experimenter); this is a task which requires integrating social and syntactic knowledge. They found that four-year-olds already do this, while three-year-olds struggle and only consistently integrate social and syntactic knowledge in the default option, i.e., when the focus is on the agent. That is, all age groups consistently produce active sentences when the experimenter looked at the agent, but three-year-olds could not consistently produce passive sentences when the experimenter was looking at the patient. This finding supports the idea that (at least some of the) abstract linguistic functions (that have been proposed) can be grounded in general cognitive and communicative principles. Language structure itself thus seems to reflect aspects of human attentional mechanisms. That is, what is attended to most often becomes the grammatical subject of the sentence that is expressed (see Chafe 1982).

To date, eye tracking has provided the most direct evidence of a relation between language, attention and vision. Eye tracking can be used to study the temporal relation between event apprehension, sentence formulation and speech execution, because people tend to look at what they are thinking about (e.g., Tanenhaus et al. 1995; Rayner 1998). Eye trackers reveal where the eye focuses and for how long. When naming objects, speakers fixate the objects long enough to recover the sounds of the words that denote them (Meyer, Sleidernik and Levelt 1998). Upon hearing a word, listeners direct their attention to a matching object. More or less, that is: objects from the same phonological and/or semantic field are often coactivated, with as result that *candy* activates *candle* and *apple* may activate *orange* (see Allopenna, Magnuson and Tanenhaus 1998; Huettig and Altmann 2005). Mishra (2015: 65–73, 112–15) reports a number of studies that have investigated the dynamic relationship between lexical access and eye movements by measuring the fixation durations on the foveal object and the timing of the shift to the second object. The attention shift between two objects appears to be affected by the visual and linguistic (e.g., number of syllables) complexity of the objects, the location of the objects and the task demands (name out loud or silently). More specifically, eye-tracking studies with multiple objects suggest that subjects only move to the next object after having retrieved the phonological form of the first fixated object (see Meyer et al. 2012 for an overview). Yet, it remains unclear which kind of attention, i.e., endogenous or exogenous attention, is crucial during language production and processing: while exogenous attention may be prominent during reading where visuo-spatial attention plays a key role, speaking may rely on endogenous attention because concepts need to be selected wilfully for articulation (Mishra 2015: 126). What is clear is that language affects the way in which we see and perceive the visual world (and vice versa) and that language influences attention shifts in the visual domain. It has long been known that patterns of looking at objects or events are heavily influenced by cognitive goals (Buswell 1935), and language can trigger an attention shift during visual exploration: we tend to direct our attention depending on what we hear (which argues against modular theories of cognition) and speech guides vision naturally and automatically in a goal-directed manner (Mishra 2015: 82, 166).

Griffin and Bock (2000) used eye tracking to examine whether speakers' eye movements were guided by an overall apprehension of the event or by salience of individual elements and whether scene apprehension, sentence formulation and voice execution were distinct phases. They found no evidence of any regions systematically attracting attention early in picture viewing, which reduces the plausibility of Osgood's (1971) salience-driven account of sentence-subject selection. By comparing eye movements during spontaneous and prepared speech, they were able to determine that scene apprehension precedes sentence formulation: conceptualization of the event precedes incremental sentence creation.

Myachykov (2007) reports on a number of studies on English, Finnish and Russian involving the visual world paradigm. Extemporaneous descriptions of visually presented events were elicited while the participants' choice of syntactic structure was manipulated with the help of perceptual, semantic and syntactic cues. In each experiment, the same categories of data were analysed: structural choices made by speakers, speech onsets at each stage of sentence formulation, and eye/voice spans for each sentence constituent (i.e., the temporal lag between the last gaze to the referent relative to the onset of the corresponding name and the name onset itself). Irrespective of language, participants relied on a sequence of quick fixations to extract the gist of the scene. In the absence of specific cues, speakers of both English and Russian behaved similarly and initially fixated the event area, proceeding to the agent, and finally to the patient. Just before uttering labels, participants tended to fixate the interest areas in a sequence mirroring the ordering of the constituents in the sentence. These gazes are thus linguistically driven, and they are likely to represent the succession of access to the referents' lexical forms reflecting the incremental nature of the sentence formulation (Myachykov, Posner and Tomlin 2007: 467). Although perceptual manipulation can attract attention to the cued referent, its effect was short-lived and only weakly biased speakers' syntactic choices. Linguistic effects (canonical or primed grammar) quite easily overrode bottom-up perceptual manipulations even when the latter were strongly biasing towards the usage of the non-preferred forms (Myachykov, Posner and Tomlin 2007: 469). Overall, Myachykov (2007: 5) concluded that:

[...] the uptake of perceptual information does not directly influence structural processing. General cognitive processes, such as attentional control and higher memorial activation actively contribute to the concept's accessibility status, but the syntactic organization of a spoken sentence constitutes a relatively independent psychological reality that can be realized partially as a product of the aforementioned operations but does not directly depend on them.

7.2   Attention and Salience

Humans and other animals have difficulty paying attention to more than one item simultaneously, so they are faced with the challenge of continuously prioritizing and integrating different bottom-up and top-down influences. Salience detection is considered a key attentional mechanism: it facilitates learning and survival by enabling organisms to focus their limited perceptual and cognitive resources on the most pertinent subset of the available data. As is the case with attention in general, most experimental research on salience stems from work on vision in psychology. Salience typically arises from visual contrasts between items and their vicinity, and similar mechanisms operate in other sensory systems. For perception researchers, the essence of salience lies in enhancing the neural and perceptual representation of locations whose local visual statistics differ significantly from the surrounding image statistics in a way that affects behaviour.

What, then, is salience in linguistics? The notion of salience has been widely used in linguistics as the explanatory factor for a diverse range of phenomena, often referring to very different aspects of language comprehension and production. Human beings are highly attuned to speech of any kind. Phonemic recognition is the most basic linguistic process that relies on orienting awareness, but it is by no means the only one. Vocal intonation (see Chafe 1994: 53–70 on intonation units) and syntax are two others. Furthermore, the term 'salience' has been used to refer to both low-level attention capturing properties of the stimulus and to top-down activation of contextually relevant elements. Recall that when attention deployment is driven top-down, it is considered to be guided by memory-dependent or anticipatory mechanisms. This contrasts with attention deployment that is bottom-up, memory-free and reactive. In this section we will ask and answer three questions. How does linguistic salience relate to perceptual salience? How can the salience of linguistic forms and variants be operationalized? And what is the relationship between salience and frequency?

7.2.1   Defining Salience in Language

There is a lack of clarity as to where the boundary between the bottom-up and top-down effect lies in language. Zarcone et al. (2016), for example, regard lexical semantic restrictions – a verb's selectional preferences – as bottom-up effects. This is in line with the definition of salience used in visual perception studies where bottom-up effects are defined as arising from properties of the stimulus. High-level predictions depend on generalized knowledge about real-world events and the typical participants in these events. This knowledge is acquired both from first-hand participation in events or from second-hand experience (including language) and is stored in our long-term memory (see McRae and Matsuki 2009).

These two categories have something in common: they are properties of entities "standing out" from a ground (perceptual in one case, cognitive in the other) and are properties we rely on to deal with limitations of our cognitive resources (attention in one case and working memory in the other). Nevertheless, salience as a stimulus-specific property is characterized as high surprisal, whereas entities which are salient with regard to the discourse or to the situation are highly predictable (low surprisal). (Zarcone et al. 2016)

Recent studies (e.g., Vogels, Krahmer and Maes 2013; Coco and Keller 2015) corroborate the view that visual cues play a role in the high-level global apprehension of the scene, which in turn affects lower (lexical-syntactic) levels of linguistic processing (Griffin and Bock 2000; Bock, Irwin and Davidson 2004). Hence, stimulus-driven visual salience influences the situation model, but only situation-driven salience affects linguistic formulation in turn. Low-level visual features help 'set the scene', using attention to filter out what is important or relevant information.

In language production, this influences how information is structured in an utterance (e.g., what is mentioned first). In language comprehension, visual saliency cues may be used to give weight to an entity (provided the listener has access to the same visual environment as the speaker), so as to adjust predictions about what will be mentioned next. Hence, what starts as a perceptual bottom-up, high-surprisal cue can become a top-down, high-predictability cue: a visually salient entity pops out as surprising, which gives it a salient status within the situation model; next, the mental representation of the salient entity will be highly accessible by virtue of its high news value. Consequently, this entity will be likely to be mentioned, and hence is predictable. (Zarcone et al. 2016)

This also implies that bottom-up and top-down levels can 'change place': a stimulus that is initially in focus because it is surprising bottom-up may, at a later stage of processing, be in focus because it has become highly predictable. Furthermore, predictions induced by the visual context interact with predictions coming from linguistic sources, be it situation-level, discourse-level or lexical-syntactic sources. These predictions may align or conflict, and hence reduce or increase processing cost respectively (Zarcone et al. 2016)

On a more general level, definitions that stress the need for expectation *violation* are in line with basic insights from learning theory, which supports the idea that an organism learns when events violate its expectations, that is, when the organism is surprised (see Rescorla and Wagner 1972: 75): it learns when it needs to make adjustments to ensure its predictions remain accurate. Rescorla and Wagner (1972: 74) explicitly state that it was Kamin's notions concerning the 'surprisingness' of an unconditioned stimulus that originally encouraged their formulations. In learning theory, surprise would work as operationalization of salience within an attentive learning tradition: there, salience weights can be adjusted, e.g., because winning cues become attended to, and thus salience can change during learning. In discrimination learning, salience is a cue property, and salience is assigned in a bottom-up fashion, e.g., because the cue has adaptive value; in the latter tradition, salience levels are inherent to a cue and do not change during learning (Petar Milin, personal communication).

Adaptation to changes in the statistics of the environment should be sensitive to surprisal (or more generally to expectation violation): the degree to which inputs differ from prior expectations is informative about how and how much learners need to adapt their future expectations. (Courville, Daw and Touretzky 2006; Qian, Jaeger and Aslin 2012)

Neurally there is evidence for the importance of surprise too. The neurotransmitter dopamine, a key player in motivated and goal-directed behaviour and in the resampling of stimuli that have been associated with rewards (Wise 2004), is also activated by surprising stimuli, such as sudden visual or auditory stimuli, that are not associated with rewards (Horvitz 2000). Dopamine has been claimed to signal the error between what you predict and expect and what you get, and to serve as prediction error system (Humphries 2017). Kakade and Dayan (2002) have proposed that dopamine activations are *novelty bonuses* that increase the probability of resampling rewarding or surprising stimuli, thereby acting as a facilitator of exploratory action and perception.

7.2.2 Defining Salience in Linguistics

In usage-based approaches, the concept salience is characterized by a high level of terminological inconsistency. There are at least four definitions in concurrent use.

There are authors who have used the concept salience loosely, such as Schmid (2007: 119–20) who distinguished cognitive salience from ontological salience. While cognitive salience refers to a temporary mental activation state, ontological salience denotes an inherent property of entities in the real world. Some things are better suited to attract our attention than others and are therefore more salient in and of themselves. But cognitive activation can be achieved by conscious selection (a concept enters working memory for processing) or via spreading activation (the activation of one concept triggers the activation of others). Salient then means loaded into working memory (whichever way) and at the centre of someone's attention.

Other linguists have been more precise, but this precision has yielded radically opposed interpretations of salience. According to Giora (2003: 15), salient is that *which is foremost on one's mind*. The meaning of a word is considered salient if it is coded in the mental lexicon. Still, the degree of salience of a given word meaning cannot be viewed as a permanent, defining characteristic, but rather as a function of a number of factors, such as frequency, conventionality, familiarity and prototypicality. The more frequent, conventional, familiar, or prototypical a given word meaning is, the greater degree of salience it holds. Giora's graded salience hypothesis revolves around two major assumptions, i.e., that (1) the salient meaning of a word is always activated and cannot be bypassed and that (2) the salient meaning is always activated first, before the less salient meanings. On the graded salience hypothesis, context plays a very limited role. Even though it can facilitate activation of a word meaning, it cannot inhibit the process of the more salient meaning activation. Other studies have likewise used top-down effects and called those salient; in these cases, salient means 'cognitively accessible' in the discourse or situation (Zarcone et al. 2016), or 'loaded into current working memory' (Schmid 2007).

In addition to Giora's hypothesis, there is also Geeraerts' (2017) view of onomasiological salience in terms of 'the relative frequency with which a *signifiant* is associated with a given *signifié*', i.e., *the frequency with which a word is used to denote an experience*. Geeraerts' onomasiological salience is identical to Schmid's 'contextual entrenchment' or 'the relative frequency of identical or similar constructions with regard to a specific pragmatic context', which we encountered in Chapter 5, Section 5.4.3, but it also links up with 'statistical pre-emption', which we discussed in Chapter 2.

In cognitive scientific traditions, finally, salient is that *which is least expected*, typically given the context based on expectations that have formed through exposure and are stored in memory. The expectation-based interpretation has given rise to a line of language-processing studies, which were introduced in Chapter 3, Section 3.3. During language processing, information ranging from transitional probabilities between words (McDonald and Shillcock 2003; Frisson, Rayner and Pickering 2005) to knowledge about events and their typical participants (Ferretti, McRae and Hatherell 2001; Bicknell et al. 2010) is exploited to narrow down predictions for upcoming input. Input that confirms the expectations facilitates processing, while a deviation from expectations increases processing costs.

Across the different views on salience, expectation plays a key role. These expectations can be confirmed or violated. Geeraerts' (2017) cognitive linguistic view of 'onomasiological salience' is the exact opposite of the definition that holds sway in the cognitive sciences: both refer to expectations derived from the probability of occurrence in the current context but Geeraerts' salience assumes *confirmation of these expectations*, whereas the standard cognitive science view on salience assumes *expectation violation*. Generally, we have expectations generated by current context (contextual expectations or probabilities), we have expectations generated by exposure to many contexts over time (context-less expectations or probabilities) or we experience a complete lack of context-generated expectations (novelty).

Surprise often – perhaps always – accompanies novelty, which may be a major reason for why the two concepts tend to be confounded (Barto, Mirolli and Baldassare 2013: 9). In sociolinguistic studies (especially dialect studies) salience is typically treated as a bottom-up phenomenon (Trudgill 1986; Kerswill and Williams 2002; Rácz 2013): a realization in one dialect stands out because speakers of other dialects do not expect it. Examples here are acoustic salience, markedness of prosodic patterns but also of syntactic constructions. Berlyne (1960) emphasized a number of relevant distinctions within the category of novelty. On the one hand, he distinguished between *short-term, long-term* and *complete novelty*. Something may never have been encountered before (complete novelty), or not encountered in the last few minutes (short-term novelty), or not encountered for some intermediate time, e.g., a few days (long-term novelty). Jaeger and Weatherholtz (2016) propose that the surprisal and frequency of lectal variants predict a variant's salience: surprisal is high when first encountering unfamiliar lectal variants. With further exposure, the association between the variant and the lect increases, while the surprisal evoked by the variant decreases. On the other hand, Berlyne distinguished between *absolute* and *relative novelty*. A stimulus is absolutely novel when some of its features have never been experienced before, whereas it is relatively novel if it has familiar features, but they occur in some combination or arrangement that has not been previously encountered (as cited in Barto, Mirolli and Baldassare 2013: 6).

7.2.3 Salience versus Frequency?

By its definition, salience refers to any (aspect of a) stimulus that makes it apparent to the perceiver. And what stands out has a better chance of being noticed and encoded in memory. We saw earlier that human beings are also highly sensitive to the frequency with which elements (co-)occur in their environment and extract this information automatically. How do salience and frequency relate? It is possible for a word sequence to have low global usage frequency yet to be salient and stand out in a circumscribed set of contexts and thereby become entrenched. But also, the higher the frequency is with which a behaviour is repeated, the higher the likelihood of the behaviour being frozen into habit. As habits are executed automatically, does this entail a reduced role for salience and attention? Could salience be an epiphenomenon of frequency, or are they two sides of the same coin?

In principle, all three linguistic definitions of salience presented in Section 7.2.1 allow operationalizing salience as an epiphenomenon of frequency. Yet, they would do this in different ways and would rely on different kinds of frequencies. While Giora (2003) relies on frequency of use and explicitly states that context is irrelevant, Geeraerts (2017) talks about the frequency with which a concept and a label are paired in a specific pragmatic context. The surprisal-based account prevalent in cognitive science is the interpretation of salience that is most clearly linked to frequency. Readers and listeners create context-based expectations about upcoming linguistic input at different levels. These different types of information are drawn upon at syntactic, lexical, semantic and pragmatic levels of representation at each point in processing to reach a provisional analysis and build expectations at all levels. The flow of information goes both ways: the encountered input activates high-level representations in a bottom-up fashion (e.g., triggering expectations for new syntactic structures, event knowledge, scenarios) and, depending on contextual information, high-level representations influence low-level predictions (Kuperberg 2016; Kuperberg and Jaeger 2016).

The statistical history of events is built on information on frequency of occurrence and co-occurrence. Since frequency effects are memory effects, and since memory is affected by how items are presented over time, the passage of linguistic elements over time is a crucial consideration. In this operationalization of salience, the nearest linguistic equivalent of a time window is a contextual frame. On a constructionist approach to language, a word's typical context or construction is a property of the stimulus, yielding bottom-up salience. Contextual frames are available at all levels of linguistic analysis, from the way in which sounds are distributed over words to the way in which words are arranged in a sentence, distributed over texts or organized in semantic networks. And they go beyond this into the interpersonal and social situation in which a word has been encountered. The availability of context can be used as a basis for an operationalization of salience. Although, at present, we lack applications that take the communicative situation into account, this is certainly within reach of the more encompassing models of language cognition that we will discuss in Chapters 8 and 9.

The degree to which an item is expected given a specific context, i.e., the expectation-based interpretation of salience typical for the cognitive sciences, can be operationalized in its simplest form by using (the logarithm of) conditional probabilities. This is known as the surprise ratio (Barlow 1990) or surprisal. The surprisal of a word is equivalent to the difference between the probability distributions of possible utterances before and after encountering that word (as captured by the Kullback–Leibler divergence), which quantifies the amount of information conveyed by that word (Levy 2008). This has given rise to a fruitful line of research: surprisal theory can account for certain patterns in language usage as well as for behavioural correlates of cognitive load during comprehension. The underlying linking hypotheses are that cognitive load is proportional to the amount of information conveyed by the input (its surprisal) given the preceding context, and that the speakers' production choices tend to keep the amount of information constant (uniform information density hypothesis, Levy and Jaeger 2007; see also Jurafsky et al. 2001; Gahl and Garnsey 2004). Evidence exists that the amount of expectation adaptation after processing unexpected linguistic input is proportional to that input's surprisal (Fine and Jaeger 2013; Arai and Mazuka 2014; for related evidence from production, see Bernolet and Hartsuiker 2010; Jaeger and Snider 2013).

Although surprisal is a potential proxy for salience, it does not appear an ideal choice, nor a fully justified one. Barto, Mirolli and Baldassare (2013: 2) classify surprisal as an information theoretical notion and consider it a concrete example of how surprise can be expressed in formal terms by looking at it as change in uncertainty. Yet, neither surprise nor surprisal are established information theoretical notions (witness here their absence from standard treatments such as Cover and Thomas 1991); surprisal is but a logarithmic transformation of probability. Weighting surprisal (i.e., the amount of information transmitted) by probability does yield entropy (Milin et al. 2009), and Hale (2016) recently proposed entropy reduction (or information gain), which indexes comprehension difficulty, as a more successful formal expression of the notion surprise.

Surprisal is successful empirically because it accounts naturally for frequency effects (Hale 2016). A surprisal-based model is typically defined by the linguistic units it takes into consideration, that is, by what kind of linguistic information (phonological, morphological, syntactic or semantic) it is conditioned on. Probabilities of (co-)occurrence, which are likely to affect or be stored in memory (Tily et al. 2009; Divjak 2017), are higher for more frequent or more typical combinations, i.e., items that can be considered expected given the context, and lower for (relatively) less frequent and more atypical combinations that are unexpected in a context. The low probability of occurrence of infrequent combinations is what makes them salient and stand out when they do occur. Although a word sequence with low global usage frequency can become entrenched because it stands out in a circumscribed set of contexts, a strong mental representation will be formed from a single instance only in special cases, such as those associated with intense emotions. It is important to note here, in anticipation of Chapter 8, that Bayesian surprise differs from surprisal in that Bayesian surprise quantifies the belief update of the model given the observation, whereas surprisal quantifies how much information the observation conveys (how predictable it is) given a current model, without taking into account a model update (Itti and Baldi 2009; Zarcone et al. 2016).

7.3   Summary and Outlook

Attention is a central component of how information is processed – it explains how certain aspects of the information stream are selected while others are suppressed to optimize performance. At first sight, it may seem that linguists have not engaged with findings from research on perceptual attention. For the most part, attention has been studied in relation to vision, but salience plays a role in other sensory modalities too, including those that are directly relevant to language, such as hearing. And it is important to bear in mind here that the concepts discussed in Chapter 6 cannot straightforwardly be transferred to linguistics: language is not a purely physiological phenomenon, and it is not a phenomenon that speaks to one sensory channel only. Moreover, a linguistic situation is multidimensional and dynamic; in real life, linguistic and non-linguistic information interact and influence attention. This makes it challenging to separate the effects of different types of attentional control from each other.

Linguists regard attention as a crucial ingredient in the structure, development and use of language. They are interested in the attentional or attention-summoning properties that language has, and they have focused on the effects of language structure in particular. The relation between language and attention has been studied from two angles; either we look at the ways in which the distribution of attention over the components of a scene is expressed in language, or we look at how language can direct attention to components of a scene. Some investigate how bottom-up attentional processes, and attention-capturing mechanisms in particular, affect the way in which a language changes over time. Others work back from the linguistic expression to determine how attention was deployed within the scene. They analyse the attention-direction devices a language offers and the mechanisms a language has to increase or decrease the salience of the parts of an expression, its reference or context.

Psychologists are more interested in the way in which language directs attention and thereby activates memory representations. The tendency to study attention from the point of view of vision has transferred to psycholinguistics where focus has been on the relation between language comprehension and visual perception; the interplay appears to be rapid, incremental and bidirectional in that language guides visual perception and non-linguistic visual information that is attended to influences language comprehension (Knoeferle 2015: 57). Psycholinguistic research has provided evidence of the effects that scene perception has on linguistic choices. Elements of a scene that are made salient by means of overt or covert cueing tend to occupy more prominent syntactic positions and, all other things being equal, can tip the choice of construction in favour of the non-default one. Eye-tracking research has added to this the finding that eye movements are time-locked to the mention of objects and this relation is modulated by the details of the syntactic presentation.

Mishra (2015: 237) concluded his survey of the relation between language and attention by saying that:

[...] the question if [sic] attention is required for language functions is not a good question to ask. [...] The question should be how different language mechanisms involve attentional states and the role played by the agent in them. The problem [sic] of linking mechanisms of attention to subtleties of language is [sic] manifold. On the one hand, we have different modes of language performance. On the other hand, we have different levels at which attention mechanisms may seem to interact with language. Although many psycholinguists who have worked on linguistic performance in these various areas talk of attention, it is difficult to find out [sic] any particular shade of attention which is common to all of them. Interestingly, not many even explicitly refer to basic components of attention such as endogenous and exogenous.

A major challenge that the field of attention studies faces is the need to standardize and operationalize definitions of attention and to integrate available findings into a cohesive and comprehensive framework (Nobre and Kastner 2014a: 1217–18). To make research on attention more directly relevant to linguists, accounts of attention need to tackle the interaction between those properties of the linguistic signal that are related to the stimulus and those that pertain to the larger discourse and situation. The accounts would also need to be compatible with processing systems that coordinate linguistic and non-linguistic information as the linguistic input is processed (Tanenhaus et al. 1995).

If research has not touched upon the wider communicative context in which an utterance is produced, this is likely so because the communicative situation is highly complex, i.e., it involves the speaker-internal relation between the message and the code, the relation between the interlocutors and the relation between the speakers and the larger social group(s) they belong to. Surprisal-based models go some way in explaining processing costs, yet do not tell us the whole story. Typically, these models do not tackle the problem of how different levels of representation interact with each other, as the probability of a linguistic unit (e.g., a phoneme, a phrase, a word, a situation model) is conditioned on preceding units at the same level (e.g., preceding phonemes, phrases, words, situation models). And they do not attempt to model the interaction between stimulus-specific properties of the linguistic signal and discourse and situation-based salience. Because of this, at present, we are still working towards a full understanding of how the various dimensions of this process fit together to generate and maintain an individual's linguistic knowledge. Significant inroads have been made, however, and work by linguists of a usage-based persuasion has been instrumental in putting attention on the linguistic research agenda.

Part IV

8   Predicting: Using Past Experience to Guide Future Action

In the previous chapters, we have seen how experiences could be encoded in memory and we have discussed the role that frequency and attention play in the process. But many questions remain to be asked and answered. One such question relates to the crucial observation that not everything can get noticed and be attended to. So, what determines which aspects of experience are selected? A popular answer suggests that we may prioritize things that are salient and surprise our cognitive system. But this leads to a new question: how can surprise arise in a cognitive system? In this chapter (and the next) we look at approaches that combine insights from memory and attention and operationalize 'noticing' as a function of the previously introduced concepts of surprise and prediction. The resulting predictive processing models could serve as stepping stones towards encompassing models of cognition, including linguistic cognition.

Recall here that much of the research into the teleology and functions of the brain, such as attention, is conducted on vision. On the traditional view, which goes back to Marr (1982), perceptual processing is dominated by a forward flow of information, transduced from the world via sensory receptors. In other words, the brain is passive and stimulus-driven: it takes input from the senses and turns this input into a 'percept'. Observed patterns are matched against available internal representations. A new view, from predictive coding and processing, reverses this approach and argues that our brains make sense of uncertain input by predicting it, i.e., by continuously formulating hypotheses about what might be generating the information our senses take in. On this account, our brains are active and try to predict the sensory signal by constructing it using stored probabilistic knowledge about the world. The goal of these predictions is to meet the incoming sensory signal with a multilevel prediction of that signal, rather than to interpret the signal after it has come in.

Clark (2015b: 19) described the self-organizing nature of a Bayesian network as 'bootstrap heaven', and this image would apply to predictive models too: you can use the prediction task as gateway to the world knowledge that you can later use to make accurate predictions. In language, for example, it helps to know the grammar of a language if you want to predict the next word in a sentence. But one way to learn about grammar – and a rather successful one, as work on large-corpus machine learning has shown – is to look for the best way to predict the next word in the sentence and to adjust your predictions for future responses according to previously encountered patterns. In other words, you can use the prediction task to discover or construct the grammar of your language, and you can use the grammar itself in future prediction tasks.

This chapter looks at a number of current proposals that assign a central place to prediction in explaining brain function: brains predict events, and this includes linguistic events. We will briefly survey the major accounts that have been proposed over the past ten years and that have either been very influential in the cognitive sciences or have interfaced directly with linguistics, and usage-based linguistics in particular. These accounts differ in terms of how they think brains make predictions. An important point of divergence concerns the question of whether predictions require stored memories. This issue is highly relevant for theories of language cognition, and representative accounts are introduced in Section 8.1 and 8.2. For a detailed overview of developments in the area I refer readers to the 2013 Frontiers Research Topic, dedicated to predictive models in cognition.

8.1   Predicting from Stored Memories

Within cognitive neuroscience, a strong trend is emerging to view brain systems as relying on memory-based predictions. The brain extracts repeating patterns and statistical regularities from its environment and stores them in memory. On the basis of these stored experiences, the brain makes predictions about the future, i.e., it predicts best actions in response to challenges. This process is guided by the statistical history of events in our environment: past experiences provide the prior knowledge needed for predicting aspects of our present and future. Tapping into the storage-retrieval metaphor of memory, some models claim that predictions are made on the basis of memories, either directly (Hawkins and Blakeslee 2004), via analogy (Bar 2011) or by relying on attractor states (Edelman 2008). A second group (introduced in Section 8.2) takes a Bayesian approach and does not posit any memory storage at all. We will review both types in turn and evaluate their usefulness for the study of language in Section 8.3.

8.1.1   The Memory–Prediction Framework (Hawkins and Blakeslee 2004)

Hawkins and Blakeslee (2004) argue that previous attempts at replicating human intelligence through artificial intelligence and neural networks have failed because human behaviour cannot be emulated without appreciation for the essence of intelligence:

The brain is not a computer, supplying by rote an output for each input it receives. Instead, it is a memory system that stores experiences in a way that reflects the true structure of the world, remembering sequences of events and their nested relationships and making predictions based on those memories. It is this memory-prediction system that forms the basis of intelligence, perception, creativity, and even consciousness. Intelligence is the capacity of the brain to predict the future by analogy to the past.

Machines that are intelligent in the way humans are would need access to all the same sensory and proprioceptive input that human bodies make available to human brains. The memory-prediction framework (Hawkins and Blakeslee 2004) addresses the role of the mammalian neocortex and its associations with the hippocampi and the thalamus in matching sensory inputs to stored memory patterns. It explains that this process leads to predictions of what will happen in the future by viewing intelligence as a result of hierarchical and recursive neural organization: predictive functionality arises from nested hierarchies of cortical modules. Hawkins and Blakeslee (2004) present a detailed model of how sequences could be stored in the six-layered hierarchical cortex. Simply put, there are higher and lower levels of cortical organization, with communication tracing both upwards (from sensory input) and downwards (from higher levels of analysis) via patterns of neural activation. What we experience is a complex interaction between external input from experience and internal input from memory, resulting in a continuous stream of online prediction.

Hawkins' proposal has been criticized on a number of points (Taylor 2005: 193). First, it does not elaborate how the theoretical proposal can be reduced to the basic biological mechanism governing the brain, i.e., that of neurons exchanging electrical spikes by means of chemical processes. Secondly, the brain is not just hierarchical, it is also distributed (Sporns et al. 2004): brain areas are highly interconnected and process information in a distributed fashion. Thirdly, attention, our 'filter' to processing the external world, has no place in Hawkins' current proposal. This leaves open the question of which aspects of experience are selected for processing.

8.1.2 The Predictive Mind (Bar 2011)

Bar (2011) investigates how the brain makes use of learned contextual regularities or how it uses prior knowledge to generate predictions and guide cognition efficiently. Generating predictability based on experience reduces uncertainty. It is also a reliable way to detect something unexpected in the bottom-up incoming sensory information. Novelty detection can guide the allocation of attention and signal that something needs encoding in memory (Bar 2011: 20–1).

On Bar's account, the brain is proactive, and its task is to generate predictions. On this assumption, the brain produces predictions continuously, unless engaged in another demanding and all-consuming task. Predictions are the result of a process in which (elementary) information is extracted rapidly from input, and analogy is used to link that information with representations that exist in memory. It is thus analogy which facilitates association and drives the prediction engine (Bar 2011: 14). This works in the following way. Memories are encoded in an associative fashion, for example, through context frames – criteria for memory encoding are salience, emotional value, surprise and novelty – and are activated holistically. Focused predictions are generated through associative activation of representations that are relevant to the analogy (Bar 2011: 13). In other words, we are not asking *What is this?* but *What is this like?* Interestingly, predictions do not require having a specific goal; predictions are generated during mind-wandering, fantasizing and revisiting memories as well. Therefore, the aim of the prediction-generation process may be to create memories that can function as scripts and guide future behaviour: there is no reason for these scripts to derive solely from real experiences. Scripts can be simulation-based too; in this way, scripts cover a wider basis of potential future actions (Bar 2011: 19).

As a side effect of accepting recognition by analogy, the (need for a) strict boundary between perception and cognition evaporates. But in order to claim that predictions rely on associative action it needs to be shown that, just like prediction, association is an ongoing process. For this to be true, there would need to be a large overlap between the 'default' cortical network and the cortical network that mediates contextual associative processing (Bar et al. 2007; Bar 2011: 17). The existence of such an overlap remains to be demonstrated.

8.1.3   Computing the Mind (Edelman 2008, 2011)

Following Putnam (1961 [1980]), Edelman (2008) proposes a computational theory of the mind. He sees computation as the formally constrained manipulation of representations. Representations and a representational capacity are necessary for cognition because 'the mind must relate to the world and the world does not fit inside a brain' (Edelman 2008: 17). If we accept this premise, then the question becomes *how* the brain or mind represents.

Edelman recognizes a number of conditions that need to be met (Edelman 2008: 40, 44, 55, 74). Crucially, each step in the process leading from perception to representation on its own must be simple to allow execution by neurons: neurons are the basic representational units in the brain but they are themselves mindless entities. To avoid the need for a homunculus, the representations should also be able to actively manipulate themselves; there should not be any need for a higher entity that performs this task. Neurons are wired together and send signals to each other by emitting all-or-none impulses. The timing and frequency of these impulses is graded and this gradedness conveys various properties of the input: every cortical neuron is tuned to a simple combination of feature values in its input domain (which can be sensory, motor or abstract). The distribution of weights (a numeric expression of importance) on the incoming connections of a neuron is determined by the statistics of that neuron's stimulation. Neurons do not count inputs, however: they detect coincidences or synchronicities. Limiting a response to coinciding inputs can be done by setting an individual neuron's firing threshold just above what a single input can achieve; it takes more than one input, then, for the neuron to fire. Generally speaking, a single neuron computes the low-dimensional statistics of its input distribution, while ensembles of neurons compute the high-dimensional statistics.

Complexity is generated by hierarchical abstractions. Top-down computational and algorithmic processes are active alongside a bottom-up implementational scheme. The top-down processes implement principles of context-dependent probabilistic learning computationally. The bottom-up process consists of structured connections carrying neural activation. These patterns unfold dynamically and support representations that are distributed, redundant and graded (Edelman 2008: 437). On this model, the representations forming memory traces are active and require no mediation; contrary to what would be expected on the dominant metaphor that represents memory in terms of storage and retrieval, the nervous system remembers what has been happening to it, and that memory shapes behaviour directly (Edelman 2008: 64–5, 156–7). Crucial in this respect are so-called attractor states or equilibria: an attractor is a set of numerical values towards which a system tends to evolve, for a wide variety of starting conditions of the system. Learning sets the synaptic weights to certain values and the effects of input and of intrinsic (feedback) activation can be balanced so that the network possesses several equilibria. Each equilibrium is only reachable from a distinct class of inputs. The resulting attractor network is thus a categorization device and implements simple associative memory: it maps each input, which can be fully described as an ordered list of initial neuron activation values, to an equilibrium-state attractor, which can be described in the same way. Each attractor thus corresponds to a particular memory maintained by the network. A strong attractor, shown in the right panel of Figure 8.1, has a wide and deep basin of attraction so every input that falls within it will cause the network to end up in the same steady state. A weak attractor has a shallow basin of attraction, as shown in the left panel of Figure 8.1, and is hence a less powerful categorization device. It is this categorization function that makes generalization possible: the response to

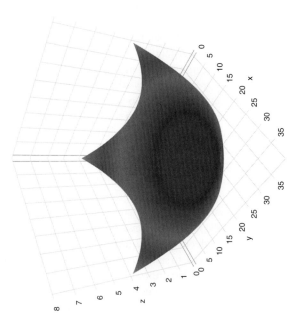

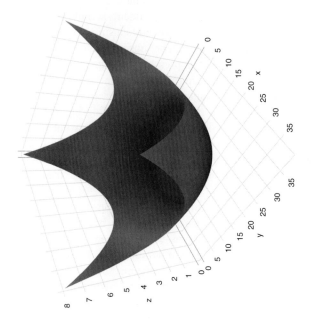

Figure 8.1 Shallow (left) and deep (right) basins of attraction

one stimulus will be extended to others, if they are sufficiently similar. This fits well with a usage-based approach, where knowing a language is thought to require categorization, generalization and abstraction. These cognitive abilities are not the topic of this book, but are critically discussed in Cordes (2017), Ramscar and Port (2015) and Baayen and Ramscar (2015).

Edelman's model offers a unified account of all the major aspects of cognition in terms of the same basic explanatory tool, that is, computation, and, on a more specific level, the same set of functions and mechanisms, that is, learning, statistical interference of structure and hierarchical abstraction. Learning is experience-driven, and therefore highly individual. Because concepts are grounded in experience through learning, they cannot be universal: no two human beings have identical perceptual histories. Due to the pervasiveness of learning, concepts also remain fluid.

On Edelman's view, learning reduces computationally to statistical inference. By taking a probabilistic approach, he puts statistics at the core of cognition (Edelman 2008: 50, 99, 187): '[S]tatistics is a mathematical framework not for capitulating in the face of uncertainty, but for managing it.' Edelman does not take a stance on whether probabilities should be interpreted in terms of expectation or prediction. In fact, we should ask ourselves: is there a real difference?

Edelman's model is the only one that comes with a specific computational implementation for language, i.e., ADIOS (Solan et al. 2005). The structure discovery procedure underlying ADIOS is very similar to what Harris (1991) proposed as discovery procedure and meshes well with the basic tenets of usage-based theories of language. Harris (1991: 32) saw the non-randomness or departure from equiprobability in the distribution of symbols and symbol sequences as a key characteristic of language: structure, which is a prerequisite for generalization, can be inferred from non-randomness (Edelman 2008: 239). Consider the following sentences that could be overheard in a bookstore: 'I would like to buy a children's book about space,' 'Could you help me buy a children's book about space?' and 'It is impossible to buy a children's book about space!' These three sentences share the pattern 'buy a children's book about space'. If other customers produce related sentences such as 'I would like to buy a scientific book about space,' or 'I would like to buy an accessible book about space,' then the algorithm could infer that 'children's', 'scientific' and 'accessible' are equivalent in this pattern. ADIOS consists of two components: (1) a Representational Data Structure (RDS) graph, and (2) a Pattern Acquisition (PA) algorithm. The algorithm learns the RDS graph by detecting patterns in input text that is segmented into the smallest possible components, for English typically root words (i.e., words stripped of their inflectional morphology). The unique components form the vertices or angular points in the preliminary RDS graph. When adjacent components are encountered in the input text, a directed edge is created between the vertices to indicate a transition from one to the other. The algorithm scans the text recursively to identify patterns that consist of a sequence of edges (words that typically follow each other such as 'buy a'), an equivalence class of vertices ('children's', 'scientific' and 'accessible') and a terminating sequence of graph edges ('book'). At each level of recursion, the set of equivalence classes is updated into progressively more complex patterns that together form a classification tree for the text. The leaves of an English tree represent parts of speech such as nouns, verbs and adjectives while the order of the branches captures patterns of their use. ADIOS can also generate sentences by selecting leaves in branch order such as noun–verb–noun–article–adjective–noun for 'He bought her a fascinating book'.

Edelman (2011: 175) highlights the existence of a partial overlap between sentences that occur in temporal proximity to each other in a conversation; these structures or constructions serve as variation sets for children, and as sources of priming for adults. On this account (Edelman 2008: 82, 277) the immediate discourse context of an utterance contains the most valuable information for a baby learner since it allows for disambiguation. For example, figurative language is a bridge between probability and structure since literal interpretations are likely given the context and metaphorical ones are unlikely. The effects of these structures or constructions and of language statistics are so tightly interconnected that it is virtually impossible to tease their effects apart: 'the statistics maintained by the language model is [sic] defined over a set of structured elements – the constructions. These, in turn, are learned by analysing the statistics of successive stimuli' (Edelman 2008: 300).

8.2   Memoryless Prediction: Bayesian Predictive Coding Frameworks

Over the past ten years, a number of influential books have appeared (Frith 2007; Hohwy 2013; Clark 2015b), promoting a Bayesian approach to the mind, or rather a Bayesian approach to how the brain implements the mind. Griffiths, Kemp and Tenenbaum (2008: 60, 63, 70) argue that Bayesian methods have value as a general framework for solving problems of induction and therefore for modelling human cognition in general: given some data, we draw conclusions about the process that might have given rise to that data and we use that knowledge to make predictions about new cases.

'Predictive processing' plausibly represents the last and most radical step in the long retreat from a passive, feed-forward, input-dominated view of the flow of neural processing. According to this emerging class of models biological brains are constantly active, trying to predict the streams of sensory stimulation before they arrive. Systems like that are most strongly impacted by sensed *deviations* from their predicted states. It is these deviations from predicted states (prediction errors) that now bear much of the information-processing burden, informing us of what is *salient and newsworthy* within the dense sensory barrage. (Clark 2015c, 14 December)

In other words, the Bayesian brain is an inference machine that actively predicts and explains any sensations it perceives. The Bayesian paradigm is said to have its roots in ideas developed by Hermann von Helmholtz on the origin of our visual experiences. However, von Helmholtz does not appear to have subscribed to the priors (estimates of how likely the hypothesis was before considering the current evidence) that are a core component of present-day Bayesian inference (see Westheimer 2008). This makes it difficult to draw a direct line between present-day implementations and the very origins of the idea.

8.2.1 The Core Idea: Prediction Error Minimization

Bayesian approaches start from the assumption that there is an ideal observer who uses evidence in the best possible way. Prediction error plays a crucial role in this process because it presents observers with an opportunity to learn. Predictions are based on what we should expect given our belief about the world; the error in our predictions provides us with information about the extent to which our beliefs need to be updated to account for the information we have just encountered. On such an approach, perception, for example, starts inside the brain, i.e., from an existing 'belief' or a model of the world that the brain uses to predict what signals the senses could or should be receiving. These predicted signals are compared with the actual signals received and any discrepancies or errors are used by the brain to improve its model of the world. This process is repeated until the prediction errors become insignificant (Frith 2007: 35, 124–7). In other words, the brain is a sophisticated hypothesis-testing mechanism that aims to minimize the prediction error between its model of the world and the sensory input it receives about the world. The mind, then, is a self-supervising system that self-calibrates through the sensory signal received from the world.

On Bayesian approaches, the brain is considered to be a Bayesian inference machine. Bayes' rule captures how we, given some evidence, update the probability of a specific hypothesis by considering the product of the likelihood of the hypothesis (i.e., the probability of the evidence given the hypothesis) and the prior probability of the hypothesis (how likely the hypothesis was before considering the current evidence). The probability assigned to the hypothesis based on this calculation is called the posterior probability. The best inference is the one with the highest posterior probability (Hohwy 2013: 17). Let us have a look at Bayes' theorem.

Following basic Boolean logic, we can ascertain that, generally, the sum of the probability that a word we encounter is 'table', and the probability that it would be any other word (i.e., not the word 'table') must sum to 1:

$$\Pr(X|I) + \Pr(\neg X|I) = 1.0$$

In the formula above X represents our variable – the indicator of the probability that the word we encounter is 'table' ($\neg X$ consequently indicates *not* 'table'), I contains all our background information and beliefs, and the vertical bar | stands for 'given' (i.e., everything to the right of this symbol is taken as being true). These two outcomes (the word being 'table' or not 'table') exhaust all possibilities, a basic inference that ensures logical *consistency* (see Cox 1946). The joint probability of two events must satisfy a similar consistency:

$$\Pr(X, Y|I) = \Pr(X|Y, I) \times \Pr(Y|I)$$

Imagine that you have compiled a very small dictionary of 100 words. Of these 100 words, 40 are nouns, and half of the nouns are masculine nouns. What is the probability of encountering a masculine noun in this dictionary then? We can quite easily work out from the information given that there are 20 masculine nouns. If we apply the formula above, it would look as follows:

$$\Pr(masculine, noun|I) = \Pr(masculine|noun, I) \times \Pr(noun|I)$$

$$\Pr(masculine|noun, I) = 0.5$$

$$\times$$

$$\Pr(noun|I) = 0.4$$

$$=$$

$$0.2$$

That is, because half of all nouns are masculine nouns the probability of encountering a masculine noun whenever you encounter a noun is 0.5; because there are 100 words in our dictionary and we know that 40 of these words are nouns, the probability of encountering a noun is 0.4; the product of 0.5 and 0.4 is 0.2, so the probability of encountering a masculine noun is 0.2. In other words, 20 per cent of instances in our small dictionary are masculine nouns; and because we have 100 words in total, we can conclude that there are 20 masculine nouns.

Logical consistency also requires that:

$$\Pr(X, Y|I) = \Pr(Y, X|I)$$

or in words: that the joint probability of having a masculine word that is a noun is the same as the joint probability that the word is a masculine noun. Then, we can replace the terms for the respective joint probabilities with their products that we have used above:

$$\Pr(X|Y, I) \times \Pr(Y|I) = \Pr(Y|X, I) \times \Pr(X|I)$$

This leads us directly to Bayes' theorem which allows us to calculate conditional probabilities that are, otherwise, hard or harder to obtain. For example, let us assume further that we know that, overall, 60 words out of our small dictionary of 100 words are marked as masculine. In other words, we know that $\Pr(masculine|I) = 0.6$, but what we do not know is the chance of seeing a noun if the word is masculine or $\Pr(noun|masculine, I)$. We can calculate this probability from the above equality formula by applying Bayes' theorem:

$$\Pr(noun|masculine, I) = \frac{\Pr(masculine|noun, I) \times \Pr(noun|I)}{\Pr(masculine|I)}$$

$$= \frac{0.5 \times 0.4}{0.6} = 0.33$$

In general, we can also use a more generic notation:

$$\Pr(hypothesis|data, I) = \frac{\Pr(data|hypothesis, I) \times \Pr(hypothesis|I)}{\Pr(data|I)}$$

The terms used in Bayes' theorem have formal names: $\Pr(hypothesis|I)$ is called the *prior* probability, which is then modified with measurements stemming from the data, through the *likelihood* function $\Pr(data|hypothesis, I)$. These two terms are crucial in establishing Bayes' relationship of proportionality, which is signalled by $\propto$:

$$\Pr(hypothesis|data, I) \propto \Pr(data|hypothesis, I) \times \Pr(hypothesis|I)$$

That is, the prior (or the belief in the hypothesis before any data is seen) is weighted by the likelihood (of the data being obtained, given the initial beliefs, i.e., our hypothesis) to yield the posterior (or updated) hypothesis (see Jaynes 2003; Sivia and Skilling 2006). Note that the product on the right-hand side is not equal (=) but proportional ($\propto$) to the posterior hypothesis. The denominator that is missing here is important as a normalization constant, as it does not depend on the hypothesis. We call it the *evidence* (sometimes also called the *marginal likelihood*). For all practical purposes, using the evidence matters only if we want to compare different models. Using the evidence to normalise the product of the prior and the likelihood puts all models that we may wish to compare on the same (comparable) scale. In all other cases, you would only use the product, ignoring the evidence. In a sense, we can think of Bayes' theorem as providing a correction for false alarms (Norris 2006: 330–1): if there is a substantial probability that a test will produce a false positive result, the rarer the event that is being predicted, the more likely it is that a positive result will be due to a false alarm.

The prediction error minimization hypothesis has been hailed as 'the first grand unified empirical theory' about how the brain implements the mind. It is also considered the first unifying account of perception, cognition and action (Clark 2015b: 2). It proposes to explain the mind via one core mechanism:

a process of comparing predicted sensory input with actual sensory input, updating hypotheses in light of the difference between predictions and observations, and generating new predictions. But predictions are not the whole story: the brain also attempts to minimize prediction error, through perception, action and attention (Clark 2013). *Perception* minimizes prediction error by trying to infer the nature of the signal source from the varying input signal and by extracting repeating patterns and statistical regularities from its environment; in this it is guided by the statistical history of events in its environment. *Action* is used by the observer to move the sensors to resample the world by actively seeking expected stimuli, for example, by moving the body so that it receives a better signal. A better signal would be a signal that better matches the generated hypothesis. Both action and perception work by reacting to prediction errors and ensuring that the external world remains synchronized with our mentally simulated world. Crucially, not all responses to error carry the same weight: *attention* assigns more weight to reliable or relevant responses than to non-reliable or irrelevant ones. Bayesian predictive models therefore rely on three core components: prediction, prediction error (minimized by perception and action) and weighting of prediction error (achieved by the system's attentional component). We will now discuss these three components in more detail.

8.2.2   The Core Mechanism: a Hierarchical, Generative Model

Predictive coding implies that the neural system actively predicts upcoming sensory information rather than passively registering it; the process of predicting is automatic and unconscious. The mechanism that drives the prediction engine, revises the model parameters and minimizes the prediction error is hierarchical and generative in nature (Clark 2015b; Hohwy 2013: 26, 41).

A generative model generates hypotheses about the expected sensory input. This model is implemented in the backwards connections in the brain. Backwards connections are required so that the brain can recognize the input and pinpoint the causes that produced that input. The easiest way to implement backwards connections is to distribute the work to a hierarchy in which each level predicts something relatively simple, guided by prediction error from the level below, and passes its inferences up to the next level. In these architectures, higher levels learn to specialize in predicting events and states of affairs that are built up from the features and properties (such as lines, shapes and edges) targeted by lower levels. But, at the same time, the lower-level response is continuously modulated by top-down predictions (Clark 2015b). This generative hierarchical model is decomposed into a likelihood (the probability of sensory data, given their causes) and a prior (the a priori probability of the causes, or estimates of how likely the causes were before considering the current sensory evidence). Perception then becomes the process of inverting the likelihood model that captures the mapping from causes to sensations to access the mappings from sensations to causes (Friston 2010: 129). How is this inversion achieved? It appears to be the case that, by distributing the current hypothesis throughout a hierarchy and viewing the hierarchy of lower and higher levels as a whole, the model is implicitly inverted: because both inputs and causes are simultaneously accessible, the mapping from sensations to causes (operationalized as the posterior probability of the causes given the sensory data) is directly available. Hence, no extra step is needed to infer inputs from possible causes, and no particular brain area needs to be designated to complete this inversion. Instead, 'representation emerges in the ongoing predictive activity of the entire hierarchy of prediction error minimization mechanisms' (Hohwy 2013: 52–5).

The idea of backward connections is not alien to linguists. Supervised connectionist models with back-propagation of error, which have been used to model language data, can be considered predecessors for predictive processing and hierarchical Bayesian processing in general (Clark 2015b: 17–18; Hohwy 2013). The back-propagation algorithms in neural networks correct error in the classification of incoming data. The problem connectionist modellers faced was to provide their models with enough training data; manually annotating data is an expensive endeavour. They also struggled to find an adequate solution that would prevent the proliferation of hidden layers. Predictive processing resolves the categorized training data problem by making the model self-supervised because the environment provides the right answer; for this reason, it qualifies as an ecologically feasible form of supervised learning. Yet, connectionist networks learn in a supervised manner and classify incoming data bottom-up rather than generating data top-down in an unsupervised fashion, as Bayesian models do. In fact, the key to Bayesian learning is to *generate* data, *not classify* it, using multilayer neural networks (Schmidhuber 2015) with efficient coding and transmission as core predictive coding strategy (Clark 2015b: 27). Efficient coding and transmission form the core of information theory, and some of its concepts have made their way into predictive processing models, as we will see in the next section.

8.2.3 Measuring Surprise

The brain 'somehow [sic] implements processing that approximates ideal ways of weighing new evidence against prior knowledge' (Clark 2015b: 8). Some of the concepts that are used in research within the predictive tradition, such as mutual information and surprisal, link in with what we have seen before (Chapter 3, Section 3.3). Yet, mutual information and surprisal are of relevance to predictive models for different reasons.

If a neural population represents a certain state in the world then they should only fire when that state is observed. If that is the case, then the neural population and the state can be considered good predictors of each other, i.e., their mutual information is high. Because there tends to be noise, ambiguity and uncertainty, the brain tries to maximize mutual information by minimizing the prediction error. It achieves this by constantly adjusting the hypotheses it generates (Hohwy 2013: 50–1). How does this work? On predictive approaches, the nervous system is considered an information channel. Any sensory state carries an amount of self information or surprisal, which is a declining function of probability: the higher the likelihood of encountering a state, the less surprised the organism will be to encounter it. The aim of the nervous system is to minimize surprisal. Surprisal minimization can be achieved, as discussed above, by minimizing the divergence between hypothesis and posterior (which is, recall, the product of the likelihood of the hypothesis, i.e., the probability of the evidence given the hypothesis, and the prior probability of the hypothesis or how likely the hypothesis was before considering the current evidence). The prediction error measures the difference between the current hypothesis and the true posterior under the model; it consists of the surprise together with the perception error. By minimizing perception error, the bound (or the upper and lower limiting value) on surprisal becomes smaller and the prediction error becomes a proxy for surprisal. This serves a double purpose: it approximates surprise so that organisms sample relevant sensory evidence and select plausible hypotheses about the causes of its sensory input. In other words, prediction error minimization describes what is required for a representation to occur, and provides a tractable task for the brain to perform on known types of input. This process is regulated by top-down predictions that control bottom-up prediction error (Hohwy 2013: 52–5).

There is an asymmetry in the flow of information across the processing hierarchy. Top-down propagation of information activates representations of expected sensory input, generated by internal models. Only the portion of sensory data that is not accounted for by the prediction at each stage – the prediction error – is propagated forward; this is a very good data-compression strategy (Clark 2015b: 29). The ascending activation updates internal models and subsequent predictions, until the prediction error is totally 'explained away' and assimilated throughout the processing hierarchy (Friston 2005).

There are several ways of formalising prediction error, and the oldest ones date back to Bush and Mosteller (1951) and Rescorla and Wagner (1972). One difference between these formalisations and the formalisation in terms of Bayesian surprise is that the former do not take into account uncertainty during inference or prediction (see Kruschke 2008 for discussion). In fact, the Rescorla–Wagner model and its computational implementations contain an update module only, no prediction module (Petar Milin, personal communication). Regardless of formalisation, however, prediction and prediction error play a central role in both learning and processing. They therefore provide a powerful way of bridging literatures (see Jaeger and Snider 2013; Kuperberg and Jaeger 2016) and we will come back to this in Chapter 9.

In addition to an error-minimization mechanism, a neurologically plausible equivalent to a 'novelty filter' on learning has been proposed: by becoming insensitive to the most highly correlated properties of the input, organisms learn to discount the statistically most predictable elements of the input signal. 'Nature's predictavores' thus come with a built-in 'biological emphasis on the newsworthy' (Clark 2015b: 29, 41). Attention, as discussed in Chapter 6, fits well into this framework: without paying conscious attention to the incoming signal, prediction errors would not carry the same import and, hence, would not alter internal models to the same extent.

8.2.4   From Prediction to Action within an Embodied Brain

Bayesian brains are proactive prediction engines, constantly anticipating the incoming sensory signal. On a Bayesian approach, organisms learn about the world by generating incoming sensory data themselves and matching their top-down predictions against bottom-up incoming sensory input; in case of mismatch, they use learning strategies to improve their model (Clark 2015b: 6). This implies that what we expect to see and hear influences what we do see and hear – perception and understanding are co-constructed, inseparable – but the precise mix of top-down and bottom-up influences is not fixed. And prediction is not the only strategy available to the organism. There is also action and we bring about the sensory stream through our bodily actions that selectively harvest sensory input. Predictions initiate actions that structure our worlds, and organisms direct their behaviour to satisfy these predictions (Clark 2015b: 6).

Clark distinguishes two versions of predictive processing, one conservative and one radical, and these provide different answers to the question of what happens when a predictive processing system deals with sensory inputs (Clark 2015a). A conservative predictive processing approach would select the hypothesis that explains the sensory data most adequately, given prior knowledge and current estimated sensory uncertainty. Prediction error, on this account, signifies information not yet explained by a hypothesis. A radical predictive processing approach requires integrating perception, cognition and action into a 'single, action-oriented, frugality-obsessed processing regime'. On this account, prediction error signals sensory information that is not yet leveraged to guide interactions with the world. The job of the prediction error signal is thus to provide 'an organism-computable anchor for self-organizing processes apt for the control of action, motion and environmental intervention'

(Clark 2015a). The brain does not search for the hypothesis that best explains the sensory data in the sense that its guiding rationale is representational. Representational fidelity is not the objective: action is: 'perceiving a structured scene is adaptively pointless unless it enables you to do something better, or to avoid doing something bad' (Clark 2015c).

While learning to deal with the world, the organism implicitly builds up a layered hierarchical representation that makes accurate predictions. But strong predictions, based on real-world knowledge or frequent structures, can sometimes lead to misinterpretations, particularly if they are compatible with certain features within bottom-up input. This so-called good enough processing (Ferreira 2003) seems superficially incompatible with predictive processing, unless the concept of information structure is invoked (Ferreira and Lowder 2016): information that is given or presupposed is processed in a good enough manner, but new or focused information is the real target of the prediction efforts.

Another interesting aspect of predictive processing models is that systems do not explicitly need to try to represent the world (Hohwy 2013: 63): a system that has learnt to predict and expect its own sensory activity can also imagine its world and dream about it: the prediction machinery can also be run 'offline', generating the kinds of neuronal activity that would be expected (predicted) in some imaginary situation. On such an account, our perceptions are – in a sense – fantasies that coincide with reality (Frith 2007: 35, 124–7). The same apparatus may make it possible for us to try out solutions in our mind, thus suggesting a bridge between offline prediction and simulation-based forms of reasoning. Yet, allowing predictive pre-activation to influence processing might lead to distortions of perceptual or interpretational reality because it affords our prior beliefs too much power (for a report on how feedback may distort prelexical processing, see Massaro 1989). If things go awry, delusions and hallucinations ensue.

8.2.5   Is a Bayesian Approach Ideal?

With the predictive coding framework (Rao and Ballard 1999; Friston 2010; Clark 2013) cognitive science completed a paradigm shift from viewing the brain as a 'transformer of ambient sensations into cognition' to 'a generator of predictions and inferences that interprets experience' (Mesulam 2008: 368). But is the Bayesian implementation of this idea ideal?

In fact, rather severe criticism has been levelled at the Bayesian framework in general (see Bowers and Davis 2012; see Griffiths et al. 2012 for a rebuttal). One aspect that has received particular criticism is the Bayesian preference for optimality. Bayesian frameworks are often said to claim that our brains have evolved to be extraordinarily good at exploiting the statistics of the environment, which enables us to perform in a close to optimal fashion. Bayesians assume that cognition is an approximately optimal response to the uncertainty and structure present in natural tasks and environments (see Anderson 1990). A common premise is, indeed, that theorising should largely be constrained by a rational analysis of what the mind ought to do in order to perform optimally. Bayesian inference then stipulates how rational learners should update their beliefs in the light of new evidence.

Bowers and Davis (2012) argue that this mathematical approach to cognition ignores many of the important constraints that stem from biological, evolutionary and processing (algorithmic) considerations. The Bayesian focus on optimality differs from most if not all other theories of cognition that have tended to assume that our motor, perception and cognitive systems *satisfice* (Simon 1956) or *meliorize* (Dawkins 1982). That is, natural selection does not produce optimal solutions but solutions that work well enough, or it produces solutions that are better but therefore not the best. In other words, our systems are adaptive and work well enough under many conditions, but are not optimal. Simon's (1957) notion of bounded rationality supports this view: humans cannot achieve full rationality because short-term memory is capacity-limited, attention spans are short and learning rates are slow.

The reason for this focus on optimality in Bayesian approaches resides at least partially in the fact that they are typically formulated at Marr's computational level and characterize the computational problems humans face and the logic by which these computations can be carried out (Marr 1982). Marr's tri-level hypothesis distinguishes between:

1 Computation: what does the system do (e.g., what problems does it solve or overcome)? And similarly, why does it do these things?
2 Algorithm/representation: how does the system do what it does? Specifically, what representations does it use and what processes does it employ to build and manipulate the representations?
3 (Physical) implementation: how is the system physically realized? What neural structures and neuronal activities implement the system?

Being specified at Marr's computational level has two implications. On the one hand, accounts proposed at the computational level cannot be directly compared to accounts proposed at the algorithmic or representational levels. On the other hand, this means that something specified at the computational level does as such not make direct claims about the algorithmic level. Nevertheless, Bayesian modellers have explored how the computational and algorithmic levels might relate, taking into account the main constraint that people must somehow be approximating Bayesian inference even though, on their view, 'there need be nothing intrinsically "Bayesian" about algorithms that approximate Bayesian inference' (Griffiths et al. 2012: 417).

At the implementational level, it has been claimed (Fletcher and Frith 2009; Clark 2013) that the neurotransmitter dopamine would be the ideal candidate for encoding precision of error units in the predictive coding framework. Currently, the most popular theory of dopamine function is the reward prediction error hypothesis (Schultz, Dayan and Montague 1997; but see Humphries 2017). Yet, behavioural evidence for competing theories has been presented. Kakade and Dayan (2002) have proposed that dopamine activations are *novelty bonuses*: they increase the probability of re-sampling typically rewarding stimuli as well as surprising stimuli. In this way, they act as a facilitator of exploratory action and perception. Redgrave and Gurney (2006: 973) contend that 'the dopamine activation response has more to do with the discovery of new actions than adjusting the relative probabilities of selecting pre-existing actions to maximize anticipated rewards.'

Bowers and Davis (2012: 8, 405) call Bayesian modelling a 'misguided approach'; why develop models that optimize at the computational level, even though we know that the brain and mind satisfice and that key model constraints will be found at the algorithmic and implementational levels? Crucially, there is relatively little support for theoretical and methodological Bayesian theories in psychology and neuroscience: Bayesian theories are so flexible that they can account for almost any pattern of results; Bayesian models are rarely compared to (often simpler) non-Bayesian models and when they are, they seldom come out as the better performer; the neuroscientific evidence is ambiguous at best and constraints from biology and evolution are typically not taken into account. Bayesian accounts have also been accused of ignoring the question of how prior beliefs, which are necessary for inference, are formed. Hierarchical generative modellers solve the question of how prior beliefs are formed by referring to the fact that the priors (i.e., the probability of causes at one level, given those at the level above) are optimized by means of the so-called free energy principle (Friston 2010: 129). The free energy principle is a mathematical formulation of how adaptive systems such as animals or brains resist the tendency to disorder that defines them. The free energy principle says that any self-organizing system that is at equilibrium with its environment must minimize surprise.

Griffiths et al. (2012) refute these objections by saying that comparing human behaviour to optimal behaviour does not necessarily imply the belief that human beings actually compute these optimal solutions. Therefore, optimality would not be the core ingredient for any neural Bayesian theory. Clark (2015b: 41) likewise stresses that researchers are not finding that human beings are Bayes optimal (i.e., that we are responding correctly relative to the absolute uncertainties in the input) in an absolute sense. Instead, we are often optimal or near optimal in characterizing the uncertainties that accompany the information we do have. In other words, we act as rational Bayesian estimators.

Overall, it needs to be borne in mind that Bayesian approaches are theoretical frameworks that provide a general perspective and a set of tools for building models. The models are falsifiable but the framework itself is not; it can only be judged on its ability to generate useful models. The merits of a Bayesian approach lie in the fact that it provides the foundation for universal laws of cognition, i.e., principles expected to hold true for any kind of intelligence anywhere in the universe. Predictions from mathematical analyses based on models of Bayesian inference thus have the potential to apply across a very wide range of domains. This makes it possible to cast a range of phenomena in one single framework. Bayesian models also insist on coherence; a coherent all-purpose model of the external world plays a crucial role in cognition. And Bayesian models emphasize understanding *why* something works: given the role uncertainty plays in life, Bayesian analysis may well play an important role in specifying the function of the different aspects of cognition. For example, Bayesian approaches may help recognize the commonalities between different mechanistic approaches to aspects of cognition that are directly relevant to language such as category learning: prototype and exemplar theory, for example, would correspond to different strategies for density estimation (Ashby and Alfonso-Reese 1995).

8.3 What Does Predictive Processing Mean for Language Cognition?

Language comprehension relies on integrating noisy sensory input obtained in a particular social setting with general world knowledge to arrive at meaning. This all happens within a time span of a few hundred milliseconds. Because of the challenge posed by the complexity and urgency of this task, it seems logical to assume that linguistic comprehension would benefit from the ability to predict upcoming material (for elaborate discussion, see the 2016 special issue (volume 31, issue 1) of *Language, Cognition and Neuroscience*).

Curiously, prediction has played a minor role in the generative theories of language and language processing that dominated the linguistic scene during the second half of the twentieth century. It was claimed that 'with infinite options available as each new word of an unfolding sentence is encountered, predicting what comes next is not just improbable but nonviable as a strategy' (Stanovich and West 1979). Early models of sentence processing relied on some form of memory buffer to store sentential elements temporarily for later integration at phrasal, clausal or sentence boundaries. Eventually, such delayed processing models became difficult to reconcile with the empirical evidence that was accumulating in favour of updating on a word-by-word basis. Notions of buffering gradually gave way to the now more widely held incremental view that words are incorporated successively into the sentential context as they are perceived and processed.

Think here of the infamous garden path sentence: 'The horse raced past the barn fell' (Bever 1970: 316). At the word 'past', it is unclear whether 'raced' is the main verb of the sentence, describing the horse's action, or a participle, describing the horse. Most hearers commit early on to the main verb interpretation and are confused when they hear the verb 'fell' – their surprise is the result of an incorrect prediction, based on the higher frequency of the main verb construction. The magnitude of the garden path effect has been shown to be graded and to depend on the predictability of the chosen parse, given the context. Kuperberg and Jaeger (2016: 32–3) list a range of observed contextual predictability effects on syntactic and lexico-semantic processing and conclude that it is logically impossible to explain these effects without assuming that the context influences the state of the language-processing system before the bottom-up input is observed.

8.3.1   From Incremental to Anticipatory Processing: Non-Predictive Accounts of Predictability

The view that language comprehension does not require buffering because it proceeds in an incremental fashion is supported by evidence from a wide variety of studies with different methodologies, including offline and online techniques. The strongest evidence to date stems from investigations of real-time, continuous language processing using techniques like eye tracking and event-related brain potentials (ERPs) from electroencephalography (EEG) that only require listening or reading (for an overview of ERPs in language research, see Kaan 2007). They also track sentence processing with high temporal resolution continuously over the course of a sentence, which makes it easier to isolate the precise processing stage implicated (Kutas, DeLong and Smith 2011: 193). What remains debated is whether prediction proceeds in a serial or parallel fashion, i.e., whether just one upcoming structure of a sentence is predicted with a certain strength at any particular time or whether the parser computes multiple syntactic parses in parallel, each with some degree of probabilistic support (Kuperberg and Jaeger 2016: 35).

Incremental, word-by-word updating models are experiencing competition from anticipatory or predictive processing models in which available contextual elements are used to activate words in advance of hearing or reading them. This idea was first proposed by McClelland and Rumelhart (1981) and McClelland and Elman (1986).

A crucial point here is the definition of 'prediction', a term which has been used in many different ways across the psycholinguistic and neuroscience literature (for an overview, see Kuperberg and Jaeger 2016). Kutas, DeLong and Smith (2011: 194–5) point out that prediction is different from predictability. Predictability means that some words could be predicted in advance from context. Even if the brain does not make a prediction in advance, once the word is encountered, it might still be processed differently depending on its predictability, i.e., how well it could have been predicted from the context. Prediction is much stronger and implies that upcoming, unseen input alters current processing. In research on language, predictability has been favoured over prediction. Reading time studies are one source of evidence that the brain is sensitive to predictability. Less predictable words – those with lower probability given the context – are read more slowly. Ehrlich and Rayner (1981) were the first to demonstrate that when a word can be predicted from the preceding context, the eyes are relatively likely to skip over the word rather than to fixate it directly. When the eyes do fixate a predictable word, they spend relatively little time on it. These effects have been confirmed in dozens of subsequent studies (for a recent overview of the eye-tracking literature, see Staub 2015).

The reading time effect is sensitive to both semantic and syntactic manipulations of predictability, and its underlying cause remains disputed. Norris (2006) has suggested that the reading time effect arises as a consequence of decoding noisy input: if the reader is presented with a noisy representation of a word because the stimulus itself is noisy, or because there is noise in the perceptual system, there will be some probability that the word that most closely matches the input will not be the intended word. If the input most closely matches a low-frequency word, there is some probability that the input was actually produced by another word, meaning that the match with the low-frequency word was a false alarm. If the other word is much more frequent than the low-frequency word, it becomes even more likely that the input was produced by the less well matching high-frequency word than by the more closely matching low-frequency word. That is, information about word frequency effectively alters the weighting of perceptual evidence. But frequency is not the only factor that can influence the prior probability of a word. Under natural reading circumstances, a variety of sources of contextual information will also alter the expected probability of words: syntactic knowledge, sentence-level semantic interpretation, discourse representations and parafoveal preview (e.g., Rayner 1998) may all alter the prior probabilities. Frequency in the Bayesian approach acts as a bias: in a perceptual identification task, a Bayesian recognizer should respond with the word with the largest posterior probability. All other things being equal, high-frequency words would therefore tend to be generated as responses more often than low-frequency words. To recognize words that have less top-down support relative to their visual competitors, more bottom-up sensory evidence needs to be acquired before an acceptable level of certainty is reached that the word has been correctly identified and this takes time. However, frequency would not improve the perceptual sensitivity of the system in terms of its ability to discriminate between a pair of words in a forced-choice task: the better the perceptual evidence, the more limited the influence of frequency and frequency can never override reliable perceptual evidence (Norris 2006: 331). Recent findings confirm this general claim and link the need for more bottom-up support to individual differences in mental speed: readers who slow down during a pattern-learning task benefit more from strong bottom-up support from the orthographic system than readers who speed up during a pattern-learning task (Milin, Divjak and Baayen 2017).

As we have seen in Chapter 3, Hale (2003) presented an entropy reduction hypothesis on which the difficulty of a word is linked to a change in the (un) certainty of how the sentence should be analysed syntactically. Likewise, Levy's surprisal theory (2008) attributes the reaction time effect to the shift in likelihood that occurs with every word that is processed (each potential whole sentence interpretation becomes more or less likely as more words are read). Words which cause a greater total likelihood shift will take longer to read and the size of the shift (typically measured as Kullback Leibler divergence) is determined by the word's predictability. Both approaches are non-predictive accounts of predictability effects as all affected processing takes place *after* the word itself is seen rather than before (Kutas, DeLong and Smith 2011: 195). In other words, these approaches measure how predictable a word that has been seen should be given experience with the contexts in which it occurs; they do not measure how predictable an unseen word should be given experience with the contexts in which it occurs. In fact, many sentence processing frameworks assume (either implicitly or explicitly) that high-level information facilitates the processing of new lower-level information only *after* this new lower-level information has been activated by the bottom-up input (Kuperberg and Jaeger 2016: 40–1). This was because they feared that lending prior beliefs too much power might distort perception or interpretation of reality. Inhibiting or suppressing predicted candidates that remain unsupported by bottom-up input might also be expensive. And, finally, predictive pre-activation might be metabolically expensive in general.

8.3.2   *Predictive Accounts of Predictability*

Yet, evidence has amassed for predictive accounts. Here too, the exact definition of the key concept is important. Kutas, DeLong and Smith (2011: 196) distinguish between *weakly predictive* and *strongly predictive* accounts.

A weakly predictive account may assume that the linguistic processor maintains a limited list of possible whole-sentence parses. Then, increased reading time may occur either when it turns out that the appropriate parse was pruned from the list for having too low a probability (Jurafsky 1996; Narayanan and Jurafsky 1998), or when new evidence turns a less preferred parse into the most likely possibility, triggering a shift in attention (Crocker and Brants 2000;

Narayanan and Jurafsky 2002). Such models are weakly predictive in the sense that they explicitly marginalize over potential sentence continuations to determine which parses are most likely and which can be pruned to reduce memory load. However, pruning can only explain effects in special cases (i.e., garden path sentences), and attention shifts only occur at relatively specific points in a sentence. Smith and Levy (2008) propose a model inspired by motor control of 'optimal preparation', in which the processor does a graded amount of anticipatory processing for each potential continuation. The actual amount of processing is determined as a trade-off between the resources spent on this anticipatory processing (preparing to process a word quickly is costly) versus the increased processing efficiency achieved if this continuation is actually encountered (sometimes preparation is worth it). Such a model expends more effort on preparing for those continuations which are more likely to be encountered, thus explaining the predictability effect on subsequent reading time of the continuation.

Evidence for strongly predictive accounts cannot be gathered using behavioural measures (Kutas, DeLong and Smith 2011: 200). Eye-tracking studies that investigated attention to visual objects during real-time language processing do yield evidence of anticipatory and predictive processing (Altmann and Kamide 2007). A range of electrophysiological studies have likewise provided support, although there remains an issue of prediction versus integration, i.e., the challenge of distinguishing between facilitation effects at a target word that arise because that word was predicted and facilitation effects at a target word that are due to it being easier to integrate once perceived. ERP studies show that we are indeed looking at prediction: there have been experiments in which the electrophysiological sign of noun prediction can be measured on a prenominal item, e.g., an adjective or article that is encountered before the actual noun is initiated. This was done with Spanish sentences (Wicha, Moreno and Kutas 2004) that contain gender-marked articles preceding target nouns of particular gender classes (in half of the cases the gender of the article mismatched the gender of the following noun or picture); with spoken Dutch sentences (Van Berkum et al. 2005) that manipulate gender marking (neuter or common) on prenominal adjectives – a feature controlled by the gender of the upcoming noun; or indefinite articles *a* versus *an* in English (DeLong, Urbach and Kutas 2005). For a recent overview of ERP evidence in this area, see the review by Delong, Troyer and Kutas (2014). Note also that Nieuwland et al. (2017) failed to replicate the crucial article-elicited N400 modulation (a negative deflection that peaks around 400 milliseconds post-stimulus onset) in an offline cloze task that measures the probability that people continue a sentence fragment with a specific word. The more commonly reported noun-elicited N400 modulation was replicated in the same close task, however. This failure to replicate the core finding casts doubt on a strong prediction view in which people routinely pre-activate the phonological form of upcoming words and suggests a more limited role for prediction during language comprehension.

Only strongly predictive accounts presuppose pre-activation; that is, only these accounts assume that the hypotheses about, e.g., syntactic structure affect information at lower levels of representation and change the *prior* distribution of belief at these lower levels, *prior* to encountering bottom-up input.[1] Facilitation does not necessarily imply predictive pre-activation. Some even argue that 'true' prediction goes beyond predictive pre-activation by entailing some kind of 'commitment' to these pre-activated candidates, ahead of encountering or combining new bottom-up input (Kuperberg and Jaeger 2016: 45). This would further increase the cost that is incurred if the chosen alternative ends up being the wrong choice. There is evidence, indeed, of 'cost' or 'punishment', i.e., when highly pre-activated input is not received, additional processing may be needed. P600 (a positive deflection that peaks around 600 milliseconds post-stimulus onset) may be related to some sort of prediction violation (and possibly also of linking across Marr's computational and algorithmic levels of analysis). Such effects may be best accounted for in frameworks of cognitive control and conflict monitoring (Kutas, DeLong and Smith 2011: 201).

8.3.3   Do We Really Make Predictions?

Linking up with Bayesian predictive processing models provides research on language with the opportunity to start developing accounts that chime with work done across a range of other disciplines. Taking a Bayesian approach to language cognition therefore offers the prospect to unite different brain functions, in that the same mode of operation is proposed to occur across all domains, at sensory, motor and cognitive levels. But are Bayesian models realistic models for language?

Rabagliati, Gambi and Pickering (2016: 95–6) point out that models of predictive learning differ from generative or usage-based models of language development which assume that learning occurs offline. The latter models, which originated within linguistics proper, largely ignore what happens while the child attempts to understand or produce a sentence (i.e., during online processing). Instead, they are interested in the end result of these processes, e.g., does the child understand the sentence or not? Is the child able to identify

---

[1] Note the distinction between pre-activation through top-down prediction and pre-activation through priming. While predictive pre-activation entails the use of high-level information within the internally represented context to pre-activate upcoming information at lower level(s) of representation, priming is assumed to stem from lingering activation due to previously processed material at lower levels of representation (Kuperberg and Jaeger 2016: 37, 39–40).

lexical items as nouns and verbs? This is because it is the end result of learning that matters to linguists. In a sense, linguistic models conceive of language development as a process occurring at a rather slow pace, and the internal grammar changes only when a considerable amount of evidence accumulates against the hypotheses about the structure of the language. Models of predictive learning are very different. In these models, the learning mechanism is not based on abstraction, but on prediction error. In particular, children can use their current linguistic knowledge to generate predictions about what they will hear next. When these predictions are checked against reality, the resulting discrepancy (the error signal) can be used to update linguistic knowledge and to enhance future predictions. This view would make implicit negative evidence available on a grand scale (Rabagliati, Gambi and Pickering 2016: 95) and explicitly connects language processing and language learning: learning takes place online, rather than after the fact. Unfortunately, as Rabagliati, Gambi and Pickering (2016: 97–8, 100) argue, we currently lack direct evidence that children make the types of predictions that would aid learning; these predictions need to be incremental, probabilistic and parallel. Adults' predictions have all of the required properties: adults make predictions incrementally, they predict on the basis of several types of cues, and they predict at different linguistic levels (from semantics to phonology). But it is not clear whether children can make predictions that are useful for learning before they have fully mastered their language, and it is even less clear whether children can use these predictions for the purpose of mastering their language.

As mentioned in Section 8.2.5 in this chapter, the predictive coding framework has been criticized for lacking too many implementational details and architectural commitments to be evaluated seriously (Rasmussen and Eliasmith 2013). Huettig and Mani (2016: 20) argue that the evidence that has been presented is not sufficient to claim that all language processing is predictive. They outline a number of issues, notably the fact that not all language users appear to predict language (there appears to be a correlation between productive vocabulary size and prediction in children and between reading ability and prediction in adults), that suboptimal input makes prediction challenging (although this is the area where most benefit would be reaped from being able to predict), and that prediction is strongly context dependent (it looks like the experimental paradigms themselves might be what induces prediction) and hindered by resource limitations such as working memory and processing speed.

Staub (2015: 323–4) concludes his survey of empirical evidence from reading by stating that:

[. . .] reading a sentence results in activation of potential upcoming words. This does not seem to involve prediction of a specific word, but rather graded *activation* of words approximately in proportion to their cloze probability.[2] Processing a word that is pre-activated in this way is then easier than it otherwise would be. The benefit of this pre-activation seems to accrue primarily in the very earliest stages of lexical processing or even during pre-lexical (i.e., feature and letter) processing. [...] If cloze probability is taken to define the notion of predictability, then the effects that we have discussed throughout this paper are unambiguously effects of predictability. But if a word's cloze probability is seen as a measure of its activation by context – and Staub et al. (2015) argue that it should be – it is no longer obvious that the effects we have been discussing are best viewed as predictability effects. Rather, notions of predictability and prediction may drop out of the explanatory picture, and the empirical effects of cloze probability may be viewed as directly reflecting pre-activation by context.

Molinaro, Monsalve and Lizarazu (2016) argue that more fine-grained psycholinguistic paradigms are needed to characterize whether prediction and production are supported by similar neurophysiological mechanisms. What is needed is evidence about the time course of neural activity through which predictive coding evolves up to the millisecond *preceding* presentation of an expected stimulus. There is some neurological evidence for the hypothesis that oscillatory activity during language processing provides a measure of predictive coding (Friston et al. 2015). This requires going back to the brainwaves we encountered briefly in Chapter 6, Section 6.3.2. Recall that slower alpha waves occur during wakeful relaxation (with closed eyes) while faster beta waves occur during normal conscious states. Gamma brainwaves are high-frequency waves that have been hypothetically related to neural consciousness. Alpha and beta oscillations are thought to index top-down processing, whereas gamma oscillations are presumed to index bottom-up processing: alpha and beta oscillatory activity reflects the forward models of lower-level (cortical or subcortical) activity (i.e., the predictions), whereas gamma-oscillatory activity indicates processing of prediction errors to update the predictions. High temporal resolution techniques with reasonable spatial brain resolution, such as MEG (and to a much lesser degree EEG) that reflect the cortical activity of large populations of pyramidal cells, can provide this critical experimental evidence. Molinaro, Monsalve and Lizarazu (2016: 51–4, 149) present preliminary findings from a sentence comprehension MEG experiment that contrasted multiword units such as *Nice to meet you* with non-fixed semantic compositional contexts – both ending in a word with cloze probability higher than 85 per cent. The findings provide initial evidence that the oscillatory dynamics (pre-stimulus beta desynchronization and post-stimulus alpha synchronization, to be precise) supporting language prediction employ a similar frequency channel to the ones involved in language production. Yet, evidence of pre-stimulus activity related to the post-stimulus perceptual processing of

---

[2] A group of subjects is asked to guess the next word of the sentence, given the first several words. A word's cloze probability is the proportion of subjects who provide that word (Taylor 1953).

a stimulus remains only partial evidence in favour of prediction during language processing.

8.4   Summary and Outlook

Of all predictive approaches, the Bayesian brain hypothesis is the one that has found strongest resonance in the area of language study. The Bayesian brain hypothesis uses Bayesian probability theory to formulate perception as a constructive process based on internal or generative models. The underlying idea is that the brain has a model of the world that it tries to optimize using sensory inputs. Crucially, the brain is an agent that actively manipulates the sensory stream by selectively harvesting sensory input through specific bodily actions. Predictions initiate actions that structure our worlds, and organisms direct their behaviour to satisfy these predictions.

Bayes-based theories of cognition are highly attractive to researchers working on language: biological implausibility has long plagued linguistic models and theories, and methodological insularity has impeded interdisciplinary approaches. A Bayesian approach promises to resolve both issues. Predictive coding has been argued to be the most appropriate framework at the neural level to shed light on the interaction between high- and low-level representations in prediction-driven language comprehension. The computations are grounded in Bayesian hierarchical inference theory which has proven its value across a range of disciplines, explaining a multitude of brain functions in a similar way. In fact, Lupyan and Clark (2015: 283) have argued that 'the learning of language may create a potent means of biasing the recruitment of prior knowledge and of artificially manipulating, at any level of processing, the weightings that determine the relative influence of different top-down expectations and incoming sensory signals.'

Yet, the Bayesian approach has also been criticized on a number of points. On an epistemological level, the objection has been raised that predictive coding frameworks have elevated a subsidiary process to ultimate goal: the brain's goal cannot be sensory prediction but must be survival through action. Moreover, Bayesian approaches are inevitably associated with the assumption that our brains have evolved to be extraordinarily good at exploiting the statistics of the environment, which enables us to be (near) optimal in solving a wide range of tasks. The ideal and rational Bayesian observer uses evidence in the best possible way to perform in a close to optimal fashion. Yet, this belief is contradicted by evidence from biological, evolutionary and (algorithmic) processing considerations; we appear to survive on good enough behaviour. Finally, the agentive representation of the brain throws up a number of questions that have profound philosophical implications: to what extent does what we expect to see and hear influence what we do see and hear? How does our individual potential for interference with 'reality' affect the sensory information we choose to harvest? And how does that, in turn, influence shared experience which underlies the formation of units of all sizes?

On a methodological level, the evidence supporting Bayesian accounts of language cognition could likewise support competing approaches. Several accounts are compatible with the results from predictability-based approaches to language, and Bayesian belief updating, which we have focused on in this chapter, is merely one of them. For example, Bayesian formalisation assumes that we hold multiple beliefs in parallel; therefore, experimental support for predictive Bayesian accounts can even be interpreted as indirect support for (non-Bayesian) parallel probabilistic prediction, a famous example of which would be the parallel-distributed connectionist models (Harm and Seidenberg 2004). Furthermore, the information theoretical construct of surprisal appears correlated with the processing times and neural activity to words during sentence comprehension. But Bayesian surprise can be implemented in many different ways at the algorithmic and neural levels, e.g., in recurrent connectionist networks, neural networks and as predictive coding models (Kuperberg and Jaeger 2016: 35–6, 48).

Over the course of this discussion, Marr's tri-level hypothesis has been mentioned on more than one occasion. The reason for the focus on optimality in Bayesian approaches has been said to reside at least partially in the fact that they are typically formulated at Marr's computational level. But Poggio (2010: 367) remarked that 'I am not sure that Marr would agree, but I am tempted to add learning as the very top level of understanding, above the computational level. [. . .] Only then may we be able to build intelligent machines that could learn to see – and think – without the need to be programmed to do it.' In the next chapter we will take a closer look at theories of learning and the insights they offer for the study of language cognition.

9 Learning: Navigating Frequency, Recency, Context and Contingency

We started out the previous chapter by asking how frequency of experience, memory and attention link together. It has long been known that 'experience is the stuff of which all learning is made' (Monsell 1991: 149), and linguists have been keen to collect frequencies of occurrence that provide a rough estimate of the differential amount of linguistic experience an average adult will have had. But the ubiquity of frequency effects does not imply that frequencies should be considered explanations or answers in their own right. Predictability-based approaches to language are one answer to this question, and in Chapter 8 we reviewed work relying on Bayesian belief updating.

> Practically all psychologists are absolutely sure that attempts to analyse and quantify human behavior will be frustrated by complexities of higher order than any encountered in the natural sciences. If some callow student ventures to doubt this truth, we have a standard argument ready to bring him into line. Look at our present theories, we tell him. Look at Hull's system or at the probabilistic models that are multiplying like overexcited paramecia. Although already too complicated for the average psychologist to handle, these theories are not yet adequate to account for the behavior of a rodent on a runway. (Estes 1957: 609)

Learning-based approaches may be what is needed to shed light on a core component of human intelligence, i.e., the ability to act without being programmed to do so (Poggio 2010: 367). This brings us to the final incarnation of our frequency question: what type of learning mechanism is needed to yield the (particular types of) frequency effects observed? In fact, several concepts from learning theory are relevant to the understanding of language learning and use. Usage-based linguistics is predicated upon the premise that the knowledge of language emerges from exposure to usage. With our linguistic abilities believed to be rooted in general cognitive abilities, this leaves a prominent role to be played by learning. Learning models 'give frequency of occurrence its rightful place as a fundamental shaper of the lexical system always dynamically responsive to experience, rather than treating it as a variable to be dealt with by means of essentially *ad hoc* assumptions applied to a model of the mature system' (Monsell 1991: 149–50). Counters in the head are only needed by theories that ignore the role of learning in language development (Baayen, Milin and Ramscar 2016: 1208).

Of all approaches to learning, the one that is most well known in usage-based circles is implicit statistical learning. As we saw in Chapter 2, statistical learning is viewed as a powerful domain-general learning mechanism and is often invoked to argue against nativist or domain-specific accounts of language and cognition. What implicit (sequence) learning has in common with language learning and processing is the ability to encode and represent sequential input, using preceding context to (implicitly) predict upcoming units (Conway et al. 2010). The human ability to extract and entrench the distributional characteristics of natural language underpins usage-based theories of grammar. A wealth of corpus-based and experimental studies has explored the richness of distributional patterns available in corpora and their potential as building blocks of language given general pattern recognition abilities. There is also plenty of research testifying to our implicit statistical learning abilities – think of the work by Saffran and colleagues (reviewed in Chapter 3, Section 3.1) who demonstrated that infants as young as nine months can use statistical properties of the input to segment a continuous speech stream into words. But researchers working in both disciplines have kept rather to themselves. Interestingly, very little work in the area of implicit learning uses a measure of pattern recognition that is *independent of language* and thereby misses the opportunity to demonstrate that the statistical learning ability is domain-general; moreover, most work relies on an artificial language-learning paradigm, which simplifies the situation language learners face in reality. These two limitations have cast doubt on the scalability of such learning to the complexity of natural language input (Johnson and Seidl 2009; Erickson and Thiessen 2015: 82–9). Furthermore, there is little evidence to date supporting a *causal* link between fundamental learning abilities related to the implicit encoding of sequential structure and the processing of language in naturalistic settings. For a discussion of how accumulated evidence regarding processing regularities in the environment is now starting to shape and constrain theories of cognitive systems, see the special issue of the *Philosophical Transactions of the Royal Society B* (volume 372, issue 1711, 2017).

The separation of learning theory and linguistics occurred six decades ago when Chomsky (1959) 'skinned' Skinner in his 'review' of *Verbal Behavior* (1957). Vigorously exiled from the linguistic landscape, learning theory is still to make a full comeback onto the linguistic scene. We will review the foundations of learning in Section 9.1. Section 9.2 surveys applications of insights from learning theory to language. Special attention is devoted to work relying on the Rescorla–Wagner learning rule, which provides an account that is highly pertinent to the challenges encountered in research on language.

9.1   Background: Learning Theory

Learning theory describes the conditions that lead to learning, how learning proceeds and how it is translated into current behaviour and long-term adaptation. The vast majority of research into learning is based on experiments conducted with animals. Animal studies offer simplicity and rigorous experimental control as the genetic background and the environment of the study participants can be engineered. Moreover, animals do not tend to interfere with experiments, for example, by guessing what the experimenter wants or by trying to please them. Interestingly, many of the insights into learning that were gathered using animals have transferred straightforwardly to situations involving human beings. Think of the concept of 'cognitive maps' that was first demonstrated using rats who were trained to learn and run a maze in search for food (Tolman, Ritchie and Kalish 1946). In the following subsections we review the core elements of early learning theory, while focusing on those that are of particular relevance for language learning.

9.1.1   Behaviour and Conditioning

Behaviourism was an influential movement, based on the conviction that psychology is the science of behaviour: psychologists should confine themselves to studying observable phenomena and measurable behaviour and stop speculating about unobservable mental states (Watson 1913, 1924). Of central interest were the mechanisms that are the result of conditioning and that link stimuli with other stimuli or responses. Although behaviourism has since gone out of fashion, it has contributed valuable insights into animal and human learning.

Conditioning allows us to investigate how animals and humans learn to associate stimuli in their environment and anticipate and handle upcoming events. Traditionally, two types of conditioning are considered: classical or respondent conditioning and instrumental or operant conditioning. Arguably, however, the two types do not differ in principle: they both advocate associative learning. But in practice, at the level of specific operations, they do differ: do subjects passively respond to the environment or do they proactively operate in it? The two main players in the conditioning field, Ivan Petrović Pavlov and Burrhus Frederic Skinner, represent a strand each.

Pavlov (1927) is famous for his respondent conditioning studies with dogs. These studies were, in essence, nothing but a serendipitous side effect of his work in physiology. Pavlov was looking at salivation in dogs in response to being fed when he accidentally noticed that his dogs would begin to salivate whenever he entered the room, even when he was not bringing them food. He then proceeded to test this association between two stimuli in a controlled manner. In respondent conditioning, behaviour is studied that is controlled by its *antecedents*. The starting point is therefore a biologically salient or potent stimulus, such as food, which naturally elicits a response, for example, salivation. During the experiment, this potent stimulus is then paired with an initially neutral stimulus, such as the sound of a bell, i.e., a bell is rung whenever food is served. As a result of learning, the neutral stimulus, i.e., the bell, elicits the salivation response that was initially elicited by the potent stimulus, i.e., the food.

Skinner (1938, 1953) studied operant conditioning to understand the relationship between behaviour and its *consequences*. He studied the relation between stimulus and response by putting rats in operant conditioning chambers (later renamed Skinner boxes) where they could press a lever and receive food *at will*. The major insight stemming from this work is that behaviour – including free or voluntary behaviour – is lawfully related to the environment: it decreases or increases according to its payoff. In other words, operant behaviour is controlled by its consequences: it allows animals and humans to continue doing things that have positive consequences and to stop doing things that yield negative consequences. The initial observations go all the way back to Thorndike's (1898) doctoral dissertation in which he described the 'law of effect'. Behaviour begins as random activity, but the stimulus–response relation is strengthened if there is a reward (in a sense, this idea is a very early precursor of the idea of reinforcement in learning). The 'law of effect' is much like Darwin's law of natural selection: random mutation generates traits that are adaptive or non-adaptive and because the organisms with the adaptive traits have a better chance to survive, the adaptive trait starts to prevail.

In the natural world, both types of conditioning operate together and are virtually inseparable; they only differ in what the organism appears to learn (Bouton 2007: 16–19, 27–9, 70). Learning under both paradigms is sensitive to the timing, novelty and magnitude of the event (Bouton 2007: 70, 83–9). First, learning is at its best when the event follows the signal or behaviour, and does so rather quickly; there appear to be optimal temporal intervals depending on the event being conditioned or learned. An effect of time on conditioning that is well known in linguistics and language pedagogy (discussed in Chapter 4, Section 4.4.2) is that of trial spacing: spaced trials yield better results than massed trials. Yet, the success of the conditioning seems to depend on the ratio between the duration of the conditional stimulus and the time between trials: increasing the time between trials improves learning but if both stimulus duration and time between trials are multiplied by the same factor, the effect of trial spacing disappears (Gibbon and Balsam 1981; Gallistel and Gibbon 2000). Secondly, conditioning occurs most rapidly if the stimuli are new to the subject – exposure to either stimulus before they are paired during conditioning can interfere with learning. Pre-exposure to the stimulus causes interference, a. k.a. latent inhibition (Siegal 1969; Lubow 1973): pre-exposure makes the stimulus less novel, hence it attracts less attention, which may affect learning. Thirdly, the strength of the unconditional and conditional stimuli is related, with stronger conditioned responses resulting from stronger unconditioned stimuli (Annau and Kamin 1961). Strength of the unconditioned stimulus determines the upper limit of learning while the intensity or salience of the conditioned stimulus determines the effectiveness; stimuli that grab the attention are more effective, but a stimulus that is too strong (e.g., fear) may be overpowering and trigger a response of its own.

Crucial to conditioning is information value: a conditional and an unconditional stimulus are only paired, and hence something is learned, if the conditional stimulus provides information about the upcoming unconditional stimulus (Bouton 2007: 93–5). In a series of landmark papers, Rescorla (1966, 1967, 1968) showed that it was contingency, not mere contiguity or temporal pairing, that generated conditioned responding. Rescorla conducted an experiment in which dogs were exposed to tones and electrical shocks under different conditions, i.e., a random condition, an excitatory condition and an inhibitory condition. Rescorla observed that the dogs learned to be afraid of a tone if the shock occurred (with a probability of 0.4) *while* the tone was played and never in the absence of the tone. Under these excitatory conditions of unique pairing, the dogs learned a positive contingency. Yet, if across the experiment the dogs were given the same number (i.e., the same frequency) of tone and shock pairings overall, but tone and shock co-occurred at random (i.e., the probability of a shock was the same regardless of whether a tone was played), the dogs did not learn to associate shock and tone. A third group of dogs heard tones and received shocks but did not receive any shocks *while* the tone was played. For the dogs in this inhibitory group, the probability of receiving a shock in the absence of a tone was the same as for the dogs in the random group but the shock never co-occurred with a tone. The tone thus signalled a decrease in the likelihood of receiving a shock, i.e., they learned a negative contingency. Rescorla (1968) specified that the background rate of the tones determined the degree to which rats conditioned to the relationship between tones and shocks. In an experiment in which the association rate between tone and shock was held constant, he observed that the higher the background rate of the tones, i.e., the more frequently they occurred alone, the less the rats conditioned to the pairing of the tone and the shock. After all, the tone did not reliably predict a shock and was, as such, not very informative. Rescorla (1988) pointed out that learning in this case is driven by prediction error: the rats predicted a tone to be followed by a shock and adjusted their expectations as experience of tones that were not followed by a shock accumulated.

Another milestone relates to the observation that conditioning typically involves compound cases, that is, two or more stimuli occurring together. Wagner, Logan and Haberlandt (1968) proceeded to designing experiments demonstrating relative validity: conditioning is a competition in which the best predictors win. Imperfect predictors can also be learned, and the amount of conditioning linked to any one cue depends on its competition with other cues (Bouton 2007: 98 100). In an exploration of compound cases, Kamin (1968, 1969) first conditioned rats to expect a foot shock upon hearing a tone. Next, he added a light to the tone to form a compound. The rats did not respond to the light alone: prior conditioning to the tone blocked conditioning of the light. This experimentally confirmed that learning only occurs when new information is presented (Bouton 2007: 95–8). Kamin (1969) interpreted blocking in terms of surprise, attention and predictability. Either the learner does not notice the second cue, or else they do notice it but do not condition to it because it is redundant and carries no new information; the relevant event is perfectly predicted by the first cue alone, which removes the motivation to take into account a second cue. Efforts to produce unblocking through surprise-triggered learning have not been consistently successful. Moreover, the available favourable evidence is subject to alternative interpretations (Rescorla and Wagner 1972; Wagner and Rescorla 1972).

A third insight, and one of importance for language, is that learning associations between conditioned and unconditioned stimuli follows an error-correction rule which adjusts the association on each trial to reflect the discrepancy between what the cue predicts and what the actual trial outcome is. Rescorla and Wagner (1972) specified that the error correction is equal to the difference between the actual trial outcome and the outcome predicted by all the cues present in the trial. Therefore, the pairing of two stimuli is not sufficient to trigger learning if another cue present already predicts the outcome. Depending on the other cues present at the trial, the pairing of stimuli can trigger an increment in association, no change, a decrement or inhibition. And if no outcome occurs, the Rescorla–Wager rule predicts unlearning, which has turned out to be not quite correct (Bouton 1994: 222).

9.1.2   Behaviourism versus Cognitivism: What Do We Learn?

The controversy surrounding the answer to the question of what we learn is one of the longest running in psychology, and one that has split the field in two. Behaviourists argued the case for habits, acquired automatically and without awareness through stimulus and response pairings that are encouraged or reinforced if the outcome is desirable for the organism. Cognitivists defend the view that higher organisms such as human beings consciously and purposefully acquire and store information that can be combined with new information and may lead to new behaviour, without the need for much stimulus–response repetition. Interestingly, despite their fierce criticism of behaviourism, cognitivists have not proposed their own theories of learning (and forgetting). Instead they shifted efforts towards memory storage and retrieval, the basic principles of which we discussed in Chapters 4 and 5.

Petri and Mishkin (1994) have argued that both views of how behaviour is acquired have received empirical support. Rather than choosing sides, they propose a model of how the brain remembers that supports both views. Memories and habits may be stored in different ways:

> [W]hile the cognitive memory system harbours cortical representations of stimulus events and their associations, the behavioural system records the probability that a stimulus will elicit a response, and this probability is determined by previously reinforced pairings. (Petri and Mishkin 1994: 36)

According to the model outlined in Petri and Mishkin (1994), two systems should be distinguished. One system is involved in developing habits or learned behaviour; this tendency to respond in a particular way in a particular situation is not necessarily available to cognition. Another system stores memories or information that is available to cognition. This two-system model aligns with the makeup of the memory system we discussed in Chapter 5. It is generally accepted that there is an implicit procedural memory system that handles habits and an explicit or declarative memory system that stores memories. Adding in knowledge about the way in which behaviour is acquired or learned yields the conclusion that different types of associations may be learned by these two different memory systems. The procedural habit system, on the one hand, would mediate the association between the stimulus and the response. It records the probability that a stimulus will elicit a response. These probabilities develop gradually as a result of repeated exposures: each exposure changes the stored response probability incrementally. No awareness is required. The declarative memory system, on the other hand, contains representations of stimuli and their associations. As such, it could mediate the association between stimulus and reinforcer, that is, a stimulus that increases the likelihood of a specific behaviour or response. The association between the response and the reinforcer could be mediated by either system, depending on the nature of the task. The locus of the probability store is likely a subcortical structure, very possibly the striatum, which makes the neurotransmitter dopamine (previously encountered in Chapter 8, Section 8.2.6) a likely candidate trigger for the bond.

Many linguists would balk at the idea of considering speakers' mastery of their mother tongue and all its intricacies a mere habit, a tendency to respond in a particular way in a particular situation. This may well have contributed to their easy rejection of behaviourist attempts to tackle language (more about which in Section 9.2.1). But language knowledge as accumulated by native speakers, i.e., without explicit instruction, has much in common with habits as described above in the passage from Petri and Mishkin. This is particularly the case for the mechanical or grammatical aspects of language, i.e., pronunciation, morphology, syntax and some areas of pragmatics; think for example of linguistic expressions of politeness. The fact that these areas might better be considered as habits might explain some of the problems second language learners encounter: instead of aiming to create habits, we tend to teach a foreign language by appealing to knowledge (grammatical rules or meaning), and thereby rely on a memory system that is not optimized for the task. Linguists would like there to be more to knowing a language than can be captured by having good habits. As Lashley (1951) pointed out, much human behaviour is highly complex, and language would be a prime example of this. It involves highly organized sequences which behaviourists would have to see as linked sequences of responses, as a chain in which each link is determined by the immediately preceding chain. But in complex behaviours, what happens at one point in the sequence is co-determined by what has preceded and what will follow, as well as by the overall goal of the action. Lashley rejected reflex chaining accounts of the sequencing of behaviour and argued instead for a more cognitive account in which behavioural sequences are typically controlled with central plans. An important feature of such plans, according to Lashley, is that they are hierarchical. This idea plays a prominent role in generativist approaches to language.

9.1.3   *Learning, Memory and Attention*

Learned information must be remembered, activated or retrieved to influence performance. Bouton (1994) argues that theories of memory and learning have been separated artificially: work on memory focuses on the representation, while work on learning highlights the development. But remembering and forgetting play an important role in conditioning experiments since the ability to learn implies the ability to remember. Conditioned stimuli have always been viewed as associated with memory representations of unconditioned stimuli. The stimulus can be considered a retrieval cue for the response (Rescorla 1974): we have seen in Chapter 4, Section 4.3 that for memories to be useful they need to be retrieved. And the strength of a memory alone does not guarantee retrieval: for this we need a good cue. Hence, classical conditioning studies that link two stimuli or a stimulus and a response can be regarded as studies into the basic mechanisms of memory retrieval. Experiments have shown that conditioned stimuli can be remembered for a very long time: for example, sixty days after training Hendersen's (1985) rats still behaved as if they accurately remembered the intensity of the shock they had received. Yet, over time, generalization occurred both in conditioned and unconditioned stimuli. This came as a surprise: it was known that memory retrieval depends on the similarity between the stimulus context at testing and at encoding and that performance could be disrupted by manipulating these background stimuli. But Riccio, Richardson and Ebner (1984) found that, as stimulus attributes were forgotten, animals started to respond to stimuli that were different from the ones they were trained on even though the context was kept constant. It also appeared that some forms of conditioning are forgotten faster than others, e.g., inhibition fades more quickly than excitation (Hendersen 1978). Yet, memories can be reactivated, showing that the information is (or can be) still available even when it is not accessible (Gordon, Smith and Katz 1979).

Forgetting has several causes, as we saw in Chapter 4: one possibility is that information fades away or decays over time, another is that conflicting information (learned before or after the target information) interferes with access to the target information, and a third is that retrieval fails. Interference and retrieval (failure) determine whether the conditioned stimulus is observed and thereby explain how learning translates into behaviour. Research on extinction has explored this in detail (Bouton 1991, 1993). In extinction, a conditioned stimulus (that signals an unconditional stimulus) loses its ability to evoke a response if it is repeatedly presented alone. This presents a way for the organism to adapt to an ever changing environment. But extinction is not unlearning, as becomes evident from cases of spontaneous recovery where the extinguished response recovers after time. Context plays a crucial role here and Bouton (1994) already suggested that this would be because the context creates different backgrounds or 'meanings' against which the relation between the conditioned and unconditioned stimulus is established. The reaction the conditioned stimulus evokes is then dependent on the specific context, one in which it is related to the unconditioned stimulus and one in which it is not related to that stimulus. Retrieval of memories for extinction appears to be highly context-dependent, and memories of extinction are likely to be forgotten outside of the extinction context.

As we saw in Chapters 6 and 7, not every aspect of experience is encoded into memory. Information that is noticed has a much higher chance of being encoded and being available for retrieval than information that was not attended to. And what gets noticed tends to be what is unexpected, what is surprising. Surprise plays a key role in the Rescorla–Wagner model: it assumes that learning occurs on a conditioning trial only if the unconditioned stimulus is surprising. Surprise decreases gradually as learning approaches its limit. This insight is similar to Kamin's blocking effect, but makes it more widely applicable: there is an element of surprise every time learning occurs. Once the unconditioned stimulus ceases to be surprising, the upper limit to learning (asymptote, also called λ) is reached and no further learning will occur. Crucially, Rescorla and Wagner proposed that all conditioned stimuli present on a trial would contribute to predicting the unconditioned stimulus. The effect of compound conditioning points to the general role of context, which is crucial for language learning. More specifically, the increment or decrement in conditioning to an individual element depends on what the other elements of the compound predict (Bouton 2007: 116).

Conversely, the Rescorla–Wagner model assumes that a stimulus is ineffective because it is not surprising. But there are other possible explanations that assign a central role to attention. Attention can be seen as a crucial condition for the formation of an association between two events. This was first described by Thorndike (1932a) who coined the 'principle of belonging', i.e., whether events are perceived as belonging together. Mackintosh (1975) proposed that the amount of attention that is paid to the conditioned stimulus determines the amount that is learned and at the same time depends on how well the conditioned stimulus predicts the event. As learning proceeds, subjects pay more attention to stronger predictors and less to the weaker predictors. Learning depends on attention and attention itself depends on previous learning: you pay attention if on a previous trial you mis-predicted the outcome (Bouton 2007: 119–23). However, Mackintosh's rules for how attention changes as a function of conditioning proved to be inaccurate. Pearce and Hall (1980) proposed instead that a conditioned stimulus will lose associability when its consequences are accurately predicted. In other words, no precious attentional resources should be wasted on a conditioned stimulus which is already well understood.

Wagner (1976, 1978) extended the Rescorla–Wagner model to explicitly incorporate surprise and attention. He suggested that learning is determined by the surprisingness of the conditioned and unconditioned stimulus on a conditioning trial. An event is surprising if it is not already present in working memory. If it is present in working memory, it is primed either as a result of self-generated priming or as a result of retrieval-generated priming; in the latter case, an item is pulled out of long-term memory by a retrieval cue. Both priming mechanisms can reduce the surprisingness of the conditioned stimulus. Learning is due to surprising stimuli getting more processing in short-term memory. Processing the conditioned stimulus in short-term memory is equivalent to paying attention to it; this increases its chances of being transferred to and stored in long-term memory (Bouton 2007: 124–30).

In the 1980s, Wagner and associates (Wagner 1981) translated the short-term memory model into connectionist terms, yielding the 'sometimes opposing process' or SOP model. When a conditioned stimulus is presented, its node is activated and activation travels along the network to activate associated nodes. The strength of the association between nodes in a network varies with learning. Activation is only temporary and analogous to being in short-term memory. There are two levels of activation: high, which equals being in focal attention, and low, which signals peripheral attention. An item stays in high activation state for a very short time only, after which it decays to low activation state, from where it reverts to inactivity. An association can only form between items that are highly activated, i.e., in focal attention, at the same time; this is the equivalent of being rehearsed in short-term memory. There are other aspects to the SOP, and the model was later expanded further to include sensory and emotional unconditioned stimulus nodes (AESOP, Wagner and Brandon 1989) and to include Pearce's configural approach (Wagner and Brandon 2001).

9.2   Applications to Linguistics

The most direct application of insights from learning theory to language is presented in the well-known monograph *Verbal Behavior* by Skinner (1957). Ironically, this book, or rather Chomsky's (1959) review of it, also ended what could have been a fruitful exchange of ideas between linguists and learning theorists. Knapp (1992: 87) points out that, for the period 1972 through 1990, the review of *Verbal Behavior* by Chomsky (1959) was cited once for each two citations of *Verbal Behavior* itself. This is a very unusual relationship between a book and one of its reviews, to say the least. Swiggers (1995: 12–13) considers Chomsky's review a 'parade-example of ideology at work': Chomsky distorted Skinner's views and very successfully promoted his own instead. Linguists uncritically accepted the views on learning from Chomsky, even though Chomsky was not research-active in the area of learning. At least a dozen competent reviews of Skinner's *Verbal Behavior* appeared, including some by prominent psychologists such as Charles Osgood (1958) and Donald Broadbent (1959), but these were largely ignored.

9.2.1   *Skinner's* Verbal Behavior

Skinner, by training an English major, moved field into strict behaviourism but never shook of his love for language. To Skinner, language was behaviour too:

What happens when a man speaks or responds to speech is clearly a question about human behaviour and hence a question to be answered with the concepts and techniques of psychology as an experimental science of behaviour. (Skinner 1957: 5)

Skinner set out to apply the basic operant model to verbal behaviour. Operants are intentional actions that have an effect on the surrounding environment. In Skinner's work on language, focus was on the verbal operant and verb operant conditioning. In order to elaborate a functional analysis of verbal behaviour, Skinner needed to identify the variables that control verbal behaviour and specify how these variables interact in eliciting a verbal response. In this equation, language is the dependent variable, and the independent variables that govern language are to be described in terms of behavioural research on animals, i.e., stimulus, response, reinforcement and motivation. Stimulus, response and reinforcement are contingent upon each other: the stimulus sets the occasion upon which the response is likely to be reinforced. Under this contingency, the stimulus becomes the occasion upon which the stimulus is likely to be emitted through a process of operant discrimination (Skinner 1957: 81). Traditional structural formulations typically used in describing language are absent from Skinner's book. It redefines the domain of interest as behaviour and organizes topics in the light of what was known about behavioural processes (Palmer 2006: 254).

A behaviourist, Skinner aimed to dispense with all that is not objective and is mentalistic, including the notion of meaning, as such concepts obscure rather than clarify. He intended to account only for the objective dimensions of verbal behaviour and to invoke only objective, non-mentalistic and non-hypothetical entities to account for it (MacCorquodale 1970: 83). Speech was analysed in terms of its 'controlling relations' which include the speaker's current motivational state, their current stimulus circumstances, their past reinforcements and their genetic constitution (MacCorquodale 1970: 83). This allowed Skinner to distinguish several kinds of elementary verbal operants, e.g., mand, tact, echoic, textual and intraverbal behaviour. There are six types of functional relations which Skinner recognizes as controlling variables of verbal operants:

1 The *mand*, is a 'verbal operant in which the response is reinforced by a characteristic consequence and is therefore under the functional control of relevant conditions of deprivation or aversive stimulation' (Skinner 1957: 35–6), i.e., a statement (order, question, advice, request, etc.) uttered when the subject wants something.

2 The *tact* is 'a verbal operant in which a response of given form is evoked (or at least strengthened) by a particular object or event or property of an object or event' (Skinner 1957: 81–2), i.e., a statement controlled by the situation, such as naming an object or thanking a host

3 *Echoic behaviour* is a response which 'generates a sound pattern similar to that of the stimulus' (Skinner 1957: 55), i.e., the repetition of words or phrases pronounced by another speaker. This is the simplest case of verbal behaviour being under the control of verbal stimuli.

4 *Textual behaviour* is a verbal response to a written stimulus which makes no demands upon linguistic competence or grammatical behaviour, such as reading of words and phrases. This is probably the most well-known example of verbal behaviour being under the control of verbal stimuli.

5 *Intraverbal behaviour* is also a verbal response under the control of other verbal behaviour but one that lacks a one-to-one behaviour and instead relies on the relation (of synonymy, or paraphrase) between words. The role of

intraverbal stimuli in instruction is to combine with echoics and textuals to produce a response which was not previously available, e.g., the response 'four' to the question 'two add two equals'.

6 The *audience:* the audience has an effect insofar as it causes the choice of a linguistic code, the choice of a language variety and the choice of the theme of conversation.

As the description of the functional relations reveals, Skinner deals with encoding on the part of the individual speaker, not with decoding on the part of the listener and not with the speech community. Stronger even, the listener is only there to provide the reinforcement needed for the behaviour to develop in the speaker: parents, for example, encourage certain vocalizations by their child. The listener is a reinforcing agent and reacts to language with conditioned reflexes of the same kind as they produce in reaction to other stimuli (Skinner 1957: 34, 357). Skinner does not study the average performance of many speakers or the reinforcing practices of verbal communities either – in his opinion, that is what linguists study (Skinner 1957: 461). Language learning, too, remains outside the scope of his investigation. Instead, Skinner presents a hypothesis about the causes of verbal behaviour, whereby verbal behaviour is the momentary response, not the inventory of possible responses, of an individual speaker on a given occasion (Skinner 1957: 28; MacCorquodale 1970: 98).

It is not difficult to see how Skinner's book would be misunderstood by readers unfamiliar with behaviourists' research on animal learning.[1] Research into animal learning is equally far removed from the complexity of human behaviour as Skinner's behaviourist analysis of language is from capturing the intricacies of human communication. Yet, it needs to be acknowledged that this approach has elucidated several fundamental principles of (animal) learning that apply far beyond the context of pigeons and rats pressing levers in cages within which the principles were established. For this reason alone, linguists should have been more critical of Chomsky's review and been more respectful of Skinner's attempt to approach linguistic behaviour in the same way.

A few remarkable facts deserve to be pointed out that are of importance for linguists but have gone largely ignored. For one, Skinner's six functional relations predate the classification of speech acts, or of performative utterances, that we find in Austin and Searle (see Swiggers 1995: 7). This is a feat that any linguist, who actually read the book, should give Skinner credit for. The fact that this was not done, points to the influence of

---

[1] Yet curiously, Osgood (1958) criticized Skinner's book for its near complete absence of experimental evidence, an absence which Broadbent (1959: 372) characterizes as 'fighting psychologists of mentalistic inclinations with their own weapons'.

Chomsky's review and the dangers of failing to read literature first hand. Secondly, and of interest to usage-based linguists in particular, is the fact that behaviourists assume a tabula rasa as the starting point for language learning, but do accept the existence of innate cognitive tendencies such as abstraction and analogy. This aligns behavioural psychologists and usage-based linguists in terms of some of their basic premises and sets them apart from Chomskyan linguists who do not explore the existence of innate tendencies but posit innate knowledge. Thirdly, Skinner (1957: 27–8) also discusses frequency, in particular the 'over-all frequency with which a response appears in a large sample of verbal behaviour'. He rightly criticizes word counts as a way to develop a formal analysis of the dependent variable, verbal behaviour, without taking into account the circumstances under which it is produced. The conditions under which a response is produced are possibly more important than the knowledge that the response is produced frequently: not all instances of a response are necessarily instances of the same operant and the frequency with which a response occurs may be due to the occurrence of the independent, controlling variables (see Divjak 2017). A change in frequency can therefore not be used to infer a change in the underlying tendency to emit certain forms. This links in directly with our discussion of the importance of context in the analysis of frequency data in Chapter 2: counting readily identifiable forms taken out of their natural (syntactic) context significantly diminishes the richness of the input from which human beings extract distributional patterns.

Unfortunately, these synergies remained undetected and hence unexplored due to the fact that Chomsky distorted Skinner's views and promoted his own instead. MacCorquodale (1970: 95) concludes:

Chomsky is totally silent, on the other hand, about what might be the form of input which would similarly engage the grammar construct when speech is to be produced, and tell it what to be grammatical about, and how to select a possible transformation to say it in, and so forth. So far as one can tell, Chomsky's one controlling variable for speech production – grammar, rules, competence – rests locked away in the brain somewhere, inert and entirely isolated from any input variables which could ever get it to say something. Unless some external input is permitted one must suppose that the grammar construct regulates itself, a repugnant notion. *No one speaks pure grammar.* All sentences have grammatically irrelevant properties; they are, in addition, about something. [...] Guthrie complained that Tolman had left the rat "lost in thought" because he provided no relation between the expectancy and behavior. Chomsky leaves the speaker lost in thought with nothing whatever to say. (MacCorquodale 1970: 95)

In fact, MacCorquodale (1970: 95) makes a very relevant remark that applies to linguistic inquiry more generally: the fact that our descriptions capture a dimension (more or less) adequately does not imply that any of this exists in the minds of speakers:

> In sum, the verbally competent person can discriminate a syntactic dimension in speech as a stimulus, and he [sic] can emit speech which has syntactic properties in the sense that a hearer can discriminate them. *This does not prove in any way that some underlying theory governs both behaviors.* A child learns both to walk and to discriminate walking. Nothing is gained by saying that therefore he has constructed a theory of walking which he uses in his perceptions and in his activities. So he may be conceived to learn to speak and to perceive speech, directly and without stopping to construct a theory or apply a rule. [italics mine] (MacCorquodale 1970: 95)

This chimes with a line of thought that has recently gained traction in cognitive linguistics as well: it is not because a phenomenon can be described in a certain way that the description is psychologically realistic, let alone real. Divjak (2015) took a closer look at what is currently considered methodological 'good practice' in the field, with the aim to draw attention to some of the assumptions that underlie usage-based methodology and thereby shape the findings, yet have gone unquestioned. One of the four challenges that was highlighted relates to our reliance on traditional categories for the annotation and analysis of linguistic data. Some of these categories have been around for millennia; the classification of words into categories, for example, predates Christianity and the rather recent concerns for psychologically plausible categories. As early as the fifth century BC, Sanskrit grammarians grouped words into classes – that would later become known as parts of speech – distinguishing between inflected nouns and verbs and uninflected pre-verbs and particles. Other linguistic categories that are well established in theoretical linguistics, regardless of framework, are, for example, phonemes, morphemes, tense, mood, and aspect. Cognitive linguistics has created its own categories, such as image schemas, trajectors and landmarks, conceptual metaphors, constructions and frames. With few exceptions, the universality of the adopted traditional linguistic categories has been questioned (e.g., Evans and Levinson 2009) and the cognitive reality of the newly introduced cognitive linguistic categories has not been systematically addressed (see Gibbs Jr. and Colston 1995). Linguistic reality and psychological reality seem to have become one, resulting in a situation whereby linguists elevate linguistic descriptions to psychological explanations and psycholinguists expect to find evidence of the cognitive reality of classifications that were designed to aid the description of language data, not to reflect the workings of the mind (compare also Eddington 2002: 212–13). Instead of trying to establish the cognitive reality of categories that were never intended to reflect the workings of the mind, it might be better to take the input as a starting point and derive categories that resemble those native speakers might derive. Models from learning theory can aid in this endeavour and we will discuss one possible approach in more detail in Sections 9.2.2 and 9.2.3.

9.2.2   Ellis: Frequency, Recency, Context and Contingency

Ellis, a cognitive psychologist interested in language, was the first to (re) introduce insights from learning theory into the analysis of language, and language development in particular. In a series of papers written after 2000, he highlights the importance of insights from learning theory for and its compatibility with a usage-based framework:

[L]anguage learning is an intuitive statistical learning problem, one that involves the associative learning of representations that reflect the probabilities of occurrence of form–function mappings. (Ellis 2006: 9)

Ellis's cognitive work on language starts from and promotes the insights obtained by Anderson and Schooler (1991) and Schooler and Anderson (1997; also Schooler 1993), within the framework of rational analysis of memory. Memory's sensitivity to statistical structure in the environment makes it possible to estimate the odds for the need of a memory trace optimally. Three factors determine this information need: frequency, recency and context (see Chapter 4, Section 4.4 for details). Language processing benefits from having what is used often and what was used most recently easily accessible in memory, and these two factors are modulated by context: an item is more likely to occur if another item that co-occurred with it in the past is currently present. In other words:

[S]omething that has been *frequently* required in the past is likely to be required now; something that has been *recently* required is likely to be required now; something that has been often required in this particular *context* is likely to be required now. (Ellis 2006: 3)

The curve typical of learning shows how learning increases with experience: the more practice (the more frequently something is done), the better the performance. This is especially the case at the initial stages of learning. After the initial stages, the effects of practice diminish and eventually reach asymptote. Learning, or the relation between practice and performance, is often described by a power law (Anderson 1982). And power functions promote robustness. Yet, Heathcote, Brown and Mewhort (2000) have argued that the evidence for a power law of practice is flawed and the power function emerges only because aggregated data is used for analysis; an exponential function fits non-averaged, individual data on practice better.

Ellis's insistence on context aligns with linguists' practice and explains their dismay upon seeing psychologists interested in language focus on words in isolation. There is, indeed, evidence that supports linguists' intuitions about the crucial importance of context. One example comes from ERP studies of word processing in sentence context. The magnitude of the N400 component (a negative voltage occurring 400 milliseconds after presentation of a word) indicates difficulty integrating a word with its sentence context. Very large N400s occur for words that are anomalous in their sentence context. N400 wave forms are influenced by word frequency, being largest for very low-frequency words. This suggests that contextual integration is most difficult for rare words. However, this frequency effect is strongest at the beginning of a sentence and diminishes for successive words in a semantically congruent sentence (but not a scrambled sentence; see van Petten 1993). In van Petten's (1993) study, by the fifth word of a sentence, the N400 frequency effect had disappeared. This suggests that when sufficient context has been encountered, low-frequency words are no more difficult to integrate into their context than are high-frequency words. A similar finding was reported in Milin, Divjak and Baayen (2017) where verbs were read in context and overall frequency of occurrence did not affect reading speed beyond initial sentence positions.

Ellis (2006: 9) concludes that 'L1 acquisition and fluent processing are as rational as other aspects of human learning and memory, and that they can be understood according to standard principles of associative learning'. In other words, to the mantra of 'frequency, recency and context' we need to add *contingency*, i.e., the reliability of a cue, a core concept from learning theory. Recall that Rescorla (1968) agreed with Pavlov (1927) that the frequency with which a stimulus was paired with an outcome was an important contributor to association learning, but he specified further that the usefulness of the cue resides in the fact that the outcome is contingent upon it. When a conditioned stimulus is associated with the presence of an unconditioned stimulus we speak of excitation, but when a conditioned stimulus is associated with the absence of an unconditioned stimulus we speak of inhibition (Bouton 2007: 89–93). Positive contingency yields excitatory conditioning, while negative contingency produces inhibitory conditioning. Both are equally fundamental to learning, but inhibition is harder to detect because the resulting behaviour is not necessarily different from the behaviour observed after a stimulus that signals nothing at all.

To implement this idea practically, Ellis relies on the one-way dependency statistic Delta P or ΔP (Allan 1980), which is related to the delta rule for associative learning in machine learning and formally equivalent to the Rescorla–Wagner learning rule (Rescorla 2008). ΔP is the probability of the outcome given the cue, or $P(O|C)$, minus the probability of the outcome in the absence of the cue, or $P(O|-C)$. When these probabilities are the same, and the outcome is just as likely when the cue is present as when it is absent, there is no covariation between the two events and $\Delta P = 0$. As ΔP approaches 1, the presence of the cue increases the likelihood of the outcome; as ΔP approaches -1, the cue decreases the chance of the outcome. In the latter case we speak of a negative association. Normative ΔP theory describes associative learning where learners have to acquire the relationship between a cue and an outcome in a situation where the cue is the only obvious causal feature present. In such situations, contingency is easy to specify. Yet in language it is rarely, if ever, the case that predictive cues appear in isolation, and most utterances contain a set of cues which co-occur with one another. The learner, then, has to determine the ones that are truly predictive (Ellis 2006: 12–14).

The probabilistic contrast model (PCM) by Cheng and Novick (1990) and Cheng and Holyoak (1995) can accommodate the *selection* requirement. PCM calculates ΔP not across all trials, but across a subset of trials (the focal set) in which the background effects are kept constant. To predict – with a reasonable degree of accuracy – what is going to happen next, we need at least a representative sample of experience of similar circumstances as basis for our judgments (the best sample we could possibly have is the totality of our linguistic experience to date). The assumption that human beings focus on a subset may not be perfectly rational but fits with findings known since Kahneman and Tversky (1972, 1973) demonstrated that human conscious inference deviates from Bayesian inference; human reasoning is not rational or Bayesian in that it tends to neglect the base rates, the prior findings. This focus on the most salient characteristic of the sample leads to predictable and systematic errors in the evaluation of uncertain events. Yet, the effects of attention reach beyond selection for scrutiny; there are also effects of salience (the perceived strength of a stimulus), overshadowing (selective attention between multiple cues, favouring the more intense one) and learned attention.

The basic 'driving forces of language learning, then, are frequency, conditioned by contingency, conditioned by selection' (Ellis 2006: 15). Ellis (2006: 15–17) concludes that all of this is readily accommodated by Rescorla and Wagner's (1972) formal model of conditioning, which was conceived to account for a range of learning phenomena that are also valuable for understanding lifelong language learning. This model of associative learning demonstrates that the amount of learning induced from a cue–outcome association depends on the salience of the cue and the importance of the outcome (Ellis 2012: 15). It has recently regained popularity, first in cognitive science and from there in psycholinguistics. This comes as no surprise:

[It] pull[s] together the findings of hundreds of experiments each designed with an empirical rigour unsurpassed outside animal learning research. Its generality of relevance makes it arguably the most influential formula in the history of conditioning theory. (Ellis 2012: 15)

Ellis, Römer and Brook O'Donnell (2016: 45–68) enumerate a large number of possible influences or determinants of learning and their interactions for the development of verb argument constructions, i.e., frequency effects (of letter chunks, items, item chunks, collocation chunks, grammar chunks and phrasal chunks), the Zipfian distribution of linguistic forms and the things to which they refer, our ability to categorize, the contingency of mapping between forms and functions, the salience and perception of linguistic forms and the ability (especially of adults) to learn implicitly as well as explicitly. To account for second language learning with principles from learning theory we need to supplement factors captured by ΔP, as well as cue salience and outcome surprise, with the effects of redundancy, blocking, overshadowing, L1 content interference and L1 perceptual tuning (Ellis 2006; Ellis and Larsen-Freeman 2006). These factors explain why certain elements may evade take-up in L2 despite availability as a result of frequency, recency and context, and are readily accommodated by associative learning theory.

However, I know associative learning theory is not the usual fare of Applied Linguistics. Pigeons' lack of pidgin, and Sniffy's apparent inability at any form of language, might well have you turning your nose up at all this animal work. 'Too much learning, too little language,' you may well be thinking, however illustrative these animal experiments are of the generality of these associative learning phenomena. But bear with me, for herein, I believe, lie important insights into first and second language acquisition both, not only for the difficulties and ordering of acquisition of different grammatical constructions in L1, but also perhaps for the biggest conundrum of all, the apparent irrationality of the shortcomings of L2 acquisition and of fossilization. (Ellis 2006: 19)

Ellis and Wulff (2015: 420) summarize research in the area of second language learning that demonstrates the relevance of blocking for language learning. Inflectional tense markings are often accompanied by (more salient) adverbs that indicate temporal reference. Accordingly, L2 learners typically prefer adverbial cues such as *today* over inflectional cues such as the verbal ending – *s* to mark present tense.

9.2.3 Naïve Discriminative Learning: a Computational Implementation of the Rescorla–Wagner Learning Rule

In explaining how learners adjust associations between two stimuli, the Rescorla–Wagner model describes how organisms learn from both positive evidence about an association between two stimuli, and from evidence that an association between two stimuli is absent (i.e., implicit negative evidence). In a series of papers, Ramscar and collaborators have explored the value of predictions derived from error-based discrimination learning for explaining challenging aspects of first language development.

9.2.3.1 *Experimenting on Language with Rescorla–Wagner*

Ramscar and Yarlett (2007) relied on learning theory to explain the development of regular and irregular plural forms for English nouns. The development of irregular nouns is particularly challenging to explain because, unlike irregular verbs that have high token but low type frequency, irregular nouns have both low type and token frequency. Generative traditions had concluded that innate mechanisms need to be postulated to explain language development because the input from which children learn is too poor to support the extraction of the set of grammatical strings that make up the adult language, especially in the light of the absence of explicit negative evidence. Relying instead on knowledge about memory and learning, Ramscar and Yarlett (2007: 931) predicted that due to its frequency advantage, strengthening of the association between –s and plural such as *houses* (and *mouses*) will dominate until learning of the regular form reaches asymptote, at which point learning of the irregular forms such as *mice* can start to pick up pace. This hypothesis was confirmed in a series of experiments which showed that recovery from overgeneralization reflects a natural learning process: children's learning mechanisms are optimized to take advantage of the frequency distributions available in the input. The findings also argued the case for taking into account cue competition: there is little point in considering how one specific representation will develop over time without considering the other concurrently available and developing representations. Of relevance for linguistics is the notion of a learning curve that reaches asymptote as a function of repetition frequency, i.e., the frequency of the joint occurrence of cue and outcome: as an unconditioned stimulus becomes less surprising, there is less learning. The complete lack of surprise puts an upper limit on learning. The Rescorla–Wagner rule specified that the prediction of an unconditioned stimulus depends on all conditioned stimuli present during a trial. The ability to handle compound conditioning is a prerequisite for language learning as it allows the rich linguistic and extralinguistic context to be taken into account.

A second finding involving cue competition that is potentially of interest for linguists is the importance of ordering features and labels in learning concepts. Ramscar et al. (2010) have demonstrated that symbolic learning, and word learning in particular, consists in learning which of a scene's semantic features are the best predictors of the phonological label used to describe it. Through computational simulation and behavioural experimentation, they showed that children extract a range of semantic features from a scene (e.g., type of objects, number of objects) and gradually learn which of these features are informative for a label. Children generate expectations about which labels they should hear for which scenes and, when they are wrong, adjust the associations between meaning and form in accordance with the Rescorla–Wagner learning rule. Due to cue competition, discrimination learning is facilitated when objects predict labels, not when labels predict objects: when objects predict labels, the properties of those objects compete for relevance, and those properties that are most relevant and discriminate the object best become highlighted in learning. Labels, on the other hand, have very few features and little cue structure, which impedes cue competition, and hence discriminative learning (Ramscar et al. 2010: 910). Learning labels from features, such *The cup is blue*, is a form of many-to-one learning: each feature of an object is a potential cue to a label for that object, and thus features can compete with one another for predictive value. By contrast, learning features from labels, e.g., *the blue cup,* is one-to-many learning: only one label is encountered at a time, and thus, essentially only a single cue is predictive of all of the many features that might be encountered in an object. Without other cues to compete with for associative value, there is no cue competition and no loss of associative value to other cues over the course of learning trials. The value of a single cue will increase when a predicted outcome appears following the cue and will decrease when a predicted outcome fails to appear following the cue (Ramscar et al. 2010: 918–19).

9.2.3.2 NDL, a Computational Implementation of the Rescorla–Wagner Learning Rule Within psycholinguistics, the Rescorla–Wagner learning rule has been used to study language processing. This was made possible through the implementation of the Rescorla–Wagner rule as the naïve discrimination learner (NDL) by Baayen et al. (2011); NDL provides a computational framework for error-driven discrimination learning. For Baayen and collaborators Rescorla–Wagner is attractive because it fits within a framework that focuses on the transfer of information in Shannon's (1948) sense:

Taking inspiration from Shannon's theory of information, our focus shifts from the internal constituency of the signal to the code encrypting and decrypting the experiences conveyed by the signal. We understand the encoding and decoding processes as fundamentally discriminative in nature, and have found the functional characterisation of discriminative learning provided by the Rescorla–Wagner equations to provide an excellent basis for computational implementation. (Baayen et al. 2016: 124)

Because NDL can handle very large numbers of outcomes given large numbers of cues, the approach scales up to what is required for the study of language in use: computations can be run on large data sets, including corpora consisting of billions of words, which makes the approach very interesting for those favouring corpus-based approaches to language. What makes the Rescorla–Wagner model particularly interesting in the framework of this book is the fact that it sheds light on how human beings learn from their own errors in language processing or development. Sensitivity to errors is what a simple frequency-based approach misses: frequency measures may capture the attested distribution (more or less) adequately, but it is important to capture negative evidence too. In Chapter 2 we discussed how negative evidence can be inferred from the attested distribution and surveyed measures such as conditional probabilities and surprisal that do so implicitly.

The choice of mathematical formalism is highly relevant, since it can greatly change what one learns from the model or what the model output means (see Stafford 2009 for an accessible discussion of the use of computational models in the study of cognition). Milin et al. (2016: 4–5) explain that core components in the naïve discriminative computational learning system are input *cues* and their *weight* in predicting learning *outcomes*. These weights are repeatedly updated as experience accumulates. Over time, some cues become discriminative (i.e., predictive) for an outcome, while many become irrelevant. The system is parsimonious in the sense that, for each outcome, only a handful of cues develop strong positive or negative connection weights to outcomes. If a given cue is consistently present when an outcome is present, their connection is strengthened. However, if a given cue is repeatedly present when the outcome is absent, the weight on the connection between them is weakened. This dynamic ensures minimal error in prediction given *all* prior experience (although strictly speaking only the immediately preceding experience is taken into account directly – Petar Milin, personal communication). As the number of available cues increases and they start to compete, the amount by which the weight on a cue's connection to an outcome can increase is affected: the more cues are present, the smaller the increase and the greater the decrease in weights will be. The error-driven learning mechanism learns by iteratively correcting erroneous predictions for upcoming events. The strengthening of weights reflects learning, and the weakening of links captures unlearning. The Rescorla–Wagner equations provide various parameters for differentiating the *salience* of cues and outcomes. There are parameters which specify the salience of an input cue i (αi), and parameters for the maximum learnability of an outcome j (λj). The importance or strength of correct ($\beta 1$) vs. incorrect ($\beta 2$) predictions, the model's error sensitivity and hence its learning rate, can be weighted differentially. The approach is called 'naïve' because the support for a given outcome is estimated independently from all other outcomes, while both cues and outcomes are specified without presupposing or relying on rich but implicit knowledge in cue and outcome representations.

Although in a typical simulation run these parameters are set to their default values, they allow for a principled account of various learning 'peculiarities' (see Milin et al. 2016: 4–5), which makes NDL interesting for those researching first and second language learning: the previously mentioned effects of salience (the perceived strength of a stimulus), overshadowing (selective attention between multiple cues, favouring the more intense one) and learned attention can, in principle, be modelled computationally. So far, however, the naïve discrimination learning measures have been mainly used as predictors of various behaviours, as measured through naming, decision and reading tasks. Baayen et al. (2011) demonstrate how known morphemic, lexical and phrasal effects observed in these tasks arise without the need for morphemic, lexical and phrasal representations. Using only letter unigrams and bigrams as cues, and representations of lexical, inflectional or derivational meanings as outcomes, they successfully accounted for paradigmatic effects on the processing of case inflections in Serbian. Moreover, they simulated the effects of frequency, family size and contextual effects on the processing of simple words, inflected words, derived words, pseudo-derived words, compounds and prepositional phrases in English. They concluded that distributional properties of words interact with fundamental principles of learning to yield the observed frequency effects (Baayen, Milin and Ramscar 2016: 1200).

Milin et al. (2017) expanded the basic orthography-based NDL architecture and work with two discrimination networks, a grapheme-to-lexome (G2L) network that links trigraphs (cues consisting of three-letter sequences) to lexomes (outcomes), and a lexome-to-lexome (L2L) network in which lexomes are both cues and outcomes. In both cases, lexomes are pointers to locations in high-dimensional semantic vector space. Several measures can be derived from each of these networks. The G2L matrix yields information about the extent to which the target lexome is activated by orthography, the amount of uncertainty with which an outcome is associated given a specific cue and the availability of a lexome irrespective of input. The L2L matrix yields indications of a lexome's semantic density, its semantic typicality, its prior availability and the extent to which other lexomes are co-activated. These discrimination-based measures of lexical processing outperformed classical lexical-distributional measures, in particular, frequency counts and measures of form similarity (e.g., neighbourhood size and density), in accounting for the behavioural data as collected in priming studies. The combination of an orthographic and a semantic network successfully captured (self-paced) reading behaviour and explained how different types of learners use orthography and semantics to guide their reading (Milin, Divjak and Baayen 2017). For a comprehensive overview and an exploration of discrimination-based measures in the context of eye movements and EEG/ERP data, see Hendrix (2015).

9.2.3.3 NDL for Linguists Although many aspects of NDL need be improved upon for it to be able to handle language at the level of detail required by linguists, NDL is attractive to cognitive linguists in particular because it is an algorithm that is psychologically and neurobiologically plausible and yields patterns that are learnable from experience. In the area of computational modelling of language, only a small number of algorithms have been proposed that can learn grammatical structure from naturalistic data. ADIOS (Solan et al. 2005), U-DOP (Bod 2009) and ConText (Waterfall et al. 2010) look for probabilistically defined similarities between language patterns and resemble analogical (Skousen 1989) and memory-based (TiMBL by Daelemans and Van den Bosch 2005) algorithms. These models, as well as parallel-distributed processing or connectionist modelling (Rumelhart and McClelland 1986; Plaut and Gonnerman 2000; Seidenberg and Gonnerman 2000), have been used to model language data within traditions that are close in spirit to cognitive linguistics. Eddington (2000) compared a connectionist, an analogical and a memory-based model on the English past tense. Theijssen et al. (2013) compared logistic regression, Bayesian networks and memory-based learning in predicting the English dative alternation. But these algorithms differ from human learning in that they do not improve in response to error, a trait which is essential from the perspective of learning theory. Milin et al. (2016) show how NDL can be used to explain the results obtained by TiMBL. Baayen (2011) compared NDL with TiMBL, logistic mixed-effects regression, classification trees and random forests, and support vector machines (SVM) on the English dative alternation. Baayen et al. (2013) compared the same set of techniques on four different morphological alternations in Russian. The classification accuracy of NDL was outperformed only by SVM.

Moreover, NDL also respects the inherently redundant nature of linguistic data. To compensate for noise in communication, language encodes bits of information redundantly: phonetic elements and word order that are highly predictable along with grammatical markers that must agree within a sentence, all help the hearer to anticipate what is coming. That diminishes the unexpectedness – the surprise effect – of the message. In learning terms: cues for outcomes tend to be highly interdependent and to a considerable extent predictable from each other. They constitute a rich and redundant feature space (see Baayen 2011: 320). The statistical techniques that are now standardly used by corpus linguists to model linguistic data (see Glynn and Fischer 2010 and Glynn and Robinson 2014 for an overview), in particular regression, require explanatory predictors to be orthogonal to avoid collinearity. Therefore, redundancy needs to be removed from the explanatory variables prior to modelling the data, hence all explanatory variables are weighted equally. And in so doing, we remove the very essence of the phenomenon we are trying to model.

Furthermore, the algorithms underlying standard statistical classifiers such as regression rely on optimization algorithms to maximize prediction accuracy. Whether humans do or do not exhibit (near) optimal behaviour remains a matter of debate (see Chapter 8, Section 8.2.5), but at the very least we can agree that regression models were not designed to mimic human learning. Although such models show good prediction accuracy, the drawback is that they yield cognitively unrealistic models of the phenomena studied and are therefore unsatisfactory to cognitive, usage-based linguists from a theoretical point of view (see Divjak 2015; Milin et al. 2016). NDL is conceived to mimic human learning, including the restrictions on memory and learning that set human learning apart from machine learning. '[A] learning rule that is "optimal" in the Bayesian sense may be favoured less by natural selection in biological systems than the Rescorla–Wagner learning rule, because the latter, as a greedy algorithm, is more robust to different configurations of cues' (Baayen et al. 2016: 125). Because the Rescorla–Wagner rule is less sensitive to changes in its parameters than the optimal rule, there is a wider range of parameter values over which the rule structure is initially viable. Consequently, the Rescorla–Wagner rule can be favoured by natural selection, ahead of other rules which yield more accurate parameters (Trimmer et al. 2012).

In linguistic circles, concerns have been raised that this preoccupation with quantification and modelling may not bring us any closer to understanding how language works. Yet, this objection appears unfounded, especially if we rely on modelling techniques based on biologically and psychologically plausible learning algorithms. Although computational models are challenged when it comes to language processing, they have certain properties that make them very attractive for researchers working on language. Computational models force us to make our assumptions explicit and to describe our procedures in minute detail. A computer will do exactly as it is told; no more, no less. It does not read your mind, it does not think, and typically has no creative problem-solving skills. The challenge thus resides into translating an idea into unambiguous, logical, step-by-step instructions. Any errors in the code that produce incorrect results are introduced by the programmer. But this can be turned into an advantage: tweaking the input data or the algorithm allows us to experiment with input and learning in ways that would be downright unethical if attempted on human beings. In this way, very controlled experiments can be run that allow us to pinpoint cause and effect. If we want empirical evidence to accrue and alter the way in which we think about language, we really should consider modelling techniques that implement principles of human behaviour and of learning. These make it possible to take a quantitative approach, while generating and testing specific hypotheses that will advance our understanding of how knowledge of language emerges from exposure to usage.

9.3   Conclusions: the Place of Frequency in a Learning Theoretic Approach to Language

What are the implications of considering learning theory for understanding the effect frequency has on language processing and representation?

We have seen that learning increases with experience: the more practice (the more frequently something is done or encountered), the better the performance. Frequency influences learning. This is especially the case at the initial stages of learning. After the initial stages, the effects of practice diminish and eventually reach asymptote. But some theories implement experience, exposure or frequency of encounter crudely as 'counters in the head'. The computational models discussed in Chapter 3 rely on resting activation levels or activation thresholds while the Bayesian models discussed in Chapter 8 set priors. Baayen, Milin and Ramscar (2016: 1208) concluded that such measures are required 'by theories that have failed to appreciate the role learning plays in discriminating between words'. Once learning is taken into account, they argue, the Zipfian distribution of objects and events and the interaction of this distribution with the properties of these objects and events, as discriminated by the speaker, will drive association strengths. Their joint effect on lexical processing will mirror this distribution (even if only imperfectly).

In other words, the fact that frequency has an effect on language processing, and by extension on language representation and change, does not justify the reification of frequency. Frequency is not an explanation in and of itself: frequency itself needs explaining and embedding in an encompassing framework. The frequency with which forms appear in language follows a Zipfian distribution; this by and large reflects the importance of the object and events these forms denote in our environment. The frequency with which forms appear in the language interacts with the properties of the objects and events captured by and associated with those forms. Our environment and the words we use to refer to the environment pattern in a way that supports learning: the Zipfian distribution yields a power law, which promotes robustness. The more frequently made associations are learned better and this is reflected in the speed and ease with which they are processed.

Furthermore, findings from learning theory also stress that we do not learn from positive evidence only: we also learn from negative evidence, including our own errors. Learning associations follow an error-correction rule which adjusts the association to reflect the discrepancy between the prediction and the outcome. Linguists have long debated whether negative evidence can be extracted from the input, and learning theory provides us with an elegant way out of this controversy: negative evidence is implicitly present in the input we receive, and the learning mechanisms human beings are equipped with are exquisitely sensitive to learning from their own errors. Learning theory thus accommodates frequency and its effects very naturally. The studies on the role of pre-emption and entrenchment discussed in Chapter 2 can easily be recast in discrimination learning terms. Both Divjak (2017) and Ambridge et al. (2018) report results that highlight the importance of taking into account the background rate of encounters with a noun or verb when it is not used in the target construction in order to determine the acceptability of the word-in-construction combination.

Learning theory can also guide the selection of linguistic categories that have a chance of being cognitively realistic. As I have argued elsewhere (Divjak 2015), at the heart of a (corpus-based) linguistic study of a language phenomenon lies the (often manual) annotation of examples. These annotations of data are typically 'linguistic' in nature, that is, they are based on categories that were designed to aid the description of a language's form and meaning. Yet '[c]ognitively real generalizations may not at all accord with generalizations arrived at by classical techniques of linguistic analysis' (Lakoff 1990: 41). In fact, there is no agreed-upon definition of what is meant by 'cognitively real-(istic)' and what level of cognitive commitment is expected. Categories that are 'consistent with our overall knowledge about cognition and the brain' (Lakoff 1990: 45) could well range from categories that can be thought of as lacking rigid boundaries (radial categories with prototype structure) to those for which there is neurological evidence, i.e., a unique neurological signature that proves that a category is treated as a processing unit in its own right by actual language users. Instead of trying to establish the cognitive reality of categories that were never intended to reflect the workings of the mind, it might be wiser to take the input as a starting point and use insights and algorithms from learning theory to derive categories that resemble those native speakers might derive, thereby safeguarding cognitive plausibility and building learnability into the very foundations of linguistic analysis. This idea will be linked back to frequency and elaborated further in the Conclusions.

10   By Way of Conclusion

We take it for granted that any infant, in only a few years' time, will master at least the basics of a highly complex symbolic system. Indeed, children achieve impressive results in a very limited time while working from what appears to be very limited input. Nativists posit that at least some knowledge needs to be present at birth for these results to be achieved so quickly. But our linguistic achievements appear to have been overestimated: the road to mastery is long, and we continue to learn throughout our lives. Moreover, there is scientific virtue in holding off on positing innate mechanisms until all alternative routes have been explored. One such alternative route is the usage-based one: it presupposes nothing but a few basic cognitive capacities that support the development of a wide range of abilities, including language, through interactions with the environment. Cognitive linguistics, unlike many other modern theories of linguistics, also aims to be a usage-based model of language structure (Langacker 1987: 46). All language units arise from and are shaped by usage events by means of the aforementioned general cognitive abilities. And frequencies of occurrence are also an excellent heuristic to measure usage (Bybee and Hopper 2001b: 2–3).

Although for long, linguistic work was predominantly descriptive in nature, and linguists aimed to capture the grammar of a language as comprehensively, elegantly and economically as possible without concern for the mental reality of their proposals, cognitive linguists are bound by two major commitments: the generalization commitment and the cognitive commitment (Lakoff 1990: 40). This means that all cognitive linguists are committed (or are assumed to be committed) to providing a characterization of the general principles governing all aspects of human language in a way that is informed by and accords with what is known about the brain and mind from other disciplines. Work in the cognitive linguistic tradition therefore likes to stress that the analyses proposed are 'in line with what is known about the mind' and abounds with claims that the proposed analysis would be cognitively realistic, if not cognitively real.

Yet, psychological and biological implausibility likewise plagues linguistic models and theories that aspire to be cognitively realistic. The general cognitive abilities that are typically mentioned in introductions to cognitive linguistics and that have given rise to the bulk of work done within this framework relate to categorization (abstraction, analogy) and imagination (imagery, metaphor, metonymy, blends). But there is also memory, attention and learning, and these have far less often been the focus of (cognitive) linguists' attention. This book aimed to close that gap because any theorizing about frequency, entrenchment and salience – core concepts in cognitive linguistic approaches to language – must engage with the main findings of research into memory, attention and learning.

10.1 Why Do Frequencies of Occurrence Play an Important Role in Usage-Based Linguistics?

The starting point for this book was the baffling preoccupation with frequencies in a discipline that has historically, for the most part, eschewed quantification. Yet, the usage-based linguist's fascination with frequency did not come out of nowhere. Subdisciplines of linguistics had become increasingly interested in the study of frequency, and insights had accumulated that were of use to the usage-based endeavour. Two different lines of inquiry can be distinguished.

First, frequency, as embodied in word frequency lists, had long played an important role for the teaching of (a foreign) language. Despite the practical purpose of most of the early word frequency counts, the problems the 'army of word counters' faced led to methodological improvements that would influence linguistics. General issues include the choice of the unit of the population, types of sampling and corpus size. Psycholinguistics was affected too: there was the discovery of the word frequency effects in psychological studies of language – frequent words are recognized faster and with fewer errors, even in less opportune conditions. This led to frequencies of occurrence being routinely considered to control for participants' experience with the lexicon of their language. Much of psycholinguistic work incorporating frequency was done in the area of processing single words, outside of their natural sentential context. The effects resulting from the crudeness of frequency counts, the absence of proper sense disambiguation and the decontextualization have no doubt impacted the findings, but the full extent of this bias remains to be understood. In contrast to psycholinguists, among corpus linguists context has always been an important issue. Work on lexicography rarely used counts of the occurrence of an individual word form in isolation: words may express different meanings depending on the *context*.

Second, some researchers went above and beyond the call for counting words and started to investigate linguistic structure using statistical methods. Zipf's first law captures the relation between word frequency and its order number in frequency dictionaries: the frequency of any word is inversely proportional to its rank in the frequency table, when both are plotted on a logarithmic scale. Zipf's second law describes a relation between the frequency of occurrence of an event and the number of different events occurring with that frequency: there are very few highly frequent words, but many rarely used words. Within usage-based linguistics the importance of the Zipfian distribution is beginning to be recognized: it has been argued that robust language learning despite learners' idiosyncratic experience is supported by the existence and convergence of Zipf-like distributions across linguistic form and function. The skewed distribution optimizes learning by providing one very high-frequency exemplar that is also prototypical in meaning.

A core observation that has supported the emergence of usage-based linguistics was the fact that adult speakers' language systems are sensitive to the frequencies of occurrence in language use. Frequency effects have been found in virtually every subdomain of language that has been studied. Due to a learner's sensitivity to frequency, each encounter affects their linguistic system; this finding supports the idea that language knowledge is usage-based. Stronger even, usage-based linguists propose that grammar itself is the result of the conventionalization of commonly used patterns: linguistic structure emerges from the repetition of linguistic patterns in language use. Finding out how linguistic patterns are mentally encoded, and how these representations vary with experience is core to the cognitive linguistic endeavour. This explains why, within usage-based theories of language, the study of frequency effects of various sorts has contributed to the understanding of the nature of grammatical organization. From here, the conviction has grown that language is a dynamic system emerging from use. Grammar is not a pre-existing, autonomous and fixed system, but a developing one that continuously adapts to usage.

10.2   How Can Frequency Be Used to Explain the Construction of a Grammar from the Ground Up?

Usage-based theories such as those proposed by Bybee (1985) and Langacker (1987, 1991) offer the theoretical freedom to identify psycholinguistic units on the basis of actual language use rather than on adult-based linguistic theory. This was a real game changer, albeit one the potential of which has not yet been fully exploited.

In an experience-based grammar, linguistic categories and linguistic structures are the result of the conventionalization of commonly used patterns. According to this account, children remember the utterances they hear and draw generalizations over these stored exemplars. "'[R]ules" of language, at all levels of analysis – from phonology, through syntax, to discourse – are structural regularities which emerge from learners' lifetime analysis of the distributional characteristics of language input' (Ellis, Römer and Brook O'Donnell

2016: 35). Frequency of occurrence and co-occurrence play a basic role in this process. Patterns each have their own activation or probability values that are determined by their relative frequencies in language use. The statistical history of events is built on information on frequency of co-occurrence.

Research suggests that human beings are quite adept at determining underlying frequency distributions and central tendencies and that they extract this information automatically; this also applies to linguistic events. Children begin with a restricted set of utterances taken directly from experience and acquired via the domain-general skills of imitation and intention reading. They then advance to productive syntax by generalizing over these utterances. This account relies on several assumptions. The most fundamental assumption is that children are able to store whole sequences of words taken directly from the input (Bannard and Matthews 2008). When children hear repeated uses of one form in similar contexts, they form productive constructions through a process of schematization (Tomasello 2003). The outcome is a linguistic construction that contains a minimum of one lexical item and one 'slot'. Important here is the fact that children are thus exposed to a range of patterns that are partly fixed, partly flexible which allows them to use both recurrence and novelty to break into the system via low-level generalizations. Cognitive abilities such as categorization and abstraction then come into play and operate on these extracted patterns to yield higher-level generalizations. But whether these low-level lexical patterns develop into higher-level abstractions, and how this process interacts with individual differences, is a fundamental question that urgently needs addressing. After all, knowing what kind of patterns actual language users operate with constitutes core knowledge for any linguistic theory laying claims to cognitive reality.

A probabilistic approach may help understand how, and to what extent, learners infer language structure from linguistic input. Taking a probabilistic standpoint makes learning language overall look more tractable: learning no longer requires (re)constructing one grammar with certainty, merely approximating it with sufficiently high probability. Unfortunately, Chomsky had formulated (misinformed) arguments against probabilistic approaches to languages that had led the field to believe that there was nothing interesting about statistical approaches to language and it took the language sciences decades to recover. Explicit mechanisms of probabilistic processing have been pursued most vigorously by connectionists, an area of study that was shaped by the seminal work in the 1980s of McClelland and Rumelhart (McClelland and Rumelhart 1981; Rumelhart and McClelland 1982). The success of probabilistic methods in computational linguistics suggested that human language development and processing might exploit probabilistic information.

The use of probability theory for psycholinguistic research became more prevalent over the next two decades and the field moved from looking at frequency effects for single words to collecting evidence that frequency plays a role in more complex relationships such as those between words and between words and syntactic structures. Grammatical rules, too, may be associated with probabilities of use, capturing what is linguistically likely, not just what is linguistically possible. In a series of papers on the dative alternation, Bresnan (2007) elaborated a probabilistic and gradient view on syntax, while Arppe (2008) and Divjak (2004, 2010) did so for (lexical) semantics. The task the learner faces on their journey to becoming a competent language user can be seen as boiling down to the challenge of learning the distribution of the probabilities of encountering an interpretation given a formal cue in a particular context, which instantiates a mapping from form to meaning conditioned by context (Manning 2003).

Probability might thus prove important as a unifying theoretical framework for understanding how the cognitive system makes the uncertain inference from speech signal to message, and vice versa. Although many cognitive scientists believe information processing to be central to cognition, it is not always clear what is meant by 'information'. The introduction of frequency into linguistics has opened up possibilities of (re)connecting with other disciplines that are more specific in this regard. An excellent example here can be found in research that has approached language processing with insights indigenous to information theory. Entropy is a concept that has been used across a vast array of disciplines, ranging from Russian literature to thermodynamics. Some researchers have brought entropy to bear on explanations of cognitive phenomena, including morphological (Kostić 1991; Moscoso del Prado Martín, Kostić and Baayen 2004; Milin, Đurđević and del Prado Martín 2009) and syntactic processing (Hale 2003; Levy 2008; Jaeger 2010; Frank 2013).

Overall, research results have made us optimistic that general cognitive computational mechanisms will explain much more of language development than the nativists have so far acknowledged.

10.3   Memory, Attention and Learning in the Emergence of Grammar

A key objective of cognitive linguistics is to determine whether and how the structure of language arises from and is shaped by usage events by means of general cognitive abilities. Cognitive abilities that are typically mentioned as crucial in this process are perception, attention, memory, categorization, abstraction and imagery (Dąbrowska and Divjak 2015: 1). Within the cognitive linguistics community, much work has been devoted to categorization and imagery, leaving aside memory and attention. Learning tends to be wholly neglected. It will have become apparent throughout this book that learning, memory and attention are intertwined in fascinating, and currently insufficiently understood, ways; this applies particularly to language cognition.

10.3.1 Memory

It is odd to think of entrenched linguistic forms as 'memories'. But entrenched forms must be memories: memories capture information that has been encoded and can influence future processing. Repeated experiences across domains are laid down in memory. There is no requirement for memories to be conscious or to be recallable. Memories are not restricted to any one dimension of our experience, nor do they exclude any dimensions. Frequency of occurrence is, in essence, the repetition of a linguistic experience, which makes our knowledge of language a complex system of (linguistic) memories.

Because memory for linguistic information is like memory for other information, frequency effects are memory effects – i.e., the effect of frequency is reflected in learning while memory reflects that learning has taken place. Surprisingly, even though language is one of the most complex human cognitive skills, if not the most complex one, the importance of memory formation and consolidation has barely influenced linguistic theories. Yet, we need knowledge of how memory works and of how the brain responds to repetition to further develop usage-based, cognitive approaches to language.

Cognitive linguists aim to endorse a sophisticated view of learning and memory-based processing. Key to this is the assumption that frequency-sensitive learning results in mental representations, if not optimized then at least suited for a particular environment. Entrenchment refers to a process of strengthening memory representations. This may result in a general reduction in processing effort or automatization, in Gestalt formation or 'unitization' or in chunking accompanied by formal reduction or 'fusion'. Frequency has long been identified as the main determinant of entrenchment. This is because the input to the processing of frequencies is repeatedly encountered events or objects that have been categorized, to avoid each perception being idiosyncratic. Little is still known about the lower or upper bounds of frequency needed to ensure entrenchment. But we know that, to turn short-term memories into long-term memories, new proteins must be synthesized within a specific time window and genes must be switched on to facilitate synaptic connectivity. This relies on a chemical process that requires repeated pulses of neurotransmitter and therefore happens only after repeated learning trials. Research shows that it may be reasonable to work from the assumption that evidence accrues from the first exposure, but that speakers cannot formulate reliable hypotheses until sufficient evidence has accumulated. There is some work suggesting that this may happen once frequency of occurrence, as counted in text corpora, reaches six times per million words (Divjak 2017).

What exactly can be entrenched has likewise remained underspecified in the literature. On a usage-based view of language there are no primordial building blocks. There is only language use. Given that entrenchment results from frequency working on input, anything can be entrenched, from a single sound over a multi-morphemic word to a formulaic expression. Linguistic units are not independent components from which larger expressions are constructed but are, instead, themselves abstracted from larger structures. Units are used and learned in context and therefore never achieve absolute autonomy, just different degrees of decontextualization. Memory is sensitive to context in multiple ways. On the one hand, encoding in memory takes into account the context in which the information was presented, making information easier to retrieve if the context is provided. On the other hand, memory is affected by how items are presented over time: information that occurs frequently and recurs regularly is more likely to be become encoded in memory.

Knowing how reliably frequency of occurrence diagnoses strength of encoding and ensures recognition and retrieval is crucial for assessing the value of frequency information for linguistic theory. And this is a third spot where the shoe pinches. Little attention has been paid to the type of memory that harbours linguistic experiences. Depending on the memory system that deals with the linguistic knowledge under scrutiny, frequency of occurrence may have differential effects. Procedural or implicit memory is memory for habit, for rather inflexible, consistent relationships between stimulus and response that are not necessarily available to cognition. A high frequency of behaviour repetition increases the likelihood that the behaviour will be frozen into habit and will be automatically chosen in subsequent decisions (Sedlmeier and Betsch 2002: 10). Declarative memory, on the other hand, is flexible, relational memory that can be consciously accessed to guide behaviour in new situations. For linguistic memories of the declarative type, and under the rule of consciousness, frequency might not achieve the same effects as for linguistic memories of the procedural type.

10.3.2   Attention

It is unlikely that it is frequency which, in and of itself, causes the observed processing advantages that have led to certain conclusions about mental representation. There is the fact that the frequency with which words occur is strongly correlated with other characteristics and a key confound is contextual. But there is also the realization that what counts are not frequencies of events but frequencies of memories – the actual uptake by an individual speaker. Information needs to be attended to before frequency can do its work; if information is not attended to, it may not be registered and encoded at all. It has been argued that attention, not repetition frequency, determines which information is, first, attended to and, then, processed and encoded in memory.

The most influential definition of attention will present attention as selective focusing on some aspects of the environment. Information selection is essential because input to the perceptual system is too rich for processing. Memory, too, is subject to processing constraints and hence requires selection: we cannot commit all aspects of our experience to memory, and neither can we retrieve all encoded information at the same time.

The question is: what captures our attention? Salience detection is considered a key attentional mechanism: it facilitates learning and survival by enabling organisms to focus their limited perceptual and cognitive resources on the most pertinent subset of the available data, while ignoring the rest. There are many, and many divergent, accounts of how the most pertinent subset of an experience is identified. Most approaches assume a tension between bottom-up versus top-down attention, a distinction which is tied to how attention comes about. There is a bottom-up, fast, primitive mechanism that biases the observer towards selecting stimuli based on stimulus salience and a second slower, top-down mechanism with variable selection criteria, which directs the 'spotlight of attention' based on goals and tasks under cognitive, volitional control.

Attention plays a double role in language because it influences event or scene perception and description. Research has provided evidence of a strong link between the distribution of attention over the environment and the organization of language used to communicate about the environment. Scene perception affects linguistic choices, and salient elements of a scene receive more prominent linguistic encoding. At the same time, attention determines the selection of linguistic elements: speakers need to select the entities they want to communicate and choose between competing words and syntactic constructions. Linguists are interested in the attentional or attention-summoning properties that language has, and they have focused on the effects of language structure on attention distribution. They work back from the linguistic expression and use the choice of one form over another to determine how attention was deployed within the scene. Psychologists who study language cognition are more interested in the way in which language directs attention and thereby activates memory representations.

Just like memory, attention is not a simple function of frequency. For linguists to predict the uptake from exposure to language accurately, frequency measures would need to incorporate a correction for attention that weights the pertinence of the unit that is being counted in the given context. In the widely used preferential looking paradigm for infants, the infants appear to pay the most attention (as indexed by eye fixations) to events which are right at the edge of the learning envelope; neither so familiar that they are boring, nor so novel that they cannot be coded and assimilated. What determines which events get noticed? Learning theory may have (the beginning of) an answer to that.

10.3.3   Learning to Predict or Predicting to Learn?

Currently, formulae used to capture frequency of occurrence and co-occurrence remain mathematical shortcuts not couched in any knowledge of what the brain does and how it learns. Frequency effects may well be ubiquitous, but they should not be considered explanations or answers in their own right. Instead, they pose a question: what type of mechanism is needed to yield the (particular types of) frequency effects observed?

There are several theories of learning that incorporate attention. But memory, especially short-term memory capacity, plays a role in noticing too, and learning theory accommodates this gracefully. One of the best researched ones is Wagner's (1976, 1978), which suggests that learning is due to surprising stimuli. On Wagner's account stimuli are surprising if they are not yet present in working memory. Due to their surprisingness they get (temporarily) more processing in short-term memory, which increases their chances of being transferred to and stored in long-term memory. If a stimulus is already in short-term memory, it will be less surprising, receive less processing time and be less likely to be transferred to and stored in long-term memory. Processing a stimulus in short-term memory is equivalent to paying attention to it. If items are rehearsed in short-term memory at the same time, an association can form between them. The association can form between two items or between an item and its context. With repeated exposure, the strength of the association increases and attention to the item, in the relevant context, will diminish. In a different context, however, the item becomes again surprising, gaining more processing in short-term memory. Sensitivity to the context can likewise be diminished or extinguished by presenting it without the item.

But which items does an organism find significant? Attention can be attracted by stimulus properties (loud, bright, etc.) or by the organism's goals (e.g., stimuli that signal events of biological significance, which aid survival). Mackintosh (1975) claims that organisms will pay attention to, and hence readily learn about, stimuli that are good predictors of important events (such as food and pain). Thus, stimuli with high associative strength, in particular stimuli that have a higher predictive value than all other stimuli present, receive most attention. Pearce and Hall (1980) proposed that controlled attention will be directed to those stimuli that need to be learned about; how much learning needs to be done is determined by the surprisingness of the event that follows. In other words, organisms will pay least attention to and learn most slowly about those stimuli that are followed by a correctly predicted event, while incorrectly predicted and hence surprising events are learned about more readily. Unfortunately, no currently available theory explains all experimental findings.

The idea that has caught on in work relating to language is that of noticing being a function of surprise and incorrect prediction rate. A relatively recent view, from predictive coding and processing, argues that our brains make sense of uncertain input by predicting it, i.e., by continuously formulating hypotheses about what might be generating the information our senses take in. Instead of passively trying to make sense of incoming stimuli, our brains try to actively predict the sensory signal by constructing it for themselves, using stored probabilistic knowledge about the world. The goal is to meet the incoming sensory signal with a multilevel prediction of that signal, not to interpret it after it has come in. The self-organizing nature of a Bayesian network is what makes it a 'bootstrap heaven': you can use the prediction task to detect or construct the grammar of your language, while the grammar itself is something that you can put to use in the prediction task in the future. Bayesian frameworks tend to claim that our brains have evolved to be extraordinarily good at exploiting the statistics of the environment, which enables us to perform in a close to optimal fashion. This focus on optimality differs from most if not all other theories of cognition that tend to accept that our systems are adaptive and work well enough under many conditions but are not optimal.

Models of predictive learning have been used to account for language learning. In these models, the learning mechanism is not based on feature checking or abstraction, but on prediction error. Children can use their current linguistic knowledge to generate predictions about what they will hear next. When these predictions are checked against reality, the resulting discrepancy can be used to update the linguistic knowledge and to enhance future predictions. In other words, these models explicitly connect language processing and language learning. Learning takes place online, rather than after the fact, thereby incorporating implicit negative evidence. This invalidates one of the major assumptions underpinning nativist approaches. Chomsky (1965) had argued that the learning problem is unsolvable without strong prior constraints on the language, given that the linguistic stimulus is poor, i.e., partial and full of errors. The language environment of the child would not provide them with enough information and information of a high enough quality to learn language, and in the absence of negative evidence there would not be a mechanism by which children would learn what not to say.

10.4   Looking Forward: What Lessons Can We Learn?

If linguists want to continue on the path of cognition, honour the cognitive commitment and make theories of language square with what is known about the mind and the brain, changes are in order in 'how we preach linguistics' and in 'how we practice linguistics'. The fact that repetition is, at the very least, not the only determinant of registration in memory makes frequency-based measures very crude approximations of the relation between what is experienced and what is encoded. We need to think about what to count, we need to think about how to count and we need to think about the conclusions we can draw from all that counting. The following three sections take up these challenges in turn.

10.4.1 Building Blocks: What to Count?

Contrary to what mainstream psycholinguistic models assume, speakers do not (and do not need to) analyse language in terms of abstract linguistic concepts when they process input (compare here Feldman et al. 2010). This has been shown across morphology (Dąbrowska 2008), syntax (Frank 2013) and semantics (Divjak, Szymor and Socha-Michalik 2015). Dąbrowska (2008) investigated questions with long-distance dependencies (e.g., *What do you think you're doing?*) and found that they tend to be quite stereotypical: the matrix clause usually consists of a *wh–* word, the auxiliary *do* or *did*, the pronoun *you* and the verb *think* or *say*, with no other elements; and they virtually never contain more than one subordinate clause. This led her to hypothesize that speakers' knowledge about such constructions is best explained in terms of relatively specific, low-level templates rather than general rules that apply 'across the board'. Frank (2013) investigated whether the cognitive processing difficulty of a word in sentence context is determined by the word's effect on the uncertainty about the sentence. In his study, surprisal and entropy reduction were estimated for actual words rather than their syntactic categories; entropy was not computed over structures but over input sequences. In addition to simplifying the estimation of entropy, this had the advantage that it does not rely on any particular grammar or other assumption about how sentences are interpreted or parsed. He reasoned that, since it is unknown which particular structures people assign to sentences, it may be more appropriate to abstract away from structures altogether and deal only with the sequential input. Yet, at the same time he added the caveat that this is a simplifying assumption that should not be taken as a claim about the cognitive process of sentence comprehension. Divjak, Szymor and Socha-Michalik (2015) report on an empirical study into the cognitive reality of linguistic classifications of modality, i.e., words such as *can/could, may/ might, must, will/would* and *shall/should.* Linguists disagree on the criteria for their classification and theoretical models distinguish as few as two and as many as six types. The results for Polish, which are replicated for Russian (Lyashevskaya et al. 2018), Czech and Croatian, point to a discrepancy between theoretical linguistic classifications and the way native speakers handle modality. Combining data from large text collections and training studies, they established that all existing linguistic classifications appear equally difficult to predict from usage for a range of statistical classifiers and are challenging to acquire and use for linguistically 'naïve' speakers. Sorting experiments showed that speakers do intuitively distinguish modal meanings, but along the lines of necessity and possibility, two concepts which are not systematically considered in linguistic theory but used to form the core of modality in Greek philosophy.

One way of checking whether accounts are comprehensive and do the work attributed to them is by implementing them computationally. Draaisma (2000: 193–4) distinguished between product and process simulations: the former imitates the result while the latter also imitates the mechanisms which will lead to that result. Over the past seventy years, inspired by the information-processing metaphor of the mind, many computational implementations of language development and representation have been proposed. Despite their success in modelling some linguistic phenomena, overall the results have not been very impressive from a linguistic point of view. In fact, we should ask why our attempts at modelling language persistently falter, despite powerful linguistic theories? I have argued elsewhere (Divjak 2015) that, despite powerful linguistic theories and computational algorithms, attempts at modelling language fail because they rely on traditional linguistic analyses and use brute-force engineering algorithms to find evidence of structures that may not exist in speakers' minds. These are, indeed, two interrelated probable causes: we are looking for cognitive evidence of generalizations that were proposed on the basis of classical techniques of linguistic analysis and for this we use computational algorithms that detect structure in data but tend to be, in essence, mere engineering solutions

Linguistic categories, which form the backbone of research on language across disciplines, were designed to describe the forms of a language and their functions as economically as possible, not to reflect the workings of the mind (Divjak 2015). Some of these categories have been around for millennia; the classification of words into categories such as nouns and verbs, for example, predates Christianity. With few exceptions, the universality of the adopted traditional linguistic categories has gone unquestioned (Evans and Levinson 2009), and the cognitive reality of the categories has not been systematically addressed. Machine learning provides powerful computational algorithms that discover patterns in sufficient amounts of data, and some do so without being explicitly told what to look for. Because language is 'never ever random', but at the same time rarely (if ever) fully predictable, it is an ideal candidate for a machine-learning approach to pattern detection. Unfortunately, we tend to force the algorithm to conform to existing linguistic classifications instead of using it to *discover* language structure. Moreover, we use machine-learning approaches that are theory-free and built to be efficient, and more often than not unconstrained by concerns about cognitive plausibility. In other words, our machines are trained to detect linguistic patterns which are inherited from early grammarians, and they typically do not learn from the data the way humans do.

10.4.2 Cognitive Models: How to Count?

Yet descriptive linguistic categories form the foundation for work on language across disciplines, from language teaching to artificial intelligence. Linguistic reality and psychological reality seem to have become conflated, resulting in a situation whereby linguists promote their descriptions as possible cognitive explanations, while psycholinguists collect behavioural evidence, assuming that linguistic descriptions must capture a cognitively reality. But, as briefly illustrated above, cognitively real generalizations may not at all accord with generalizations arrived at by classical techniques of linguistic analysis. To be successful at modelling, and understanding, language learning and representation, we will need algorithms simulating the process of human learning in a biologically and psychologically plausible way. We will also need to understand and represent the language process better, i.e., by including what we know about the role memory and attention play in this process.

Currently, very few such algorithms are available, and those that are available are in their infancy. Although linguistics, and cognitive linguistics in particular, has undergone a 'quantitative turn' over the past ten to fifteen years (Janda 2013), focus has been on introducing statistical methods to linguistics (Baayen 2008; Johnson 2008; Gries 2009; Levshina 2015), without further consideration of their cognitive reality or unreality, for that matter. In many publications from across the wider language sciences, predictions are derived from data that has been extracted from large text collections and subjected to statistical modelling. Predictions derived from such models are then compared to data from experimental tasks. There are two issues with this approach. For one, text collections are amalgamations: the patterns that emerge are an average that may not represent a single individual language user. Experiments, however, are taken by individuals who bring their own set of cognitive skills and their own history of exposure to language to the experiment. Currently, statistical models of linguistic data do not typically account for such individual differences, hence their predictions represent average behaviour. This poses a challenge when comparing textual and experimental results. Linguists, who typically run an experimental study after a corpus-based study, often refer to this process as 'validation' (see the discussion in Klavan and Divjak 2016a). In addition to the amalgamation problem, this choice of words, unfortunately, creates the impression that behavioural data is inherently more valuable than textual data, be it transcribed spoken language or originally written language. But for language, textual data is the result of one of the most natural types of linguistic behaviour, and 'observing' the output qualifies as an 'observational study' or a 'natural experiment', which is quite popular in disciplines where experimental manipulation of groups and treatments would be unethical. It may be important to note that both textual and experimental data can be considered behavioural data since both are forms of human behaviour; in this sense, textual data (as reflection of speaking or writing) is often more natural than experimental data, which tends to have low ecological validity. Through observation, we get a real picture of the phenomenon as it manifests itself in natural settings.

In a natural setting, so many factors may influence a phenomenon that it becomes difficult if not impossible to establish cause and effect; although this can be (partially) countered by taking a multivariate approach, at present we lack an exhaustive list of potentially influential factors (Divjak 2010), and we need experiments to check whether the factors we have identified by modelling observational data do indeed cause a particular behaviour. It is also well known that there is a greater risk of selection bias in observational studies than in experimental studies, and this is certainly true for most studies based on small and medium-sized corpora; billion-word corpora may overcome this problem simply by being very large. A third set of issues relates to the observer themselves: although observer bias, where the observer's interests colour the observations, may well affect the annotations that are added to the corpus data, observer effect tends to manifest itself mainly when the data consists of transcribed recordings of conversations, as in acquisition corpora where a researcher was present during the recorded interactions. And finally not every pattern that we can detect in a large dataset will have been picked up by every speaker, and this problem is only becoming more acute as the size of datasets increases and statistical modelling techniques become more sensitive. We need experiments – at least for now – to set upper and lower boundaries to what could be psychologically relevant and to calibrate our models.

Yet, we should not forget about the product: to use as outcomes for our modelling endeavours, we need cognitively plausible descriptions of the linguistic knowledge adult language users develop in natural settings. And this knowledge need not coincide at all with what is described in grammars of a language. As demonstrated in a study on tense, aspect and mood in Russian (Milin, Divjak and Baayen 2017), readers can rely on simple letter sequences that are linked directly to an experience and embed crucial information about the experience (i.e., Is it over, ongoing or coming up? Was it something that they completed, or simply did for a while? Was it an order?). Using an 80 million–word subtitle corpus, a naïve discrimination learning model found that basic usage patterns consisting of letter triplets predict the time it takes to read and integrate these verbs into a sentence significantly better than all tense, aspect and mood markers combined. Crucially, in this case, the most strongly activated trigraphs captured the letter combinations that uniquely identified a particular tense, aspect and mood constellation. This challenges the idea that theoretical linguistic constructs such as tense, aspect and mood are needed to explain how native speakers of Russian process events in real time. It also demonstrates that honouring the scientific principle of parsimony (naivety and simplicity) in the structures that are hypothesized to exist, and in the way in which behaviour is explained, is a powerful research stance, in particular for designing effective language learning strategies. Sequences that combine form and function should lie at the core of what is taught to language learners to ensure that second language learning unfolds in a natural fashion and gives learners the best possible chance of achieving near native performance. This does not mean that three-letter combinations are the way forward when it comes to modelling any textual input other than that received through reading, and models relying on perceptually more plausible units such as syllables (Vihman 1996) are underway (see work by done the Out of Our Minds team, https://outofourminds.bham.ac.uk)

10.5   By Way of Conclusion

Frequency of occurrence was introduced as a way to account for experience, then took on a life of its own. Operationalizing frequency as counts of occurrences seems to date back to early psycholinguistic attempts to capture familiarity, or experience, with an item at a time when word frequency lists were in full swing in educational research. It is this basic operationalization of frequency as counts of occurrence, i.e., as proxy for exposure, that has held sway in (usage-based) linguistics. In its crude form, this measure indiscriminately captures available input only, i.e., exposure, and it captures it as a function of the composition of a particular text corpus. More sophisticated implementations from quantitative linguistics suffer from this same drawback. Although some measures account for context better than others, the effect of a lack of occurrence (or negative evidence) remains only indirectly available. The effect of cognitive capacities that regulate uptake and the individual differences that affect these capacities are currently not implemented in any of the available frequency measures. Measures based on insights from learning theory incorporate the effects of frequency of exposure (or lack thereof) on learning directly. Yet, current implementations that have been used to model language, such as NDL, do not typically aim to model the effects of (individual differences in) memory and attention either. Once they do, it would be ideal for linguists who aspire to provide cognitively realistic accounts to take the input as a starting point and use insights and algorithms from learning theory to derive linguistic categories that resemble those native speakers might derive, thereby safeguarding cognitive plausibility and building learnability into the very foundations of linguistic analysis. Implementing the requirement for cognitive reality in linguistic analysis at the theoretical, methodological and descriptive levels will yield profound new insights into the knowledge speakers have of their language. Providing researchers across disciplines with linguistic abstractions that matter to the cognitive systems of speakers paves the way for cognitively plausible models of language. Such models will induce a step change in research on language and language-related cognition across disciplines and will make it possible for us to unravel and harness the language-learning power that the human mind is equipped with.

References

Abney, S. 1996. 'Statistical Methods and Linguistics.' In Judith L. Klavans and Philip Resnik (eds.), *The Balancing Act: Combining Symbolic and Statistical Approaches to Language* (CogNet: Cambridge, MA).

Adelman, J. S., G. D. Brown, and J. F. Quesada. 2006. 'Contextual diversity, not word frequency, determines word-naming and lexical decision times', *Psychological Science*, 17: 814–23.

Alegre, M., and P. Gordon. 1999. 'Frequency effects and the representational status of regular inflections', *Journal of Memory and Language*, 40: 41–61.

Alekseev, P. M. 2005. 'Frequency Dictionaries (Häufigkeitswörterbücher).' In Reinhard Köhler, Gabriel Altmann and Rajmund G. Piotrowski (eds.), *Quantitative Linguistik. Ein internationales Handbuch. Quantitative Linguistics. An international Handbook* (Walter de Gruyter: Berlin, New York).

Alkire, M. T., A. G. Hudetz, and G. Tononi. 2008. 'Consciousness and anesthesia', *Science*, 322: 876–80.

Allan, L. G. 1980. 'A note on measurement of contingency between two binary variables in judgement tasks', *Bulletin of the Psychonomic Society*, 15: 147–9.

Allen, K., F. Pereira, M. Botvinick, and A. E. Goldberg. 2012. 'Distinguishing grammatical constructions with fMRI pattern analysis', *Brain and Language*, 123: 174–82.

Allén, S. 1970. *Nusvensk frekvensordbok baserad på tidningstext. 1, Graford. Homografkomponenter = Graphic words. Homograph components* (Almqvist and Wiksell International: Stockholm).

1971. *Nusvensk frekvensordbok baserad på tidningstext. 2, Lemman = Lemmas* (Almqvist and Wiksell International: Stockholm).

1975. *Nusvensk frekvensordbok baserad på tidningstext. 3, Ordförbindelser = Collocations* (Almqvist and Wiksell International: Stockholm).

1980. *Nusvensk frekvensordbok baserad på tidningstext. 4, Ordled. Betydelser = Morphemes. Meanings* (Almqvist and Wiksell International: Stockholm).

Allopenna, P. D., J. S. Magnuson, and M. K. Tanenhaus. 1998. 'Tracking the time course of spoken word recognition using eye movements: evidence for continuous mapping models', *Journal of Memory and Language*, 38: 419–39.

Altmann, G. T. M., and Y. Kamide. 2007. 'The real-time mediation of visual attention by language and world knowledge: linking anticipatory (and other) eye movements to linguistic processing', *Journal of Memory and Language*, 57: 502–18.

Ambridge, B. 2013. 'How do children restrict their linguistic generalizations? An (un-) grammaticality judgment study', *Cognitive Science*, 37: 508–43.

2018. 'Against stored abstractions: a radical exemplar model of language acquisition.' Available at SSRN: http://dx.doi.org/10.2139/ssrn.3219847

Ambridge, B., L. Barak, E. Wonnacott, C. Bannard, and G. Sala. 2018. 'Effects of both pre-emption and entrenchment in the retreat from verb overgeneralization errors: four reanalyses, an extended replication, and a meta-analytic synthesis', *Collabra: Psychology*, 4.

Ambridge, B., A. Bidgood, K. E. Twomey, J. M. Pine, C. F. Rowland, and D. Freudenthal. 2015. 'Pre-emption versus entrenchment: towards a construction-general solution to the problem of the retreat from verb argument structure overgeneralization', *PLoS ONE*, 10: e0123723.

Ambridge, B., E. Kidd, C. F. Rowland, and A. L. Theakston. 2015. 'The ubiquity of frequency effects in first language acquisition', *Journal of Child Language*, 42: 239–73.

Ambridge, B., and E. V. M. Lieven. 2011. *Child Language Acquisition: Contrasting Theoretical Approaches* (Cambridge University Press: Cambridge).

       2015. 'A Constructivist Account of Child Language Acquisition.' In Brian MacWhinney and William O'Grady (eds.), *The Handbook of Language Emergence* (Wiley Blackwell: Hoboken, NJ).

Ambridge, B., J. M. Pine, and C. F. Rowland. 2012. 'Semantics versus statistics in the retreat from locative overgeneralization errors', *Cognition*, 123: 260–79.

Ambridge, B., J. M. Pine, C. F. Rowland, and F. Chang. 2012. 'The roles of verb semantics, entrenchment, and morphophonology in the retreat from dative argument-structure overgeneralization errors', *Language*, 88: 45–81.

Ambridge, B., J. M. Pine, C. F. Rowland, D. Freudenthal, and F. Chang. 2014. 'Avoiding dative overgeneralization errors: semantics, statistics or both?', *Language, Cognition and Neuroscience*, 29: 218–43.

Ambridge, B., A. Theakston, E. V. M. Lieven, and M. Tomasello. 2006. 'The distributed learning effect for children's acquisition of an abstract grammatical construction', *Cognitive Development*, 21: 174–93.

Anderson, J. R. 1982. 'Acquisition of cognitive skill', *Psychological Review*, 89: 369–406.

       1990. *The Adaptive Character of Thought* (Lawrence Erlbaum: Hillsdale, NJ, Hove, London).

Anderson, J. R., and R. Milson. 1989. 'Human memory: an adaptive perspective', *Psychological Review*, 96: 703–19.

Anderson, J. R., and L. J. Schooler. 1991. 'Reflections of the environment in memory', *Psychological Science*, 2: 396–408.

Anderson, M. C., E. L. Bjork, and R. A. Bjork. 2000. 'Retrieval-induced forgetting: evidence for a recall-specific mechanism', *Psychonomic Bulletin and Review*, 7: 522–30.

Anderson, M. C., and B. A. Spellman. 1995. 'On the status of inhibitory mechanisms in cognition: memory retrieval as a model case', *Psychological Review*, 102: 68–100.

Andersson, R., F. Ferreira, and J. M. Henderson. 2011. 'I see what you're saying: the integration of complex speech and scenes during language comprehension', *Acta Psychologica*, 137: 208–16.

Annau, Z., and L. J. Kamin. 1961. 'The conditioned emotional response as a function of intensity of the US', *Journal of Comparative and Physiological Psychology*, 54: 428–32.

Antić, E. 2012. 'Relative Frequency Effects in Russian Morphology.' In Stefan Th. Gries and Dagmar Divjak (eds.), *Frequency Effects in Language Learning and Processing. Vol. 1* (De Gruyter Mouton: Berlin, Boston).

Arai, M., and R. Mazuka. 2014. 'The development of Japanese passive syntax as indexed by structural priming in comprehension', *The Quarterly Journal of Experimental Psychology*, 67: 60–78.

Arnon, I., and E. V. Clark. 2011. 'Why brush your teeth is better than teeth: children's word production is facilitated in familiar sentence-frames', *Language Learning and Development*, 7: 107–29.

Arnon, I., and N. Snider. 2010. 'More than words: frequency effects for multi-word phrases', *Journal of Memory and Language*, 62: 67–82.

Aronoff, M. 1976. *Word Formation in Generative Grammar* (MIT Press: Cambridge, MA).

Arppe, A. 2008. 'Univariate, bivariate and multivariate methods in corpus-based lexicography: a study of synonymy', dissertation, University of Helsinki.

Arppe, A., G. Gilquin, D. Glynn, M. Hilpert, and A. Zeschel. 2010. 'Cognitive corpus linguistics: five points of debate on current theory and methodology', *Corpora*, 5: 1–27.

Arppe, A., and J. Järvikivi. 2007. 'Every method counts: combining corpus-based and experimental evidence in the study of synonymy', *Corpus Linguistics and Linguistic Theory*, 3: 131–59.

Ashby, F. G., and L. A. Alfonso-Reese. 1995. 'Categorization as probability density estimation', *Journal of Mathematical Psychology*, 39: 216–33.

Aslin, R. N., J. R. Saffran, and E. L. Newport. 1998. 'Computation of conditional probability statistics by eight-month-old infants', *Psychological Science*, 9: 321–4.

Awh, E., A. V. Belopolsky, and J. Theeuwes. 2012. 'Top-down versus bottom-up attentional control: a failed theoretical dichotomy', *Trends in Cognitive Sciences*, 16: 437–43.

Ayres, L. P. 1913. *Psychological tests in vocational guidance* (Russell Sage Foundation: New York).

  1915. *A Measuring Scale for Ability in Spelling* (Russell Sage Foundation: New York).

Baayen, R. H. 1993. 'On Frequency, Transparency, and Productivity.' In Geert Booij and Jaap van Marle (eds.), *Yearbook of Morphology 1992* (Kluwer Academic: Dordrecht).

  2001. *Word frequency distributions* (Kluwer Academic: Dordrecht, Boston).

  2003. 'Probabilistic Approaches to Morphology.' In Rens Bod, Jennifer Hay and Stefanie Jannedy (eds.), *Probabilistic linguistics* (MIT Press: Cambridge, MA).

  2008. *Analyzing Linguistic Data: A Practical Introduction to Statistics* (Cambridge University Press: Cambridge, UK, New York).

  2010. 'Demythologizing the word frequency effect: a discriminative learning perspective', *The Mental Lexicon*, 5: 436–61.

  2011. 'Corpus linguistics and naïve discriminative learning', *Brazilian Journal of Applied Linguistics*, 11: 295–328.

Baayen, R. H., A. Endresen, L. A. Janda, A. Makarova, and T. Nesset. 2013. 'Making choices in Russian: pros and cons of statistical methods for rival forms', *Russian Linguistics*, 37: 253–91.

Baayen, R. H., and P. Hendrix. 2011. 'Sidestepping the combinatorial explosion: towards a processing model based on discriminative learning', *Language and Speech*, 56 (3): 329–347

Baayen, R. H., R. Lieber, and R. Schreuder. 1997. 'The morphological complexity of simplex nouns', *Linguistics*, 35: 861–77.

Baayen, R. H., P. Milin, D. F. Durdevic, P. Hendrix, and M. Marelli. 2011. 'An amorphous model for morphological processing in visual comprehension based on naïve discriminative learning', *Psychological Review*, 118: 438–81.

Baayen, R. H., P. Milin, and M. Ramscar. 2016. 'Frequency in lexical processing', *Aphasiology*, 30: 1174–220.

Baayen, R. H., and M. Ramscar. 2015. 'Abstraction, Storage, and Naïve Discriminative Learning.' In Ewa Dąbrowska and Dagmar Divjak (eds.), *Handbook of Cognitive Linguistics* (De Gruyter Mouton: Berlin, Boston).

Baayen, R. H., C. Shaoul, J. Willits, and M. Ramscar. 2016. 'Comprehension without segmentation: a proof of concept with naïve discriminative learning', *Language, Cognition and Neuroscience*, 31: 106–28.

Baayen, R. H., L. H. Wurm, and J. Aycock. 2007. 'Lexical dynamics for low-frequency complex words. A regression study across tasks and modalities', *The Mental Lexicon*, 2: 419–63.

Baddeley, A. 1986. *Working Memory* (Clarendon: Oxford).

———. 1993. 'Working Memory or Working Attention?' In Alan Baddeley and Lawrence Weiskrantz (eds.), *Attention: Selection, Awareness and Control. A Tribute to Donald Broadbent* (Oxford University Press: Oxford).

Baddeley, A. 2000. 'Short-Term and Working Memory.' In E. Tulving and F. I. M. Craik (eds.), *The Oxford Handbook of Memory* (Oxford University Press: New York).

Baddeley, A. 2003. 'Working memory and language: an overview', *Journal of Communication Disorders*, 36: 189–208.

Baddeley, A., and G. Hitch. 1993. 'The recency effect: implicit learning with explicit retrieval?', *Memory and Cognition*, 21: 146–55.

Baddeley, A., and G. J. Hitch. 1974. 'Working Memory.' In G. A. Bower (ed.), *Recent Advances in Learning and Motivation* (Academic Press: New York).

Baddeley, A., V. Lewis, M. Eldridge, and N. Thomson. 1984. 'Attention and retrieval from long-term memory', *Journal of Experimental Psychology: General*, 113: 518–40.

Bahrick, H. P. 1984. 'Semantic memory content in permastore: fifty years of memory for Spanish learned in school', *Journal of Experimental Psychology: General*, 113: 1–29.

Bahrick, H. P., L. E. Bahrick, A. S. Bahrick, and P. E. Bahrick. 1993. 'Maintenance of foreign language vocabulary and the spacing effect', *Psychological Science*, 4: 316–21.

Baldwin, D. 1995. 'Understanding the Link between Joint Attention and Language.' In Chris Moore and Philip J. Dunham (eds.), *Joint Attention: Its Origins and Role in Development* (Lawrence Erlbaum: Hillsdale, NJ).

Balota, D. A., M. J. Yap, K. A. Hutchison, and M. J. Cortese. 2012. 'Megastudies: Large-Scale Analysis of Lexical Processes.' In James S. Adelman (ed.), *Visual Word Recognition* (Psychology Press: London).

Balota, D. A., M. J. Yap, K. A. Hutchison, M. J. Cortese, B. Kessler, B. Loftis, J. H. Neely, D. L. Nelson, G. B. Simpson, and R. Treiman. 2007. 'The English lexicon project', *Behavior Research Methods*, 39: 445–59.

Banaji, M. R., and R. G. Crowder. 1989. 'The bankruptcy of everyday memory', *American Psychologist*, 44: 1185–93.

Bannard, C., and D. Matthews. 2008. 'Stored word sequences in language learning: the effect of familiarity on children's repetition of four-word combinations', *Psychological Science*, 19: 241–8.

Bar, M. 2011. *Predictions in the Brain: Using Our Past to Generate a Future* (Oxford University Press: New York, Oxford).

Bar, M., E. Aminoff, M. Mason, and M. Fenske. 2007. 'The units of thought', *Hippocampus*, 17: 420–8.

Barðdal, J. 2008. *Productivity: Evidence from Case and Argument Structure in Icelandic* (John Benjamins: Amsterdam).

Barlow, H. 1990. 'Conditions for versatile learning, Helmholtz's unconscious inference, and the task of perception', *Vision Research*, 30: 1561–71.

Baroni, M. 2008. 'Word Frequency Distributions.' In Anke Lüdeling and Merja Kytö (eds.), *Corpus Linguistics. An International Handbook* (Mouton de Gruyter: Berlin).

Barrouillet, P., S. Bernardin, S. Portrat, E. Vergauwe, and V. Camos. 2007. 'Time and cognitive load in working memory', *Journal of Experimental Psychology: Learning, Memory, and Cognition*, 33: 570–85.

Bartlett, F. C. 1932. *Remembering: A Study in Experimental and Social Psychology* (Cambridge University Press: Cambridge, UK).

Barto, A., M. Mirolli, and G. Baldassare. 2013. 'Novelty or surprise?', *Frontiers in Psychology*, 4: 1–15.

Bear, M. F., B. W. Connors, and M. A. Paradiso. 2016. *Neuroscience: Exploring the Brain* (Wolters Kluwer: Philadelphia).

Beckner, C., R. Blythe, J. L. Bybee, M. H. Christiansen, W. Croft, N. C. Ellis, J. Holland, J. Ke, D. Larsen-Freeman, and T. Schoenemann. 2009. 'Language is a complex adaptive system: position paper', *Language Learning*, 59: 1–26.

Behrens, H., and S. Pfänder (eds.). 2016. *Experience Counts: Frequency Effects in Language* (De Gruyter: Berlin, Boston).

Berlyne, D. E. 1960. *Conflict, Arousal and Curiosity* (McGraw-Hill: New York).

Bernolet, S., and R. J. Hartsuiker. 2010. 'Does verb bias modulate syntactic priming?', *Cognition*, 114: 455–61.

Besner, D., and G. W. Humphreys. 1991. *Basic Processes in Reading: Visual Word Recognition* (Lawrence Erlbaum: Hillsdale, NJ).

Bever, T. G. 1970. 'The Cognitive Basis for Linguistic Structure.' In John R. Hayes (ed.), *Cognition and the Development of Language* (John Wiley: New York).

Bicknell, K., J. L. Elman, M. Hare, K. McRae, and M. Kutas. 2010. 'Effects of event knowledge in processing verbal arguments', *Journal of Memory and Language*, 63: 489–505.

Biederman, I., A. L. Glass, and E. W. Stacy. 1973. 'Searching for objects in real-world scenes', *Journal of Experimental Psychology*, 97: 22–7.

Blevins, J. 2013. 'The information-theoretic turn', *Psihologija*, 46: 355–75.

2016. *Word and Paradigm Morphology* (Oxford University Press: Oxford).

Bloomfield, L. 1914. 'Sentence and word', *Transactions of the American Philological Society*, 45: 65–75.

1933. *Language* (Allen and Unwin: London).

Blumenthal-Dramé, A. 2017. 'Entrenchment from a Psycholinguistic and Neurolinguistic Perspective.' In Hans-Jörg Schmid (ed.), *Entrenchment and the Psychology of Language Learning: How We Reorganize and Adapt Linguistic Knowledge* (De Gruyter Mouton and APA: Berlin).

Blumenthal-Dramé, A. 2012. *Entrenchment in Usage-Based Theories: What Corpus Data Do and Do Not Reveal about the Mind* (Mouton De Gruyter: Berlin).

Blything, R. P., B. Ambridge, and E. V. M. Lieven. 2014. 'Children use statistics and semantics in the retreat from overgeneralization', *PLoS ONE*, 9: e110009.

Bock, K. 1986. 'Syntactic persistence in language production', *Cognitive Psychology*, 18: 355–87.

Bock, K., and V. Ferreira. 2014. 'Syntactically Speaking.' In Matthew Goldrick, Victor Ferreira and Michele Miozzo (eds.), *The Oxford Handbook of Sentence Production* (Oxford University Press: New York).

Bock, K., and Z. M. Griffin. 2000. 'The persistence of structural priming: transient activation or implicit learning?', *Journal of Experimental Psychology*, 129: 177–92.

Bock, K., D. E. Irwin, and D. J. Davidson. 2004. 'Putting First Things First.' In John M. Henderson and Fernanda Ferreira (eds.), *The Interface of Language, Vision, and Action: Eye Movements and the Visual World* (Psychology Press: New York).

Bock, K., and W. J. M. Levelt. 2002. 'Language Production: Grammatical Encoding.' In Gerry T. M. Altmann (ed.), *Psycholinguistics: Critical Concepts in Psychology* (Routledge: London).

Bod, R. 2009. 'From exemplar to grammar: a probabilistic analogy-based model of language learning', *Cognitive Science*, 33: 752–93.

Bod, R., J. Hay, and S. Jannedy. 2003a. 'Introduction.' In Rens Bod, Jennifer Hay and Stefanie Jannedy (eds.), *Probabilistic Linguistics* (MIT Press: Cambridge, MA, London).

2003b. *Probabilistic Linguistics* (MIT Press: Cambridge, MA, London).

Boldrini, M. 1948. *Le statistiche letterarie e i fonemi elementari nella poesia* (Milano).

Bolinger, D. 1976. 'Meaning and memory', *Forum Linguisticum*, 1: 1–14.

Bontrager, T. 1991. 'The development of word frequency lists prior to the 1944 Thorndike–Lorge list', *Reading Psychology*, 12 (2): 91–116.

Bouton, M. E. 1991. 'Context and Retrieval in Extinction and in Other Examples of Interference in Simple Associative Learning.' In Lawrence Dachowski and Charles F. Flaherty (eds.), *Current Topics in Animal Learning: Brain, Emotion, and Cognition* (Earlbaum: Hillsdale, NJ.).

1993. 'Context, time, and memory retrieval in the interference paradigms of Pavlovian learning', *Psychological Bulletin*, 114: 80–99.

1994. 'Conditioning, remembering, and forgetting', *Journal of Experimental Psychology: Animal Behavior Processes*, 20: 219–31.

2007. *Learning and Behavior. A Contemporary Synthesis* (Sinauer Associates: Sunderland, MA).

Bowers, J. S., and C. J. Davis. 2012. 'Bayesian Just-So Stories in psychology and neuroscience', *Psychological Bulletin*, 138: 389–414.

Boyd, J. K. 2014. 'Statistical Pre-emption.' In Patricia Brooks and Vera Kempe (eds.), *Encyclopedia of Language Development* (SAGE Reference: Los Angeles).

Boyd, J. K., F. Ackerman, and M. Kutas. 2012. 'Adult learners use both entrenchment and preemption to infer grammatical constraints.' In *2012 IEEE International Conference on Development and Learning and Epigenetic Robotics (ICDL)*, 1–2.

Boyd, J. K., and A. E. Goldberg. 2011. 'Learning what not to say: categorization, statistical pre-emption, and discounting in a-adjective production', *Language*, 87: 55–83.

Boye, K., and E. Engberg-Pedersen. 2010. 'Introduction.' In Kasper Boye and Elisabeth Engberg-Pedersen (eds.), *Language Usage and Language Structure* (De Gruyter Mouton: Berlin, New York).

Bradshaw, J. L. 1984. 'A guide to norms, ratings, and lists', *Memory and Cognition*, 12: 202–6.

Braine, M. D. S., and P. Brooks. 1995. 'Verb Argument Structure and the Problem of Avoiding an Overgeneral Grammar.' In Michael Tomasello and William E. Merriman (eds.), *Beyond Names for Things: Young Children's Acquisition of Verbs* (Lawrence Erlbaum: Hillsdale, NJ).

Branigan, H. P., and M. J. Pickering. 2017. 'Structural Priming and the Representation of Language', *Behavioral and Brain Sciences*, 40.

Brase, G. L., L. Cosmides, and J. Tooby. 1998. 'Individuation, counting, and statistical inference: the role of frequency and whole-object representations in judgment under uncertainty', *Journal of Experimental Psychology: General*, 127: 3–21.

Bresnan, J. 2007. 'Is Syntactic Knowledge Probabilistic? Experiments with the Dative Alternation.' In Sam Featherston and Wolfgang Sternefeld (eds.), *Roots: Linguistics in Search of Its Evidential Base* (Mouton de Gruyter: Berlin).

Bresnan, J., A. Cueni, T. Nikitina, and R. H. Baayen. 2007. 'Predicting the Dative Alternation.' In Gerlof Boume, Irene Kraemer and Joost Zwarts (eds.), *Cognitive Foundations of Interpretation* (Royal Netherlands Academy of Science: Amsterdam).

Bresnan, J., and M. Ford. 2010. 'Predicting syntax: processing dative constructions in American and Australian varieties of English', *Language*, 86: 186–213.

Bright, T. 1588. *Characterie. An Arte of shorte, swifte, and secrete writing by character* (Windet, I.: London).

Broadbent, D. E. 1958. *Perception and Communication* (Pergamon Press: London).
1959. 'Review of verbal behavior', *British Journal of Psychology*, 50: 371–3
1967. 'Word-frequency effect and response bias', *Psychological Review*, 74: 1–15.
1971. *Decision and Stress* (Academic Press: Oxford).

Brooks, P., and M. Tomasello. 1999. 'How children constrain their argument structure constructions', *Language*, 75: 720–38.

Browne, C., B. Culligan, and J. Phillips. 2013. 'New General Service List', www.newgeneralservicelist.org.

Bruner, J. S. 1978. 'From Communication to Language: A Psychological Perspective.' In Ivana Markova (ed.), *The Social Context of Language* (Wiley: New York).

Brysbaert, M., and B. New. 2009. 'Moving beyond Kučera and Francis: a critical evaluation of current word frequency norms and the introduction of a new and improved word frequency measure for American English', *Behavior Research Methods*, 41: 977–90.

Bush, R. R., and F. Mosteller. 1951. 'A mathematical model for simple learning', *Psychological Review*, 58: 313–23.

Buswell, G. T. 1935. *How People Look at Pictures: A Study of the Psychology of Perception in Art* (University of Chicago Press: Chicago).

Bybee, J. L. 1985. *Morphology: A Study of the Relation between Meaning and Form* (John Benjamins: Amsterdam, Philadelphia).

———— 1994. 'Productivity, Regularity and Fusion: How Language Use Affects the Lexicon.' In Rajendra Singh and Richard Desrochers (eds.), *Trubetzkoy's Orphan: Proceedings of the Montreal Roundtable 'Morphonology: Contemporary Responses'* (John Benjamins: Amsterdam, Philadelphia).

———— 1995. 'Regular morphology and the lexicon', *Language and Cognitive Processes*, 10: 425–55.

———— 2001. *Phonology and Language Use* (Cambridge University Press: Cambridge, UK).

———— 2003. 'Mechanisms of Change in Grammaticization: The Role of Frequency.' In Brian D. Joseph and Richard D. Janda (eds.), *Handbook of Historical Linguistics* (Blackwell: Oxford).

———— 2006. 'From usage to grammar: the mind's response to repetition', *Language*, 82: 711–33.

———— 2007. *Frequency of Use and the Organization of Language* (Oxford University Press: New York, Oxford).

———— 2008. 'Usage-Based Grammar and Second Language Acquisition.' In Peter Robinson and Nick C. Ellis (eds.), *Handbook of Cognitive Linguistics and Second Language Acquisition* (Routledge: New York).

———— 2010. *Language, Usage and Cognition* (Cambridge University Press: Cambridge, UK).

———— 2013. 'Usage-Based Theory and Exemplar Representation.' In Thomas Hoffman and Graeme Trousdale (eds.), *The Oxford Handbook of Construction Grammar* (Oxford University Press: Oxford).

———— 2015. *Language change* (Cambridge University Press: New York).

Bybee, J. L., and C. Beckner. 2009. 'Usage-Based Theory.' In Bernd Heine and Heiko Narrog (eds.), *The Oxford Handbook of Linguistic Analysis* (Oxford University Press: Oxford).

Bybee, J. L., and D. Eddington. 2006. 'A usage-based approach to Spanish verbs of "becoming"', *Language*, 82: 323–55.

Bybee, J. L., and P. Hopper. 2001a. *Frequency and the Emergence of Linguistic Structure* (John Benjamins: Amsterdam, Philadelphia).

———— 2001b. 'Introduction.' In Joan L. Bybee and Paul Hopper (eds.), *Frequency and the Emergence of Linguistic Structure* (John Benjamins: Amsterdam, Philadelphia).

Bybee, J. L., and S. Thompson. 2000. 'Three Frequency Effects in Syntax.' In *The Twenty-Third Annual Meeting of the Berkeley Linguistics Society: General Session and Parasession on Pragmatics and Grammatical Structure.*, 65–85 (Berkeley Linguistics Society: Berkeley).

Caldwell-Harris, C. L., J. Berant, and S. Edelman. 2012. 'Measuring Mental Entrenchment of Phrases with Perceptual Identification, Familiarity Ratings, and Corpus Frequency Statistics.' In Stefan Th. Gries and Dagmar Divjak (eds.), *Frequency Effects in Cognitive Linguistics (Vol. 1): Statistical Effects in Learnability, Processing and Change* (De Gruyter Mouton: The Hague).

Calkins, M. W. 1894. 'Association', *Psychological Review*, 1: 476–83.

Calude, A. S., and S. Miller. 2009. 'Are clefts contagious in conversation?', *English Language and Linguistics*, 13: 127–32.

Caplan, D., and G. S. Waters. 1999. 'Verbal working memory and sentence comprehension', *Behavioral and Brain Sciences*, 22: 77–94.

Carey, S., and E. Bartlett. 1978. 'Acquiring a single new word.' In *Proceedings of the Stanford Child Language Conference*, 17–29.

Carpenter, S. K., N. J. Cepeda, D. Rohrer, and S. H. K. Kang. 2012. 'Using spacing to enhance diverse forms of learning: review of recent research and implications for instruction', *Educational Psychology Review*, 24: 369–78.

Casenhiser, D. M., and G. M. L. Bencini. 2015. 'Argument Structure Constructions.' In Ewa Dąbrowska and Dagmar Divjak (eds.), *Handbook of Cognitive Linguistics* (De Gruyter Mouton: Berlin, Boston).

Castel, A. D., and F. I. M. Craik. 2003. 'The effects of aging and divided attention on memory for item and associative information', *Psychology and Aging*, 18: 873–85.

Cattell, J. M. 1886. 'The time it takes to see and name objects', *Mind*, 11: 63–5.

Chafe, W. 1979. 'The Flow of Thought and the Flow of Language.' In Talmy Givón (ed.), *Discourse and Syntax* (Academic Press: New York).

    1982. 'Integration and Involvement in Speaking, Writing, and Oral Literature.' In Deborah Tannen (ed.), *Spoken and Written Language: Exploring Orality and Literacy* (Ablex: Norwood, NJ).

    1994. *Discourse, Consciousness, and Time: The Flow and Displacement of Conscious Experience in Speaking and Writing* (The University of Chicago Press: Chicago).

    1998. 'Language and the Flow of Thought.' In Michael Tomasello (ed.), *The New Psychology of Language: Cognitive and Functional Approaches to Language Structure* (Lawrence Erlbaum: Mahwah, NJ).

Chater, N., and C. D. Manning. 2006. 'Probabilistic models of language processing and acquisition', *Trends in Cognitive Sciences*, 10: 335–44.

Chelazzi, L., E. K. Miller, J. Duncan, and R. Desimone. 1993. 'A neural basis for visual search in inferior temporal cortex', *Nature*, 363: 345–7.

Cheng, P. W., and K. J. Holyoak. 1995. 'Adaptive Systems as Intuitive Statisticians: Causality, Contingency, and Prediction.' In J.-A. Meyer and H. Roitblat (eds.), *Comparative Approaches to Cognition* (MIT Press: Cambridge, MA).

Cheng, P. W., and L. R. Novick. 1990. 'A probabilistic contrast model of causal induction', *Journal of Personality and Social Psychology*, 58: 545–67.

Cherry, E. C. 1953. 'Some experiments on the recognition of speech, with one and with two ears', *Journal of the Acoustical Society of America*, 25: 975–9.

Choi, S., and M. Bowerman. 1991. 'Learning to express motion events in English and Korean: the influence of language-specific lexicalization patterns', *Cognition*, 41: 83–121.

Chomsky, N. 1957. *Syntactic Structures* (Mouton: The Hague).

    1959. 'A review of B. F. Skinner's *Verbal Behavior*', *Language*, 35: 26–58.

    1965. *Aspects of the Theory of Syntax* (MIT Press: Cambridge, MA).

Christiansen, M. H, and I. Arnon (eds.). 2017. *More Than Words: The Role of Multiword Sequences in Language Learning and Use*, *TopiCS*, Special issue, 9 (3): 542–51.

Chun, M. M. 2000. 'Contextual cueing of visual attention', *Trends in Cognitive Sciences*, 4: 170–8.

Chun, M. M., J. D. Golomb, and N. B. Turk-Browne. 2011. 'A taxonomy of external and internal attention', *Annual Review of Psychology*, 62: 73–101.

Chun, M. M., and Y. Jiang. 1998. 'Contextual cueing: implicit learning and memory of visual context guides spatial attention', *Cognitive Psychology*, 36: 28–71.

Chun, M. M., and M. K. Johnson. 2011. 'Memory: enduring traces of perceptual and reflective attention', *Neuron*, 72: 520–35.

Chun, M. M., and N. B. Turk-Browne. 2007. 'Interactions between attention and memory', *Current Opinion in Neurobiology*, 17: 177–84.

Church, K., and W. Gale. 1995. 'Poisson mixtures', *Natural Language Engineering*, 1: 163–90.

Church, K. W., and P. Hanks. 1990. 'Word association norms, mutual information, and lexicography', *Computational Linguistics*, 16: 22–9.

Clark, A. 2013. 'Whatever next? Predictive brains, situated agents, and the future of cognitive science', *The Behavioral and Brain Sciences*, 36: 181–204.

2015a. 'Conservative versus radical predictive processing,' blog, John Schwenkler (ed.), *The Brains Blog*.

2015b. *Surfing Uncertainty* (Oxford University Press: Oxford).

2015c. 'Surfing uncertainty: prediction, action and the embodied mind,' blog, John Schwenkler (ed.), *The Brains Blog*.

Clark, E. V. 1993. *The Lexicon in Acquisition* (Cambridge University Press: Cambridge, UK).

Clarke, W. F. 1921. 'Writing vocabularies', *The Elementary School Journal*, 10: 349–51.

Clausner, T. C., and W. Croft. 1997. 'Productivity and schematicity in metaphors', *Cognitive Science*, 21: 247–82.

Coco, M. I., and F. Keller. 2015. 'The interaction of visual and linguistic saliency during syntactic ambiguity resolution', *The Quarterly Journal of Experimental Psychology*, 68: 46–74.

Cohen, N. J., and L. R. Squire. 1980. 'Preserved learning and retention of pattern-analyzing skill in amnesia: dissociation of knowing how and knowing that', *Science*, 210: 207–9.

Colleman, T., and S. Bernolet. 2012. 'Alternation Biases in Corpora vs. Picture Description Experiments: Do-Biased and Pd-Biased Verbs in the Dutch Dative Alternation.' In Dagmar Divjak and Stefan Th. Gries (eds.), *Frequency Effects in Language Representation* (De Gruyter Mouton: Berlin, New York).

Coltheart, M., K. Rastle, C. Perry, R. Langdon, and J. Ziegler. 2001. 'DRC: A dual route cascaded model of visual word recognition and reading aloud', *Psychological Review*, 108: 204–56.

Condon, E. U. 1928. 'Statistics of vocabulary', *Science*, 67: 1.

Conway, C. M., A. Bauernschmidt, S. S. Huang, and D. B. Pisoni. 2010. 'Implicit statistical learning in language processing: word predictability is the key', *Cognition*, 114: 356–71.

Conway, M. A., C. W. Pleydell-Pearce, S. E. Whitecross, and H. Sharpe. 2003. 'Neurophysiological correlates of memory for experienced and imagined events', *Neuropsychologia*, 41: 334–40.

Cooper, R. M. 1974. 'The control of eye fixation by the meaning of spoken language: a new methodology for the real-time investigation of speech perception, memory, and language processing', *Cognitive Psychology*, 6: 84–107.

Corbetta, M., and G. Shulman. 2002. 'Control of goal-directed and stimulus-driven attention in the brain', *Nature Reviews: Neuroscience*, 3: 215–29.

Cordes, A.-K. 2017. 'The Roles of Analogy, Categorization, and Generalization in Entrenchment.' In Hans-Joerg Schmid (ed.), *Entrenchment and the Psychology of Language Learning: How We Reorganize and Adapt Linguistic Knowledge* (De Gruyter Mouton and APA: Berlin).

Cosmides, L., and J. Tooby. 1996. 'Are humans good intuitive statisticians after all? Rethinking some conclusions from the literature on judgment under uncertainty', *Cognition*, 58: 1–73.

Courville, A. C., N. D. Daw, and D. S. Touretzky. 2006. 'Bayesian theories of conditioning in a changing world', *Trends in Cognitive Sciences*, 10: 294–300.

Cover, T. M., and J. A. Thomas. 1991. *Elements of Information Theory* (Wiley: New York; Chichester).

2006. *Elements of Information Theory* (John Wiley and Sons, Inc: Hoboken, NJ).

Cowan, N. 1988. 'Evolving conceptions of memory storage, selective attention, and their mutual constraints within the human information-processing system', *Psychological Bulletin*, 104: 163–91.

2001. 'The magical number 4 in short-term memory: A reconsideration of mental storage capacity', *Behavioral and Brain Sciences*, 24: 87–114.

Cox, R. T. 1946. 'Probability, frequency and reasonable expectation', *American Journal of Physics*, 14: 1–13.

Craik, F. I., and E. Tulving. 1975. 'Depth of processing and the retention of words in episodic memory', *Journal of Experimental Psychology: General*, 104: 268–94.

Craik, F. I., R. Govoni, M. Naveh-Benjamin, and N. D. Anderson. 1996. 'The effects of divided attention on encoding and retrieval processes in human memory', *Journal of Experimental Psychology: General*, 125: 159–80.

Craik, F. I. M., and R. S. Lockhart. 1972. 'Levels of processing: a framework for memory research', *Journal of Verbal Learning and Verbal Behavior*, 11: 671–84.

Crick, F., and C. Koch. 1998. 'Consciousness and neuroscience', *Cerebral Cortex*, 8: 97–107.

Crocker, M. W., and T. Brants. 2000. 'Wide-coverage probabilistic sentence processing', *Journal of Psycholinguistic Research*, 29: 647–69.

Croft, W. 2009. 'Toward a Social Cognitive Linguistics.' In Vyvyan Evans and Stephanie Pourcel (eds.), *New Directions in Cognitive Linguistics* (John Benjamins: Amsterdam, Philadelphia).

Croft, W., and D. A. Cruse. 2004. *Cognitive Linguistics* (Cambridge University Press: Cambridge, UK).

Cutler, A. 1981. 'Making up materials is a confounded nuisance, or: will we be able to run any psycholinguistic experiments at all in 1990', *Cognition*, 10: 65–70.

Dąbrowska, E. 2000. 'From formula to schema: the acquisition of English questions', *Cognitive Linguistics*, 11: 83–102.

2004. 'Rules or schemas? Evidence from Polish', *Language and Cognitive Processes*, 19: 225–71.

2008. 'Questions with long-distance dependencies: a usage-based perspective', *Cognitive Linguistics*, 19: 391–425.

2015. 'Individual Differences in Grammatical Knowledge.' In Ewa Dąbrowska and Dagmar Divjak (eds.), *Handbook of Cognitive Linguistics* (De Gruyter: Berlin).

Dąbrowska, E., and D. Divjak. 2015. 'Introduction.' In Ewa Dąbrowska and Dagmar Divjak (eds.), *Handbook of Cognitive Linguistics* (De Gruyter de Mouton: Berlin, Boston).

Daelemans, W., and A. Van den Bosch. 2005. *Memory-Based Language Processing* (Cambridge University Press: Cambridge).

Dahan, D., and M. K. Tanenhaus. 2005. 'Looking at the rope when looking for the snake: conceptually mediated eye movements during spoken-word recognition', *Psychonomic Bulletin and Review: A Journal of the Psychonomic Society, Inc.*, 12: 453–9.

Dahl, Ö. 2013. 'Tense-aspect-mood-evidentiality (TAME) and the Organization of Human Memory.' In Karina Veronica Molsing and Anna Maria Tramunt Ibaños (eds.), *Time and TAME in Language* (Cambridge Scholars Publishing: Newcastle upon Tyne).

Davis, M. H., and M. G. Gaskell. 2009. 'A complementary systems account of word learning: neural and behavioural evidence', *Philosophical Transactions of the Royal Society B*, 364: 3773–800.

Dawkins, R. 1982. *The Extended Phenotype: The Gene as the Unit of Selection* (Freeman: Oxford).

De Pisapia, N., G. Repovš, and T. S. Braver. 2008. 'Computational Models of Attention and Cognitive Control.' In Ron Sun (ed.), *The Cambridge Handbook of Computational Psychology* (Cambridge University Press: Cambridge UK).

de Saussure, F. 1916/1966. *Course in General Linguistics* (McGraw-Hill Book Co.: New York).

De Smet, H., and H. Cuyckens. 2007. 'Diachronic Aspects of Complementation: Constructions, Entrenchment and the Matching Problem.' In C. M. Cains and G. Russom (eds.), *Studies in the History of the English Language III: Managing Chaos, Strategies for identifying Change in English* (Mouton de Gruyter: Berlin).

Dell, G. S. 1986. 'A spreading activation theory of retrieval in language production', *Psychological Review*, 93.

Dell, G. S., M. F. Schwartz, N. Martin, E. M. Saffran, and D. A. Gagnon. 1997. 'Lexical access in aphasic and nonaphasic speakers', *Psychological Review*, 104: 801–939.

Delong, K. A., M. Troyer, and M. Kutas. 2014. 'Pre-processing in sentence comprehension: sensitivity to likely upcoming meaning and structure', *Language and Linguistics Compass*, 8: 631–45.

DeLong, K. A., T. P. Urbach, and M. Kutas. 2005. 'Probabilistic word pre-activation during language comprehension inferred from electrical brain activity', *Nature Neuroscience*, 8: 1117–21.

Dennet, D. 1979. *Brainstorms. Philosophical Essays on Mind and Psychology* (Harvester Press: Hassocks).

Dennis, S., and M. S. Humphreys. 2001. 'A context noise model of episodic word recognition', *Psychological Review*, 108.

Desimone, R., and J. Duncan. 1995. 'Neural mechanisms of selective visual attention', *Annual Review of Neuroscience*, 18: 193.

Deutsch, J. A., and D. Deutsch. 1963. 'Attention: some theoretical considerations', *Psychological Review*, 70: 80–90.

Dewey, G. 1923. *Relative Frequency of English Speech Sounds* (Harvard University Press: Cambridge, MA).

Diessel, H. 2007. 'Frequency effects in language acquisition, language use, and diachronic change', *New Ideas in Psychology*, 25: 108–27.

Divjak, D. 2003. 'On trying in Russian: a tentative network model for near(er) synonyms', *Slavica Gandensia*, 30: 25–58.

——— 2004. 'Degrees of verb integration: conceptualizing and categorizing events in Russian', Ph.D. thesis, Katholieke Universiteit, Leuven, Belgium.

——— 2008. 'On (In)Frequency and (Un)Acceptability.' In Barbara Lewandowska-Tomaszczyk (ed.), *Corpus Linguistics, Computer Tools and Applications: State of the Art* (Peter Lang: Frankfurt a. Main).

——— 2010. *Structuring the Lexicon: A Clustered Model for Near-Synonymy* (De Gruyter Mouton: Berlin; New York).

——— 2015. 'Four Challenges for Usage-Based Linguistics.' In Jocelyne Daems, Eline Zenner, Kris Heylen, Dirk Speelman and Hubert Cuycken (eds.), *Change of Paradigms: New Paradoxes. Recontextualizing Language and Linguistics* (De Gruyter: Berlin).

——— 2017. 'The role of lexical frequency in the acceptability of syntactic variants: evidence from that-clauses in Polish', *Cognitive Science*, 41: 354–82.

——— 2018. 'Binding Scale Dynamics: Fact or Fiction?' In Daniël Van Olmen, Tanja Mortelmans and Frank Brisard (eds.), *Aspects of Linguistic Variation: Studies in Honor of Johan van der Auwera* (De Gruyter: Berlin).

Divjak, D., and A. Arppe. 2013. 'Extracting prototypes from exemplars: what can corpus data tell us about concept representation?', *Cognitive Linguistics*, 24: 221–74.

Divjak, D., A. Arppe, and R. H. Baayen. 2016. 'Does Language-as-Used Fit a Self-Paced Reading Paradigm? (The Answer May Well Depend on the Statistical Model You Use).' In Anja Gattnar, Tanja Anstatt and Christina Clasmeier (eds.), *Slavic Languages and the Black Box* (Narr-Verlag: Tübingen).

Divjak, D., and C. L. Caldwell-Harris. 2015. 'Frequency and Entrenchment.' In Ewa Dąbrowska and Dagmar Divjak (eds.), *Handbook of Cognitive Linguistics* (Walter de Gruyter: Berlin, Boston).

Divjak, D., E. Dąbrowska, and A. Arppe. 2016. 'Machine meets man: evaluating the psychological reality of corpus-based probabilistic models', *Cognitive Linguistics*, 27: 1–34.

Divjak, D., and S. T. Gries. 2006. 'Ways of trying in Russian clustering behavioral profiles', *Journal of Corpus Linguistics and Linguistic Theory*, 2: 23–60.

——— 2012. *Frequency Effects in Language Representation* (De Gruyter Mouton: Berlin).

Divjak, D., N. Levshina, and J. Klavan. 2016. 'Cognitive linguistics: looking back, looking forward', *Cognitive Linguistics*, 27: 447–63.

Divjak, D., N. Szymor, and A. Socha-Michalik. 2015. 'Towards a usage-based categorization of Polish modals', *Russian Linguistics*, 39: 327–49.

Draaisma, D. 2000. *Metaphors of Memory: A History of Ideas about the Mind* (Cambridge University Press: Cambridge, UK).

Drobisch, M. W. 1866. 'Ein statistischer Versuch über die Formen des lateinischen Hexameters', *Berichte über die Verhandlungen der Königlich-Sächsische Gesellschaft, Philologisch-Historische Classe*, 18: 75–139.

Dror, I. E., and D. P. Gallogly. 1999. 'Computational analyses in cognitive neuroscience: in defense of biological implausibility', *Psychonomic Bulletin and Review*, 6: 173–82.

Duncan, J. 1996. 'Cooperating Brain Systems in Selective Perception and Action.' In T. Inui and J. L. McClelland (eds.), *Attention and Performance XVI* (MIT Press: Cambridge, MA).

Duncan, J., and G. Humphreys. 1992. 'Beyond the search surface: visual search and attentional engagement', *Journal of Experimental Psychology: Human Perception and Performance*, 18: 578–88.

Duncan, J., and G. W. Humphreys. 1989. 'Visual search and stimulus similarity', *Psychological Review*, 96: 433–58.

Ebbinghaus, H. 1885a. *Memory: A Contribution to Experimental Psychology* (Dover: New York).

1885b. *Über das Gedächtnis. Untersuchungen zur experimentellen Psychologie* (Duncker and Humblot: Leipzig).

Eddington, D. 2000. 'Analogy and the dual-route model of morphology', *Lingua*, 110: 281–98.

2002. 'Why quantitative?', *Linguistics*, 40: 209–16.

Edelman, S. 2006. 'Bridging Language with the Rest of Cognition: Computational, Algorithmic and Neurobiological Issues and Methods.' In Monica Gonzalez-Marquez, Irene Mittelberg, Seana Coulson and Michael J. Spivey (eds.), *Methods in Cognitive Linguistics* (John Benjamins: Amsterdam, Philadelphia).

2008. *Computing the Mind: How the Mind Really Works* (Oxford University Press: Oxford).

2011. 'On Look-Ahead in Language: Navigating A Multitude of Familiar Paths.' In Moshe Bar (ed.), *Predictions in the Brain: Using Our Past to Generate a Future* (Oxford University Press: New York, Oxford).

Egeth, H. E., and S. Yantis. 1997. 'Visual attention: control, representation, and time course', *Annual Review of Psychology*, 48: 269–97.

Ehrlich, S. F., and K. Rayner. 1981. 'Contextual effects on word perception and eye movements during reading', *Journal of Verbal Learning and Verbal Behavior*, 20: 641–55.

Eldridge, R. C. 1911. *Six Thousand Common English Words* (Niagara Falls).

Ellis, N. C. 2002. 'Frequency effects in language processing: a review with implications for theories of implicit and explicit language acquisition', *Studies in Second Language Acquisition*, 24: 143–88.

2006. 'Language acquisition as rational contingency learning', *Applied Linguistics*, 27: 1–24.

2012. 'What Can We Count in Language, and What Counts in Language Acquisition, Cognition, and Use?' In Stefan Th. Gries and Dagmar Divjak (eds.), *Frequency Effects in Language Learning and Processing (Vol. 1)* (Mouton de Gruyter: Berlin).

2016. 'Online processing of Verb–Argument Constructions: lexical decision and meaningfulness', *Language and Cognition*, special issue, 8 (3): 391–420.

Ellis, N. C., and F. Ferreira-Junior. 2009. 'Construction learning as a function of frequency, frequency distribution, and function', *Modern Language Journal*, 93: 370–85.

Ellis, N. C., and D. Larsen-Freeman. 2006. 'Language emergence: implications for applied linguistics: introduction to the special issue', *Applied Linguistics*, 27: 558–89.

Ellis, N. C., U. Römer, and M. Brook O'Donnell. 2016. *Usage-Based Approaches to Language Acquisition and Processing: Cognitive and Corpus Investigations of Construction Grammar* (Wiley: West Sussex).

Ellis, N. C., and R. Simpson-Vlach. 2009. 'Formulaic language in native speakers: triangulating psycholinguistics, corpus linguistics, and education', *Corpus Linguistics and Linguistic Theory*, 5: 61–78.

Ellis, N. C., and S. Wulff. 2015. 'Second Language Acquisition.' In Ewa Dąbrowska and Dagmar Divjak (eds.), *Handbook of Cognitive Linguistics* (Gruyter de Mouton: Berlin, Boston).

Elman, J. L. 1990. 'Finding structure in time', *Cognitive Science*, 14: 179–211.

1991. 'Distributed representations, simple recurrent networks, and grammatical structure', *Machine Learning*, 7: 195–225.

1993. 'Learning and development in neural networks: the importance of starting small', *Cognition*, 48: 71–99.

2003. 'Development: it's about time', *Developmental Science*, 6: 430–3.

2009. 'On the meaning of words and dinosaur bones: lexical knowledge without a lexicon', *Cognitive Science*, 33: 547–82.

Elman, J. L., and E. A. Bates. 1996. 'Learning rediscovered', *Science*, 274: 1849–50.

Elman, J. L., E. A. Bates, D. M. Johnson, A. Karmiloff-Smith, D. Parisi, and K. Plunkett. 1996. *Rethinking Innateness: A Connectionist Perspective on Development* (MIT Press: Cambridge, MA, London).

Engle, R. W., S. W. Tuholski, J. E. Laughlin, and A. R. A. Conway. 1999. 'Working memory, short-term memory, and general fluid intelligence: a latent-variable approach', *Journal of Experimental Psychology: General*, 128: 309–31.

Epstein, R. 2016. 'The empty brain,' https://bit.ly/2I8K5hy

Erickson, L. C., and E. D. Thiessen. 2015. 'Statistical learning of language: theory, validity, and predictions of a statistical learning account of language acquisition', *Developmental Review*, 37: 66–108.

Erk, S., M. Kiefer, J. Grothe, A. P. Wunderlich, M. Spitzer, and H. Walter. 2003. 'Emotional context modulates subsequent memory effect', *NeuroImage*, 18: 439–47.

Erker, D., and G. R. Guy. 2012. 'The role of lexical frequency in syntactic variability: variable subject personal pronoun expression in Spanish', *Language*, 88: 526–57.

Estes, W. K. 1950. 'Toward a statistical theory of learning', *Psychological Review*, 57: 94–107.

1957. 'Of models and men', *American Psychologist*, 12: 609–17.

Estoup, J. B. 1902. *Gammes sténographiques. Recueil de textes choisis pour l'acquisition méthodique de la vitesse, précédé d'une introduction par J.-B. Estoup* (Institut Sténographique: Paris).

Evans, J. S. B. T., S. J. Handley, N. Perham, D. E. Over, and V. A. Thompson. 2000. 'Frequency versus probability formats in statistical word problems', *Cognition*, 77: 197–213.

Evans, J. S. B. T., and D. Over. 1996. *Rationality and Reasoning* (Psychology Press: Hove).

Evans, N., and S. C. Levinson. 2009. 'The myth of language universals: language diversity and its importance for cognitive science', *Behavioral and Brain Sciences*, 32: 429–92.

Evert, S. 2005. 'The statistics of word co-occurrences: word pairs and collocations', paper, University of Stuttgart.

2008. 'Corpora and Collocations.' In Anke Lüdeling and Merja Kytö (eds.), *Corpus Linguistics: An International Handbook* (Mouton De Gruyter: Berlin).

Faucett, L., and I. Maki. 1932. *A Study of English Word-Values Statistically Determined from the Latest Word-Counts* (Matsumura Sanshodo: Oxford).

Fauconnier, G. 1985. *Mental Spaces: Aspects of Meaning Construction in Natural Language* (MIT Press: Cambridge, MA).

Feldman, J. A., J. Gips, J. J. Horning, and S. Reder. 1969. 'Grammatical complexity and inference', paper, Computer Science Department, Stanford University, Stanford, CA.

Feldman, L. B., A. Kostić, D. M. Basnight-Brown, D. Filipović Ðurđević, and M. J. Pastizzo. 2010. 'Morphological facilitation for regular and irregular verb formations in native and non-native speakers: little evidence for two distinct mechanisms', *Bilingualism: Language and Cognition*, 13: 119–35.

Fennell, B. A. 2001. *A History of English. A Sociolinguistic Approach* (Blackwell: Oxford).

Fernandes, M. A., and M. Moscovitch. 2002. 'Factors modulating the effect of divided attention during retrieval of words', *Memory and Cognition*, 30: 731–44.

Ferreira, F. 2003. 'The misinterpretation of noncanonical sentences', *Cognitive Psychology*, 47: 164–203.

Ferreira, F., and M. W. Lowder. 2016. 'Chapter six: prediction, information structure, and good-enough language processing', *Psychology of Learning and Motivation*, 65: 217–47.

Ferrer i Cancho, R., and R. V. Solé. 2001. 'Two regimes in the frequency of words and the origins of complex lexicons: Zipf's law revisited', *Journal of Quantitative Linguistics*, 8: 165–73.

Ferretti, T. R., K. McRae, and A. Hatherell. 2001. 'Integrating verbs, situation schemas, and thematic role concepts', *Journal of Memory and Language*, 44: 516–47.

Filipović-Ðurđević, D., and P. Milin. 2019. 'Information and Learning in Processing Adjective Inflection', *Cortex*, 116: 209–227.

Filipović-Ðurđević, D., and S. Zdravković. 2013. *Uvod u kognitivne neuronauke* (Gradska narodna biblioteka Zrenjanin: Zrenjanin, RS).

Fillmore, C. J. 1979. 'On Fluency.' In Charles J. Fillmore, Daniel Kempler and William S.-Y. Wang (eds.), *Individual Differences in Language Ability and Language Behavior* (Academic Press).

1982. 'Frame Semantics.' In Linguistics Society of Korea (ed.), *Linguistics in the Morning Calm* (Hanshin Publishing: Seoul).

1985. 'Frames and the semantics of understanding', *Quaderni di Semantica*, 6: 222–54.

Fine, A. B., and T. F. Jaeger. 2013. 'Evidence for implicit learning in syntactic comprehension', *Cognitive Science*, 37: 578–91.

Firth, J. R. 1937/1964. *The Tongues of Men and Speech* (Oxford University Press: London).

Fletcher, P. C., and C. D. Frith. 2009. 'Perceiving is believing: a Bayesian approach to explaining the positive symptoms of schizophrenia', *Nature Reviews Neuroscience*, 10: 48.

Fodor, J. A. 1983. *The Modularity of Mind* (MIT Press: Cambridge, MA).

Ford, M. 1983. 'A method for obtaining measures of local parsing complexity throughout sentences', *Journal of Verbal Learning and Verbal Behavior*, 22: 203–18.

Ford, M., and J. Bresnan. 2010. 'Using Convergent Evidence from Psycholinguistics and Usage.' In Manfred Krug and Julia Schlüter (eds.), *Research Methods in Language Variation and Change* (Cambridge University Press: Cambridge, UK).

2013a. '"They Whispered Me the Answer" in Australia and the US: A Comparative Experimental Study.' In Tracy Holloway King and Valeria de Paiva (eds.), *From Quirky Case to Representing Space: Papers in Honor of Annie Zaenen* (CSLI Publications: Stanford).

2013b. 'Using Convergent Evidence from Psycholinguistics and Usage.' In Manfred Krug and Julia Schulter (eds.), *Research Methods in Language Variation and Change* (Cambridge University Press: Cambridge, UK).

Forrest, L. 1996. 'Discourse Goals and Attentional Processes in Sentence Production: The Dynamic Construal of Events.' In Adele Goldberg (ed.), *Conceptual Structure, Discourse, and Language* (CSLI Publications: Stanford).

Förstemann, E. 1852. 'Numerische Lautverhältnisse im Griechischen, Lateinischen und Deutschen.' In *Germanische Zeitschrift für Vergleichende Sprachforschung auf dem Gebiete des Deutschen, Griechischen und Lateinischen 1*.

Forster, K. I. 1976. 'Accessing the Mental Lexicon.' In F. Wales and E. Walker (eds.), *New Approaches to Language Mechanisms* (North Holland: Amsterdam).

1981. 'Priming and the effects of sentence and lexical contexts on naming time: evidence for autonomous lexical processing', *Quarterly Journal of Experimental Psychology*, 33: 465–95.

Forster, K. I., and S. Chambers. 1973. 'Lexical access and naming time', *Journal of Verbal Learning and Verbal Behavior*, 12: 627–35.

Frakes, W. B., and R. Baeza-Yates (eds.). 1992. *Information Retrieval: Data Structures and Algorithms* (Prentice Hall: Englewood Cliffs, NJ).

Frank, S. L. 2013. 'Uncertainty reduction as a measure of cognitive load in sentence comprehension', *Topics in Cognitive Science*, 5: 475–94.

French, N. R., C. W. Carter Jr, and W. Koenig Jr. 1930. 'The words and sounds of telephone conversations', *Bell System Technical Journal*, 9: 290–324.

Friederici, A. D. 2011. 'The brain basis of language processing: from structure to function', *Physiological Review*, 91 (4): 1357–92.

Fries, C. C., and A. A. Traver. 1950. *English Word Lists: A Study of Their Adaptability for Instruction: Prepared for the Committee on Modern Languages of the American Council on Education* (George Wahr: Ann Arbor).

Frisson, S., K. Rayner, and M. J. Pickering. 2005. 'Effects of contextual predictability and transitional probability on eye movements during reading', *Journal of Experimental Psychology: Learning, Memory, and Cognition*, 31: 862–77.

Friston, K. J. 2005. 'A Theory of cortical responses', *Philosophical Transactions: Biological Sciences*, 360: 815–36.

2010. 'The free-energy principle: a unified brain theory?', *Nature Reviews Neuroscience*, 11: 127.

Friston, K. J., D. Pinotsis, A. M. Bastos, and V. Litvak. 2015. 'LFP and oscillations: what do they tell us?', *Current Opinion in Neurobiology*, 31: 1–6.

Frith, C. D. 2007. *Making up the Mind: How the Brain Creates Our Mental World* (Blackwell: Malden, MA).

Fuster, J. M. 2009. 'Cortex and memory: emergence of a new paradigm', *Journal of Cognitive Neuroscience*, 21: 2047–72.

Gahl, S., and S. M. Garnsey. 2004. 'Knowledge of grammar, knowledge of usage: syntactic probabilities affect pronunciation variation', *Language*, 80: 748–75.

Gallistel, C. R. 1990. *The Organization of Learning* (Bradford Books/MIT Press: Cambridge, MA).

Gallistel, C. R., and J. Gibbon. 2000. 'Time, rate, and conditioning', *Psychological Review*, 107: 289–344.

Gardner, M. K., E. Z. Rothkopf, R. Lapan, and T. Lafferty. 1987. 'The word frequency effect in lexical decision: finding a frequency-based component', *Memory and Cognition*, 15: 24–8.

Gaskell, M. G. 2007. *The Oxford Handbook of Psycholinguistics* (Oxford University Press: Oxford).

Geeraerts, D. 2010a. 'Recontextualizing Grammar: Underlying Trends in Thirty Years of Cognitive Linguistics.' In Elżbieta Tabakowska, Michał Choiński and Łukasz Wiraszka (eds.), *Cognitive Linguistics in Action: From Theory to Application and Back* (De Gruyter Mouton: Berlin, New York).

2010b. 'Schmidt Redux: How Systematic Is the Linguistic System If Variation Is Rampant.' In Kasper Boye and Elisabeth Engberg-Pedersen (eds.), *Language Usage and Language Structure* (De Gruyter Mouton: Berlin, New York).

2017. 'Entrenchment as Onomasiological Salience.' In Hans-Joerg Schmid (ed.), *Entrenchment and the Psychology of Language Learning: How We Reorganize and Adapt Linguistic Knowledge* (De Gruyter Mouton and APA: Berlin).

Geeraerts, D., S. Grondelaers, and P. Bakema. 1994. *The Structure of Lexical Variation. Meaning, Naming and Context* (Mouton de Gruyter: Berlin, New York).

Geeraerts, D., G. Kristiansen, and Y. Peirsman. 2010. *Advances in Cognitive Sociolinguistics* (De Gruyter Mouton: Berlin, New York).

Geertzen, J., J. P. Blevins, and P. Milin. 2016. 'The informativeness of linguistic unit boundaries', *Italian Journal of Linguistics*, 28: 25–48.

Gernsbacher, M. A. 1984. 'Resolving 20 years of inconsistent interactions between lexical familiarity and orthography, concreteness, and polysemy', *Journal of Experimental Psychology: General*, 113: 256–81.

Gibbon, J., and P. D. Balsam. 1981. 'Spreading Association in Time.' In C. M. Locurto, H. S. Terrace and J. Gibbon (eds.), *Autoshaping and Conditioning Theory* (Academic Press: New York).

Gibbs Jr., R. W., and H. L. Colston. 1995. 'The cognitive psychological reality of image schemas and their transformations', *Cognitive Linguistics*, 6: 347–78.

Gigerenzer, G. 2002. *Calculated Risks: How to Know When Numbers Deceive You* (MIT Press: Cambridge, MA).

Gigerenzer, G., and U. Hoffrage. 1995. 'How to improve Bayesian reasoning without instruction: frequency formats', *Psychological Review*, 102: 684–704.

Giles, H. 1973. 'Accent mobility: a model and some data', *Anthropological Linguistics*, 15: 87–105.

Gilquin, G. 2006. 'The verb slot in causative constructions: finding the best fit', *Constructions*, 1: 1–46.

Giora, R. 2003. *On Our Mind: Salience, Context, and Figurative Language* (Oxford University Press: Oxford).

Giuliano, V. E. 1965. 'Postscript: A Personal Reaction to Reading the Conference Manuscripts.' In Mary Elizabeth Stevens, Vincent E. Giuliano and Laurence B. Heilprin (eds.), *Statistical Association Methods for Mechanized Documentation. Symposium Proceedings Washington 1964* (US Government Printing Office: Washington, DC).

Givón, T. 1979. *On Understanding Grammar* (Academic Press: New York).

    1983. *Topic Continuity in Discourse: Quantified Cross-Language Studies* (John Benjamins: Amsterdam).

    1988. 'The Pragmatics of Word-Order: Predictability, Importance and Attention.' In M. Hamond, E. A. Moravcsik and J. Wirth (eds.), *Studies in Syntactic Typology* (John Benjamins: Amsterdam).

    1992. 'The grammar of referential coherence as mental processing instructions', *Linguistics*, 30: 5–55.

Glanzer, M., and A. R. Cunitz. 1966. 'Two storage mechanisms in free recall', *Journal of Verbal Learning and Verbal Behavior*, 5: 351–60.

Gleitman, L., D. January, R. Nappa, and J. Trueswell. 2007. 'On the give-and-take between event apprehension and utterance formulation', *Journal of Memory and Language*, 57.

Glynn, D., and K. Fischer. 2010. *Quantitative Methods in Cognitive Semantics: Corpus-Driven Approaches* (De Gruyter Mouton: Berlin).

Glynn, D., and J. A. Robinson. 2014. *Corpus Methods for Semantics: Quantitative Studies in Polysemy and Synonymy* (John Benjamins: Amsterdam; Philadelphia).

Gobet, F. 2017. 'Entrenchment, Gestalt formation, and Chunking.' In Hans-Joerg Schmid (ed.), *Entrenchment and the Psychology of Language Learning: How We Reorganize and Adapt Linguistic Knowledge* (De Gruyter Mouton and APA: Berlin).

Gold, E. M. 1967. 'Language identification in the limit', *Information and Control*, 10: 447–74.

Goldberg, A. E. 1995. *Constructions: A Construction Grammar Approach to Argument Structure* (University of Chicago Press: Chicago).

    2006. *Constructions at Work: The Nature of Generalization in Language* (Oxford University Press: Oxford).

    2009. 'The nature of generalization in language', *Cognitive Linguistics*, 20: 93–127.

    2011a. 'Corpus evidence of the viability of statistical pre-emption', *Cognitive Linguistics*, 22: 131–54.

    2011b. 'Partial productivity of constructions as induction', *Linguistics*, 49: 1237–69.

    2013. 'Constructionist Approaches to Language.' In Thomas Hoffmann and Graeme Trousdale (eds.), *Handbook of Construction Grammar* (Oxford University Press: Oxford).

Goldberg, A. E., D. Casenhiser, and N. Sethuraman. 2004. 'Learning argument structure generalizations', *Cognitive Linguistics*, 15: 289–316.

Gómez, R. L. 2007. 'Statistical Learning in Infant Language Development.' In M. Gaskell (ed.), *The Oxford Handbook of Psycholinguistics* (Oxford University Press: Oxford).

Gómez, R. L., and L. Gerken. 1999. 'Artificial grammar learning by one-year-olds leads to specific and abstract knowledge', *Cognition*, 70: 109–35.

Goodman, J. C., P. S. Dale, and P. Li. 2008. 'Does frequency count? parental input and the acquisition of vocabulary', *Journal of Child Language*, 35: 515–31.

Gordon, P. C., R. Hendrick, and W. H. Levine. 2002. 'Memory-load interference in syntactic processing', *Psychological Science*, 13: 425–30.

Gordon, W. C., G. J. Smith, and D. S. Katz. 1979. 'Dual effects of response blocking following avoidance learning', *Behaviour Research and Therapy*, 17: 479–87.

Goulden, R., P. Nation, and J. Read. 1990. 'How large can a receptive vocabulary be?', *Applied Linguistics*, 11: 341–63.

Green, C. 2017. 'Usage-based linguistics and the magic number four', *Cognitive Linguistics*, 28.

Gries, S. T. 2003. *Multifactorial Analysis in Corpus Linguistics: A Study of Particle Placement* (Continuum Press: London, New York).

——— 2005a. 'Null-hypothesis significance testing of word frequencies: a follow-up on Kilgarriff', *Corpus Linguistics and Linguistic Theory*, 1: 277–94.

——— 2005b. 'Syntactic priming: a corpus-based approach', *Journal of Psycholinguistic Research*, 34: 365–99.

——— 2008. 'Dispersions and adjusted frequencies in corpora', *International Journal of Corpus Linguistics*, 13: 403–37.

——— 2009. *Statistics for Linguistics with R: A Practical Introduction* (Mouton de Gruyter: Berlin, New York).

——— 2010. 'Dispersions and Adjusted Frequencies in Corpora: Further Explorations.' In Stefan Th. Gries, Stefanie Wulff and Mark Davies (eds.), *Corpus Linguistic Applications: Current Studies, New Directions* (Rodopi: Amsterdam).

——— 2012. 'Frequencies, probabilities, association measures in usage-/exemplar-based linguistics: some necessary clarifications', *Studies in Language*, 36: 477–510.

——— 2014. 'Frequencies, Probabilities, Association Measures in Usage-/Exemplar-Based Linguistics: Some Necessary Clarifications.' In Nikolas Gisborne and Willem Hollmann (eds.), *Theory and Data in Cognitive Linguistics* (John Benjamins: Amsterdam, Philadelphia).

——— 2015. ' More (old and new) misunderstandings of collostructional analysis: on Schmid and Küchenhoff (2013)', *Cognitive Linguistics*, 26: 505–36.

Gries, S. T., and D. Divjak. 2012. *Frequency Effects in Language Learning and Processing* (De Gruyter Mouton: Berlin, Boston).

Gries, S. T., and N. C. Ellis. 2015. 'Statistical measures for usage-based linguistics', *Language Learning*, 65: 228–55.

Gries, S. T., B. Hampe, and D. Schönefeld. 2005. 'Converging evidence: bringing together experimental and corpus data on the association of verbs and constructions', *Cognitive Linguistics*, 16: 635–76.

Gries, S. T., and M. Hilpert. 2010. 'Modeling diachronic change in the third person singular: a multifactorial, verb-and author-specific exploratory approach', *English Language and Linguistics*, 14: 293–320.

Gries, S. T., and A. Stefanowitsch. 2004. 'Extending collostructional analysis: a corpus-based perspectives on "alternations"', *International Journal of Corpus Linguistics*, 9: 97–129.

Griffin, Z. M., and K. Bock. 2000. 'What the eyes say about speaking', *Psychological Science*, 11: 274–9.

Griffiths, T. L., N. Chater, D. Norris, and A. Pouget. 2012. 'How the Bayesians got their beliefs (and what those beliefs actually are): comment on Bowers and Davis (2012)', *Psychological Bulletin*, 138 (3): 415–22.

Griffiths, T. L., C. Kemp, and J. B. Tenenbaum. 2008. 'Bayesian Models of Cognition.' In Ron Sun (ed.), *The Cambridge Handbook of Computational Psychology* (Cambridge University Press: Cambridge, UK).

Grondelaers, S., and D. Speelman. 2007. 'A variationist account of constituent ordering in presentative sentences in Belgian Dutch', *Corpus Linguistics and Linguistic Theory*, 3: 161–93.

Grosjean, F. 1980. 'Spoken word recognition processes and the gating paradigm', *Perception and Psychophysics*, 28: 267–83.

Gross, M. 1972. *Mathematical Methods in Linguistics* (Prentice Hall: Englewood Cliffs, NJ).

Guderian, S., B. H. Schott, A. Richardson-Klavehn, and E. Düzel. 2009. 'Medial temporal theta state before an event predicts episodic encoding success in humans', *Proceedings of the National Academy of Sciences of the United States of America*, 106: 5365–70.

Gülzow, I., and N. Gagarina (eds.). 2007. *Frequency Effects in Language Acquisition. Defining the Limits of Frequency as an Explanatory Concept* (De Gruyter Mouton: Berlin, Boston).

Gunter, T. C., and A. D. Friederici. 1999. 'Concerning the automaticity of syntactic processing', *Psychophysiology*, 36: 126–37.

Gupta, P. 2012. 'Word Learning as the Confluence of Memory Mechanisms: Computational and Neural Evidence.' In M. Faust (ed.), *Handbook of the Neuropsychology of Language* (Wiley: Oxford).

Gurevich, O., M. A. Johnson, and A. E. Goldberg. 2010. 'Incidental verbatim memory for language', *Language and Cognition*, 2: 45–78.

Hahne, A., and A. D. Friederici. 1999. 'Electrophysiological evidence for two steps in syntactic analysis: early automatic and late controlled processes', *Journal of Cognitive Neuroscience*, 11: 194.

———— 2002. 'Differential task effects on semantic and syntactic processes as revealed by ERPs', *Cognitive Brain Research*, 13: 339–56.

Hale, J. 2001. 'A Probabilistic Early Parser as a Psycholinguistic Model'. In *NAACL '01: Proceedings of the Second Meeting of the North American Chapter of the Association for Computational Linguistics on Language Technologies* (Pittsburgh, PA).

———— 2003. 'The information conveyed by words in sentences', *Journal of Psycholinguistic Research.*, 32: 101–23.

———— 2016. 'Information-theoretical complexity metrics', *Language and Linguistics Compass*, 10: 397–412.

Hall, J. F. 1954. 'Learning as a function of word-frequency', *American Journal of Psychology*, 67: 138–40.

Halliday, M. A. K. 1976. 'Theme and Information in the English Clause.' In G. Kress (ed.), *Halliday: System and Function in Language* (Oxford University Press: London).

1991. 'Corpus Studies and Probabilistic Grammar.' In Karin Aijmer and Bengt Altenberg (eds.), *English Corpus Linguistics: Studies in Honour of Jan Svartvik* (Longman: London).

1993. 'Quantitative Studies and Probabilities in Grammar.' In Michael Hoey (ed.), *Data, Description, Discourse. Papers on the English Language in Honour of John McH. Sinclair* (Harper Collins: London).

Harder, P. 2010. *Meaning in Mind and Society. A Functional Contribution to the Social Turn in Cognitive Linguistics* (De Gruyter Mouton: Berlin, New York).

Harm, M. W. and M. S. Seidenberg. 2004. 'Computing the meanings of words in reading: cooperative division of labor between visual and phonological processes', *Psychological Review*, 111: 662–720.

Harper, D. N., A. P. McLean, and J. C. Dalrymple-Alford. 1993. 'List item memory in rats: effects of delay and delay task', *Journal of Experimental Psychology: Animal Behavior Processes*, 19: 307–16.

Harris, Z. 1954. 'Distributional structure', *Word*, 10: 146–62.

1991. *A Theory of Language and Information: A Mathematical Approach* (Clarendon Press: Oxford).

Hart, B., and T. R. Risley. 1995. *Meaningful Differences in the Everyday Experience of Young American Children* (P.H. Brookes: Baltimore, MD, London).

Hartsuiker, R. J., S. Bernolet, S. Schoonbaert, S. Speybroeck, and D. Vanderelst. 2008. 'Syntactic priming persists while the lexical boost decays: evidence from written and spoken dialogue', *Journal of Memory and Language*, 58: 214–38.

Hasher, L., and R. T. Zacks. 1979. 'Automatic and effortful processes in memory', *Journal of Experimental Psychology: General*, 108: 356–88.

1984. 'Automatic processing of fundamental information: The case of frequency of occurrence', *American Psychologist*, 39: 1372–88.

Hawkins, J., and S. Blakeslee. 2004. *On Intelligence* (Henry Holt: New York).

Hay, J. 2001. 'Lexical frequency in morphology: is everything relative?', *Linguistics: An Interdisciplinary Journal of the Language Sciences*, 39: 1041–70.

Heathcote, A., S. Brown, and D. Mewhort. 2000. 'The power law repealed: the case for an exponential law of practice', *Psychonomic Bulletin and Review*, 7: 185–207.

Hebb, D. O. 1949. *The Organization of Behavior* (Wiley: New York).

Heister, J., and R. Kliegl. 2012. 'Comparing Word Frequencies from Different German Text Corpora.' In Kay-Michael Würzner and Edmund Pohl (eds.), *Lexical Resources in Psycholinguistic Research* (Universitätsverlag Potsdam: Potsdam).

Hendersen, R. W. 1978. 'Forgetting of conditioned fear inhibition', *Learning and Motivation*, 9: 16–30.

1985. 'Fearful Memories: The Motivational Significance of Forgetting.' In F. R. Brush and J. B. Overmier (eds.), *Affect, Conditioning, and Cognition: Essays on the Determinants of Behaviour* (Lawrence Erlbaum: Hillsdale, NJ).

Henderson, J. 2004. 'Lookahead in Deterministic Left-Corner Parsing.' In *Proceedings of the Workshop on Incremental Parsing: Bringing Engineering and Cognition Together* (Barcelona).

Henderson, J. M. 2003. 'Human gaze control during real-world scene perception', *Trends in Cognitive Sciences*, 7: 498–504.

Hendrix, P. 2015. 'Experimental explorations of a discrimination learning approach to language processing', paper, University of Tübingen.

Herdan, G. 1956. *Language as Choice and Chance* (Noordhoff: Groningen).

— 1960. *Type-Token Mathematics: A Textbook of Mathematical Linguistics* (Mouton: The Hague).

— 1964. *Quantitative Linguistics* (Butterworths: London).

— 1966. *The Advanced Theory of Language as Choice and Chance* (Springer-Verlag: Berlin, New York).

Hernandez, P. J., and T. Abel. 2008. 'The role of protein synthesis in memory consolidation: progress amid decades of debate', *Neurobiology of Learning and Memory*, 89: 293–311.

Hewitt, K. 1973. *Context Effects in Memory: A Review* (Cambridge University Psychological Laboratory: Cambridge, UK).

Hills, T. T., J. Maouene, B. Riodan, and L. B. Smith. 2010. 'The associative structure of language: contextual diversity in early word learning', *Journal of Memory and Language*, 63: 259–73.

Hilpert, M., and H. Diessel. 2017. 'Entrenchment in Construction Grammar.' In Hans-Jörg Schmid (ed.), *Entrenchment and the Psychology of Language Learning: How We Reorganize and Adapt Linguistic Knowledge* (De Gruyter Mouton and APA: Berlin).

Hintz, F., and F. Huettig. 2015. 'The Complexity of the Visual Environment Modulates Language-Mediated Eye Gaze.' In Ramesh Mishra, Narayanan Kumar Srinivasan and Falk Huettig (eds.), *Attention and Vision in Language Processing* (Springer: New Delhi).

Hintzman, D. L., and L. D. Stern. 1978. 'Contextual variability and memory for frequency', *Journal of Experimental Psychology: Human Learning and Memory*, 4: 539–49.

Hoffmann, T., and G. Trousdale (eds.). 2013. *The Oxford Handbook of Construction Grammar* (Oxford University Press: Oxford).

Hohwy, J. 2013. *The Predictive Mind* (Oxford University Press: Oxford).

Hopfield, J. J. 1982. 'Neural networks and physical systems with emergent collective computational abilities', *Proceedings of the National Academy of Sciences of the United States of America*, 79: 2554–8.

Hopper, P. 1987. 'Emergent Grammar.' In *Proceedings of the Thirteenth Annual Meeting of the Berkeley Linguistics Society* (Berkeley).

Hopper, P., and S. Thompson. 1980. 'Transitivity in discourse and grammar', *Language*, 56: 251–99.

— 1984. 'The discourse basis for lexical categories in universal grammar', *Language*, 60: 703–52.

Horn, E. 1926. *A Basic Writing Vocabulary: 10,000 Frequently Used Words in Writing* (University of Iowa: Iowa City).

Horning, J. 1969. 'A study of grammatical inference', dissertation, ProQuest Dissertations Publishing.

Horvitz, J. C. 2000. 'Mesolimbocortical and nigrostriatal dopamine responses to salient nonreward events', *Neuroscience*, 96: 651–6.

Howes, D. H. 1957. 'On the relation between the intelligibility and frequency of occurrence of English words', *Journal of the Acoustical Society of America*, 29: 296–305.

Howes, D. H., and D. L. Solomon. 1951. 'Visual duration threshold as a function of word-probability', *Journal of Experimental Psychology* 416: 401–10.

Huettig, F., and G. T. M. Altmann. 2004. 'The On-Line Processing of Ambiguous and Unambiguous Words in Context: Evidence from Head-Mounted Eye-Tracking.' In M. Carreiras and C. Clifton (eds.), *The On-Line Study of Sentence Comprehension: Eyetracking, ERP and Beyond* (Psychology Press: New York).

Huettig, F., and G. T. M. Altmann. 2005. 'Word meaning and the control of eye fixation: semantic competitor effects and the visual world paradigm', *Cognition: International Journal of Cognitive Science*, 96: B23–B32.

2007. 'Visual-shape competition during language-mediated attention is based on lexical input and not modulated by contextual appropriateness', *Visual Cognition*, 15: 985–1018.

Huettig, F., and N. Mani. 2016. 'Is prediction necessary to understand language? Probably not', *Language, Cognition and Neuroscience*, 31: 19–31.

Huettig, F., and J. McQueen. 2007. 'The tug of war between phonological, semantic and shape information in language-mediated visual search', *Journal of Memory and Language*, 57: 460–82.

Huettig, F., P. T. Quinlan, S. A. McDonald, and G. T. M. Altmann. 2006. 'Models of high-dimensional semantic space predict language-mediated eye movements in the visual world', *Acta Psychologica*, 121: 65–80.

Huettig, F., J. Rommers, and A. S. Meyer. 2011. 'Using the visual world paradigm to study language processing: a review and critical evaluation', *Acta Psychologica*, 137: 151–71.

Humphries, M. 2017. 'The Crimes against Dopamine: For They Be Many and Grievous.' https://medium.com/the-spike/the-crimes-against-dopamine-b82b082d5f3d.

Huttenlocher, J., W. Haight, A. Bryk, M. Seltzer, and T. Lyons. 1991. 'Early vocabulary growth: relation to language input and gender', *Developmental Psychology*, 27: 236–48.

Hwang, H., and E. Kaiser. 2009. 'The Effects of Lexical vs. Perceptual Primes on Sentence Production in Korean: An Online Investigation of Event Apprehension and Sentence Formulation.' In *22nd CUNY Conference on Sentence Processing* (Davis, CA).

Ibbotson, P., E. V. M. Lieven, and M. Tomasello. 2013. 'The attention-grammar interface: eye-gaze cues structural choice in children and adults', *Cognitive Linguistics*, 24: 457–81.

Imamizu, H., T. Kuroda, T. Yoshioka, and M. Kawato. 2004. 'Functional magnetic resonance imaging examination of two modular architectures for switching multiple internal models', *The Journal of Neuroscience: The Official Journal of the Society for Neuroscience*, 24: 1173.

Indefrey, P., and W. J. M. Levelt. 2004. 'The spatial and temporal signatures of word production components', *Cognition*, 92: 101–44.

Itti, L., and P. Baldi. 2009. 'Bayesian surprise attracts human attention', *Vision Research*, 49: 1295–306.

Itti, L., and C. Koch. 2000. 'A saliency-based search mechanism for overt and covert shifts of visual attention', *Vision Research*, 40: 1489–506.

Itti, L., C. Koch, and E. Niebur. 1998. 'A model of saliency-based visual-attention for rapid scene analysis', *IEEE Transactions on Pattern Analysis and Machine Intelligence*, 20: 1254–9.

Jackendoff, R. 1983. *Semantics and Cognition* (MIT Press: Cambridge, MA).

——— 2007. 'Linguistics in cognitive science: the state of the art', *The Linguistic Review*, 24 (4): 347–401.

Jaeger, F. 2010. 'Redundancy and reduction: speakers manage syntactic information density', *Cognitive Psychology*, 61: 23–62.

Jaeger, T. F., and N. E. Snider. 2013. 'Alignment as a consequence of expectation adaptation: syntactic priming is affected by the prime's prediction error given both prior and recent experience', *Cognition*, 127: 57–83.

Jaeger, T. F., and K. Weatherholtz. 2016. 'What the Heck Is Salience? How Predictive Language Processing Contributes to Sociolinguistic Perception', *Frontiers in Psychology*, 7.

James, W. 1890. *The Principles of Psychology* (London).

Janda, L. A. 2013. *Cognitive Linguistics: the Quantitative Turn. The Essential Reader* (De Gruyter Mouton: Berlin).

Jaynes, E. T. 2003. *Probability Theory: the Logic of Science* (Oxford University Press: Oxford).

Jespersen, O. 1924/1976. 'Living Grammar.' In D. D. Bornstein (ed.), *Readings in the Theory of Grammar* (Winthrop Publishers: Cambridge, MA).

Jiang, Y., and A. W. Leung. 2005. 'Implicit learning of ignored visual context', *Psychonomic Bulletin and Review*, 12: 100–6.

Johns, B. T., M. Dye, and M. N. Jones. 2014. 'The Influence of Contextual Variability on Word Learning' In P. Bello, M. Guarani, M. McShane and B. Scassellati (eds.), *36th Annual Conference of the Cognitive Science Society*.

——— 2016. 'The influence of contextual diversity on word learning', *Psychonomic Bulletin and Review*, 23: 1214–20.

Johns, B. T., T. M. Gruenenfelder, D. B. Pisoni, and M. N. Jones. 2012. 'Effects of word frequency, contextual diversity, and semantic distinctiveness on spoken word recognition', *The Journal of the Acoustical Society of America*, 132: EL74–EL80.

Johnson, E. K., and A. H. Seidl. 2009. 'At 11 months, prosody still outranks statistics', *Developmental Science*, 12: 131.

Johnson, K. 2008. *Quantitative Methods in Linguistics* (Blackwell: Oxford).

Johnson, M. 1987. *The Body in the Mind. The Bodily Basis of Meaning, Imagination, and Reason* (University of Chicago Press: Chicago, London).

Jones, L. V., and J. M. Wepman. 1966. 'A spoken word count', paper, Language Research Associates, Chicago.

Jones, M. N., B. T. Johns, and G. Recchia. 2012. 'The role of semantic diversity in lexical organization', *Canadian Journal of Experimental Psychology/Revue canadienne de psychologie expérimentale*, 66: 115–24.

Jones, S., M. L. Murphy, C. Paradis, and C. Willners. 2012. *Antonyms in English: Construals, Constructions and Canonicity* (Cambridge University Press: Cambridge, UK).

Joos, M. 1936. 'Review of G.K. Zipf, *The Psychobiology of Language*', *Language*, 12: 196–210.

Juhasz, B. J. 2005. 'Age-of-acquisition effects in word and picture identification', *Psychological Bulletin*, 131: 684–712.

Juilland, A. G., D. R. Brodin, and C. Davidovitch. 1970. *Frequency Dictionary of French Words* (Mouton: The Hague).

Jurafsky, D. 1996. 'A probabilistic model of lexical and syntactic access and disambiguation', *Cognitive Science: A Multidisciplinary Journal of Artificial Intelligence, Linguistics, Neuroscience, Philosophy, Psychology*, 20: 137–94.

——— 2003. 'Probabilistic Modeling in Psycholinguistics: Linguistic Comprehension and Production.' In Rens Bod, Jennifer Hay and Stefanie Jannedy (eds.), *Probabilistic Linguistics* (MIT Press: Cambridge, MA, London).

Jurafsky, D., A. Bell, M. Gregory, and W. D. Raymond. 2001. 'Probabilistic Relations between Words: Evidence from Reduction in Lexical Production.' In Joan Bybee and Paul Hopper (eds.), *Frequency and the Emergence of Linguistic Structure* (John Benjamins: Amsterdam, Philadelphia).

Jurafsky, D., and J. H. Martin. 2014. *Speech and Language Processing* (Pearson: London).

Jusczyk, P. 2000. *The Discovery of Spoken Language* (MIT Press: Cambridge, MA).

Kaan, E. 2007. 'Event-related potentials and language processing: a brief overview', *Language and Linguistics Compass*, 1: 571–91.

Kaeding, F. W. 1898. *Häufigkeitswörterbuch der deutschen Sprache: Festgestellt durch einen Arbeitsausschuß der deutschen Stenographiesysteme* (Steglitz bei Berlin: Selbstverslag der Herausgebers: Berlin).

Kahneman, D., and A. Treisman. 1984. 'Changing Views of Attention and Automaticity.' In R. Parasuraman and D. R. Davies (eds.), *Varieties of Attention* (Academic Press: New York).

Kahneman, D., and A. Tversky. 1972. 'Subjective probability: a judgment of representativeness', *Cognitive Psychology*, 3: 430–54.

——— 1973. 'On the psychology of prediction', *Psychological Review*, 80: 237–51.

Kakade, S., and P. Dayan. 2002. 'Dopamine: generalization and bonuses', *Neural Networks*, 15: 549–59.

Kamin, L. J. 1968. '"Attention-like" Processes in Classical Conditioning.' In M. R. Jones (ed.), *Miami Symposium on the Prediction of Behavior: Aversive Stimulation* (University of Miami Press: Miami).

——— 1969. 'Predictability, Surprise, Attention and Conditioning.' In B. A. Campbell and R. M. Church (eds.), *Punishment and Aversive Behavior* (Eppleton-Century-Crofts: New York).

Kan, I. P., and S. L. Thompson-Schill. 2004. 'Selection from perceptual and conceptual representations', *Cognitive, Affective, and Behavioral Neuroscience*, 4: 466–82.

Kendall, M. G. 1952. 'Obituary: George Udny Yule', *Journal of the Royal Statistical Society. Series A (General)*, 115: 156–61.

Kendall, T., J. Bresnan, and G. Van Herk. 2011. 'The dative alternation in African American English: researching syntactic variation and change across sociolinguistic datasets', *Corpus Linguistics and Linguistic Theory*, 7: 229–44.

Kent, G. H., and A. J. Rosanoff. 1910. 'A study of association in insanity', *American Journal of Insanity*, 67: 37–96.

Kerswill, P., and A. Williams. 2002. '"Salience" as an Explanatory Factor in Language Change: Evidence from Dialect Levelling in Urban England.' In Mari C. Jones and Edith Esch (eds.), *Language Change: the Interplay of Internal, External, and Extra-Linguistic Factors* (Mouton de Gruyter: Berlin; New York).

Kilgarriff, A. 2005. 'Language is never ever ever random', *Corpus Linguistics and Linguistic Theory*, 1: 263–76

Kiyonaga, A., and T. Egner. 2013. 'Working memory as internal attention: toward an integrative account of internal and external selection processes', *Psychonomic Bulletin and Review*, 20: 228–42.

Klavan, J. 2012. *Evidence in Linguistics: Corpus-Linguistic and Experimental Methods for Studying Grammatical Synonymy* (University of Tartu Press: Tartu).

Klavan, J., and D. Divjak. 2016a. 'The cognitive plausibility of statistical classification models: comparing textual and behavioral evidence', *Folia Linguistica, Special Issue: From Methodology Back to Theory: How Does Corpus-Based Research Feed Back into Functional Linguistic Theories?*, 50: 355–84.

——— 2016b. 'The Cognitive Plausibility of Statistical Classification Models: Comparing Textual and Behavioral Evidence', *Folia Linguistica*.

Knapp, T. J. 1992. 'Verbal behavior: the other reviews', *The Analysis of Verbal Behavior*, 10: 87.

Knoeferle, P. 2015. 'Visually Situated Language Comprehension in Children and in Adults.' In Ramesh Mishra, Narayanan Kumar Srinivasan and Falk Huettig (eds.), *Attention and Vision in Language Processing* (Springer: New Delhi).

Knoeferle, P., P. Pyykkönen-Klauck, and M. W. Crocker (eds.). 2016. *Visually Situated Language Comprehension* (John Benjamins: Amsterdam, Philadelphia).

Knudsen, E. I. 2007. 'Fundamental components of attention', *Annual Review of Neuroscience*, 30: 57–78.

Koch, C., and S. Ullman. 1985. 'Shifts in selective visual attention: towards the underlying neural circuitry', *Human Neurobiology*, 4: 219–27.

Köhler, R., G. Altmann, and R. G. Piotrowski (eds.). 2005. *Quantitative Linguistik. Ein internationales Handbuch. Quantitative Linguistics. An international Handbook* (De Gruyter: Berlin, New York).

Komenský, J. A. 1631. *Janua linguarum reserata sive seminarium linguarum et scientiarum omnium* ([s.l.]).

Kostić, A. 1991. 'Informational approach to processing of inflected morphology: standard data reconsidered', *Psychological Research*, 53: 62–70.

——— 1995. 'Informational Load Constraints on Processing Inflected Morphology.' In Laurie Beth Feldman (ed.), *Morphological Aspects of Language Processing* (Lawrence Erlbaum: Hillsdale, NJ).

Kostić, A., T. Markovíc, and A. Baucal. 2003. 'Inflectional Morphology and Word Meaning: Orthogonal or Co-Implicative Domains?' In R. Harald Baayen and R. Schreuder (eds.), *Morphological Structure in Language Processing* (Mouton de Gruyter: Berlin).

Kristiansen, G., and R. Dirven. 2008. *Cognitive Sociolinguistics: Language Variation, Cultural Models, Social Systems* (Mouton de Gruyter: Berlin, New York).

Krug, M. 2003. 'Frequency as a Determinant in Grammatical Variation and Change.' In Günter Rohdenburg and Britta Mondorf (eds.), *Determinants of Grammatical Variation in English* (Mouton de Gruyter: Berlin, New York).

Kruschke, J. 2008. 'Bayesian approaches to associative learning: from passive to active learning', *Learning and Behavior*, 36: 210–26.

Kučera, H., and W. N. Francis. 1967. *Computational Analysis of Present-Day American English* (Brown University Press: Providence).

Küchenhoff, H., and H.-J. Schmid. 2015. 'Reply to "More (old and new) misunderstandings of collostructional analysis: on Schmid and Küchenhoff" by Stefan Th. Gries', *Cognitive Linguistics*, 26: 537–47.

Kuhl, B. A., and M. M. Chun. 2014. 'Memory and Attention.' In Anna C. Nobre and Sabine Kastner (eds.), *The Oxford Handbook of Attention* (Oxford University Press: Oxford).

Kuperberg, G. R. 2016. 'Separate streams or probabilistic inference? What the N400 can tell us about the comprehension of events', *Language, Cognition and Neuroscience*, 31: 602–16.

Kuperberg, G. R., and T. F. Jaeger. 2016. 'What do we mean by prediction in language comprehension?', *Language, Cognition and Neuroscience*, 31: 32–59.

Kutas, M., K. A. DeLong, and N. J. Smith. 2011. 'A Look around at What Lies Ahead: Prediction and Predictability in Language Processing.' In Moshe Bar (ed.), *Predictions in the Brain : Using Our Past to Generate a Future* (Oxford University Press: New York, Oxford).

Lakoff, G. 1987. *Women, Fire, and Dangerous Things: What Categories Reveal about the Mind* (University of Chicago Press: Chicago, London).

1990. 'The invariance hypothesis: is abstract reason based on image-schemas?', *Cognitive Linguistics*, 1: 39–74.

Lakoff, G., and M. Johnson. 1980. *Metaphors We Live By* (University of Chicago Press: Chicago).

Landauer, T. K., and S. T. Dumais. 1997. 'A solution to Plato's problem: the latent semantic analysis theory of acquisition, induction, and representation of knowledge', *Psychological Review*, 104: 211–40.

Langacker, R. W. 1987. *Foundations of Cognitive Grammar* (Stanford University Press: Stanford).

1991. *Foundations of Cognitive Grammar: Descriptive Application* (Stanford University Press: Stanford).

2008. *Cognitive Grammar: A Basic Introduction* (Oxford University Press: New York).

2015. 'Construal.' In Ewa Dąbrowska and Dagmar Divjak (eds.), *Handbook of Cognitive Linguistics* (De Gruyter Mouton: Berlin, Boston).

2016. 'Working towards a synthesis', *Cognitive Linguistics*, 27: 465–77.

2017. 'Entrenchment in Cognitive Grammar.' In Hans-Joerg Schmid (ed.), *Entrenchment and the Psychology of Language Learning: How We Reorganize and Adapt Linguistic Knowledge* (De Gruyter Mouton and APA: Berlin).

Lashley, K. S. 1930. 'Basic neural mechanisms in behavior', *Psychological Review*, 37: 1–24.

1951. 'The Problem of Serial Order in Behavior.' In J. L. Jeffress (ed.), *Cerebral mechanisms in behaviour: the Hixon symposium* (Wiley: New York).

Lavie, N. 2005. 'Distracted and confused? Selective attention under load', *Trends in Cognitive Sciences*, 9: 75–82.

Lavie, N., and P. Dalton. 2014. 'Load Theory of Attention and Cognitive Control.' In Anna C. Nobre and Sabine Kastner (eds.), *The Oxford Handbook of Attention* (Oxford University Press: Oxford).

Lavie, N., and Y. Tsal. 1994. 'Perceptual load as a major determinant of the locus of selection in visual attention', *Perception and Psychophysics*, 56: 183–97.

Lee, C., M. Grossman, J. Morris, M. B. Stern, and H. I. Hurtig. 2003. 'Attentional resource and processing speed limitations during sentence processing in Parkinson's disease', *Brain and Language*, 85: 347–56.

Leech, G., P. Rayson, and A. Wilson. 2014. *Word Frequencies in Written and Spoken English: Based on the British National Corpus* (Routledge: London, New York).

Leitner, S. 1974. *So lernt man leben* (Droemer Knaur, Munich).

Levelt, W. J. M. 2013. *A History of Psycholinguistics: The Pre-Chomskyan Era* (Oxford University Press: Oxford).

Levelt, W. J. M., and S. Kelter. 1982. 'Surface form and memory in question answering', *Cognitive Psychology*, 14: 78–106.

Levshina, N. 2015. *How to Do Linguistics with R: Data Exploration and Statistical Analysis* (John Benjamins Publishing Company: Amsterdam, Philadelphia).

Levy, R. 2008. 'Expectation-based syntactic comprehension', *Cognition*, 106: 1126–77.

Levy, R., and F. Jaeger. 2007. 'Speakers optimize information density through syntactic reduction.' In *Proceedings of the 20th Conference on Neural Information Processing Systems (NIPS)*.

Lewis, D. 1969. *Convention* (MIT Press: Cambridge, MA).

Li, C. N. 1976. *Subject and Topic* (Academic Press: New York).

Lidz, J., H. Gleitman, and L. Gleitman. 2003. 'Understanding how input matters: verb learning and the footprint of universal grammar', *Cognition: International Journal of Cognitive Science*, 87: 151–78.

Lieven, E. V. M. 2010. 'Input and first language acquisition: evaluating the role of frequency', *Lingua*, 120: 2546–56.

Lieven, E. V. M., and M. Tomasello. 2008. 'Children's First Language Acquisition from a Usage-Based Perspective.' In Peter Robinson and Nick C. Ellis (eds.), *Handbook of Cognitive Linguistics and Second Language Acquisition* (Routledge: New York).

Linder, K., and A. Hohenberger. 2009. 'Introduction: concepts of development, learning, and acquisition', *Linguistics*, 47: 211–39.

Lisac, J., and P. Milin. 2006. 'T-vrednost i zajednička informacija kao mere jačine asocijativne veze u srpskom jeziku', *Psihologija*, 39: 57–74.

Loftus, G. R., and N. H. Mackworth. 1978. 'Cognitive determinants of fixation location during picture viewing', *Journal of Experimental Psychology: Human Perception and Performance*, 4: 565–72.

Lohnas, L. J., S. M. Polyn, and M. J. Kahana. 2011. 'Contextual variability in free recall', *Journal Of Memory And Language*, 64: 249–55.

Lubow, R. E. 1973. 'Latent inhibition', *Psychological Bulletin*, 79: 398–407.

Lukatela, G., B. Gligorijević, A. Kostić, and M. T. Turvey. 1980. 'Representation of inflected nouns in the internal lexicon', *Memory and Cognition*, 21: 415–23.

Lukatela, G., Z. Mandić, B. Gligorijević, A. Kostić, M. Savić, and M. T. Turvey. 1978. 'Lexical decision for inflected nouns', *Language and Speech*, 21: 166–73.

Lund, K., and C. Burgess. 1996. 'Producing high-dimensional semantic spaces from lexical co-occurrence', *Behavior Research Methods, Instruments, and Computers*, 28: 203–8.

Lupyan, G., and A. Clark. 2015. 'Words and the world: predictive coding and the language-perception-cognition interface', *Current Directions in Psychological Science*, 24: 279–84.

Lutosławski, W. 1897. *The Origin and Growth of Plato's Logic: With an Account of Plato's Style and of the Chronology of His Writings* (Longmans, Green and Co: London).

Lyashevskaya, O., M. Ovsjannikova, N. Szymor, and D. Divjak. 2018. 'Looking for Contextual Cues to Differentiating Modal Meanings: A Corpus-Based Study.' In Mikhail Kopotev, Olga Lyashevskaya and Arto Mustajoki (eds.), *Quantitative Approaches to the Russian Language* (Routledge: Abingdon, New York).

Lyne, A. A. 1985. *The Vocabulary of French Business Correspondence: Word Frequencies, Collocations, and Problems of Lexicometric Method* (Slatkine-Champion: Geneva, Paris).

MacCorquodale, K. 1970. 'On Chomsky's review of Skinner's *Verbal Behavior*', *Journal of the Experimental Analysis of Behavior*, 13: 83–99.

MacKay, D. G. 1982. 'The problems of flexibility, fluency, and speed-accuracy trade-off in skilled behavior', *Psychological Review*, 89: 483–506.

Mackintosh, N. J. 1975. 'A theory of attention: variations in the associability of stimuli with reinforcement', *Psychological Review*, 82: 276–98.

Mackworth, N. H., and A. J. Morandi. 1967. 'The gaze selects informative details within pictures', *Attention, Perception and Psychophysics*, 2: 547–52.

MacWhinney, B. 1977. 'Starting points', *Language*, 53: 152–68.

1978. *The Acquisition of Morphophonology* (University of Chicago Press: Chicago).

1998. 'Models of emergence of language', *Annual Review of Psychology*, 49: 199–227.

Mandelbrot, B. 1953. 'An Informational Theory of the Statistical Structure of Languages.' In Willis Jackson (ed.), *Communication Theory* (Butterworth: Woburn, MA).

Manning, C. D. 2003. 'Probabilistic Syntax.' In Rens Bod, Jennifer Hay and Stefanie Jannedy (eds.), *Probabilistic Linguistics* (MIT Press: Cambridge, MA, London).

Manning, C. D., and H. Schütze. 1999. *Foundations of Statistical Natural Language Processing* (MIT Press: Cambridge, MA).

Mariotti, F. 1880. *Dante e la statistica delle lingue* (Rome).

Marr, D. 1982. *Vision: A Computational Investigation into the Human Representation and Processing of Visual Information* (W. H. Freeman: San Francisco).

Marslen-Wilson, W. D., and L. K. Tyler. 2007. 'Morphology, language and the brain: the decompositional substrate for language comprehension', *Philosophical Transactions of the Royal Society B: Biological Sciences*, 362: 823–36.

Massaro, D. W. 1989. 'Testing between the TRACE model and the fuzzy logical model of speech perception', *Cognitive Psychology*, 21: 398–421.

Matthews, D., and C. Bannard. 2010. 'Children's production of unfamiliar word sequences is predicted by positional variability and latent classes in a large sample of child-directed speech', *Cognitive Science*, 34: 465–88.

Matthews, D., and G. Krajewski. 2015. 'First Language Acquisition.' In Ewa Dąbrowska and Dagmar Divjak (eds.), *Handbook of Cognitive Linguistics* (De Gruyter Mouton: Berlin, Boston).

Matthews, P. H. 1972. *Inflectional Morphology: A Theoretical Study Based on Aspects of Latin Verb Conjugation* (Cambridge University Press: Cambridge, UK).

Maye, J., J. F. Werker, and L. Gerken. 2002. 'Infant sensitivity to distributional information can affect phonetic discrimination', *Cognition*, 82: B101–B11.

McClelland, J. L. 2013. 'Incorporating rapid neocortical learning of new schema-consistent information into complementary learning systems theory', *Journal of Experimental Psychology: General*, 142 (4): 1190–1210.

McClelland, J. L., and J. Bybee. 2007. 'Gradience of gradience: a reply to Jackendoff', *The Linguistic Review*, 24: 437–55.

McClelland, J. L., and J. L. Elman. 1986. 'The TRACE model of speech perception', *Cognitive Psychology*, 18: 1–86.

McClelland, J. L., and D. E. Rumelhart. 1981. 'An interactive activation model of context effects in letter perception: I. An account of basic findings', *Psychological Review*, 88: 375–407.

——— 1985. 'Distributed memory and the representation of general and specific information', *Journal of Experimental Psychology: General*, 114: 159–88.

McDonald, S., and R. C. Shillcock. 2001. 'Rethinking the word frequency effect: The neglected role of distributional information in lexical processing', *Language and Speech*, 44: 295–323.

McDonald, S. A., and R. C. Shillcock. 2003. 'Eye movements reveal the on-line computation of lexical probabilities during reading', *Psychological Science*, 14: 648–52.

McRae, K., and K. Matsuki. 2009. 'People use their knowledge of common events to understand language, and do so as quickly as possible', *Lang Linguist Compass*, 3: 1417–29.

Meltzer, N. S., and R. Herse. 1969. 'The boundaries of written words as seen by first graders. journal of literacy research', *Journal of Literacy Research*, 1: 3–14.

Mesulam, M. 2008. 'Representation, inference, and transcendent encoding in neuro-cognitive networks of the human brain', *Annals of Neurology*, 64: 367–78.

Meyer, A. S., A. M. Sleidernik, and W. J. M. Levelt. 1998. 'Viewing and naming objects: eye movements during noun phrase production', *Cognition*, 66: B25–33.

Meyer, A. S., L. Wheeldon, F. van der Meulen, and A. Konopka. 2012. 'Effects of speech rate and practice on the allocation of visual attention in multiple object naming', *Frontiers in Psychology*, 3.

Mikolov, T., K. Chen, G. Corrado, and J. Dean. 2013. 'Efficient estimation of word representations in vector space', paper, *CoRR*, abs/1301.3781.

Milin, P., D. Divjak, and R. H. Baayen. 2017. 'A learning perspective on individual differences in skilled reading: exploring and exploiting orthographic and semantic discrimination cues', *Journal of Experimental Psychology: Learning, Memory, and Cognition*, 43: 1730–51.

Milin, P., D. Divjak, S. Dimitrijević, and R. H. Baayen. 2016. 'Towards cognitively plausible data science in language research', *Cognitive Linguistics*, 27: 507–26.

Milin, P., D. F. Đurđević, and F. M. del Prado Martín. 2009. 'The simultaneous effects of inflectional paradigms and classes on lexical recognition: evidence from Serbian', *Journal of Memory and Language*, 60: 50–64.

Milin, P., L. B. Feldman, M. Ramscar, P. Hendrix, and R. H. Baayen. 2017. 'Discrimination in Lexical Decision', *PLoS ONE*, 12.

Milin, P., V. Kuperman, A. Kostić, and R. H. Baayen. 2009. 'Words and Paradigms Bit by Bit: An Information-Theoretic Approach to the Processing of Inflection and Derivation.' In J. P. Blevins and J. Blevins (eds.), *Analogy in Grammar: Form and Acquisition* (Oxford University Press: Oxford).

Miller, G. 1957. 'Some effects of intermittent silence', *American Journal of Psychology*, 70: 311–14.

Miller, G. A. 1956. 'The magical number seven, plus or minus two: some limits on our capacity for processing information', *Psychological Review*, 63: 81–97.

Mishra, R. K., N. Singh, A. Pandey, and F. Huettig. 2012. 'Spoken language-mediated anticipatory eye-movements are modulated by reading ability: evidence from Indian low and high literates', *Journal of Eye Movement Research*, 5: 1–10.

Mishra, R. K. 2015. *Interaction between Attention and Language Systems in Humans: a Cognitive Science Perspective* (Springer: New Delhi).

Mishra, R. K., N. Srinivasan, and F. Huettig. 2015. *Attention and Vision in Language Processing* (Springer: New Delhi).

Mitchell, D. C., F. Cuetos, M. M. B. Corely, and M. Brysbaert. 1995. 'Exposure-based models of human parsing: evidence for the use of coarse-grained (nonlexical) statistical records', *Journal of Psycholinguistic Research*, 24: 469–88.

Molinaro, N., I. F. Monsalve, and M. Lizarazu. 2016. 'Is there a common oscillatory brain mechanism for producing and predicting language?', *Language, Cognition and Neuroscience*, 31: 145–58.

Monsell, S. 1991. 'The Nature and Locus of Word Frequency Effects in Reading.' In Derek Besner and Glyn W. Humphreys (eds.), *Basic Processes in Reading: Visual Word Recognition* (Lawrence Erlbaum: Hillsdale, NJ).

Montemurro, M. A. 2001. 'Beyond the Zipf–Mandelbrot law in quantitative linguistics', *Physica A*, 300: 567–78.

Moore, K. E. 2014. *The Spatial Language of Time: Metaphor, Metonymy and Frames of Reference* (John Benjamins: Amsterdam & Philadelphia).

Moray, N. 1959. 'Attention in dichotic listening: affective cues and the influence of instructions', *Quarterly Journal of Experimental Psychology*, 11: 56–60.

Morrison, C. M., and A. W. Ellis. 1995. 'The roles of word frequency and age of acquisition in word naming and lexical decision', *Journal of Experimental Psychology: Learning, Memory, and Cognition*, 21: 116–33.

Morrison, C. M., A. W. Ellis, and P. T. Quinlan. 1992. 'Age of acquisition, not word frequency, affects object naming, not object recognition', *Memory and Cognition*, 20: 705–14.

Morton, J. 1969. 'Interaction of information in word recognition', *Psychological Review*, 76: 165–78.

Moscoso del Prado Martín, F., A. Kostić, and R. H. Baayen. 2004. 'Putting the bits together: an information theoretical perspective on morphological processing', *Cognition*, 94: 1–18.

Mukherjee, J. 2005. *English Ditransitive Verbs: Aspects of Theory, Description and a Usage-Based Model* (Rodopi: Amsterdam).

Mulligan, N. W. 1997. 'Attention and implicit memory tests: the effects of varying attentional load on conceptual priming', *Memory and Cognition*, 25: 11–17.

1998. 'The role of attention during encoding in implicit and explicit memory', *Journal of Experimental Psychology: Learning, Memory, and Cognition*, 24: 27–47.

Murphy, G. 2002. *The Big Book of Concepts* (MIT Press: Cambridge, MA, London).

Murray, W. S., and K. I. Forster. 2004. 'Serial mechanisms in lexical access: the rank hypothesis', *Psychological Review*, 111: 721–56.

Myachykov, A. 2007. 'Integrating perceptual, semantic and syntactic information in sentence production', unpublished Ph.D. dissertation, University of Glasgow.

Myachykov, A., S. Garrod, and C. Scheepers. 2010. 'Perceptual Priming of Syntactic Choice during English and Finnish Sentence Production.' In R. Mishra and N. Srinivasan (eds.), *Language and Cognition: State of the Art* (Lincom Europa: Munich).

2012. 'Determinants of structural choice in visually situated sentence production', *Acta Psychologica*, 141: 304–15.

Myachykov, A., M. I. Posner, and R. S. Tomlin. 2007. 'A parallel interface for language and cognition in sentence production: theory, method, and experimental evidence', *The Linguistic Review*, 24: 457–74.

Myachykov, A., D. Thompson, C. Scheepers, and S. Garrod. 2011. 'Visual attention and structural choice in sentence production across languages', *Language and Linguistics Compass*, 5: 95–107.

Myachykov, A., and R. S. Tomlin. 2008. 'Perceptual priming and syntactic choice in Russian sentence production', *Journal of Cognitive Science*, 9: 31–48.

Myachykov, A., R. S. Tomlin, and M. I. Posner. 2005. 'Attention and empirical studies of grammar', *The Linguistic Review*, 22: 347–64.

Narayanan, S., and D. Jurafsky. 1998. 'Bayesian Models of Human Sentence Processing.' In *COGSCI-98* (Lawrence Erlbaum: Hillsdale, NJ).

2002. 'A Bayesian Model Predicts Human Parse Preference and Reading Times in Sentence Processing' In *Advances in Neural Information Processing Systems*, 14.

Nevat, M., M. T. Ullman, Z. Eviatar, and T. Bitan. 2017. 'The neural bases of the learning and generalization of morphological inflection', *Neuropsychologia*, 98: 139–55.

New, B., M. Brysbaert, J. Veronis, and C. Pallier. 2007. 'The use of film subtitles to estimate word frequencies', *Applied Psycholinguistics*, 28: 661–77.

Newmeyer, F. J. 2003. 'Grammar is grammar and usage is usage', *Language*, 79: 682–707.

Newport, E. L. 1990. 'Maturational constraints on language learning', *Cognitive Science*, 14: 11–28.

Niceforo, A. 1916. *La misura della vita* (Torino).

Nieuwland, M., S. Politzer-Ahles, E. Heyselaar, K. Segaert, E. Darley, N. Kazanina, S. Von Grebmer Zu Wolfsthurn, F. Bartolozzi, V. Kogan, A. Ito, D. Mézière, D. J. Barr, G. Rousselet, H. Ferguson, S. Busch Moreno, X. Fu, J. Tuomainen, E. Kulakova, E. Matthew Husband, and F. Huettig. 2017. 'Limits on prediction in language comprehension: a multi-lab failure to replicate evidence for probabilistic pre-activation of phonology'. In *bioRxiv*.

Nobre, A. C., and S. Kastner. 2014a. 'Attention: Time Capsule 2013.' In Anna C. Nobre and Sabine Kastner (eds.), *The Oxford Handbook of Attention* (Oxford University Press: Oxford).

(eds.). 2014b. *The Oxford Handbook of Attention* (Oxford University Press: Oxford).

Norcliffe, E., and A. E. Konopka. 2015. 'Vision and Language in Cross-Linguistic Research on Sentence Production.' In Ramesh Mishra, Narayanan Kumar Srinivasan and Falk Huettig (eds.), *Attention and Vision in Language Processing* (Springer: New Delhi).

Norman, D. A., and T. Shallice. 1986. 'Attention to Action: Willed and Automatic Control of Behaviour.' In R. J. Davidson, G. E. Schwartz and D. Shapiro (eds.), *Consciousness and Self-Regulation: Advances in Research and Theory* (Springer US: New York).

Norris, D. 2006. 'The Bayesian reader: explaining word recognition as an optimal Bayesian decision process', *Psychological Review*, 113: 327–57.

Nosofsky, R. M. 1988. 'Similarity, frequency and category representation', *Journal of Experimental Psychology: Learning, Memory, and Cognition*, 14: 54–65.

Núñez, R., and K. Cooperrider. 2013. 'The tangle of space and time in human cognition', *Trends in Cognitive Sciences*, 17: 220–9.

O'Brien, D. P., A. Roazzi, R. Athias, and M. D. C. Brandao. 2007. 'What Sorts of Reasoning Modules Have Been Provided by Evolution? Some Experiments Conducted among Tukano Speakers in Brazilian Amazonia concerning Reasoning about Conditional Propositions and about Conditional Probabilities.' In Maxwell J. Roberts (ed.), *Integrating the Mind: Domain General versus Domain Specific Processes in Higher Cognition* (Psychology Press: New York).

O'Regan, J. K., R. A. Rensink, and J. J. Clark. 1999. 'Change-blindness as a result of "mudsplashes"', *Nature*, 398: 34.

Oakley, T. 2009. *From Attention to Meaning: Explorations in Semiotics, Linguistics, and Rhetoric* (Peter Lang: Bern).

Oberauer, K. 2002. 'Access to information in working memory: exploring the focus of attention', *Journal of Experimental Psychology: Learning, Memory, and Cognition*, 28: 411–21.

2009. 'Design for a working memory', *The Psychology of Learning and Motivation*, 51: 45–100.

Oldfield, R. C., and A. Wingfield. 1965. 'Response latencies in naming objects.', *Quarterly Journal of Experimental Psychology*, 17: 273–81.

Olson, D. R., and N. Filby. 1972. 'On the comprehension of active and passive sentences', *Cognitive Psychology*, 3: 361–81.

Osgood, C. E. 1958. 'A question of sufficiency', *Contemporary Psychology: a Journal of Reviews*, 3: 209–12.

1971. 'Exploration in semantic space: a personal diary', *Journal of Social Issues*, 27: 5–64.

Osgood, C. E., and K. Bock. 1977. 'Salience and Sentencing: Some Production Principles.' in S. Rosenberg (ed.), *Sentence Production: Developments in Research and Theory* (Lawrence Erlbaum: Hillsdale, NJ).

'Out of Our Minds'. https://outofourminds.shef.ac.uk.

Padó, U., M. W. Crocker, and F. Keller. 2009. 'A probabilistic model of semantic plausibility in sentence processing', *Cognitive Science*, 33: 794–838.

Paller, K. A., and A. D. Wagner. 2002. 'Observing the transformation of experience into memory', *Trends in Cognitive Sciences*, 6: 93–102.

Palmer, D. C. 2006. 'On Chomsky's appraisal of Skinner's Verbal Behavior: a half century of misunderstanding', *The Behavior Analyst*, 29: 253–67.

Pavlov, I. P. 1927. *Conditioned Reflexes: An Investigation of the Physiological Activity of the Cerebral Cortex* (Oxford University Press: London).

Pearce, J. M. 1997. *Animal Learning and Cognition: An Introduction (2nd ed.)* (Psychology Press: Hove).

Pearce, J. M., and G. Hall. 1980. 'A model for Pavlovian learning: variations in the effectiveness of conditioned but not of unconditioned stimuli', *Psychological Review*, 87: 532–52.

Pecina, P. 2009. *Lexical Association Measures: Collocation Extraction* (UFAL: Praha).

Pelucchi, B., J. F. Hay, and J. R. Saffran. 2009. 'Statistical learning in a natural language by eight-month-old infants.', *Child Development*, 80: 674–85.

Perruchet, P., and B. Poulin-Charronnat. 2012. 'Word Segmentation: Trading the (New, but Poor) Concept of Statistical Computation for the (Old, but Richer) Associative Approach.' In P. Rebuschat and J. N. Williams (eds.), *Statistical Learning and Language Acquisition* (De Gruyter: Berlin).

Petri, H. L., and M. Mishkin. 1994. 'Behaviorism, cognitivism and the neuropsychology of memory', *American Scientist*, 82: 30–7.

Piantadosi, S. T. 2014. 'Zipf's word frequency law in natural language: a critical review and future directions', *Psychonomic Bulletin and Review*, 21: 1112–30.

Pickering, M. J., and H. P. Branigan. 1998. 'The representation of verbs: evidence from syntactic priming in language production', *Journal of Memory and Language, 39* (4): 633–51.

Pierrehumbert, J. B. 2001. 'Exemplar Dynamics: Word Frequency, Lenition and Contrast.' In Joan Bybee and Paul Hopper (eds.), *Frequency Effects and the Emergence of Lexical Structure* (John Benjamins: Amsterdam, Philadelphia).
    2006. 'The next toolkit', *Journal of Phonetics*, 34: 516–30.

Pimsleur, P. 1967. 'A memory schedule', *Modern Language Journal*, 51: 73–5.

Pine, J. M. 1994. 'The Language of Primary Caregivers.' In C. Gallaway and B. J. Richards (eds.), *Input and Interaction in Language Acquisition* (Cambridge University Press: Cambridge, UK).

Pinker, S. 1984. *Language Learnability and Language Development* (Harvard University Press: Cambridge, MA, London).

Plaut, D. C., and L. M. Gonnerman. 2000. 'Are non-semantic morphological effects incompatible with a distributed connectionist approach to lexical processing?', *Language and Cognitive Processes*, 15: 445–85.

Poeppel, D. 2012. 'The *maps problem* and the *mapping problem*: two challenges for a cognitive neuroscience of speech and language', *Cognitive Neuropsychology*, 29: 34–55.

Poggio, T. A. 2010. 'Afterword to Vision.' In David Marr (ed.), *Vision* (MIT Press: Cambridge, MA).

Porter, H. N. 1951. *The Early Greek Hexameter* (Yale University Press: New Haven).

Posner, M. I. 1980. 'Orienting of attention', *The Quarterly Journal of Experimental Psychology*, 32: 3–25.

Postle, B. R. 2006. 'Working memory as an emergent property of the mind and brain', *Neuroscience*, 139: 23–38.

Prat, C. S., B. L. Yamasaki, R. A. Kluender, and A. Stocco. 2016. 'Resting-state qEEG predicts rate of second language learning in adults', *Brain and Language*, 157–8:44–50.

Prentice, J. 1967. 'Effects of cuing actor vs. cuing object on word order in sentence production', *Psychonomic Science*, 8.

Pullum, G., and B. Scholz. 2002. 'Empirical assessment of stimulus poverty arguments', *The Linguistic Review*, 19: 8–50.

Pulvermüller, F., Y. Shtyrov, A. S. Hasting, and R. P. Carlyon. 2008. 'Syntax as a reflex: neurophysiological evidence for early automaticity of grammatical processing', *Brain and Language*, 104: 244–53.

Putnam, H. 1963. 'Brains and Behavior'. In Ronald J. Butler (ed.), *Analytical Philosophy*, second series (Blackwell: Oxford).

Qian, T., F. T. Jaeger, and R. N. Aslin. 2012. 'Learning to represent a multi-context environment: more than detecting changes', *Frontiers in Psychology*, 3.

Rabagliati, H., B. Ferguson, and C. Lew-Williams. 2019. 'The profile of abstract rule learning in infancy: meta-analytic and experimental evidence', *Developmental Science*, 22.

Rabagliati, H., C. Gambi, and M. J. Pickering. 2016. 'Learning to predict or predicting to learn?', *Language, Cognition and Neuroscience*, 31: 94–105.

Rácz, P. 2013. *Salience in Sociolinguistics: A Quantitative Approach* (De Gruyter Mouton: Berlin and Boston).

Rainer, F. 2016. 'Blocking.' In Mark Aronoff (ed.), *Oxford Research Encyclopedias* (Oxford University Press: Oxford).

Ramón y Cajal, S. 1894. 'La fine structure des centres nerveux', *Proceedings of the Royal Society of London. Series B, Biological Sciences*, 55: 443–68.

Ramscar, M., and R. Port. 2015. 'Categorization (without Categories).' In Ewa Dąbrowska and Dagmar Divjak (eds.), *Handbook of Cognitive Linguistics* (De Gruyter Mouton: Berlin, Boston).

Ramscar, M., and D. Yarlett. 2007. 'Linguistic self-correction in the absence of feed-back: a new approach to the logical problem of language acquisition', *Cognitive Science*, 31: 927–30.

Ramscar, M., D. Yarlett, M. Dye, K. Denny, and K. Thorpe. 2010. 'The effects of feature-label-order and their implications for symbolic learning', *Cognitive Science*, 34: 909–57.

Rao, R. P., and D. H. Ballard. 1999. 'Predictive coding in the visual cortex: a functional interpretation of some extra-classical receptive-field effects', *Nature Neuroscience*, 2: 79–87.

Rasmussen, D., and C. Eliasmith. 2013. 'God, the devil, and the details: fleshing out the predictive processing framework', *The Behavioral and Brain Sciences*, 36: 223.

Raymond, W. D., and E. L. Brown. 2012. 'Are Effects of Word Frequency Effects of Context Of Use? An Analysis of Initial Fricative Reduction in Spanish.' In Stefan Th Gries and Dagmar Divjak (eds.), *Frequency Effects in Language. Vol 2: Learning and Processing* (Mouton de Gruyter: The Hague).

Rayner, K. 1998. 'Eye movements in reading and information processing: 20 years of research', *Psychological Bulletin*, 124: 372–422.

Rebuschat, P. 2013. 'Statistical Learning' In P. Robinson (ed.), *The Routledge Encyclopedia of Second Language Acquisition* (Routledge: London).

Redgrave, P., and K. Gurney. 2006. 'The short-latency dopamine signal: a role in discovering novel actions?', *Nature Reviews Neuroscience*, 7: 967.

Reicher, G. M. 1969. 'Perceptual recognition as a function of meaningfulness of stimulus material', *Journal of Experimental Psychology*, 82: 275–80.

Rescorla, R. A. 1966. 'Predictability and number of pairings in Pavlovian fear conditioning', *Psychonomic Science*, 4: 383–4.

———. 1967. 'Pavlovian conditioning and its proper control procedures', *Psychological Review*, 74: 71–80.

———. 1968. 'Probability of shock in the presence and absence of cs in fear conditioning', *Journal of Comparative and Physiological Psychology*, 66: 1–5.

———. 1974. 'Effect of inflation of the unconditioned stimulus value following conditioning', *Journal of Comparative and Physiological Psychology*, 86: 101–6.

———. 1988. 'Pavlovian conditioning: it's not what you think it is', *American Psychologist*, 43: 151–60.

———. 2008. 'Rescorla–Wagner model', *Scholarpedia*, 3 (3): 2237.

Rescorla, R. A., and R. A. Wagner. 1972. 'A Theory of Pavlovian Conditioning: Variations in the Effectiveness of Reinforcement and Non-Reinforcement.' In H. Black and W. F. Prokasy (eds.), *Classical Conditioning II* (Appleton-Century-Crofts: New York).

Riccio, D. C., R. Richardson, and D. L. Ebner. 1984. 'Memory retrieval deficits based upon altered contextual cues: A paradox', *Psychological Bulletin*, 96: 152–65.

Roark, B. 2001. 'Probabilistic top-down parsing and language modeling', *Computational Linguistics*, 27: 249–76.

Robenalt, C., and A. E. Goldberg. 2015. 'Judgment evidence for statistical pre-emption: it is relatively better to vanish than to disappear a rabbit, but a lifeguard can equally well backstroke or swim children to shore', *Cognitive Linguistics*, 26: 467–504.

Roediger, H. 1980. 'Memory metaphors in cognitive psychology', *Memory and Cognition*, 8: 231–46.

Roediger, H., and R. G. Crowder. 1975. 'The spacing of lists in free recall', *Journal of Verbal Learning and Verbal Behavior*, 14: 590–602.

Roelofs, A. 1997. 'The WEAVER model of word-form encoding in speech production', *Cognition*, 64: 249–84.

Rogalsky, C., and G. Hickok. 2009. 'Selective attention to semantic and syntactic features modulates sentence processing networks in anterior temporal cortex', *Cerebral Cortex*, 19: 786–96.

Rogers, T. T., and J. L. McClelland. 2004. *Semantic Cognition: A Parallel Distributed Processing Approach* (MIT Press: Cambridge, MA).

Rosch, E. 1975. 'Cognitive representation of semantic categories.', *Journal of Experimental Psychology* 104: 192–233.

Rubenstein, H., L. Garfield, and J. A. Millikan. 1970. 'Homographic entries in the internal lexicon', *Journal of Verbal Learning and Verbal Behavior*, 9: 487–94.

Rumelhart, D. E., and J. L. McClelland. 1982. 'An interactive activation model of context effects in letter perception, 2: the contextual enhancement effect and some tests and extensions of the model', *Psychological Review*, 89: 60–94.

——1986. 'On Learning the Past Tense of English Verbs.' In D. E. Rumelhart and J. McClelland (eds.), *Parallel Distributed Processing* (MIT Press: Cambridge, MA).

Saffran, J. R. 2001a. 'The use of predictive dependencies in language learning', *Journal of Memory and Language*, 44: 493–515.

——2001b. 'Words in a sea of sounds: The output of statistical learning', *Cognition*, 81: 149–69.

——2002. 'Constraints on statistical language learning', *Journal of Memory and Language*, 47: 172–96.

——2003. 'Statistical language learning: mechanisms and constraints', *Current Directions in Psychological Science* 12: 110–14.

Saffran, J. R., R. N. Aslin, and E. L. Newport. 1996. 'Statistical Learning by Eight-Month-Old Infants', *Science*: 1926–8.

Saffran, J. R., E. L. Newport, and R. N. Aslin. 1996. 'Word segmentation: the role of distributional cues', *Journal of Memory and Language*, 35: 606–21.

Saffran, J. R., and D. P. Wilson. 2003. 'From syllables to syntax: multi-level statistical learning by 12-month-old infants', *Infancy*, 4: 273–84.

Sahlgren, M. 2006. 'The word–space model: using distributional analysis to represent syntagmatic and paradigmatic relations between words in high-dimensional vector spaces', PhD Dissertation, Stockholm University.

Saling, L. L., and J. G. Phillips. 2007. 'Automatic behaviour: efficient not mindless', *Brain Research Bulletin*, 73: 1–20.

Salverda, A. P., and G. T. M. Altmann. 2011. 'Attentional capture of objects referred to by spoken language', *Journal of Experimental Psychology: Human Perception and Performance*, 37: 1122–33.

Sankoff, D., and W. Labov. 1979. 'On the uses of variable rules', *Language in Society*, 8: 189–222.

Saussure, F. d. 1916. *Cours de linguistique général* (Payot: Paris).

Savin, H. B. 1963. 'Word-frequency effect and errors in the perception of speech', *Journal of the Acoustical Society of America*, 35: 200–6.

Scaife, M., and J. S. Bruner. 1975. 'The capacity for joint visual attention in the infant', *Nature*, 253: 255–6.

Scarborough, D. L., C. Cortese, and H. S. Scarborough. 1977. 'Frequency and repetition effects in lexical memory', *Journal of Experimental Psychology: Human Perception and Performance*, 3: 1–17.

Schmid, H.-J. 2000. *English Abstract Nouns as Conceptual Shells. From Corpus to Cognition* (Mouton de Gruyter: Berlin, New York).

——2007. 'Entrenchment, Salience and Basic Levels.' In Dirk Geeraerts and Hubert Cuyckens (eds.), *The Oxford Handbook of Cognitive Linguistics* (Oxford University Press: Oxford).

2010. 'Does Frequency in Text Instantiate Entrenchment in the Cognitive System.' In Dylan Glynn and Kerstin Fischer (eds.), *Quantitative Methods in Cognitive Semantics: Corpus-Driven Approaches* (Walter de Gruyter: Berlin).

2015. 'A blueprint of the entrenchment-and-conventionalization model', *Yearbook of the German Cognitive Linguistics Association* 5: 1–27.

2016a. 'A blueprint of the entrenchment-and-conventionalization Model', *Yearbook of the German Cognitive Linguistics Association*, 3: 3–26.

2016b. 'Why cognitive linguistic must embrace the pragmatic and social dimensions of language and how it could do so more seriously', *Cognitive Linguistics*, 27: 543–58.

(ed.). 2017a. Entrenchment and the Psychology of Language Learning: How We Reorganize and Adapt Linguistic Knowledge (De Gruyter Mouton and APA: Berlin).

2017b. 'A Framework for Understanding Linguistic Entrenchment and its Psychological Foundations.' In Hans-Joerg Schmid (ed.), *Entrenchment and the Psychology of Language Learning: How We Reorganize and Adapt Linguistic Knowledge* (De Gruyter Mouton and APA: Berlin).

Schmid, H.-J., and H. Küchenhoff. 2013. 'Collostructional analysis and other ways of measuring lexicogrammatical attraction: theoretical premises, practical problems and cognitive underpinnings', *Cognitive Linguistics*, 24: 531–77.

Schmidhuber, J. 2015. 'Deep learning in neural networks: an overview', *Neural Networks*, 61: 85–117.

Schooler, L. J. 1993. 'Memory and the statistical structure of the environment', paper, Carnegie Mellon University.

Schooler, L. J., and J. R. Anderson. 1997. 'The role of process in the rational analysis of memory', *Cognitive Psychology*, 32.

Schreuder, R., and R. H. Baayen. 1997. 'How complex simplex words can be', *Journal of Memory and Language*, 37: 118–39.

Schriefers, H., A. S. Meyer, and W. J. M. Levelt. 1990. 'Exploring the time course of lexical access in language production: picture-word interference studies', *Journal of Memory and Language*, 29: 86–102.

Schultz, W., P. Dayan, and P. Montague. 1997. 'A neural substrate of prediction and reward', *Science*, 275: 1593–9.

Schupp, H. T., J. Stockburger, M. Codispoti, M. Junghöfer, A. I. Weike, and A. O. Hamm. 2007. 'Selective visual attention to emotion', *Journal of Neuroscience*, 27: 1082–9.

Schwanenflugel, P., and E. Shoben. 1983. 'Differential context effects in the comprehension of abstract and concrete verbal materials', *Journal of Experimental Psychology: Learning, Memory, and Cognition*, 9: 82–102.

Schwartz, B. L. 2011. Memory: Foundations and Applications (SAGE: Los Angeles, London).

Sedlmeier, P., and T. Betsch. 2002. Etc.: Frequency Processing and Cognition (Oxford University Press: Oxford, New York).

Seidenberg, M. S., and L. M. Gonnerman. 2000. 'Explaining derivational morphology as the convergence of codes', *Trends in Cognitive Sciences*, 4: 353–61.

Seidenberg, M. S., and J. L. McClelland. 1989. 'A distributed, developmental model of word recognition and naming', *Psychological Review*, 96: 523–68.

Serences, J. T., and S. Kastner. 2014. 'A Multi-Level Account of Selective Attention.' In Anna C. Nobre and Sabine Kastner (eds.), *The Oxford Handbook of Attention* (Oxford University Press: Oxford).

Settles, B., and B. Meeder. 2016. 'A Trainable Spaced Repetition Model for Language Learning.' In *54th Annual Meeting of the Association for Computational Linguistics*, 1848–58 (Association for Computational Linguistics: Berlin).

Shannon, C. E. 1948. 'A mathematical theory of communication', *Bell System Technical Journal*, 27: 379–423.

Shaoul, C. 2012. 'The processing of lexical sequences', PhD Dissertation, University of Alberta.

Shukla, M., J. Gervain, J. Mehler, and M. Nespor. 2012. 'Linguistic Constraints on Statistical Learning in Early Language Acquisition.' In P. Rebuschat and J. William (eds.), *Statistical Learning and Language Acquisition* (Mouton de Gruyter: Berlin, Boston).

Shukla, M., M. Nespor, and J. Mehler. 2007. 'An interaction between prosody and statistics in the segmentation of fluent speech', *Cognitive Psychology*, 54: 1–32.

Siegal, S. 1969. 'Generalization of latent inhibition', *Journal of Comparative and Physiological Psychology*, 69: 157–9.

Simon, H. A. 1956. 'Rational choice and the structure of the environment', *Psychological Review*, 63: 129–38.

——— 1957. *Models of Man, Social and Rational: Mathematical Essays on Rational Human Behavior in a Social Setting* (Wiley, Chapman and Hall: New York, London).

Simons, D. J., and D. T. Levin. 1997. 'Change blindness', *Trends in Cognitive Sciences*, 1: 261–7.

Singer, W., and C. M. Gray. 1995. 'Visual feature integration and the temporal correlation hypothesis', *Annual Review of Neuroscience*, 18: 555–86.

Sivia, D., and J. Skilling. 2006. *Data Analysis: a Bayesian Tutorial* (Oxford University Press: Oxford).

Skinner, B. F. 1937. 'The distribution of associated words', *Psychological Record*, 1: 71–6.

——— 1938. *The Behavior of Organisms: an Experimental Analysis* (Appleton-Century: New York).

——— 1953. *Science and Human Behavior* (Simon and Schuster:New York).

——— 1957. *Verbal Behavior* (Appleton-Century-Crofts.: New York).

Skousen, R. 1989. *Analogical Modeling of Language* (Kluwer Academic Publishers: Dordrecht).

Smith, N. J., and R. Levy. 2008. 'Optimal Processing Times in Reading: a Formal Model and Empirical Investigation.' In *Proceedings of the 30th Annual Conference of the Cognitive Science Society* (Cognitive Science Society: Austin, TX).

Snider, N., and I. Arnon. 2012. 'A Unified Lexicon and Grammar? Compositional and Non-Compositional Phrases in the Lexicon.' In Dagmar Divjak and Stefan Th. Gries (eds.), *Frequency Effects in Language Representation* (De Gruyter Mouton: Berlin, Boston).

Solan, Z., D. Horn, E. Ruppin, and S. Edelman. 2005. 'Unsupervised learning of natural languages', *Proceedings of the National Academy of Sciences of the United States of America*, 102: 11629–34.

Sporns, O., D. R. Chialvo, M. Kaiser, and C. C. Hilgetag. 2004. 'Organization, development and function of complex brain networks', *Trends in Cognitive Sciences*, 8: 418–25.

Squire, L. R., and E. R. Kandel. 2009. *Memory: From Mind to Molecules* (Roberts and Company: Totnes).

Stafford, T. 2009. 'What Use Are Computational Models of Cognitive Processes?' In J. Mayor, N. Ruh and K. Plunkett (eds.), *Connectionist Models of Behaviour and Cognition* (World Scientific: Singapore).

Stanovich, K., and R. West. 1979. 'Mechanisms of sentence context effects in reading: automatic activation and conscious attention', *Memory and Cognition*, 7: 77–85.

Staub, A. 2015. 'The effect of lexical predictability on eye movements in reading: critical review and theoretical interpretation', *Language and Linguistics Compass*, 9: 311–27.

Staub, A., M. Grant, L. Astheimer, and A. Cohen. 2015. 'The influence of cloze probability and item constraint on cloze task response time', *Journal of Memory and Language*, 82: 1–17.

Stefanowitsch, A. 2008. 'Negative entrenchment: a usage-based approach to negative evidence', *Cognitive Linguistics*, 19: 513–31.

2011. 'Constructional pre-emption by contextual mismatch: a corpus-linguistic investigation', *Cognitive Linguistics*, 22: 107–30.

2013. 'Collostructional Analysis.' In G. Trousdale and T. Hoffmann (eds.), *The Oxford Handbook of Construction Grammar* (Oxford University Press: Oxford).

Stefanowitsch, A., and S. T. Gries. 2003. 'Collostructions: investigating the interaction between words and constructions', *International Journal of Corpus Linguistics*, 8: 209–43.

2005. 'Co-varying collexemes', *Corpus Linguistics and Linguistic Theory*, 1: 1–43.

Steinhauer, K., and J. E. Drury. 2012. 'On the early left-anterior negativity (ELAN) in syntax studies', *Brain and Language*, 120: 135–62.

Stevens, M. E., V. E. Giuliano, and L. B. Heilprin (eds.). 1965. *Statistical Association Methods for Mechanized Documentation. Symposium Proceedings Washington 1964* (U.S. Government Printing Office: Washington, DC).

Steyvers, M., and K. J. Malmberg. 2003. 'The effect of normative context variability on recognition memory', *Journal of Experimental Psychology: Learning, Memory, and Cognition*, 29: 760–6.

Stolcke, A. 1995. 'An efficient probabilistic context-free parsing algorithm that computes prefix probabilities', *Computational Linguistics*, 21: 165–202.

Stone, J. V. 2015. *Information Theory: a Tutorial Introduction* (Sebtel Press: Sheffield).

2018. *Principles of Neural Information Theory: Computational Neuroscience and Metabolic Efficiency* (Sebtel Press: Sheffield).

Stroop, J. R. 1935. 'Studies of interference in serial verbal reactions', *Journal of Experimental Psychology*, 18: 643–62.

Styles, E. A. 2005. *Attention, Perception and Memory: An Integrated Introduction* (Psychology Press: Hove, New York).

Suppes, P. 1970. 'Probabilistic Grammar for Natural Languages.' In *Psychology Series*, 34 (Stanford University: Stanford, CA).

Suttle, L., and A. E. Goldberg. 2011. 'Partial productivity of constructions as induction', *Linguistics*, 49: 1237–69.

Swiggers, P. 1995. 'How Chomsky skinned Quine, or what "verbal behavior" can do', *Language Sciences*, 17: 1–18.

Szmrecsanyi, B. 2006. *Morphosyntactic Persistence in Spoken English: a Corpus Study at the Intersection of Variationist Sociolinguistics, Psycholinguistics, and Discourse Analysis* (Mouton de Gruyter: Berlin, New York).

2013. 'Diachronic probabilistic grammar', *English Language and Linguistics*, 1: 41–68.

Taft, M. 1979. 'Recognition of affixed words and the word frequency effect', *Memory and Cognition*, 7: 263–72.

Takashima, A., and I. Bakker. 2016. 'Memory Consolidation.' In Hans-Joerg Schmid (ed.), *Entrenchment, and the Psychology of Language Learning: How We Reorganize and Adapt Linguistic Knowledge* (De Gruyter Mouton: Washington, DC).

Talmy, L. 1985. 'Lexicalization Patterns: Semantic Structure in Lexical Forms.' In Timothy Shopen (ed.), *Language Typology and Syntactic Description. Vol. 3: Grammatical Categories and the Lexicon* (Cambridge University Press: Cambridge, UK).

1995. 'The cognitive culture system', *The Monist*, 78: 80–114.

2000. *Toward a Cognitive Semantics* (MIT Press: Cambridge, MA).

2007. 'Attention Phenomena.' In Dirk Geeraerts and Hubert Cuyckens (eds.), *Oxford Handbook of Cognitive Linguistics* (Oxford University Press: Oxford).

Tanenhaus, M. K., M. J. Spivey-Knowlton, K. M. Eberhard, and J. C. Sedivy. 1995. 'Integration of visual and linguistic information in spoken language comprehension', *Science*, 268: 1632–4.

Tannenbaum, P. H., and F. Williams. 1968. 'Generation of active and passive sentences as a function of subject or object focus', *Journal of Verbal Learning and Verbal Behavior*, 7: 246–50.

Taylor, J. G. 2005. '*On Intelligence*: Book review', *Artificial Intelligence*, 169: 192–5.

Taylor, J. R. 1995. *Linguistic Categorization: Prototypes in Linguistic Theory* (Oxford University Press: Oxford).

2012. *The Mental Corpus. How Language is Represented in the Mind* (Oxford University Press: Oxford).

Taylor, W. L. 1953. '"Cloze Procedure": a new tool for measuring readability', *Journalism and Mass Communication Quarterly*, 30: 415–33.

Těšitelová, M. 1992. *Quantitative Linguistics* (Academia: Praha).

Theakston, A. 2004. 'The role of entrenchment in children's and adults' performance on grammaticality judgment tasks', *Cognitive Development*, 19: 15–34.

Theeuwes, J., A. V. Belopolsky, and C. N. L. Olivers. 2009. 'Interactions between working memory, attention and eye movements', *Acta Psychologica*, 132: 106–14.

Theijssen, D., L. ten Bosch, L. Boves, B. Cranen, and H. van Halteren. 2013. 'Choosing alternatives: using Bayesian networks and memory-based learning to study the dative alternation', *Corpus Linguistics and Linguistic Theory*, 9: 227–62.

Thomas, M. S. C., and J. L. McClelland. 2008. 'Connectionist Models of Cognition.' In Ron Sun (ed.), *The Cambridge Handbook of Computational Psychology* (Cambridge University Press: Cambridge, UK).

Thompson, R. K., and L. M. Herman. 1977. 'Memory for lists of sounds by the bottle-nosed dolphin: convergence of memory processes with humans?', *Science*, 195: 501–3.

Thompson, S. A., and P. J. Hopper. 2001. 'Transitivity, Clause Structure, and Argument Structure: Evidence from Conversation.' In Joan Bybee and Paul Hopper (eds.), *Frequency Effects and the Emergence of Linguistic Structure* (John Benjamins: Amsterdam, Philadelphia).

Thorndike, E. L. 1898. 'Animal intelligence: an experimental study of the associative processes in animals', *Psychological Monographs: General and Applied*, 2: i-109.

1921. *The Teacher's Word Book* (Teachers College, Columbia University: New York).

1932a. *The Fundamentals of Learning* (AMS Press: New York).

1932b. *A Teacher's Word Book of the Twenty Thousand Words Found Most Frequently and Widely in General Reading for Children and Young People* (Teacher's College, Columbia University: New York).

1937. 'On correlations between measurements which are not normally distributed', *Journal of Educational Psychology*, 28: 367–70.

Thorndike, E. L., and I. Lorge. 1944. *The Teacher's Word Book of 30,000 Words* (Teacher's College, Columbia University: New York).

Tily, H., S. Gahl, I. Arnon, and N. E. Snider. 2009. 'Syntactic probabilities affect pronunciation variation in spontaneous speech', *Language and Cognition*, 1: 147–65.

Tolman, E. C., B. F. Ritchie, and D. Kalish. 1946. 'Studies in spatial learning. II. Place learning versus response learning', *Journal of Experimental Psychology*, 36: 221–9.

Tomasello, M. 2000. 'First steps toward a usage-based theory of language acquisition', *Cognitive Linguistics*, 11: 61–82.

2003. *Constructing a language: A Usage-Based Theory of Language Acquisition* (Harvard University Press: Boston).

Tomlin, R. 1995. 'Focal Attention, Voice, and Word order.' In P. Downing and M. Noonan (eds.), *Word Order in Discourse* (John Benjamins: Amsterdam).

1997. 'Mapping Conceptual Representations into Linguistic Representations: The Role of Attention in Grammar.' In J. Nuyts and E. Pederson (eds.), *Language and Conceptualization* (Cambridge University Press: Cambridge, UK).

Tomlin, R., L. Forrest, M. M. Pu, and M. H. Kim. 2010. 'Discourse Semantics.' In Teun A. van Dijk (ed.), *Discourse Studies: A Multidisciplinary Introduction* (Sage: London).

Tomlin, R., and A. Myachykov. 2015. 'Attention and Salience.' In Ewa Dąbrowska and Dagmar Divjak (eds.), *Handbook of Cognitive Linguistics* (De Gruyter Mouton: Berlin).

Treisman, A. M. 1960. 'Contextual cues in selective listening', *The Quarterly Journal of Experimental Psychology*, 12: 242–8.

Treisman, A. M., and G. Gelade. 1980. 'A feature-integration theory of attention', *Cognitive Psychology*, 12: 97–136.

Tremblay, A., and R. H. Baayen. 2010. 'Holistic Processing of Regular Four-Word Sequences: A Behavioral and ERP Study of the Effects of Structure, Frequency, and Probability on Immediate Free Recall.' In D. Wood (ed.), *Perspectives on Formulaic Language: Acquisition and Communication* (Continuum: London).

Tremblay, A., B. Derwing, G. Libben, and C. Westbury. 2011. 'Processing advantages of lexical bundles: evidence from self-paced reading and sentence recall tasks', *Language Learning*, 61: 569–613.

Tribus, M. 1961. *Thermostatics and Thermodyamics* (D. van Nostrand: New York).

Trimmer, P. C., J. M. McNamara, A. I. Houston, and J. A. R. Marshall. 2012. 'Does natural selection favour the Rescorla–Wagner rule?', *Journal of Theoretical Biology*, 302: 39–52.

Trudgill, P. 1986. *Dialects in Contact* (Basil Blackwell: Oxford, New York).

Tulving, E., and W. Donaldson. 1972. *Organization of Memory* (Academic Press: New York, London).

Tulving, E., and D. L. Schacter. 1990. 'Priming and human memory systems', *Science*, 247: 301–6.

Tulving, E., and D. M. Thomson. 1973. 'Encoding specificity and retrieval processes in episodic memory', *Psychological Review*, 80: 352–73.

Turing, A. M. 1969. 'Intelligent Machinery.' In B. Meltzer and D. Mitchie (eds.), *Machine Intelligence 5* (Edinburg University Press: Edinburgh).

Turk-Browne, N. B., D. J. Yi, and M. M. Chun. 2006. 'Linking implicit and explicit memory: common encoding factors and shared representations', *Neuron*, 49: 917–27.

Turner, E. A., and R. Rommetveit. 1968. 'Focus of attention in recall of active and passive sentences', *Journal of Verbal Learning and Verbal Behavior*, 7: 543–8.

Ullman, M. T. 2001. 'The declarative/procedural model of lexicon and grammar', *Journal of Psycholinguistic Research*, 30: 37–69.

——— 2004. 'Contributions of memory circuits to language: the declarative/procedural model', *Cognition*, 92: 231–70.

Urrutibétheity, H. N. 1972. 'The statistical properties of the Spanish lexicon', *Cahiers de lexicologie*, 20: 79–95.

Van Berkum, J. J. A., C. M. Brown, P. Zwitserlood, V. Kooijman, and P. Hagoort. 2005. 'Anticipating upcoming words in discourse: evidence from ERPs and reading times', *Journal of Experimental Psychology*, 31: 443–67.

van der Heijden, A. H. C., and S. Bem. 1997. 'Successive approximations to an adequate model of attention', *Consciousness and Cognition*, 6: 413–28.

van Petten, C. 1993. 'A comparison of lexical and sentence-level context effects and their temporal parameters', *Language and Cognitive Processes*, 8: 485–532.

Vander Beke, G. E. 1930. *French Word Book* (Macmillan: New York).

Verkoeijen, P. P. J. L., R. M. J. P. Rikers, and H. G. Schmidt. 2004. 'Detrimental influence of contextual change on spacing effects in free recall', *Journal of Experimental Psychology: Learning, Memory, and Cognition*, 30: 796–800.

Vihman, M. M. 1996. *Phonological Development: The Origins of Language in the Child* (Blackwell: Cambridge, MA, Oxford).

Vogels, J., E. Krahmer, and A. Maes. 2013. 'Who is where referred to how, and why? The influence of visual saliency on referent accessibility in spoken language production', *Language and Cognitive Processes*, 28: 1323–49.

Von Ehrenfels, C. 1890. 'Ueber "Gestaltqualitaeten"', *Vierteljahrsschrift fuer wissenschaftliche Philosophie*, 14: 249–92.

Wagner, A. R. 1976. 'Priming in STM: An Information-Processing Mechanism for Self-Generated or Retrieval-Generated Depression in Performance.' In T. J. Tighe and R. N. Leaton (eds.), *Habituation: Perspectives from Child Development, Animal Behavior, and Neurophysiology* (Lawrence Erlbaum: Hillsdale, NJ).

1978. 'Expectancies and the Priming of STM.' In S. H. Hulse, H. Fowler and W. K. Honig (eds.), *Cognitive Processes in Animal Behavior* (Lawrence Erlbaum: Hillsdale, NJ).

1981. 'SOP: A Model of Automatic Memory Processing in Animal Behavior.' In N. E. Spear and R. R. Miller (eds.), *Information Processing in Animals: Memory Mechanisms* (Lawrence Erlbaum: Hillsdale, NJ).

Wagner, A. R., and S. E. Brandon. 1989. 'Evolution of a Structured Connectionist Model of Pavlovian Conditioning (ÆSOP).' In S. B. Klein and R. R. Mowrer (eds.), *Contemporary Learning Theories: Pavlovian Conditioning and the Status of Traditional Learning Theories* (Lawrence Erlbaum: Hillsdale, NJ).

2001. 'A Componential Theory of Pavlovian Conditioning.' In R. R. Mowrer and S. B. Klein (eds.), *Handbook of Contemporary Learning Theories* (Lawrence Erlbaum: Mahwah, NJ).

Wagner, A. R., F. A. Logan, and K. Haberlandt. 1968. 'Stimulus selection in animal discrimination learning', *Journal of Experimental Psychology*, 76: 171–80.

Wagner, A. R., and R. A. Rescorla. 1972. 'Inhibition in Pavlovian Conditioning: Application of a Theory.' In R. A. Boakes and M. S. Halliday (eds.), *Inhibition and Learning* (Academic Press.: London).

Waterfall, H. R., B. Sandbank, L. Onnis, and S. Edelman. 2010. 'An empirical generative framework for computational modeling of language acquisition', *Journal of Child Language*, 37: 671–703.

Waters, G., D. Caplan, and S. Yampolsky. 2003. 'On-line syntactic processing under concurrent memory load', *Psychonomic Bulletin and Review: A Journal of the Psychonomic Society, Inc.*, 10: 88–95.

Watson, J. B. 1913. 'Psychology as the behaviorist views it', *Psychological Review*, 20: 158.

1924. *Behaviorism* (People's Institute: New York).

West, M. 1953. *A General Service List of English Words* (Longman, Green and Co: London).

Westheimer, G. 2008. 'Was Helmholtz a Bayesian?', *Perception*, 37: 642–50.

Whaley, C. P. 1978. 'Word-nonword classification time', *Journal of Verbal Learning and Verbal Behavior*, 17: 143–54.

Wheeler, D. D. 1970. 'Processes in word recognition', *Cognitive Psychology*, 1: 59–85.

Wicha, N. Y. Y., E. M. Moreno, and M. Kutas. 2004. 'Anticipating words and their gender: an event-related brain potential study of semantic integration, gender expectancy, and gender agreement in Spanish sentence reading', *Journal of Cognitive Neuroscience*, 16: 1272–88.

Wiechmann, D. 2008. 'On the computation of collostruction strength: testing measures of association as expressions of lexical bias', *Corpus Linguistics and Linguistic Theory*, 4: 253–90.

Wingfield, A. 1968. 'Effects of frequency on identification.', *American Journal of Psychology*, 81: 226–34.

Wise, R. A. 2004. 'Dopamine, learning and motivation', *Nature Reviews Neuroscience*, 5: 483.

Wolfe, J. M., K. R. Cave, and S. L. Franzel. 1989. 'Guided search: an alternative to the feature integration model for visual search', *Journal of Experimental Psychology: Human Perception and Performance*, 15: 419–33.

Wolk, C., J. Bresnan, A. Rosenback, and B. Szmrecsanyi. 2013. 'Dative and genitive variability in Late Modern English: exploring cross-constructional variation and change', *Diachronica*, 30: 382–419.

Wolters, G., and A. Prinsen. 1997. 'Full versus divided attention and implicit memory performance', *Memory and Cognition*, 25: 764–71.

'Word Encoding by Activation and VERification', www.socsci.ru.nl/ardiroel/weaver++.htm.

Wray, A. 2002. *Formulaic Language and the Lexicon* (Cambridge University Press: Cambridge, UK).

Wu, W. 2014. *Attention* (Routledge: London).

Xiao, R. Z. 2008. 'Well-Known and Influential Corpora'. In A. Lüdeling and M. Kytö *Corpus Linguistics: An International Handbook* (Mouton de Gruyter: Berlin).

Yang, C. D. 2004. 'Universal grammar, statistics or both?', *Trends in Cognitive Sciences*, 8: 451–6.

—— 2015. 'For and against frequencies', *Journal of Child Language*, 42: 287–93.

Yates, F. 1984. 'Tests of significance for 2 x 2 contingency tables', *Journal of the Royal Statistical Society. Series A*, 147: 426–63.

Yule, G. U. 1944. *The Statistical Study of Literary Vocabulary* (Cambridge University Press: London).

Zacks, R. T., and L. Hasher. 2002. 'Frequency Processing: A Twenty-Five Year Perspective.' In P. Sedlmeier and T. Betsch (eds.), *Frequency Processing and Cognition* (Oxford University Press: New York).

Zarcone, A., M. van Schijndel, J. Vogels, and V. Demberg. 2016. 'Salience and attention in surprisal-based accounts of language processing', *Frontiers in Psychology*, 7: 844.

Zeldes, A. 2012. *Productivity in Argument Selection: From Morphology to Syntax* (De Gruyter Mouton: Berlin).

Zevin, J. D., and M. S. Seidenberg. 2004. 'Age-of-acquisition effects in reading aloud: Tests of cumulative frequency and frequency trajectory', *Memory and Cognition*, 32: 31–8.

Zhou, D. W., D. D. Mowrey, P. Tang, and Y. Xu. 2015. 'Percolation model of sensory transmission and loss of consciousness under general anesthesia', *Physical Review Letters*, 115: 108103.

Zipf, G. K. 1932. *Selected Studies of the Principle of Relative Frequencies in Language* (MIT Press: Cambridge, MA).

—— 1935. *The Psycho-Biology of Language: an Introduction to Dynamic Philology* (MIT Press: Cambridge, MA).

—— 1949. *Human Behaviour and the Principle of Least Effort : an Introduction to Human Ecology* (Hafner: New York).

Zlatev, J. 2016. 'Turning back to experience in cognitive linguistics via phenomenology', *Cognitive Linguistics*, 27: 559–72.

Index

ability
  cognitive, 5, 6, 8, 9, 11, 16, 17, 27, 78, 183, 184, 211, 233, 260, 263, 264
  computational, 75, 104
  linguistic, 6, 11, 43, 233
  pattern recognition, 234
abstraction, 17, 36, 42, 44, 46, 47, 57, 78, 79, 121, 136, 147, 209, 211, 229, 246, 261, 263, 264, 269
  high-level, 48, 263
  linguistic, 42, 70, 78, 107, 275
account
  predictive, 179, 226, 227, 228
acquisition
  language, 5, 16, 17, 75, 136, 251
activation, 40, 73, 82, 96, 104, 120, 126, 129, 135, 138, 139, 149, 171, 175, 180, 193, 196, 207, 208, 209, 218, 220, 222, 226, 228, 229, 242, 258, 263
activity
  brain, 101, 110
algorithm, 83, 92, 134, 144, 147, 151, 211, 217, 221, 256, 257, 259, 271, 272, 274
analysis
  rational, 221, 248
approach
  Bayesian, 206, 212, 213, 219, 221, 223, 225, 228, 231, 232
  behavioural, 117
  cognitive, 6, 117
  cognitive linguistic, 99, 128, 261
  constructionist, 47, 198
  constructivist, 78
  corpus linguistic, 58
  corpus-based, 31, 254
  emergentist, 118
  exemplar, 43
  generativist, 240
  information theoretic, 96
  predictive, 11, 218, 231
  probabilistic, 72, 77, 78, 79, 80, 81, 84, 85, 87, 88, 211, 263

  quantitative, 57, 257
  statistical, 23, 78, 81, 263
  usage-based, 10, 15, 17, 19, 70, 72, 128, 134, 136, 139, 195, 211, 265
area
  brain, 110, 169, 207, 217
association
  semantic, 57
  statistical, 58, 59, 64, 66
asymptote, 2, 241, 248, 252, 258
attention
  automatic, 167
  bottom-up, 167, 168, 169, 177, 200, 267
  divided, 178, 179
  endogenous, 192
  exogenous, 167, 170, 187, 192
  focal, 139, 166, 167, 243
  selective, 164, 165, 169, 171, 175, 177, 185, 250, 255
  top-down, 167, 169, 267
  visual, 162, 164, 166, 167, 172, 173
automaticity, 134, 138, 163
automatization, 133, 137, 151, 156, 265
axon, 111, 113, 114

behaviour
  human, 161, 206, 222, 240, 243, 245, 257, 273
  linguistic, 2, 66, 152, 245, 272
  verbal, 6, 243, 244, 245, 246
behaviourism, 5, 6, 102, 239, 243
behaviourist, 102, 110, 174, 238, 239, 240, 244, 245, 246
belief
  prior, 220, 222, 226
  updating, 232, 233
brain
  Bayesian, 213, 219, 231
brainwaves, 178, 230

capacity
  cognitive, 5, 40, 142, 162, 260, 274